A SWORD FOR THE CONVICTED

Recent Titles in
Contributions in Criminology and Penology

Police Administration and Progressive Reform: Theodore Roosevelt as Police Commissioner of New York
Jay Stuart Berman

Policing Multi-Ethnic Neighborhoods: The Miami Study and Findings for Law Enforcement in the United States
Geoffrey P. Alpert and Roger G. Dunham

Minorities and Criminality
Ronald Barri Flowers

Marijuana: Costs of Abuse, Costs of Control
Mark Kleiman

Doing Time in American Prisons: A Study of Modern Novels
Dennis Massey

Demographics and Criminality: The Characteristics of Crime in America
Ronald Barri Flowers

Taking Charge: Crisis Intervention in Criminal Justice
Anne T. Romano

Beyond Punishment: A New View on the Rehabilitation of Criminal Offenders
Edgardo Rotman

Police Pursuit Driving: Controlling Responses to Emergency Situations
Geoffrey P. Alpert and Roger G. Dunham

Vigilantism: Political History of Private Power in America
William C. Culberson

Chinese Subculture and Criminality: Non-traditional Crime Groups in America
Ko-lin Chin

A SWORD FOR THE CONVICTED

Representing Indigent Defendants on Appeal

David T. Wasserman

Foreword by James B. Jacobs

CONTRIBUTIONS IN CRIMINOLOGY AND PENOLOGY, NUMBER 30
Marvin Wolfgang, *Series Adviser*

GREENWOOD PRESS
New York • Westport, Connecticut • London

Library of Congress Cataloging-in-Publication Data

Wasserman, David T.
A sword for the convicted : representing indigent defendants on appeal / David T. Wasserman ; foreword by James B. Jacobs.
p. cm. — (Contributions in criminology and penology, ISSN 0732–4464 ; no. 30)
Includes bibliographical references.
ISBN 0–313–26881–9 (lib. bdg. : alk. paper)
1. Appellate procedure—New York (N.Y.) 2. Criminal procedure—New York (N.Y.) 3. Legal aid—New York (N.Y.) 4. Appellate procedure—New York (State) 5. Criminal procedure—New York (State) 6. Legal aid—New York (State) I. Title. II. Series.
KFX2093.W37 1990
347.747'08—dc20
[347.47078] 89–25909

British Library Cataloguing in Publication Data is available.

Library of Congress Catalog Card Number: 89–25909
ISBN: 0–313–26881–9
ISSN: 0732–4464

First published in 1990

Greenwood Press, 88 Post Road West, Westport, CT 06881
An imprint of Greenwood Publishing Group, Inc.

Printed in the United States of America

The paper used in this book complies with the Permanent Paper Standard issued by the National Information Standards Organization (Z39.48–1984).

10 9 8 7 6 5 4 3 2 1

Contents

Figures and Tables

FIGURES

TABLES

Foreword

In this monograph, David Wasserman presents a comprehensive analysis of indigent criminal appeals in New York City. At the outset, he shows how these appeals have increased massively in number and as a percentage of the state's appellate court docket, and links this growth to Warren Court decisions of the 1960s which expanded the rights of criminal defendants. He then explains how the vastly increased caseload has created a challenge, if not a crisis, for the appellate courts and for the provision of indigent appellate legal services.

Based on careful sampling, Wasserman presents systematic data on the outcomes of criminal appeals in recent years and on the comparative competencies of New York City's two indigent legal services providers: the Legal Aid Society's Criminal Appeals Bureau (CAB) and the appellate division's assigned counsel system (18b). He also provides a fascinating and creative comparison of briefs by CAB and 18b attorneys based upon a grading scheme applied by retired appellate court judges.

Two major problems in the processing of indigent criminal appeals quickly become apparent. First, because there are no economic or other disincentives for appealing, there are a high number of appeals which fail to raise plausible issues for relief. The widespread perception that criminal appeals are often frivolous leads judges to take criminal appeals less seriously, thereby jeopardizing those defendants who have meritorious claims. Second, this same problem affects the organization and ethics of legal defense practice. How should legal service providers allocate their time and energy in a world of limited resources and overwhelming numbers of clients? Wasserman offers a policy review and analysis of reform options that have surfaced in New York and elsewhere around the United States to address both of these problems, and then offers a number of interesting proposals of his own.

The strength of this study can be attributed to the author's unique capacities to address the subject of indigent criminal appeals as a participant observer, quantitative researcher, and policy analyst. Wasserman is adept at tracing and explicating legal doctrines affecting appeals and the provision of legal services—for example, the constitutional right of indigent defendants to the effective assistance of appellate counsel. Having himself practiced as a criminal appeals attorney for four years, Wasserman is in a position to write confidently about the pressures and dilemmas which confront organizations and individuals in the provision of appellate criminal defense services. He is also a skilled empirical researcher who has defined his samples with care and analyzed his data with sophistication. The result is a first-rate quantitative empirical analysis of a process which for too long has been dominated by impressionistic accounts or by dataless doctrinal analyses. The extensive data and analysis presented in the monograph will provide a point of departure for scholars, students, and policymakers for many years to come.

Wasserman employs multiple perspectives in investigating the subject of indigent criminal appeals. He defines the topic broadly and is extremely reflective about the origins and consequences of the developments he observes. Nevertheless, I would like to offer three observations that, from my perspective, give the book even broader significance.

(1) *Criminal appeals are but the last stage of a criminal justice process which, all along the way, fails to conform to the model of rights propounded in Supreme Court decisions and other juridical pronouncements.*

As we read Wasserman's monograph, we cannot forget that criminal appeals are but the last stage of a criminal justice process that is problematic from start to finish. Nowhere is the gap between law on paper and law in action greater than in the operation of the criminal justice system. Supreme Court decisions portray neutral and detached magistrates protecting criminal suspects from overreaching by police and prosecutors. They portray criminal defendants, represented by vigorous defense lawyers, standing innocent until proven guilty under the watchful eyes of alert and impartial trial judges, and convicted defendants represented by vigorous appellate defenders bringing errors and injustices to the attention of vigilant appellate tribunals. In this mythical account, indigency is no bar to justice. The poor defendant is assured legal counsel from the point of arrest, through the lineup, preliminary hearings, plea bargain or hearing, and appeal. Unfortunately, this picture, which stirs pride in the hearts and minds of much of the American population, would be unrecognizable to criminal defendants in New York City and most other cities throughout the United States.

American society has yet to come to terms with the implications of its promise to provide all criminal defendants, including the majority who are indigent, a full adversary procedure which requires the state to test its prosecutorial case against vigorous cross examination. Perhaps most fundamentally, it has failed to come to grips with its promise to provide effective assistance of counsel at both the trial and appellate stages of the criminal process. It would be completely unrealistic to expect consistently searching appellate review in a system which does not provide high quality justice at any other stage of the criminal justice process.

(2) *The implications of costless criminal appeals should cause us to reconsider our traditional notions about the purposes and functions of appeals.*

In the 1960s, the Supreme Court extended the right of free appellate counsel to indigent criminal defendants. Since convicted defendants, even those who plead guilty, have nothing to lose in filing appeals, there was a vast increase in the number of criminal appeals and in their proportion of the appellate docket. However, the judicial system had never been intended, structured, or staffed to deal with "automatic appeals." The traditional notion of appeal conjured up a litigant willing to expend his own money to press a specific complaint before a review panel. Since most cases were not appealed, appellants typically had reasonably important and interesting issues to call to the attention of an appellate tribunal and the appellate tribunal could approach each case individually, weighing the merits of the unique arguments about facts, law, and policy.

The advent of costless appeals challenges the whole idea of what appeals are designed to accomplish. We have now created a norm that all criminal defendants, even those who have pled guilty, can and probably should appeal. It seems obvious that, under these circumstances, an appellate court will inevitably tend to lump such appeals into large and undifferentiated categories. Equally important, this reality alters expectations about the appellate court's role. Perhaps it is now implicitly assumed that an appellate court's job is to take a second look at every criminal conviction but only to see that the rules were followed and that the process was formally complied with. Only the most egregious violations of law will stand out in this review process, and the appellate courts could be expected to be more and more concerned with expediting the ever accumulating caseload. Inevitably, no matter how much it is decried, the advent of costless criminal appeals has extended the reality of assembly-line justice to the appellate courts.

(3) *The budgetary, organizational, and ethical problems of appellate indigent legal providers need to be understood in the more general context of providing diverse social services to the poor.*

The provision of appellate legal services to the poor must be placed in the context of providing all sorts of services to the poor—for example, social services and health, education, and welfare. In none of these spheres are poor people provided services anything like the equivalent of the services that are regularly available to and consumed by the middle class, much less the upper classes. Many of the problems that Wasserman defines as afflicting the provision of appellate legal services to indigent criminal defendants are problems that exist or have their equivalent in other social service contexts. This is especially true of the enormous organizational and morale problems affecting appellate defender organizations and their personnel. Like other social services for the poor, indigent appellate representation will never be high prestige work and therefore the systemic and organizational problems of recruitment, retention, and morale will always be a serious challenge. Moreover, there will never be enough money to do the job properly; budgets will always lag behind programmatic needs.

James B. Jacobs
New York University School of Law
October 1989

Preface

This book examines the professional and administrative challenges of providing zealous advocacy for every defendant wishing to appeal. It addresses some of the questions I lived with during the four years I spent representing indigent defendants in their state appeals. For most of my brief professional career, I was a staff attorney with the Criminal Appeals Bureau (CAB) of the New York City Legal Aid Society, the unit charged with representing most of the indigent defendants in New York City who appeal their convictions and sentences. The CAB staff regarded itself as an elite, providing convicted indigents with the zealous, highly skilled representation that a discriminating private client would expect. At the same time, many of us had vexing doubts about the value of our services to our clients and to the protection of defendants' rights.

Although people unfamiliar with criminal appeals sometimes thought of us as the lawyers who "got dangerous criminals off on technicalities," we knew only too well that very few of our clients "got off," and almost none on "technicalities." Few forms of legal practice provide so little tangible benefit to the client for so much time and effort. While each CAB staff attorney briefed about 20 appeals a year, producing several hundred pages of carefully crafted factual narrative and legal argument, only one or two appeals would usually result in any kind of favorable action and only three or four yielded a written opinion.

We CAB lawyers regarded our low rate of success as an unavoidable feature of a system of review in which every convicted indigent, regardless of the merits of his case, was guaranteed free appellate counsel. Though we undoubtedly shared the tendency of most litigators to overestimate the strength of our cases, we did not really believe that most of our appeals should have been decided in the defendant's favor, given the issues the court could resolve, the information it could consider in resolving them, and the present state of the law. Our clients had typically been convicted on strong, if not overwhelming, evidence and sentenced to terms that seemed reasonable, if not lenient, by prevailing standards. They may have been badly treated by the police who arrested them, the judges before whom they appeared, or the attorneys who represented them, but this was hard to establish from the records we had before us.

Although we were obliged to represent every eligible defendant seeking to appeal, we frequently wished for more cases in which we could rectify serious error, raise issues at the frontiers of criminal and constitutional law, or challenge prevailing police, prosecutorial, or judicial practices. In CAB, such selectivity was a perquisite of rank: our supervisors were able to pick the cases they briefed, to concentrate on interesting issues or innocent clients. While we believed that we owed our clients our fullest efforts regardless of their chances of success, we were privately relieved when clients with weak cases withdrew their appeals or were reassigned to substitute counsel.

Still, we took a certain amount of pleasure even in our routine work. It was a challenge to fashion the strongest possible arguments from a frozen record, to discover poignant or amusing details that might spark the court's interest in an otherwise routine case, or to suggest a plausible scenario or rationale to accommodate recalcitrant facts or law. For some of us, it was liberating to work on a nearly hopeless appeal, freed of the encumbering anxiety that often accompanies a close case.

Even if these efforts were gratifying to the attorney, however, it was not clear if they benefitted anyone else. Given the low odds of success, the effort we devoted to routine cases sometimes seemed extravagant. In a large majority of our cases, our clients could have done no worse with more perfunctory briefing, and it was hard to know whether our efforts had made a difference in the small minority of appeals receiving favorable action. Moreover, given the frequency with which the courts affirmed silently or uninformatively, it was hard to know if our advocacy played a significant role in clarifying the law or calling attention to improper practices.[1]

These were serious questions for an enterprise which consumed a large share of New York City's criminal defense budget. Nearly one out of every six dollars the city paid to the Legal Aid Society in 1985 for criminal defense went to CAB, where 14 percent of the Society's attorneys produced less than 2 percent of its dispositions.[2] Even if the effort we put into weak and routine cases raised the odds of favorable action very slightly—from nil to negligible, we said—there may have been other areas of criminal defense in which increased funding would have yielded far more substantial results.

The justification for devoting such a large share of defense resources to appellate representation was also called into question by the high proportion of criminal cases resolved by guilty plea—about 90 percent of all felony convictions in New York City. A guilty plea largely forecloses review of the defendant's factual guilt or legal liability. Only a small proportion of defendants challenged their guilty pleas, and a majority of appeals appeared to come from the 15 percent of indicted defendants who go to trial.[3]

The grounds on which CAB won appeals often seemed irrelevant to the plea-bargaining process which resolved most cases. The bargains struck by most defendants would rarely be affected by reversals based on improper jury instructions, inflammatory prosecutorial rhetoric, logically inconsistent verdicts, the failure to submit a lesser-included offense or alternative defense, the invalidity of a prior out-of-state conviction for sentence-enhancement purposes. CAB successes in these areas merely seemed to refine the process of adjudication for the small minority of defendants who went to trial.

This disproportion would have been less troublesome if the cases brought to trial were the closest or most difficult—those with the greatest possibility of error or the greatest significance for criminal justice administration. The literature on criminal case-processing suggests, however, that just the opposite may be true—that cases with significant issues of factual guilt and legal liability get bargained away, while the cases most likely to go to trial are those where the evidence is too strong and the charges too serious for an acceptable plea bargain.[4] While legislative restrictions on plea bargaining in New York had enlarged the pool of defendants with nothing to lose by going to trial, the proportion of "sure-loser" cases among those tried had very likely remained quite high.

Moreover, defendants convicted at trial ran little or no risk in appealing—except in unusual circumstances, they could not receive a higher sentence on retrial. In contrast, plea defendants with viable search, confession, and identification issues often declined to raise them, for fear of jeopardizing a good deal. To an unsympathetic observer, it might have appeared that the state was lavishing resources on the appeal rather than the adjudication of criminal cases and on the review of some of its least problematic convictions.

My concern about the value and priority of appellate representation was sharpened by the release in 1985 of the McConville/Mirsky draft report on trial-level representation for indigent defendants in New York City. That report revealed a wholesale departure from the Assigned Counsel Plan adopted in 1966, under which the Legal Aid Society (LAS) would represent all indigent defendants who did not present a "conflict of interest," with a panel of private attorneys (called the "18b panel" after the authorizing statute) providing high-quality representation in what were expected to be a small number of conflict cases.

McConville and Mirsky found that the Criminal Defense Division (CDD) of LAS was taking a much smaller share of the caseload than originally expected, in part because it was "shedding" large numbers of cases with no apparent conflict of interest, typically taking the least culpable and heavily implicated defendants. A large share of the cases in which CDD was relieved went to a small number of private attorneys supported solely or principally by criminal assignments, who often failed to provide their clients with the most basic defense services. McConville and Mirsky concluded that CDD was an integral part of a system whose real purpose was to process cases cheaply and expeditiously, not to protect the rights of accused indigents.

While the McConville/Mirsky report dealt exclusively with trial-level representation, it forced CAB attorneys to confront the possibility that they themselves might be failing to live up to their contractual obligations. Although CAB claimed to take all indigent appeals that did not present a conflict of interest, it was clear that the 18b panel was receiving a far larger share of the appellate caseload than the Assigned Counsel Plan had intended. The McConville/Mirsky report also deepened the concern which many CAB attorneys felt about the quality of representation received by the defendants LAS declined to represent, confirming their worst impressions of 18b representation on the trial level.

More broadly, the report's findings raised the disturbing possibility that the primary effect of indigent appellate representation, if not its intended function, was cosmetic. For observers troubled by the lack of adversary confrontation and judicial oversight at the trial level, a vigorous appellate process provided a reassuring, if belated, display of adversary zeal and searching judicial scrutiny. The kinds of victories CAB won contributed to the comforting appearance that nothing could be terribly wrong in the trial courts: if convictions were reversed for such apparently minor errors as "prosecutorial vouching" and "burden-shifting reasonable doubt instructions," then more serious injustices could hardly escape rectification.

The draft report, and the ensuing public controversy, also suggested the role that CAB might play in "legitimating" LAS in the eyes of its critics, providing a highly visible but not very disruptive example of the Society's zeal for its clients. CAB's occasional United States Supreme Court victory and frequent wins in the New York Court of Appeals did more for the Society's image than a string of trial acquittals or favorable plea bargains, and made up for a lot of bad publicity about case-shedding in the arraignment parts. Most of us, however, had not gone into indigent defense to engage in a form of corporate public relations.

To address these difficult issues about the quality and impact of indigent appellate representation in New York City, I felt that it was necessary to assess the performance of the City's appellate defenders in a systematic empirical study. I approached Professor James Jacobs, Director of the New York University Center for Research in Crime and Justice, which had sponsored the research by McConville and Mirsky, to see if he was willing to support a similar investigation of indigent appellate defense in New York City. Professor Jacobs was enthusiastic and urged me to design a study that would look beyond the comparative performance of New York's appellate defenders to the role of appellate representation in the criminal justice system.

The study I designed examined first-level felony appeals, which constitute the bulk of the indigent appellate caseload in New York City and which, as appeals of right, confront the appellate defender with the challenge of providing zealous representation for cases of widely varying merit. The questions I sought to address fell into three categories: (1) those concerning the implementation of the Assigned Counsel Plan on appeal—Was CAB representing all the defendants it was supposed to? Was the quality of representation it provided significantly better than that provided by the 18b appellate panel? Were both defenders providing minimally adequate representation on appeal? (2) those concerning the effect of appellate representation on case outcomes—Did one defender get significantly better results for its clients than the other? Was the difference greater for certain kinds of cases? Was it possible to attribute better outcomes to superior advocacy? (3) those concerning the role of appellate representation in correcting error and serving as a catalyst for reform in the criminal justice system—What kinds of errors led to reversal? What role did appellate attorneys play in bringing about their rectification? How could those attorneys play a greater role in correcting systemic abuses of their clients' rights?

Two features of New York City's system of appellate representation and review gave these inquiries a significance well beyond the city limits. First, the disparity in resources between New York's institutional appellate defender and its backup panel of private attorneys was as great as in any jurisdiction with a "mixed" system of indigent appellate defense. Second, its appellate courts have review powers as broad as any in the nation, and have not employed the screening mechanisms which, in other jurisdictions, limit the input of appellate counsel in routine cases. If the money spent on criminal appellate representation makes a difference in quality and outcome, that difference should be apparent in a comparison of New York's two appellate defenders. If appellate representation plays a significant role in correcting errors and improving the operation of the criminal justice system, those effects should be visible in an analysis of New York City's appellate dispositions.

To ensure my objectivity in evaluating the performance of an organization that had provided me with four years of rewarding employment, I structured the study to avoid any need for my personal judgments on the quality or impact of the representation provided by either defender. I also joined the 18b appellate panel to broaden my perspective on indigent appellate practice. Equally important, I came to rely on Professor Jacobs's keen eye for bias and preconception. I proceeded with confidence that his relentless questioning would help expose and counteract any sympathies or antipathies that might affect my conduct of the investigation. I also benefitted greatly from the observations and insights of Professor Mirsky, whose own research had made him skeptical of the Legal Aid Society's self-presentation.

I began my research on a fairly blank slate. Criminal appellate representation has been the subject of a fair amount of practice commentary but almost no research or scholarly writing.[5] Empirical research on appeals has focused on appellate decision-making and case management,[6] while research on indigent defense has concentrated on trials and pretrial proceedings.[7] There have been numerous studies of appellate caseload, docket control, and dispositions, but only one study of appellate lawyering, making only passing reference to criminal appeals.[8] There have been several important studies of trial representation for indigent defendants, but no comparable studies of indigent appellate representation. The law review writing on criminal appellate representation has focused almost exclusively on the single problem of frivolous criminal appeals, failing to provide a broader context in which that problem might be understood.[9]

A handful of empirical studies on criminal appellate dispositions set the stage for my research, revealing the formidable challenge faced by an appellate defender in a contemporary American jurisdiction. In his study of first-level criminal appeals in a first-level appellate court in California, Thomas Davies found a preponderance of cases involving serious offenses and very strong evidence, a set of judicial norms discouraging reversal even in the face of serious error, and an 84 percent affirmance rate.[10] Davies's findings also suggested a formidable challenge for the appellate researcher in developing a measure of attorney influence sensitive enough to detect the limited and subtle effects that skilled advocacy might be expected to have in such a setting.

Using New York City as a research setting, this book examines the organizational, tactical, and ethical challenges of providing zealous advocacy for every convicted indigent wishing to appeal. It examines the unique form of representation that has emerged in the 25 years since the Supreme Court recognized the right to free appellate counsel in *Douglas v. California* (1963).[11] The end product, I hope, is an integrated piece of research and policy analysis of interest to participants in the criminal justice system in New York City, appellate lawyers and judges in other jurisdictions, specialists in constitutional criminal law and legal ethics, and social scientists interested in criminal adjudication.

The book is divided into three parts. Part I examines, through existing research and commentary, the impact of *Douglas* on the nature of appellate representation, on the appellate courts, and on the organization of defense services. It argues that the upsurge in criminal appeals and the outward success of the due process revolution have made the job of assigned appellate counsel more difficult but no less important than in the days before *Douglas*.

It focuses on New York City, where the challenge of indigent appellate representation has been heightened by the volume of criminal appeals, the lack of judicial screening mechanisms, and the expansive review powers of the appellate courts.

Part II presents an empirical study of criminal appeals in New York City, assessing the quality and impact of its appellate defenders, their division of the indigent appellate caseload, and the grounds on which they prevail. The study finds significant disparities in the quality of representation provided by the city's institutional and assigned defenders. Despite an extremely low reversal rate, it also finds strong evidence that these differences in quality affect the odds of success and the rectification of significant error. At the same time, it finds that the appellate court rarely confronts systemic problems in the investigation, prosecution, and defense of criminal cases, and that the correction of serious injustice depends to a large extent on the fortuitous presence of procedural error.

Part III examines the implications of this research for the analysis of indigent appellate defense developed in Part I. It considers measures for improving the quality of assigned appellate counsel and proposals for resolving the tension between the adversary role and the appellate review function. It analyzes the vexing problem of "equalizing" legal protection for indigent defendants in a system of appellate review dominated by a fee-for-service model. It concludes that the quality of appellate representation can be upgraded by a number of practical reforms, but that the tension between zealous advocacy and "efficient" appellate review is an inherent feature of a criminal justice system with limited resources and an adversary form of adjudication.

NOTES

1. During my four years at CAB, I shared this ambivalence and uncertainty about the value of zealous appellate advocacy. Of the 50-odd cases I had briefed, only six had ended with a reversal, modification, or sentence reduction. Few of my cases raised basic issues of constitutional law or factual innocence, but almost all had at least one issue worthy of the court's serious consideration.

The issues on which I had won favorable action ran the gamut from matters of fundamental justice to genuine technicalities. On the one extreme, I represented an elderly nursing home operator with a distinguished record, bankrupted when the state improperly withheld thousands of dollars of medicaid reimbursement, and then charged him with failing to pay wages during the five weeks before his nursing home was forced to close. Following the letter of a law making failure to pay wages a "strict-liability" offense, the trial court refused to hear testimony from the employees' own union representative, who had urged the staff to continue working during that period in the hopes of obtaining the reimbursement owed by the state. Acting "in the interest of justice," the appellate court reversed the conviction and barred re-prosecution.

On the other extreme, I obtained a sentence reduction for a defendant convicted of robbery on overwhelming evidence in an eminently fair trial. The defendant had been sentenced as a second felony offender on the basis of an invalid predicate offense—a Louisiana auto burglary that would not have constituted a felony in New York. The appellate court reduced his minimum term from one and a half years to a year, a paper victory since he had already been incarcerated for two years.

The cases I lost also ran a wide gamut, from those in which the court appeared to ignore important issues or serious misconduct because of the practical consequences of reversal, to those in which the issues were too slight to warrant extended discussion. A challenge to Kings County grand jury selection procedures, fully litigated at the trial level, appeared to fall into the first category: the informal practices of the jury commissioner had made a "volunteer" system out of the "draft" clearly mandated by statute, but a reversal would have meant the dismissal of thousands of other indictments obtained during the period when the illegal practices were in effect.

Several other cases presented legal issues or alleged misconduct which may not have compelled reversal, but warranted a carefully reasoned opinion rather than a silent affirmance: the constitutionality of "duplicative" statutes, permitting the same conduct to be charged as a high-grade felony or a low-grade misdemeanor, the use of an apparently bogus arrest threat to discourage the defense from calling a material witness. In several other cases, the issues were important but the setting in which they arose made the case an unattractive forum for their resolution, either because the prejudice suffered by the defendant from the alleged error was negligible, or because his attorney had not even requested the omitted judicial action.

Another group of cases involved the application of inherently imprecise legal standards, such as "reasonable suspicion," where the facts did not compel, but certainly would have permitted, a reversal. There were also a number of cases in which I argued for a reduced sentence on the basis of strong mitigating factors of which the trial court had already taken some account. Finally, there were a handful of cases in which the arguments I made were virtual throwaways, interesting, sometimes clever, but with little legal or moral force and virtually no chance of prevailing.

2. McConville and Mirsky, "Criminal Defense of the Poor in New York City," *New York University Review of Law and Social Change* 15 (1987): 581, 864 n.1190.

3. These figures are derived from the 1977 Vera Institute report on *Felony Arrests: Their Prosecution and Disposition in New York's Criminal Courts*, 1–9, based on data from 1971, and are thus somewhat dated. More recent work on plea bargaining in other jurisdictions certainly suggests that the rate of plea bargaining has not changed dramatically.

4. See Mather, *Plea Bargaining or Trial? The Process of Criminal Case Disposition* (Lexington, Mass.: Lexington Books, 1979), 60–63.

5. See Purver and Taylor, *Handling Criminal Appeals* (Rochester, N.Y.: Lawyer's Cooperative, 1980); Steinberg, "The Criminal Appeal," in Carpentier, ed., *Counsel on Appeal* (New York: McGraw-Hill, 1968).

6. See Meador, *Appellate Courts: Staff and Process in the Crisis in Volume* (St. Paul, Minn.: West, 1974); Carrington, Meador, and Rosenberg, *Justice on Appeal* (St. Paul, Minn.: West, 1976); Leflar, *Internal Operating Procedures of Appellate Courts* (Chicago: American Bar Foundation, 1976).

7. See Herman, Single, and Boston, *Counsel for the Poor: Criminal Defense in*

Urban America (Lexington, Mass.: D. C. Heath, 1977); McConville and Mirsky, "Criminal Defense of the Poor."

8. Marvell, *Appellate Courts and Lawyers: Information Gathering in the Adversary System* (Westport, Conn.: Greenwood Press, 1978).

9. See Pengilly, "Never Cry *Anders*: The Ethical Dilemma of Counsel Appointed to Pursue a Frivolous Appeal," *Criminal Justice Journal* 9 (1986): 45, 52; Hermann, "Frivolous Criminal Appeals," *New York University Law Review* 47 (1972): 701, 715–16.

10. Davies, "Affirmed: A Study of Criminal Appeals and Decision-Making Norms in a California Court of Appeal," *American Bar Foundation Research Journal* 82 (1982): 543.

11. 372 U.S. 353.

Acknowledgments

My research on indigent appellate defense was completed and most of this book written when I was Marden and Marshall Fellow at New York University Law School's Center for Research in Crime and Justice. My greatest debt is to the Center's Director, Jim Jacobs, who prodded, cajoled, inspired, and browbeat me into completing a large-scale research project and writing a book about it. He was indispensable at every stage of the study, guiding its design, reviewing its progress, editing the emerging manuscript, assembling an impressive group of scholars to read the first draft, and extending my fellowship to twice its original length to permit me to complete the research and writing.

Jim's colleagues at NYU Law School were extremely supportive as well. I consulted frequently with Chet Mirsky, whose work with Mike McConville on indigent trial defense in New York City provided a point of departure and frame of reference, and Graham Hughes, who lent a sharp critical eye and a formidable knowledge of criminal law. The book benefited greatly from the advice of the readers Jim recruited: Sally Hillsman, Associate Director of Research at the VERA Institute of Criminal Justice; Randy Hertz of the NYU Clinic; Jo Dixon from the NYU Sociology Department; and Steve Kelban, Director of the NYU Root-Tilden program.

The organizations I studied—the Criminal Appeals Bureau of the Legal Aid Society (CAB) and the Assigned Counsel Panels of the First and Second Judicial Departments—were always cooperative and often generous in providing access to their records and insight into their work. The Legal Aid Society allowed me to examine all records which did not contain confidential client information. In addition, I received unstinting support and assistance from Philip Weinstein, CAB Attorney-in-Charge; Elaine Friedman, Managing Attorney; Judith Romanowski, Assistant Managing Attorney; and Susan Salomon, Assistant Attorney-in-Charge. I received valuable insight and suggestions from thoughtful former colleagues at CAB, including Rob Precht, Abe Clott, and Sarah Burr. The greatest resource that CAB provided, however, was the encyclopedic knowledge and passionate conviction of Andrew Fine, Associate Attorney-in-Charge. His views on criminal justice and appellate advocacy, though quite different from my own, inform and animate this book.

I also received considerable assistance from the administrators of the Assigned Counsel Panels in two Judicial Departments I studied: Geoffrey Rawls in the First and Malvina Nathanson in the Second. Though our approaches to criminal appellate advocacy and the provision of appellate defense sometimes differed, they provided critical support for my research. The Appellate Division Clerks in both Departments were extremely helpful and patient, giving me and my research assistants the run of their offices and file rooms, and helping us out when we got lost or confused. I learned a lot from talking with Joshua Rosenkranz and Ira Mickenberg, the attorneys in charge of the First Department Office of the Appellate Defender, and I gained valuable comparative perspectives from conversations with Robert Calhoun, Director of the California First District Appellate Project, and Joy Chapper, who has done extensive research on appellate courts for the National Center for State Courts.

I was served by a number of talented and conscientious research assistants, who performed with diligence and good humor the often dull and repetitive tasks I assigned them: David Eichenthal, Alice Frankl, Allan Herman, and Eric Machmer were among the most helpful and persevering. I was ably assisted by Paul Larkins, who directed a group of CAB paralegals in coding confidential material from their files. Ariel Dodson did an impressive and expeditious job of preparing graphics for the book. Robert Gilmore provided invaluable assistance in selecting appropriate statistical tests and in other aspects of the data collection and analysis.

Part I

INDIGENT APPELLATE REPRESENTATION IN THE QUARTER CENTURY AFTER *DOUGLAS*: CHALLENGES AND CONSTRAINTS

Part I of this book traces the doctrinal and administrative history of the right to assigned appellate counsel from the promise of *Douglas v. California* in 1963 to the realities of an overcrowded appellate docket in the mid–1980s. It introduces a theme that will be developed throughout the book: that the creation of an unqualified right to appellate counsel altered the character of indigent appellate representation, placing counsel's duty of zealous representation for each client into conflict with the courts' increasingly strong commitment to conserving judicial resources for more deserving cases. Aspects of this conflict will surface in Chapter 4, where I observe judicial impatience with zealous advocacy for marginal cases; in Chapter 8, where I argue that a defender organization faces a structural conflict of interest in representing a majority or large plurality of indigent appellants; and in Chapter 10, where I offer a critique of proposals and experiments to limit the review of weak and routine criminal appeals.

Part I also presents New York City as a strategic site for studying the performance and impact of assigned appellate counsel in the post-*Douglas* era; it examines how appellate defenders have met the challenge of providing zealous representation for routine appeals before overburdened courts. The appellate defenders who face that challenge in New York City differ greatly in resources, political influence, and reputation. A comparison of their performance reveals a great deal about the variations in quality and impact that are possible under the constraints of contemporary appellate review.

Chapter 1 analyzes the guarantee of appellate counsel within the due process revolution that produced it. It argues that the adaptation of the criminal justice system to the doctrinal upheaval of the Warren Court era has made the role of assigned appellate counsel more difficult, less productive, but no less valuable to the individual defendant. It reviews some of the strategies that have been adopted to ease the tension between counsel's obligation under *Douglas* to brief every nonfrivolous case with single-minded zeal and the courts' desire to control their swollen dockets.

Chapter 2 describes the basic features of criminal appeals and the evolving powers of the appellate courts in New York, placing the developments reviewed in Chapter 1 into a broader historical context. The expansion of appellate review in the late nineteenth and early twentieth centuries was accompanied by a rejection of technical error as a basis for appellate action; appellate courts acquired the power to correct a wider range of errors, but they also acquired the habit of exercising those powers very sparingly. Both aspects of this trend are epitomized by New York's Appellate Division, which has among the most extensive powers and conservative dispositions of any first-level appellate court in the nation. This contrast heightens the tension between counsel's obligation to obtain the fullest possible review for each client and the court's desire to conserve its resources.

Chapter 3 describes the provisions for indigent appellate defense in New York City and tracks the divergent growth of the City's two appellate defense organizations: the Criminal Appeals Bureau (CAB) of the Legal Aid Society and the assigned counsel or "18b" panel for appeals. It introduces two themes that will be developed later in the book: the disparity in resources between the two defenders, and the commitment of CAB to an intensive but highly circumscribed form of representation. The comparison of the two defenders will be extended in Part II, which studies the quality and impact of their representation. CAB policy will be examined in Part III, which discusses the role of appellate defense in a contemporary criminal justice system.

1

The Right to Assigned Appellate Counsel and the Transformation of Criminal Appeals

This chapter examines the doctrinal origins of the right to assigned appellate counsel and assesses the significance of that right in the aftermath of the due process revolution that established it. It traces the evolution of criminal appellate representation over 25 years of swollen caseloads and doctrinal retrenchment. Two related themes emerge from this retrospective: First, the guarantee of free appellate counsel to indigent defendants has made the work of assigned appellate representation considerably more difficult by increasing the volume of criminal appeals beyond the court's capacity to give each case a full hearing and by reducing the average merit of the indigent appeals heard by the court. Second, the outward success of the due process revolution has diminished the comparative importance of appellate review in the criminal defense system by improving the performance of the police, prosecutors, and judges and by insulating the remaining sources of systematic injustice from appellate scrutiny.

These related developments have not eliminated the value of counseled appeals to indigent defendants, but they have made them seem a comparative luxury in a system where many indigent defendants plead guilty without the benefit of even minimal investigation or preparation by their assigned trial counsel. In the chapters that follow, in which we examine the development and performance of New York City's appellate defenders, we will continue to confront the priority of zealous appellate representation for routine appeals in a system with grave deficiencies in trial defense and adjudication.

THE CONSTITUTIONAL BASIS FOR THE RIGHT TO APPELLATE COUNSEL

Though the Supreme Court recognized the indigent defendant's rights to trial and appellate counsel the same term, those rights have very different doctrinal sources. The state's obligation to provide trial counsel for indigent defendants is based on the explicit constitutional guarantees of due process and a fair trial. Over twenty-five years ago, in *Gideon v. Wainwright* (1963), a unanimous Supreme Court held that "reason and reflection require us to recognize that in our adversary system of criminal justice, any person haled into court, who is too poor to hire a lawyer, cannot be assured a fair trial unless counsel is provided for him."[1]

In contrast, the Supreme Court has never even recognized a constitutional right to appeal a criminal conviction, let alone a right to the assistance of counsel on a criminal appeal. In *McKane v. Durston* (1894), it held that the due process clause does not require the states to provide appellate review for criminal convictions.[2] The rationale for this holding was reaffirmed as recently as 1974 in *Ross v. Moffitt*, which rejected the claim that indigent defendants are entitled to assigned representation in discretionary appeals:

> It is ordinarily the defendant, rather than the state, who initiates the appellate process, seeking not to fend off the efforts of the State's prosecutor, but rather to overturn a finding of guilt made by a judge or jury below. The defendant needs an attorney not as a shield to protect him against being "haled into court" by the State and stripped of the presumption of innocence, but rather as a sword to upset the prior determination of guilt.[3]

Although under no constitutional obligation to do so, all states have guaranteed defendants convicted by trial of a felony the right to a first appeal.[4] Until 1963, however, that right was rarely implemented by the appointment of free appellate counsel for indigent defendants. Rather, under the pre-*Douglas* standard in California, *People v. Hyde* (1956), the state would usually provide a lawyer only if the court found that counsel would be "of advantage to the defendant or helpful to the appellate court," a discretionary judgment made by the appellate court on the motion of the indigent defendant.[5]

In *Douglas v. California* (1963),[6] the U.S. Supreme Court held that such a screening procedure denied indigents "equal protection of the law" under the Fourteenth Amendment:

> [T]he rich man can require the court to listen to the arguments of counsel, while the poor man cannot. There is lacking that equality demanded by the Fourteenth Amendment where the rich man . . . enjoys the benefit of counsel's examination into the record, research of the law, and marshalling of arguments on his behalf, while the indigent . . . is forced to shift for himself. The indigent, when the record is unclear

or the errors are hidden, has only the right to a meaningless ritual, while the rich man has a meaningful appeal.[7]

This proposition did not go unchallenged. The dissent argued that the majority had overstated the need for appellate counsel, since an appeal lacked "the large variety of tactical and strategic problems that must be resolved at the trial," and even the uncounseled indigent would receive "the benefit of [the Court's] expert and conscientious legal appraisal of the merits of his case on the basis of the trial record."[8] The argument that appellate counsel was unnecessary, or less important than trial counsel, has frequently resurfaced in the policy debates on the implementation of *Douglas* during the past 25 years.

The critical assumption made by the *Douglas* majority and challenged by the dissent was that the "argument of counsel" would frequently have a significant impact on the outcome of the case, that the court would often ignore subtle or hidden errors unless they were pressed by an adversary advocate. This position was more fully articulated by Judge Fuld of the New York Court of Appeals, in *People v. Emmett* (1969) which reversed a lower appellate court judgment reached before counsel had a chance to file his brief:

> Nor may it be successfully argued that, since an appellate tribunal may have the record before it, it is competent to review a case and pass upon its merits without waiting for the defendant's counsel.... There is no substitute for the single-minded advocacy of appellate counsel. Experience has demonstrated that they not infrequently advance contentions which might otherwise escape the attention of judges of busy appellate courts, no matter how conscientiously and carefully those judges read the records before them.[9]

The importance of the "single-minded advocacy" of appellate counsel was reaffirmed in the Supreme Court's second major decision on appellate counsel. In *Anders v. California* (1967), the Court refused to permit counsel to withdraw from an assigned appeal merely by filing a "no merit" letter. The Court held that this common practice improperly shifted to counsel the screening function which had been performed by the court before *Douglas*: "The constitutional requirement of substantial equality can only be attained when counsel acts in the role of an active advocate on behalf of his client as opposed to an *amicus curiae*."[10]

Anders did not prohibit assigned counsel from withdrawing, but required counsel wishing to do so to file a brief which discussed all potential issues and ended with the conclusion that they were all frivolous. In requiring counsel to draw this adverse conclusion, *Anders* created a dilemma which two decades of lower court decisions have not resolved: "[C]ounsel is . . . required to perform one or the other of two tasks, both of which are impossible or unethical: either argue the merits of claims which are meritless, or explain to the court why those claims are meritless without taking a position adverse to the clients interests."[11] Several states, including New York, have made counsel's task possible, if not clearly ethical, by requiring her to take a position adverse to her client's interests and to argue the frivolity of all possible issues.[12] Other states have sought to reduce the adverse impact on the client in two different ways, either permitting the attorney to raise frivolous issues or to withdraw without arguing their frivolity, satisfying the court in some other manner that she has done her adversarial best.

In most jurisdictions, the courts have made withdrawal more difficult than continued representation. As Pengilly complains:

> [T]he work necessary to compile something approximating an "*Anders* brief" will consume more time than any ten "merit" briefs which could be written.... What is worse, though, is the fact that the motion to withdraw is always denied: after spending many unpleasant hours in preparing an *Anders* brief, counsel will be tersely informed that the case is not wholly frivolous and instructed to file a merit brief—and when this is done, the conviction will be summarily affirmed.... The experience is one that is rarely repeated.[13]

Because the cost of raising frivolous issues is rarely as high, particularly if counsel has the good sense not to press them at oral argument, *Anders* has encouraged assigned counsel to resolve any doubts in favor of continued representation.

Under *Douglas* and *Anders*, then, most, if not all, of the indigent appeals which had previously been screened by court staff would now receive full briefing by appellate counsel. Not surprisingly, *Douglas* and *Anders* contributed to a tremendous upsurge in the volume of indigent criminal appeals and a significant decline in their average merit. These developments have threatened to make the promise of *Douglas* an empty one by diminishing the quality of appellate review for all criminal appeals. Ironically, *Douglas* may have achieved equal protection only by giving the "rich man" and "poor man" alike the right to a meaningless ritual rather than a meaningful appeal.

THE GROWTH OF CRIMINAL APPEALS AND THE CHANGING ROLE OF ASSIGNED APPELLATE COUNSEL

The Growth of Criminal Appeals

Douglas did not produce a sudden upsurge in criminal appeals, but accelerated a trend of two decades. The number of civil and criminal appeals increased steadily after World War II, perhaps reflecting a general increase in "litigiousness" or "claims-consciousness."[14] If the California data collected by Thomas Davies are representative, criminal appeals began increasing at a faster rate than civil appeals by the mid–1950s.[15]

In the 1960s, criminal appeals grew even more quickly, comprising an increasing share of the appellate docket. Davies found that California criminal appeals increased *500 percent* between 1960 and 1970;[16] Paul Carrington (1969) reported a 200 percent increase in federal criminal appeals nationwide from 1960 to 1967.[17] In the 1970s, the volume of criminal appeals continued to rise, though at a less dramatic rate. Justice Department Bureau of Criminal Justice statistics show that criminal filings increased 102 percent from 1973 to 1983, compared with 112 percent for civil appeals and 52 percent for criminal trials.[18] This rate of growth cannot be wholly explained by increases in the crime or conviction rate: criminal appeals grew twice as fast as the FBI Crime Index and trial-court criminal filings between 1973 and 1983.[19]

It is not possible to estimate how much the Supreme Court's decisions in *Douglas* and *Anders* affected this phenomenal growth, but their contribution may have been limited by a number of factors. For one thing, a number of states had already recognized the right to free appellate counsel before *Douglas.*[20] For another, indigent defendants were always free to file their own briefs, though the percentage that did so is likely to have been quite low in an era when jailhouse lawyering was still in its infancy. Still, there is no doubt that the Court's decisions encouraged more indigents to apply for counsel by recognizing their right to have counsel appointed and, more generally, by making a first appeal seem a routine part of the process of criminal adjudication.[21] The volume of retained appeals may also have been affected: paying clients may have become less selective about challenging their own convictions in coming to see appeals as the rule rather than the exception.

The states could have responded to *Douglas* by amending their statutes or constitutions to make *all* criminal appeals discretionary, but none did. Since they were unwilling to abridge the right to appeal, however, and could hardly prevent affluent defendants from securing the assistance of counsel, the states were constrained to provide appellate counsel for indigent defendants. In Chapter 3, we will discuss the various mechanisms they adopted to supply appellate counsel to all convicted indigents wishing to appeal.

The demand for appellate counsel in the years following *Douglas* far outstripped the supply. State funding for appellate defense was rarely adequate for the increasing number of indigent appeals. Equally important, the size of the appellate courts failed to keep pace with the volume of civil and criminal appeals. From 1973 to 1983, when appellate filings increased 108 percent, appellate judgeships increased only 36 percent.[22] The stress of an increased caseload clearly lowered the quality of appellate review. McCrate et al. illustrated the problem with a striking contrast: while the major contemporary study of appellate decision-making concluded that an appellate judge could decide no more than 100 cases per year without "jeopardizing the essential qualities of the appellate process,"[23] the average appellate judge in New York in 1980 was responsible for well over 200 decisions a year.[24]

Criminal appeals account for only part of the increased caseload, but they have borne the brunt of the austerity measures adopted to conserve judicial resources.[25] The economies imposed on criminal appeals have been justified by the prevailing belief among judges and court administrators that the "free ride" which *Douglas* gave to indigent criminal appellants had led to a preponderance of frivolous appeals. While that impression may be exaggerated, it clearly has some basis in fact.

The Decline in Average Merit

Although the merits of cases obviously cannot be measured as accurately as the volume of cases, there can be little doubt that *Douglas* and *Anders* contributed to a decline in the average merit of indigent appeals. However inadequate the pre-*Douglas* screening mechanisms may have been at selecting the most meritorious cases for appointment of counsel, they almost certainly did better than chance. While judicial screeners may have passed over many cases with unclear records and hidden errors, they were likely to have identified most cases with obvious legal uncertainties and egregious errors. The elimination of judicial screening virtually guaranteed that the average indigent appeal would have less merit, especially since an unknown proportion of convicted indigents were now appealing simply because they had no reason not to, rather than from any perceived injustice or error. There may also have been a decline in the average merit of retained appeals: influenced by the trend among indigent defendants, affluent defendants may have insisted on appellate challenges that they previously would have declined to pay for.

Robert Hermann (then head of Special Litigation for the New York City Legal Aid Society) was among the first to recognize that the provision of free appeals to indigent defendants had led to an increase in the proportion of meritless appeals and a decline in the quality of appellate briefing. *Anders* had made it considerably easier for counsel to submit a perfunctory brief than to withdraw from the appeal. As Hermann explained:

> Counsel may write a sketchy digest of the testimony and simply state in conclusory fashion that . . . the evidence was insufficient to sustain the verdict. . . . He may accurately state the law at present but argue without amplification that the court should reconsider the issue. He may file a brief raising matters obviously lacking in merit and waive oral argument.[26]

Hermann contended that the growing number of meritless appeals and perfunctory briefs jeopardized the quality of review for all defendants:

Even though it is the regular business of judges to winnow from a mass of claims those which are substantial, the task becomes more bothersome and more routinized as the volume of such work grows. This in turn results in a judicial *Weltschmerz* which colors the court's attitudes toward all criminal appeals and has a perceptible effect on the chances of success on appeal of those defendants who may have meritorious grounds for obtaining a reversal.[27]

Hermann is typical of the commentators in this area in regarding frivolous appeals as the principal culprit in the growing judicial impatience with criminal appeals.[28] There is reason to doubt this explanation, however, simply because there appears to be no judicial consensus on the frivolity of particular issues.[29] Davies has gone as far as to argue that the perception of "frivolity" merely reflects judicial resentment at the increasing share of the appellate docket taken up by criminal cases, cases which are relatively low in professional rewards.[30]

Whether or not the problem of frivolous appeals was exaggerated, many appellate judges found their criminal caseload becoming less interesting as it became larger. At the same time, most appellate judges continued to recognize the vital interests at stake in criminal litigation and the possibility of serious injustice. While 74 percent of the judges surveyed in *Appellate Justice in New York* felt that criminal appeals were more likely to be frivolous than any other kind of appeal, 78 percent felt that they warranted at least as much time as they devoted to them. The dominant perception seemed to be that criminal appeals required, but rarely rewarded, close judicial scruntiny.[31]

The Decline in the Reversal Rate

In *Griffin v. Illinois* (1955), which led the way to *Douglas* by requiring free trial transcripts for indigent appellants, the Supreme Court cited findings showing that "a substantial proportion of criminal convictions are reversed by state appellate courts."[32] A comprehensive survey of state supreme court dispositions between 1870 and 1970 revealed that the average rate of reversal for criminal defendant appeals was 36.7 percent—a very substantial proportion indeed.[33] This level of success is not surprising, since the formidable barriers faced by indigent defendants and the economic costs to nonindigent defendants may well have assured that most of the cases which were appealed raised plausible claims of error.

Once the appellate courts began reviewing a large majority of trial convictions rather than a select minority, it was almost inevitable that the reversal rate would decline. While statistics on criminal appellate dispositions are far too sketchy to present a close picture of nationwide trends, it is clear from the available data that the reversal rate has dropped considerably in the last 30 years. Davies's statistics from the First Judicial District in California show the reversal rate reaching a 50-year high of 30 percent in the mid–1950s, plummeting to less than 5 percent by 1960, rising back sharply to 25 percent in the mid–1960s, then declining slowly, but unsteadily, to 5 percent in the mid–1970s.[34]

While Davies offers state-specific explanations for some of the more jagged edges on this curve,[35] the overall pattern suggests a heightened concern for defendants' rights in the early 1950s (when California and other states were beginning to assign appellate counsel in select cases), another burst of intervention at the onset of the due process revolution, and then a gradual decline as the expansion of defendants' rights was offset by the growing number of low-merit appeals, the adaptation of the criminal justice system to the reforms of the Warren Court era, and the doctrinal brakes applied by the Burger Court.[36]

Comparative data on the reversal rates for retained and assigned cases during this period are not available, and we can only speculate on whether retained appeals were affected to the same extent as indigent appeals. First, we do not know whether the average merit of retained appeals declined as sharply: while nonindigent as well as indigent defendants may have become more rights-conscious and litigious, the former still faced the same economic disincentives in appealing. Changes in court practice and legal doctrine may have affected the two groups of defendants differently, discouraging retained appeals while defeating assigned ones. Second, even if the merit of retained appeals declined as well, there may have been a lag in judicial perceptions: retained appeals may have received the benefit of a selectivity which most affluent defendants no longer exercised.

The Pressure to Control the Criminal Appellate Docket and its Impact on Appellate Counsel

Over the past fifteen years, a variety of proposals have been made to limit the volume of low-merit appeals and to conserve judicial resources for more meritorious cases. One approach, directed towards prospective appellants, has attempted to equalize the positions of indigent and nonindigent defendants. Before *Douglas*, many indigent convictions that would have been appealed if the client had money were not appealed for want of counsel. After *Douglas* and *Anders*, assigned counsel undoubtedly briefed large numbers of cases that conscientious retained counsel would have discouraged their clients from pursuing, cases that had little or no practical chance of success. It was left to state legislatures and court administrators to devise constitutional means for giving indigent defendants the same incentive as affluent ones to forego unpromising appeals.

In the 1970s, a number of schemes were proposed for encouraging selectivity by indigent defendants without "penalizing" the exercise of their constitutional right to assigned appellate counsel. Carrington et al. proposed a scheme to give the indigent defendant the option of pocketing the estimated expense of an appeal.[37] The indigent defendant would supposedly face the same kind of decision about exercising his right to appellate counsel as the nonindigent defendant. No jurisdiction has tried out this proposal; perhaps the political resistance to paying off convicted criminals is simply too great, or perhaps lawmakers feel queasy about "bribing" defendants not to exercise a constitutional right.

A second strategy for reducing the volume of low-merit appeals was based on the belief that many or most indigent appellants "are not motivated by meritorious legal claims but by dissatisfaction with the sentence received."[38] Thus, a number of commentators have proposed simplified procedures for sentence review, as a less costly outlet for disgruntled defendants. Unfortunately, jurisdictions which have tried this approach have not seen any decline in ordinary "judgment" appeals.[39] The proponents of simple sentencing review may have misunderstood or oversimplified the reasons why most convicted defendants appealed. It may also have been that expedited sentence review spawned more appeals than it diverted.

The most common judicial response to increasing volume and declining merit has been to screen criminal cases *after* the assignment of counsel in order to expedite the disposition of "routine" appeals from indigent and nonindigent defendants alike, while reserving full-dress appellate review for "significant" or "complex" cases.[40] In some states, a large share of criminal appeals are diverted for summary disposition after preliminary briefing by counsel. In others, the court permits oral argument only in a minority of cases. Additionally, many appellate courts impose strict page limits on briefs and time limits on oral argument. Thus, in an increasing number of jurisdictions, neither the rich man nor the poor man may "compel the court to listen to the arguments of counsel" to the extent that the rich man once could.

These "fast tracking" mechanisms and other restrictions on appellate advocacy do not offend equal protection, since they apply to both retained and assigned cases. Still, they call into question the underlying rationale for *Douglas*, in their willingness to substitute the "expert and conscientious legal appraisal" of the court and its staff for the "single-minded advocacy" of counsel. In so doing, they reflect the continuing vitality of the *Douglas* dissent.

Although the post-*Douglas* screening mechanisms limit the involvement of appellate counsel in many cases, they also protect counsel from judicial pressure to perform the screening function themselves: to reserve oral argument for "truly significant" cases, to write shorter and more perfunctory briefs for routine cases, and, in general, to modulate the zeal of their advocacy to reflect the differential merit of their cases. In states without judicial screening mechanisms, appellate counsel frequently experience pressure to screen cases in this manner. William Hellerstein, founder of the New York

Legal Aid Society's Criminal Appeals Bureau, has offered some striking examples:

> I recall a particular afternoon on which I had argued three cases when, at the conclusion of my last argument, the presiding judge asked me which of the three I "really wanted." On another occasion, a judge telephoned to ask whether there was some way our office could indicate, perhaps by an asterisk on the brief's last page, which cases we "really thought should be reversed." On still another occasion, a judge called me the morning after an argument to ask if I was "truly serious" about the case.[41]

These judges may have been more unusual in their candor than their sentiment (albeit a little tongue-in-cheek, as Hellerstein concedes): overburdened appellate courts may find it easier to approve zealous representation for all defendants in theory than to encourage it in practice.[42]

The impatience of the appellate bench with "routine" criminal appeals confronts an appellate defense organization with a kind of Sophie's choice: either to condemn many or most of its clients to cursory review by making an implicit judgment on the worth of their cases, or to risk cursory review for all its cases. To avoid this unhappy dilemma, some institutional attorneys welcome the judicial screening: although it restricts the representation they are able to provide for many clients, it places the onus of selection on the court.[43] I will return to this dilemma in Chapter 8, where I argue that judicial pressure on appellate attorneys to perform a screening function may create a conflict of interest for an institutional defender in representing a large share of all criminal appellants. In Chapter 10, I argue that judicial screening cannot eliminate that conflict without sacrificing the accuracy of the appellate process.

The Role of Assigned Appellate Counsel Two Decades after *Douglas*

The character of assigned appellate advocacy has undergone a fundamental change since, and largely because of, *Douglas* and *Anders*. Instead of trying to persuade a bench that had already singled out her case for close scrutiny, the assigned attorney[44] is now, at least in jurisdictions without judicial screening procedures, trying to engage the interest of a court that has lost control over its docket.[45] The greatest challenge for appellate counsel may simply be to get the court's attention.

The mass representation of indigent appellants has placed a severe strain on the traditional role of adversary counsel. To judges who believe, as many do, that most criminal appeals have little or no merit, the assigned attorney who engages in single-minded advocacy for each case with any arguable merit may seem to be "crying wolf." As indigent defendants compete for the court's limited attention, the assigned attorneys who represent them face the challenge of "remaining true to each client's cause while simultaneously retaining the full confidence of the court."[46]

There is considerable doubt that this challenge can be met, a doubt reflected in the conflicting conclusions reached by two of the pioneers of indigent appellate representation.

> [L]awyers will be forced to make difficult and delicate judgments assessing the meaning of their clients' rights to the effective assistance of counsel and to the equal protection of the laws on appeal, while simultaneously reckoning with . . . their continued credibility as . . . advocates. . . . For a lawyer who regularly appears before the same appellate court in criminal cases to treat each case as equally meritorious is . . . to attempt without avail to solve the problem of his professional effectiveness on behalf of all his clients by pretending or assuming that it does not exist. (Hermann, 1972)[47]

> The challenge . . . can be accomplished only by a tactful and gracious performance in each court appearance which communicates the unstated but apparent message that for institutional appellate counsel the obligation to a client is no different than that owed by the bar at large. It is the obligation to argue each case on its own merits and to the fullest extent possible in the advancement of the clients' cause. (Hellerstein, 1987)[48]

These conclusions may not be technically inconsistent, but they reflect a fundamental disagreement about whether it is possible for an assigned appellate attorney to provide "single-minded advocacy" for each client without sacrificing her effectiveness.

It could be argued that these doubts reflect an underlying tension between the traditional adversary model and the accurate review of a high volume of dispositions in which errors are infrequent and fairly technical. Such review requires close attention, expertise, and perhaps a strong predisposition to find error, but it does not require the single-minded zeal of adversary counsel. The adversary model may commit counsel to a form of representation that serves neither the system nor the individual defendant.

The tension between the adversary role and the appellate review function is most visible when counsel's adversary duties impair the review of her client's case and reduce his chances for favorable action. This conflict surfaced twenty years after *Douglas* in *Jones v. Barnes* (1983), which considered whether assigned counsel had an obligation to raise all nonfrivolous issues pressed by the client, however weak or distracting.[49] *Jones* involved a divergence between the constitutional basis for assigning appellate counsel—to increase the indigent's odds of favorable action—and the duty of counsel in an adversary system—to pursue her client's goals, even if they *reduce* his chances of favorable action.

The conflict in *Jones* was a familiar one to criminal appellate attorneys: the client wanted assigned counsel to raise issues that, while not frivolous, were judged by the attorney to weaken the overall effectiveness of the appeal by blurring its focus and diffusing the impact of stronger points. After the affirmance of a direct appeal in which these issues were raised in a *pro se* supplemental brief, the client sought habeas relief, claiming that he had been denied the effective assistance of appellate counsel. The Second Circuit agreed, holding that effective appellate counsel must argue all nonfrivolous points requested by his client "to the full extent of his professional abilities."

The Court rejected this standard on the grounds that effective appellate advocacy required the careful selection, not the indiscriminate briefing, of nonfrivolous issues. The concurring and dissenting opinions both noted, however, that the ABA Standards for Criminal Appeals required the attorney to defer to his client's decision to raise an issue on appeal, whether or not he agreed with it. The dissent obscured the tension between the attorney's professional duties and the constitutional basis for his assignment by ignoring the narrow basis on which *Douglas* had been decided. Relying on *Faretta v. California* (1975),[50] which recognized the defendant's right to represent himself, the dissent stated that "the function of counsel under the Sixth Amendment is to protect the dignity and autonomy of a person by *assisting* him in making choices that are his to make, although counsel may be able to better decide which tactics will be most effective for the defendant."[51] If this autonomy-enhancing role is the function of counsel under the Sixth Amendment, however, it was certainly not the basis for assigning counsel to indigent appellants under the Fourteenth. This is not to say that the *Jones* majority was correct; it may be that "the effective assistance of counsel" requires a deference to the client's ends that will sometimes defeat the purpose of assigning counsel. In releasing assigned counsel from the duty to serve her clients' ends, the Supreme Court may have strengthened the effectiveness of assigned counsel, but, as the *Jones* dissent insisted, it left indigent defendants with something less than full adversarial representation.

Jones pitted the duties of adversary counsel against the client's own constitutionally protected interests. In later chapters, we will explore the conflict between those duties and the interests of other clients and the courts. Chapter 8 analyzes the conflicts of interest inherent in seeking the same or similar relief for a large proportion of the defendants appearing before the same tribunal. Chapter 10 reviews the measures that have been proposed and adopted to limit zealous advocacy for the sake of more efficient and reliable appellate review. A quarter century after *Douglas*, the tension between the duties of zealous advocacy and the pressures of mass representation remains unresolved.

THE DUE PROCESS REVOLUTION AND THE LIMITATIONS ON CRIMINAL APPELLATE REVIEW

In the remainder of the chapter, we will consider how the role of appellate counsel has been affected by the doctrinal containment of, and institutional adaptation to, the due process revolution of which *Douglas* was a part. While the Burger Court preserved most of the due process reforms of the preceding era, it often made their appellate enforcement more difficult. The growing familiarity of the police, prosecutors, and trial courts with those due process safeguards not only reduced the frequency of error but the proportion of errors accessible to appellate review. Most importantly, perhaps, the official acceptance of plea bargains and their growing insulation from appellate review limited the enforcement of many Warren Court reforms to a small minority of aggressively litigated cases.

Douglas was decided two years after *Mapp v. Ohio* (1961)[52] applied the exclusionary rule to the states, the same term that *Gideon v. Wainwright* required appointed counsel for all indigent defendants at trial, and less than three years before *Miranda v. Arizona* (1966)[53] and *United States v. Wade* (1967)[54] established stringent safeguards for elicited confessions and identifications. These and kindred decisions invalidated thousands of convictions; imposed formidable requirements on police, prosecutors, and judges; and greatly increased the possibilities for reversible error in subsequent criminal proceedings. In the mid–1960s, criminal convictions appeared more vulnerable to appellate review than ever before, and the role of appellate counsel more critical.[55]

Two developments combined to restore a presumption of regularity to criminal proceedings and to limit the role of appellate counsel: doctrinal retrenchment and institutional adaptation. The first development may well have been less significant than the second in its impact on routine appeals. While the due process revolution begun by the Warren Court had waned by the early 1970s, its reforms remained largely intact over the next decade. By and large, the Burger Court halted but did not dismantle the work of its predecessor.[56]

A Contained Revolution: The Review of Unpreserved Errors, Factual Accuracy, and Ineffective Representation

The Burger Court accepted most of the central tenets of the Warren Court revolution, particularly its "incorporation" of Fourth, Fifth, and Sixth Amendment rights and its application of the exclusionary rule to state criminal prosecutions. In several areas, however, it curtailed the appellate enforcement of Warren Court reforms, either by restoring procedural barriers to appellate review or by setting very demanding standards for reversal. What follows is a sample of those areas, not a comprehensive survey.

Procedural Default and Unpreserved Error. Perhaps the single most significant limitation on appellate review effected by the Burger Court was its restoration of a strict standard of procedural default. In *Fay v. Noia* (1963), a Warren Court majority had permitted federal review of all alleged issues for which the state courts had not been "deliberately bypassed," including all those alleged errors which trial or appellate counsel failed to raise through ignorance or neglect.[57]

While *Fay* only concerned the scope of federal habeas review, its impatience with procedural disqualifications threatened to undermine the default doctrine itself, which required appellate courts to consider only those errors "preserved" by timely objection.[58] Had the state courts adopted a similar standard and committed themselves to the review of all errors that had not been knowingly waived or deliberately bypassed, the scope of appellate review and the role of appellate counsel would have been greatly enlarged. Any movement in this direction was discouraged by the Burger Court's reversion in *Wainwright v. Sykes* (1977) to a more traditional default standard, requiring very good "cause" and very severe "prejudice" to overcome state procedural default.[59]

Factual Accuracy and Factual Review. The reforms of the Warren court era had only a limited effect on the appellate review of factual accuracy. While several Warren Court reforms enhanced the reliability of criminal trials and reduced the probability that an innocent person would be convicted, the Court did little to facilitate the appellate enforcement and refinement of those safeguards.[60] The most important reform in this area, the establishment of due process guidelines for line-ups and other identification procedures in the *Wade* trilogy, was undermined by the permissive standard of admissibility adopted in *Neil v. Biggars* (1972),[61] and *Manson v. Braithwaite* (1977),[62] which allowed police suggestiveness to be outweighed by independent evidence of eyewitness accuracy.

A second critical area of reform, the imposition of a duty on the prosecution to disclose exculpatory evidence, *Brady v. Maryland* (1963), was similarly eviscerated.[63] In the absence of a specific request by the defense for the unknown evidence, the Burger Court in *United States v. Agurs* (1976) limited the duty to disclose to evidence that had "a reasonable likelihood of affecting the jury."[64] As a practical matter, this meant that a prosecutor could conceal evidence with impunity unless the defense could show on appeal that it was highly exculpatory.

In both the identification and disclosure areas, the Burger Court seemed to show a greater concern for the possibility of factual error in the specific case than the deterrence of unreliable practices which reduce the general accuracy of criminal adjudication. Unfortunately, as Louis Seidman has argued, that concern for factual innocence did not carry over to Burger Court decisions on habeas corpus or guilty pleas. Nor did it lead to the development of constitutional standards for the appellate review of trial-court fact-finding.

While the Court recognized the "reasonable doubt" standard as the constitutionality mandated burden of proof in criminal cases, *In Re Winship* (1970),[65] its adoption of that standard had only a limited effect on appellate review: the trial courts were required to charge the jury on the reasonable doubt standard, but the appellate courts were not required to review its application by the jury, only the bare legal sufficiency of the evidence.[66] Thus, appellate review of the evidence was frequently a shield for the state, leading to findings of harmless error, but rarely a sword for the defense, leading to reversals of doubtful convictions.

Ineffective Assistance of Counsel. Ineffective assistance may be both the best documented source of trial level injustice and the most resistant to appellate review.[67] The poor quality of the trial defense bar has been recognized by observers as diverse as Warren Burger[68] and Richard Abel.[69] Most of the damage, however, is done at the pretrial stage, by the wholesale failure to investigate and prepare. Many courthouse regulars are familiar enough with trial practice to improvise a hostile cross-examination or an impassioned summation on a few hours' notice, creating the semblance of adversary confrontation for an appellate court reluctant to second-guess their performance.

While the constitutional standard of effectiveness has actually been raised by the Burger court, so has the required showing of prejudice. Under *Strickland v. Washington* (1984), the defendant no longer has to show a "farce and mockery of justice" to establish ineffectiveness, merely a "lack of reasonable competence" on the part of his attorney.[70] To *prevail* on an ineffectiveness claim, however, he must also show a "significant probability" of a better outcome with competent representation. By inviting the reviewing court to assess prejudice before examining counsel's performance, *Strickland* encouraged the appellate neglect of ineffectiveness claims.

After *Strickland*, two factors severely limit the review of ineffectiveness claims. The first is a de facto presumption of competence. Appellate courts will strive to find, or simply assume, a tactical basis for all but the most egregious mistakes and omissions of trial counsel—a posture that reflects either an unwarranted confidence in the defense bar or a misplaced professional courtesy. The second factor is the required showing of prejudice. The very failure to prepare and investigate on which many ineffectiveness claims are based will often prevent the defendant from establishing a significant probability of a different outcome—it is impossible to say what the case would have looked like if the defendant had better representation. For this reason, ineffective assistance is often a self-insulating injustice.

The review of effectiveness in plea cases is even more limited. The presumption of competence, the requirement of prejudice, and the acceptance of "hardball" negotiating tactics combine to render the appellate review of counsel's effectiveness in plea cases virtually meaningless.[71] As Schulhofer has argued:

> [A] creative court can almost always find in the plea bargain some quid pro quo for the attorney's refusal to press an available defense.... The courts usually assume

that investigation would not affect the ultimate terms of the bargain, or even that the very act of raising a defense claim "might jeopardize plea negotiation."

Thus, appellate courts not only tolerate coerciveness in the bargaining process but rely on it to justify the complete absence of an adversary defense. Except for conceded error in the advice given the defendant,[72] there is virtually no mistake or omission so egregious that it can establish counsel's ineffectiveness in negotiating a facially valid guilty plea.[73] As a result, the defendant's right to effective assistance in plea cases is virtually unenforceable on appeal.

The Due Process Revolution and the Appeal of Guilty Pleas

The major constitutional reforms of the 1960s had only a limited effect on the review of the 85 percent to 95 percent of defendants convicted by plea.[74] It has been argued that the Warren Court revolution greatly increased the rate of plea dispositions, not only by approving the practice of plea bargaining, but by making trials far more expensive and time-consuming.[75] Plea bargaining won judicial approval with its promise of conserving judicial resources, and appellate courts have vigorously enforced that promise. While adhering to the formal requirement that the waiver of basic constitutional rights must be fully knowing and voluntary, the courts have in fact relentlessly curtailed appellate inquiry into the voluntariness of the plea.

In *Brady v. United States* (1970), which upheld the validity of plea bargaining, the Supreme Court also ruled that a guilty plea could operate as a waiver of virtually all issues concerning the defendant's factual guilt and the constitutionality of the police and prosecutorial conduct leading to his conviction.[76] For many defendants, the procedural safeguards established by the Warren Court would only affect the "shadow" in which their bargaining took place by altering the default option if plea negotiations broke down.

Brady not only accepted the guilty plea as a comprehensive waiver of constitutional rights, but adopted a fairly relaxed standard for assessing the "knowing and voluntary" character of that waiver. Brady himself had entered his plea to escape a death sentence if convicted at trial. While the Court found that sentence unconstitutional, it upheld a plea which had been entered to avoid its imposition. The Court understood the defendant to be taking a calculated gamble in deciding whether to plead guilty, and held him to the consequences of that gamble if his attorney's advice was not manifestly unreasonable.

Lower court cases following *Brady* did not demand a very searching appellate review of the "knowing and voluntary" character of guilty pleas. While *Boykin v. Alabama* (1969) had required the trial court to ascertain on the record that the defendant "has a full understanding of what the plea connotes and of its consequences,"[77] appellate courts came to display both a ready acceptance of strictly pro forma inquiries and a high tolerance for omissions in, and departures from, the standard form.[78] At the present time, an appellate court will rarely disturb a counseled guilty plea unless the plea or sentencing minutes contain protestations of innocence, glaring discrepancies between the plea allocation and the elements of the offense, or affirmative evidence of misunderstanding or coercion.[79]

The insulation of guilty pleas from appellate review has largely confined the enforcement of constitutional rights to the small minority of defendants going to trial. To adapt Yale Kamisar's metaphor, most defendants never get beyond the crowded "gatehouse" of the calendar part, in which rough justice is hastily dispensed, to the capacious "mansion" of the trial courtroom, in which the defendants' rights are ceremoniously respected. The appellate courts, unable or unwilling to review what has not been transcribed, can only inspect the mansion and the small part of the gatehouse open to public viewing.[80]

The treatment of the guilty plea as a comprehensive and irrevocable waiver would be less disturbing if the closest, most difficult, and most ambiguous cases went to trial—if trials were really public forums for resolving controversial legal and factual issues. In fact, the literature on criminal case-processing suggests that the opposite is the case—significant issues of factual guilt, legal sufficiency, and state misconduct are likely to be bargained away, while the cases that go to trial are most often those where the evidence is too strong and the charges too serious for an acceptable discount.[81]

While a guilty plea forecloses most appealable issues in most jurisdictions, it usually does not waive the right to appeal. Even with severe restrictions on appellate review, the assignment of counsel for all plea appeals serves two important purposes. First, it increases the likelihood of corrective action in the small minority of pleas with serious facial errors. Second, it gives counsel the opportunity to investigate defendants' claims of off-the-record improprieties, which can be reviewed by the trial court in most jurisdictions through a motion to vacate judgment.[82] Many pleas, however, offer little hope for a direct or collateral attack, and their appeal merely increases the proportion of marginal and frivolous cases handled by appellate counsel.[83]

The Institutionalization of the Due Process Revolution

The routine work of appellate representation may have been less affected by the containment of the due process revolution than by its outward success. In response to the widespread publicity attending the Warren Court's major decisions in criminal procedure and the bureaucratic pressures they generated, the police, prosecutors, and judges changed their conduct. Warrants were obtained more frequently, suspects were routinely "Mirandized," line-ups were standardized, and suppression hearings became a standard feature of the trial court proceedings. Defendants' rights were better protected than they had been in previous generations.[84]

The Warren Court also made the participants in the criminal justice system acutely conscious of appellate scrutiny. By and large, they learned to say, if not always do, the right thing. Police officers became accustomed to articulating the "reasonable and articulable suspicion" which *Terry* required for a stop-and-frisk; trial judges accompanied discretionary rulings of any importance with assurances that they had carefully weighed the relevant factors. The traditional deference which appellate courts accord to trial court findings of fact severely limited their willingness to look behind trial records that were free of facial error. If police, prosecutorial, and judicial misconduct had become less common, it also became better concealed.

This subversion of the due process revolution may have been inherent in the form it took. The Warren Court extended the reach of appellate review in several areas by formalizing due process requirements; the most familiar examples are the *Miranda* warnings and the *Boykin* plea "catechism."[85] This formalism was double-edged, however: while it enhanced the appellate enforcement of due process norms, by setting clear minimum standards, it also facilitated their violation, by giving police, prosecutors, and judges clear instructions on how to avoid a searching review of their conduct. It provided a formula, not only for perjury, but perhaps more damaging, for nominal or perfunctory compliance.

The formal compliance of the trial participants with due process norms creates a deceptive appearance of regularity in the official record. The trial and appellate courts in New York, for example, can now view a videotape of almost every homicide confession made in the city, but these confessions are made to an assistant district attorney after hours of unrecorded police interrogation, at a time when the defendant's fright, confusion, intoxication, withdrawal symptoms, and physical injuries are no longer visible. A transcript, photograph, and sometimes videotape are now available for New York lineups, allowing the court to observe any suggestiveness in the array or the procedure but not in the earlier and often more critical stages of the identification process, such as the witness's prior exposure to the defendant's mugshot in the file of "usual suspects." A complete plea allocution will contain the defendant's repeated affirmations that he understands and accepts the terms and consequences of his plea; only the occasional breakdown of the process exposes the defendant's confusion or his attorney's impatient coaching.

This appearance of regularity poses a formidable challenge for appellate counsel, strengthening the presumption of regularity in the trial court proceedings. While there are procedural devices for looking behind the facade presented by the trial court record, their use by a reviewing court is usually discretionary. In order to enlarge the record, appellate counsel must convince the reviewing court that the record is seriously incomplete or distorted; in order to do that, she needs to go outside the record. This is not strictly a "catch 22"—counsel can always submit evidentiary affidavits with a motion to enlarge the record, but the trial and appellate courts usually give little credence to paper submissions.

CONCLUSION

The guarantee of appellate counsel on appeal has clearly made the task of indigent appellate representation more difficult than it was in an era when only "meritorious" indigent appeals received benefit of counsel. Twenty-five years after *Douglas*, the cases argued by assigned appellate counsel have less average merit, the courts before which they argue are less patient and attentive, and the odds of success are considerably lower.

At the same time, the value of appellate counsel to the individual defendant may be greater than ever. As criminal procedures have become more complex, and police, prosecutors, and trial judges more sophisticated, the proportion of subtle and obscure error may have increased, even as the overall frequency of discoverable error has declined. Moreover, skilled appellate counsel may have become even more critical to overcome the increasingly strong presumption of regularity afforded by the appellate courts to routine criminal prosecutions.

In 1985, the Supreme Court reaffirmed the importance of appellate representation in holding that the Fourteenth Amendment required the effective assistance of counsel on appeal. Writing for the majority in *Evitts v. Lucey* (1985), Justice Brennan asserted that skilled counsel was indispensable for the criminal defendant seeking to challenge his conviction:

> To prosecute the appeal, a criminal appellant must face an adversary proceeding that, like a trial, is governed by intricate rules that to a lay person would be hopelessly forbidding. An unrepresented appellant, like an unrepresented defendant at trial—is unable to protect the vital interests at stake.... [T]he promise of *Douglas* that a criminal defendant has a right to counsel on appeal—like the promise of *Gideon* that a criminal defendant has a right to counsel at trial—would be a futile gesture unless it comprehended the right to the effective assistance of counsel.[86]

NOTES

1. 372 U.S. 335.
2. 153 U.S. 684.
3. 417 U.S. 600.
4. American Bar Association, *Standards on Criminal Appeals* (1970): 16–17.
5. 51 Cal. 2d 152, 154.
6. 372 U.S. 353.
7. Ibid. 358.

8. Ibid. 392.

9. 25 N.Y. 2d 354, 356.

10. 386 U.S. 738, 744.

11. Pengilly, "Never Cry *Anders*: The Ethical Dilemma of Counsel Appointed to Pursue a Frivolous Appeal," *Criminal Justice Journal* 9 (1986): 45, 52.

12. In 1988, the Supreme Court upheld this approach against an argument that *Anders* prohibited counsel from arguing against her client's interests in this manner. In *McCoy v. Court of Appeals of Wisconsin*, 108 S.Ct. 175, the majority emphasized that the challenged rule allowed the appellate court to assure that the attorney was really seeking to withdraw because he found the appeal devoid of merit, not merely, like the judicial screeners before *Douglas*, because its issues were not strong or interesting enough to warrant the court's attention. The dissent argued that in insisting on this assurance, the rule merely replaced a speculative threat to equal protection with its certain denial: under the Wisconsin rule, the indigent client with a marginal appeal faced the prospect of an adverse brief from assigned counsel, while the paying client faced nothing more prejudicial than the task of obtaining a second, more favorable opinion.

13. Pengilly, "Never Cry *Anders*," 63.

14. Davies, "Gresham's Law Revisited: Expedited Processing Techniques and the Allocation of Appellate Resources," *Justice Systems Journal* 6 (1981): 372, 384.

15. Ibid.

16. Ibid.

17. Carrington, "Crowded Dockets and the Courts of Appeals: The Threat to the Function of Review and the National Law," *Harvard Law Review* 82 (1969): 542, 586.

18. Bureau of Justice Statistics Bulletin, *The Growth of Criminal Appeals: 1973–1983 Trends* (Washington, D.C.: Government Printing Office, 1985), 3.

19. Ibid. Criminal appeals have lagged slightly behind prison commitments, however. Because of differences among the relevant baselines, "it is very difficult to construct any valid measure of the rate of appeal." Davies, "Affirmed: A Study of Criminal Appeals and Decision-Making Norms in a California Court of Appeal," *American Bar Foundation Research Journal* 82 (1982): 543, 572.

20. See Special Committee to Study Defender Systems, *Equal Justice for the Accused* (New York: Doubleday, 1959): Appendix. New York, however, assigned counsel only at the discretion of the appellate court, *People v. Breslin* 4 N.Y.2d 73 (1958).

21. Another factor which undoubtedly contributed to the growth of indigent appeals was the elimination of any practical threat of a higher sentence for defendants convicted at trial. In *North Carolina v. Pearce*, 395 U.S. 711 (1969), the Court held that the trial judge would have to overcome a strong presumption of vindictiveness to impose a higher sentence after a second trial. Although subsequent decisions have weakened the presumption and limited the circumstances in which it is applicable, the risk of a higher sentence following a successful trial appeal remains slight. Unlike *Douglas, Pearce* may have removed a deterrent which operated mainly against defendants with highly meritorious appeals, for whom the possibility of retrial and the threat of a higher sentence would have been greatest.

22. Bureau of Justice Statistics Bulletin, *The Growth of Criminal Appeals*, 3. Although "social loafing" and other group-size studies suggest that an *x* percent

increase in size will produce significantly less than an *x* percent increase in productivity. Luskin, "Social Loafing on the Bench: The Case of Calendars and Caseloads" (paper prepared for 1986 Annual Meeting, Law & Society Assn. Chicago, Ill.). A comprehensive study of appellate court output, found that in most jurisdictions, appellate court output went up in direct proportion to the number of new judges appointed. Marvell, "A Time-Series Cross-Section Study of Methods to Increase Appellate Court Decision Output," (paper prepared for 1987 Annual Meeting, Law & Society Assn., Washington, D.C.), 28.

23. McCrate et al., *Appellate Justice in New York* (Chicago: American Judicature Society, 1982): 101–2.

24. The "benchmark" of 100 decisions per judge was set by Carrington, Meador, and Rosenberg in *Justice on Appeal* (St. Paul, Minn.: West Publishing Co., 1976): 42–48, based on the authors' estimates of the time required for the different steps in appellate decision-making under standard working conditions.

25. See "Symposium: The Appellate Judiciary—Its Strengths, Its Woes, and Some Suggestions for Reform," *Maryland Law Review* 4 (1983): 42; Davies, "Gresham's Law Revisited."

26. Hermann, "Frivolous Criminal Appeals," *New York University Law Review* 47 (1972): 701, 715–16.

27. Ibid. 703.

28. Carrington et al., *Justice on Appeal*, 60, 91–96.

29. This lack of consensus has been amply demonstrated on the civil side by the continuing controversy over the application of FRCP Rule 11, amended in 1983 to allow federal judges to impose sanctions on attorneys raising frivolous claims and defenses. Reviewing the enforcement of the amended rule in its first four years, Federal District Judge William Schwartzer concluded that:

> Undoubtedly there are claims and defenses in whose patent lack of merit most judges would generally agree, but they are rare.... No one as yet has come up with a definition of frivolousness that would allow one to predict with some certainty whether a claim is so far beyond the pale that no judge would listen to it sympathetically; an attempt to do so would be disingenuous. (Schwartzer, "Rule 11 Revisited," *Harvard Law Review* 101 [1988]: 1013, 1016, 1018.)

Judges convinced that "they know frivolity when they see it" might be surprised by their discrepant reactions to specific cases. A 1985 Federal Judicial Center study of Rule 11 sanctions, cited by Schwartzer, found general agreement among the judges surveyed on only 1 of 10 hypothetical fact situations.

30. Davies, "Gresham's Law Revisited."

31. McCrate et al., *Appellate Justice in New York*, Appendix.

32. 351 U.S. 12.

33. Wheeler, Cartwright, Kagan, and Friedman, "Do the Haves Come Out Ahead?: Winning and Losing in State Supreme Courts, 1870–1970," *Law & Society Review* 21 (1987): 403, 426. While the reversal rate for first-level appellate courts would have been lower than for second-level courts, since they generally would have had less discretion in the appeals they heard, many of the state supreme courts included in this survey *were* first-level appellate courts for most or all of the period covered.

34. Ibid. 578.

35. Davies, "Affirmed," 578–82.

36. For a general discussion of the Burger Court's approach to criminal justice, see Seidman, "Factual Guilt and the Burger Court: An Examination of Continuity and Change in Criminal Procedure," *Columbia Law Review* 80 (1980): 437.

37. Carrington et al., *Justice on Appeal*, 93–95.

38. Botler, DeVita, Kallas, Ruane and Weisbrot, "Project. The Appellate Division of the Supreme Court of New York: An Empirical Study of Its Powers and Functions as an Intermediate State Court," *Fordham Law Review* 47 (1978): 929, 1008.

39. See Chapters 2 and 5, which discuss the steady growth of the overall criminal caseload in the Second Department of the New York Appellate Division, despite its adoption of an expedited procedure for sentence appeals.

40. See "Symposium: The Appellate Judiciary"; Davies, "Gresham's Law Revisited."

41. Hellerstein, "Appellate Advocacy for the Defense—A Joyful Challenge," *The Defender* 39 (1987): 37.

42. Judicial pressure to compromise the adversary role is not limited to assigned counsel, of course, or to criminal cases. Thomas Marvell noted a general tendency of appellate courts to demand a disclosure of adverse authority and facts that is often not in the client's best interests and is not always required by professional ethics. In effect, counsel are told that their full disclosure in one case, though damaging to their clients' interests, will enhance their credibility in other cases. The dilemma is more acute for assigned appellate counsel in criminal cases because of the kind of disclosure demanded—an assessment of the "real merits" of the case—and the magnitude of damage to the client—the summary affirmance of his conviction. Marvell, *Appellate Courts and Lawyers: Information Gathering in the Adversary System* (Westport, Conn.: Greenwood Press, 1978).

43. See Olson and Chapper, "Screening and Tracking Criminal Appeals: The Rhode Island Experience," *Justice Systems Journal* 8 (1983): 20.

44. Throughout this book, I will employ the convention of referring to defendants as "he" and appellate lawyers as "she," pronouns which are reasonably faithful to present demographics and which reduce confusion about antecedants. I will use the expression "appellate defender" to refer to any organization or individual representing individual defendants on appeal, using "institutional appellate defender" to refer exclusively to appellate defense organizations.

45. It did not take long for commentators to recognize the difficulty of assigned appellate representation under *Douglas*. In a 1968 New York City Bar Association symposium on appellate advocacy, Harris Steinberg enthused that "Legal Aid lawyers, volunteers, and assigned counsel are bringing their skill, imagination, and idealism to criminal appeals, and the beneficial results are growing more apparent every day." Judge Breitel of the New York Court of Appeals was less optimistic, however, observing that the "virtually absolute right to an appeal and the assignment of counsel" meant that "a large number of substantive appeals had become largely pro forma, regardless of how able or astute the counsel that may be assigned to them." "The Criminal Appeal" in Carpentier, ed., *Counsel on Appeal* (New York: McGraw-Hill, 1968): 23–26.

46. Hellerstein, "Appellate Advocacy," 39.

47. Hermann, "Frivolous Criminal Appeals," 703–4.

48. Hellerstein, "Appellate Advocacy," 39.

49. 463 U.S. 745.

50. 422 U.S. 806.
51. 463 U.S. at 759.
52. 367 U.S. 643.
53. 384 U.S. 486.
54. 388 U.S. 218.
55. Seidman notes that after *Gideon* was decided, Florida had to release *1,000* convicted, incarcerated defendants. "Factual Guilt and the Burger Court," 430.
56. Ibid. 448.
57. 372 U.S. 391.
58. See Hughes, "Sandbagging the Constitution: Federal Habeas Corpus and the Procedural Default Principal," *NYU Review of Law and Social Change* 16 (1988): 321.
59. 433 U.S. 72.
60. Seidman, "Factual Guilt and the Burger Court."
61. 409 U.S. 188.
62. 432 U.S. 682.
63. 373 U.S. 83.
64. 427 U.S. 97.
65. 397 U.S. 358.
66. *Jackson v. Virginia*, 443 U.S. 407 (1979). Robert Gregory argues that by requiring all reasonable inferences to be construed in favor of the prosecution, *Jackson* makes it virtually impossible to enforce the reasonable doubt standard in sufficiency review. "Whose Reasonable Doubt? Reconsidering the Role of the Reviewing Court in the Criminal Decision Making Process," *American Criminal Law Review* 24 (1987): 911.
67. See Levine, "Preventing Defense Counsel Error—An Analysis of Some Ineffectiveness Claims and Their Implications for Professional Regulation," *Toledo Law Review* 15 (1984): 1275.
68. Burger, "The Special Skills of Advocacy: Are Specialized Training and Certification of Advocates Essential to Our System of Justice?" *Fordham Law Review* 42 (1973): 227.
69. Abel, "Legal Aid," *U.C.L.A. Law Review* 32 (1985): 474.
70. 466 U.S. 668.
71. See *Bordenkircher v. Hayes* 434 U.S. 357 (1978).
72. Even then, the court may decline to review that concession if it contradicts a statement made by the defendant in the plea allocution or involves an off-the-record promise. See *Matter of Benjamin S.*, 55 N.Y. 2d 116, 121 (1982). At least in theory, however, the appellate court must consider off-the-record representations and promises, however much they conflict with the allocution, in reviewing a claim that the allocution itself was made involuntarily or without the effective assistance of counsel. To the extent that *Benjamin S.* merely denies specific performance of off-the-record promises, see *People v. Rodriguez*, 123 A.D.2d 404, 405 (1986); it is consistent with this requirement.
73. As Schulhofer has noted,

> [t]he attorney who accepts a plea offer immediately, without doing these things [researching legal defenses, interviewing witness or filing motions], can plausibly claim that he made a sound tactical choice, that additional effort would entail delay and, with it, the risk of losing the early plea offer. Indeed, the formal requirements of effective assistance do not, even in

theory, require the defense attorney to make the same investigation before accepting a plea that is required in preparation for trial. Schulhofer, "Criminal Justice Discretion as a Regulatory System," *Journal of Legal Studies* 17 (1988): 43, 58.

74. A Bureau of Justice Statistics survey of 27 states found that guilty pleas accounted for 88 percent of all felony convictions in 1981. B.J.S. Final Report, "The Prosecution of Felony Arrests" (Washington, D.C.: Government Printing Office, 1986).

75. See Alschuler, "Plea-Bargaining and its History," *Law & Society Review* 13 (1979): 211, 238–39.

76. 397 U.S. 742. Even in states which permit the appeal of all issues raised in preplea hearings, there is a strong deterrent to appeal in the threat of a higher sentence on reprosecution. Lower courts applying *North Carolina v. Pearce* have consistently rejected a presumption of vindictiveness where a defendant who successfully challenges his plea gets a higher sentence after trial. The threat may discourage the most meritorious plea appeals, for which the prospect of reversal and reprosecution is most salient.

77. 395 U.S. at 242–244.

78. For a striking illustration of the latter trend, see *People v. Harris et al.*, 61 N.Y. 2d 9 (1983).

79. The New York Court of Appeals has even taken the position that appellate courts cannot consider, or at least enforce, documented off-the-record promises; see *Matter of Benjamin S.*

80. The almost exclusive appellate focus on trials recalls the anecdote about the man determinedly searching for his keys beneath a street light, even though he had dropped them some distance away. Like the man in the story, the appellate courts seem committed to looking for error where they can see it, not where it is most likely to be present. In Chapter 11, I will review the propsects for illuminating a greater area by giving appellate courts the power to hear additional evidence.

81. See Mather, *Plea Bargaining or Trial? The Process of Criminal Case Disposition* (1979): 60–63.

82. The chances for reversal may be very slim, however, even when appellate counsel is able to establish that the defendant was seriously confused or misled, since the defendant will have given his sworn assurance, at his plea, that this was not the case. The courts sometimes seem to operate on an estoppel theory in reviewing guilty pleas; see *Matter of Benjamin S.*

83. The time demanded by a simple plea case is increased by the need to communicate with the client about the risks of a higher sentence if the plea is vacated, a far greater risk than the trial defendant faces under *North Carolina v. Pearce*. Some prosecutors' offices have adopted a policy of refusing charge reductions to defendants whose pleas are vacated on appeal, giving them the choice of a trial on or plea to the top count of the indictment. If the risk of a higher sentence is negligible in such jurisdictions, it is only because the odds of reversal are.

84. While two early and widely cited studies cast doubt on the deterrent effect of the exclusionary rule: Oaks, "Studying the Exclusionary Rule in Search and Seizure, *University of Chicago Law Review* 30 (1970): 665; and Spiotto, "An Empirical Study of the Exclusionary Rule and Its Alternatives," *Journal of Legal Studies* 2 (1973): 243, a number of later studies questioned their methodology and

found evidence of significant police compliance in some jurisdictions. See Canon, "Is the Exclusionary Rule in Failing Health? Some New Data and a Plea Against a Precipitous Conclusion," *Kentucky Law Journal* 62 (1974): 681; Horowitz, *The Courts and Social Policy* (Washington, D.C.: Brookings Institution, 1976).

85. *Boykin v. Alabama*, 395 U.S. 742 (1970).

86. 469 U.S. 387.

2

An Introduction to Criminal Appeals and First-Level Appellate Review in New York

This chapter offers a capsule history of criminal appeals and an introduction to the organization and powers of New York's intermediate appellate courts, providing an institutional and historical context for the developments described in Chapter 1. The evolution of criminal appeals over the past century, while greatly expanding the review powers of the appellate courts, has also increased the difficulty of obtaining favorable action in routine criminal appeals. These contrasting trends are especially striking in New York, whose first-level appellate courts have among the broadest powers, greatest volume, and fewest screening devices found in any American jurisdiction, and whose appellate defenders face the corresponding challenge of appearing before a virtually unrestricted but severely overburdened tribunal.

BACKGROUND: THE FUNCTIONS AND LIMITATIONS OF APPELLATE REVIEW IN CRIMINAL CASES

Appellate review is conventionally held to serve two distinct but overlapping functions: correcting the errors made in individual cases, particularly in the exercise of discretion, and clarifying and refining the law.[1] The term "error" covers a multitude of sins. In its narrowest sense, it means a mistake in applying the law made by the trial court, duly objected to by counsel, and thus "preserved" for the appellate court's review. In a broader sense, it can refer to virtually anything that went wrong from the inception of the case.

In a criminal context, there are three basic ways that something can go wrong. The first, most elemental, is the conviction of an innocent person, particularly one who did not even commit the acts that are the subject of the criminal complaint. The second is an infirmity in the procedures that culminated in conviction—the failure of the police, prosecutor, judge, or jury to play by the prescribed rules. Since such failure usually becomes appellate error only if the trial judge fails to take the appropriate corrective action, from a mistrial to a curative instruction, this form of error shades into judicial regulation. The third is the correctness of the court's evidentiary and other rulings, and its instructions to the jury, a concern that shades into law articulation.[2] While the first type of error is the most basic, it is also, as we will discuss in Chapter 7, the least accessible to appellate review.

The nature of appellate review in an adversary system limits the opportunity to correct these errors. Appellate courts are not roving commissions charged with investigating and rectifying injustice wherever they find it; they are passive tribunals limited to correcting certain types of error brought before them by the affected party in an appropriate manner. They are, for the most part, confined to reviewing the actions of the trial courts: an injustice suffered by the defendant only becomes a reviewable error if it is committed, ratified, or inadequately "cured" by that court.

Reflecting and defining the basic posture of the appellate court, there are several traditional restrictions on appellate review in American jurisdictions—on reviewing the facts, on taking new evidence, on considering objections not made to the trial court, and on reviewing errors that did not prejudice the party complaining about them.[3] These restrictions are sometimes contained in constitutions or statutes, but they are more often established by convention and habit, assumed rather than justified.

First, appellate courts are generally supposed to decide the law, not the facts. While the distinction between legal and factual judgments is notoriously slippery, there are some kinds of determinations a British or American appellate court will not make: it will not sit as a "second jury" and try a case de novo, and it will not reverse simply because it suspects the credibility of witnesses that the trial-level factfinder could reasonably have believed. In some jurisdictions, however, appellate courts may decide whether the jury's verdict was "against the weight of the evidence," and they must, under the U.S. Constitution, decide if the evidence against the defendant was "legally sufficient" to sustain a conviction.[4] We will discuss these distinctions later in this chapter when we review the unusually broad powers of New York's Appellate Division.

Second, American appellate courts do not receive any new evidence, but decide the case on the basis of the "record" created in the trial court. If that record contains gaps or ambiguities, or otherwise needs to be supplemented, the court may "remand" the case to the trial court for clarification or expansion.[5] While these first two limitations seem to go hand-in-hand, they are distinct: an appellate court could be empowered to try a case de novo, but only on the trial court record; in deciding an issue of law, the court could receive new statistical, demographic, or other general evidence. (*Brown v. Board of Education* is perhaps the most familiar example.)

Third, American appellate courts will generally not consider an issue unless it was "preserved" by an objection to the trial court.[6] Appellate courts commonly require objections to be raised at a time when remedial action is still possible, in sufficient detail to apprise the trial court of the grounds on which it is raised. Some courts even require that the arguments made to the trial court be essentially the same as those made on appeal. Almost all courts have some exceptions to their preservation rules; among the most common are matters going to the trial court's jurisdiction, errors that are "plain" or obvious from the record, and matters of fundamental justice. Some jurisdictions, notably New York, give their first-level appellate courts the power to review any unpreserved error "in the interests of justice."

Fourth, appellate courts will not review an error unless it actually harmed the complaining party. This prejudice requirement precludes the review of any misconduct, however egregious, perpetrated against a defendant who is ultimately acquitted. It also precludes anyone but the aggrieved defendant from raising the error—the court will not review a conviction *sua sponte*, or at the instigation of a conscience-stricken prosecutor.[7]

A final aspect of appellate review important for the appeal of criminal convictions it the division of labor between the first and second level appellate courts in the roughly 50 percent of American jurisdictions that have a "two-tier" appellate structure.[8] Typically, the first-level court hears all appeals-of-right, while the second-level court selects a small number for further review. In an influential essay, James Hopkins argued that the error-correction function must predominate in a first-level appellate court, as the court of last resort for most cases, with the regulation of trial court discretion as an important secondary function. The primary function of the second-level court is to decide important issues of law and to resolve the disagreements among the lower courts. Hopkins argued that the first-level court can enhance this function by screening cases for the higher court, spotting and framing emerging issues for its consideration.[9]

A CAPSULE HISTORY OF CRIMINAL APPELLATE REVIEW: FROM THE WRIT OF ERROR TO THE HARMLESS ERROR RULE

Historically, the limitation on factual review had an eminently practical basis: until the development of shorthand and stenography, it was not feasible to keep a running record of the trial proceedings, and thus a reviewing court had no reliable access to the evidence presented.[10] For centuries following the Norman Conquest, the standard form of appeal was the "writ of error," which permitted the court to review only those errors which appeared in a record consisting solely of "the process, the pleadings, and the judgments, together with various entries made by the clerk. It did not include the testimony and exhibits, the rulings on admissibility, or the instructions of the court."[11] Obviously, most serious errors would not appear on such a narrow record, and almost any error that did appear would be a technicality.[12]

Even a skeletal record, however, may have served to alert the reviewing court to an unjust or cruel outcome, especially at a time when so many minor offenses were punished by torture and execution. There is little doubt that appellate judges used technicalities then as they now use fairly minor procedural errors, to avoid or mitigate serious injustice that would otherwise fall beyond their reach. As Harris Steinberg noted:

> Judges, too, are human, and if correcting Latin grammatical errors appears to be a useful way to avoid boiling a curly-haired ten year old who stole sixpence, it is no wonder that the appellate courts of several centuries ago were willing to mask their real reasons for acting as they did with a solemn false face of hypertechnicality.[13]

However enlightened this use of technicalities, the correction of injustice depended to a large extent on the fortuitous presence of a technical error. Although the powers of appellate courts have been greatly expanded, that is still true. As we will see in Chapter 7, the appellate habit of relying on technical errors to reverse troublesome convictions has survived the legal necessity to do so.

The American states took over the British machinery for appellate review and modified it very slowly. In New York, appeal in criminal cases was limited to the writ of error until 1881, when the state's first criminal code created a broader remedy of appeal.[14] After that, however, the powers of the appellate courts increased dramatically. The 1894 Constitution established the Appellate Division of the Supreme Court as the state's first-level appellate court, giving it the power to make factual determinations, review the trial court's exercise of discretion, and exercise its own discretion in considering unpreserved errors. A 1914 statute confirmed its power to review a jury's findings of fact; a 1925 constitutional amendment gave it the power to make its own factual findings.[15]

These powers, unusually broad for an American appellate court, derived from the Appellate Division's status as "a branch of the Supreme Court, vested with all the powers of the trial court."[16] The one trial court power the Appellate Division did not explicitly receive, and has consistently abjured, is the power to enlarge the record by calling witnesses or taking evidence.

The reform movement that broadened the review powers of the appellate courts in the late 19th and early 20th century also rejected the emphasis on errors of form and detail that had, of necessity, prevailed for most of the history of Anglo-American appeals. Few jurisdictions displayed these dual aspects of appellate reform more prominently than New York, which pioneered in both the expansion of appellate review powers and the rejection of "technical errors or defects" as a basis for reversal. The 1881 Code of Criminal Procedure declared, in language that now appears in Sec. 470.05 of the Criminal Procedure Law, that "an appellate court must determine an appeal without regard to technical errors or defects which do not affect the substantial rights of the parties."

This provision was among the earliest of the "harmless error" rules, adopted in most jurisdictions by the late 1920s in response to a perception that the appellate courts had become "impregnable citadels of technicalities."[17] According to Justice Rutledge in *Kotteakos v. U.S.* (1946), "so great was the threat of reversal in many jurisdictions that the criminal trial became a game for sewing reversible error in the record, only to have repeated the same matching of wits when a new trial had become thus obtained."[18] This account is surely exaggerated: it overlooks the devices the appellate courts must have utilized to avoid automatic reversal for strictly technical errors, and the selective use of technicalities to rectify substantial injustice. Thus, Davies (1982) notes that although the California Supreme Court was reported to have reversed 52.4 percent of appealed convictions between 1870 and 1879,[19] a study of criminal appeals filed in one California county during that period concluded that there were virtually no reversals attributable to legal formalism, and "precious little sign of appellate coddling."[20]

Although the New York courts had imposed a harmlessness test before the adoption of the 1881 Code, the standard came very close to a rule of automatic reversal. The post-Code cases continued to set a fairly strict standard for finding error harmless, similar to the test for constitutional error ultimately adopted in *Chapman v. California* (1967).[21] The problem with this standard was that, in focusing on the outcome-affecting potential of the error, it failed to distinguish between trivial or strictly formal lapses and serious errors that happened to occur in cases with strong independent evidence; between minor irregularities with no effect on the defendant's "substantial rights" and significant violations of those rights with no apparent effect on the outcome of the case.

The conflation of these two forms of "harmlessness" undermined the review function of the appellate courts. As Justice Traynor of the California Supreme Court pointed out:

> It is one thing to tolerate as harmless the errors that involve only the "mere etiquette of trials" or "the formalities or minutiae of the procedure." It is quite another to tolerate as harmless the errors that do such violence to the substantial rights of litigants as to debase the judicial process itself, whose very purpose is to assure justice.[22]

Unlike a misspelling in the indictment, a jury instruction which shifts the burden of proof to the defendant, or a bench ruling which prevents him from offering a weak alibi, affects the defendant's "substantial rights" even if it has no conceivable affect on the outcome of the particular case. In disregarding such errors as "harmless," the courts severely limited their ability to regulate criminal trials, where serious error and misconduct frequently coexist with very strong evidence.

This broad notion of "harmlessness" subverts the appellate review of criminal cases in two further ways. First, it makes a number of errors self-insulating, especially the ineffective assistance of counsel. The evidence against the defendant will often look overwhelming to the appellate court just because it has never been subject to adversary testing. Second, a harmless error rule gives the appellate court almost unfettered discretion in deciding which errors to correct: a counterfactual judgment that an error would probably, or almost certainly, not have affected the verdict often is far more difficult to dispute than a legal determination that no error has occurred and is far more susceptible to the influence of hindsight and bias.

The class of serious but "harmless" rights violations has been significantly enlarged by the imposition of the exclusionary rule on the states. *Mapp v. Ohio* (1961) made it a constitutional error for a state judge to admit evidence obtained in violation of the Fourth, Fifth or Sixth Amendments.[23] Since such evidence was often admitted in cases where it was unnecessary for a conviction, the states' harmless error rules threatened to exempt much police conduct from the threat of exclusion or at least from the appellate enforcement of that sanction. *Chapman v. California* confronted this threat to the exclusionary rule by requiring reversal unless there was no "reasonable possibility" that the tainted evidence could have affected the verdict.

This harmless error standard, strict as it appears, still denies the defendant an appellate remedy when the admission of illegally obtained evidence merely "gilded the lily" in a case with overwhelming evidence.[24] Even if the exclusionary rule is only intended to sanction police misconduct, with the defendant an incidental beneficiary, its deterrent affect may be substantially reduced by this exception to its appellate enforcement.[25] Moreover, the exception carved out by *Chapman* may be considerably broader in practice than on paper. Psychological research has shown that even experts greatly underestimate the possibility that "things might have been otherwise," a judgment involving much the same cognitive difficulty as disregarding inadmissible evidence.[26] The tendency to discount alternative outcomes is amplified by the practical consequences of acknowledging "a reasonable possibility" of such an outcome. Thus, even the stringent language of the Chapman test may do little to restrain a court disposed to maintain the status quo.

Some indication of the harm wrought by the harmless error rule is reported by Davies, who observed in his study of California criminals appeals that the rule appeared to insulate most criminal cases, and many acknowledged errors, from the threat of reversal. His study confirmed that most criminal cases going to trial and ending in conviction had evidence strong enough to trivialize the impact of any single procedural or evidentiary error, however egregious: only one in six of the trial appeals Davies examined suggested doubts about factual guilt; in a quarter of all trial appeals, the court acknowledged error but deemed it harmless.[27]

In *People v. Crimmins* (1970) the New York Court of Appeals adopted a standard considerably less demanding than *Chapman*'s for nonconstitutional error: an error committed in a trial where the independent evidence of guilt was "overwhelming" will not require reversal unless there is a "significant probability" (despite the overwhelming evidence) that the jury would have acquitted without the error.[28] In holding that the defendant's constitutional rights demanded more stringent protection than his nonconstitutional ones, *Crimmins* implicitly recognized that the importance of the rights affected must be distinguished from the causal impact of their violation on the verdict. Unfortunately, the practical affect of *Crimmins* was to increase the difficulty of obtaining reversals for serious nonconstitutional errors.

The development of the harmless error rule as a constraint on the appellate review of criminal convictions had a significant effect on the function of appellate counsel. Although the appellate lawyer must have the technical expertise to spot an increasing number of potential procedural and statutory errors, her primary function is not as a legal technician but as a factual advocate. She must convince a court empowered but reluctant to reverse convictions on a large number of grounds that the errors she raises are not trivialized by the weight of the prosecution evidence. In Chapter 7, we will analyze the reversals won by appellate counsel in New York and observe the critical role of factual advocacy in obtaining them.

CRIMINAL APPEALS BEFORE THE APPELLATE DIVISION

The New York Appellate Division embodies, in extreme form, both aspects of the historical process described in the last section. It has among the most expansive review powers of any first-level appellate court in the United States, but a strong commitment to exercising those powers sparingly in the large volume of criminal appeals brought before it. To understand the challenge of indigent appellate representation in New York, it is necessary to review its powers and practices in some detail.

The Appellate Division of the state Supreme Court is the court of first and last resort for most criminal appellants in New York State. All defendants convicted of a felony or misdemeanor in the Trial Division of the state Supreme Court have the statutory right to appeal their convictions to the Appellate Division,[29] and neither the state's highest court, the New York

Court of Appeals, nor any federal court will ordinarily review their convictions until the Appellate Division has done so. Few criminal appeals get beyond the Appellate Division. The state Court of Appeals hears criminal appeals on a discretionary basis, and it takes less than 5 percent of the defense appeals affirmed by the Appellate Division.

The Appellate Division is divided into four departments: the First (AD1) covers New York (Manhattan) and Bronx counties alone; the Second (AD2) covers Kings (Brooklyn), Queens, Richmond (Staten Island) and seven other counties; the Third and Fourth cover the rest of the state. AD1 and AD2 each has 15 appointed justices, who may serve up to the age of 70 and on a year by year basis thereafter. The justices hear cases in panels of four or five, with a simple majority required to alter the trial court judgment or order.

The Review Powers of the Appellate Division

The convicted defendant may appeal directly to the Appellate Division or challenge his conviction by motion before the trial court which imposed it.[30] While similar claims can be raised before the appellate and trial courts, the Appellate Division is restricted to the record created in the trial court. It cannot consider new evidence, although it can order the trial court to do so, thereby "enlarging the record." The trial court itself can conduct a postconviction hearing on any new evidence concerning the defendant's guilt or the propriety of the proceedings.

While the Appellate Division has more restricted access to information than the trial court, it has a far wider scope of review, perhaps the most extensive of any intermediate appellate court in the country. First, it can and must review all "questions of law"—all claims of constitutional and nonconstitutional error "preserved" by a timely and specific objection from the trial attorney.[31] While the Appellate Division is bound by the direct authority of the Court of Appeals, it enjoys greater law-making authority than many intermediate appellate courts. Its departments have almost as much autonomy as the circuits of the U.S. Courts of Appeal: the decisions of each department are not binding on the others, and the Court of Appeals sometimes permits them to develop different approaches, using them as laboratories for doctrinal experimentation. As a result, the "law" of the different departments may differ for significant periods of time, and the courts often have the opportunity to develop and refine conflicting positions in unresolved areas.

Second, the Appellate Division can and must review all "questions of fact."[32] While it is not supposed to substitute its own judgment for the fact finder's, it can reverse any verdict it finds to be "against the weight of the evidence"—even if it finds the evidence legally sufficient and believes that a rational fact finder could have accepted it. Unlike a judgment that the evidence is legally insufficient, such a finding is not reviewable by the state's highest court. The Appellate Division must also decide a large number of "mixed questions of law and fact" which the state Court of Appeals declines to review, concerning the application of constitutional standards to particular facts, such as the reasonableness of police suspicion or the voluntariness of the defendant's consent to a search.

Finally, the Appellate Division has both the power and obligation to review the case in "the interests of justice": to consider any and all unpreserved errors and the overall fairness of the procedure and the outcome.[33] At its unguided and unreviewable discretion, it can reverse a conviction because of an unprotested error. Even if the evidence is legally sufficient and the verdict is not against the weight of the evidence, the court can reverse in the interest of justice simply because it is "left with a very disturbing feeling that guilt has not been satisfactorily established," as in *People v. Kidd* (1980).[34] The Appellate Division also has the interests-of-justice power to reduce to the statutory minimum any sentence that it finds "unduly harsh or severe."[35] Neither the Court of Appeals nor the trial court has this sweeping interest-of-justice review power; the Court of Appeals is strictly confined to questions of law.

The powers of the Appellate Division are further augmented by the right of the defendant to raise issues which would be foreclosed from review in other jurisdictions. The defendant who pleads guilty can raise any constitutional issue that was the subject of a hearing before the trial court—the admissibility of the defendant's statements (*Huntley* hearing), of physical evidence seized by the police (*Mapp* hearing), or of police-arranged identifications (*Wade* hearing).[36] In many jurisdictions, a guilty plea waives all such suppression issues.

Given the Court's extensive review powers, it is arguable that no appeal of a New York trial conviction can be frivolous—it is always possible to claim, however unconvincingly, that the verdict is against the weight of the evidence, and almost always possible to discover some unprotested error, however trivial. While the Court's powers increase the number of possible issues for appeal they do not necessarily increase the odds of reversal. A survey of AD1 dispositions in 1965 and 1975 concluded that the Court used its powers quite sparingly:

> [T]he Appellate Division's powers are extremely broad and highly discretionary, but ... certain judicial and constitutional constraints are imposed in recognition of the possible abuse that such broad powers may entail.... [W]ith an acute awareness of the responsibility inherent in appellate review, the court generally indulges in presumptions and draws inferences freely in order to sustain the lower court's decision; it rarely will do so in order to reverse the lower court.[37]

The tension between the Court's sweeping review powers and its conservative disposition is heightened by two additional facts: it is severely overburdened, and it has no official mechanisms for screening or expediting criminal appeals. These conditions create a difficult environment for indigent appellate representation.

The Volume of Appeals

A 1982 study reported that the number of appeals decided statewide by the Appellate Division had increased more than 200 percent in the past 20 years, while the number of trials had gone up only 60 percent.[38] In AD1, the increase was 167 percent; in AD2, a staggering 316 percent. The authors calculated that the 1980 totals represented 208 and 233 dispositions per judge in AD1 and AD2, respectively. As noted in Chapter 1, these averages are more than twice the recommended limit of 100 cases per judge. Criminal cases accounted for a disproportionate share of this increase: the AD1 survey cited above revealed that criminal cases had gone from 19.3 percent of the criminal docket in 1965 to 31.3 percent in 1975.[39]

Since 1980, both the volume and the proportion of criminal appeals have increased. In AD2, the only department to keep separate count, criminal decisions went up almost 40 percent between 1980 and 1985, while civil decisions increased by only 5 percent. Almost as many criminal as civil decisions, 1876 vs. 2085, respectively, were rendered by AD2 in 1985.[40]

Despite this trend, the bulk of the Appellate Division's time still appears to be taken up by civil cases. Decisions on motions, which mainly concern civil matters, increased even faster than decisions on judgments: more than 150 percent in AD2 and 350 percent in AD1 between 1968 and 1983. In 1980, AD2 heard oral argument in only 37 percent as many criminal as civil cases; while the percentage had risen by 1985, it was still only 52 percent.[41]

The Absence of Screening Mechanisms

The Appellate Division has not responded to the growing number of criminal appeals by adopting any of the case-screening procedures common in other jurisdictions (described in Chapter 1). All AD1 and AD2 criminal appeals may be argued orally and all receive the same formal consideration up to the first conference on their disposition.[42] Routine appeals are not subject to summary disposition procedures or diverted to central staff processing. Because the absence of screening commits the Appellate Division to the full review of all criminal cases, the Court must rely on counsel's selectivity and discrimination to keep its caseload manageable.

The pressure on counsel is especially severe in the scheduling of oral argument. Both departments urge counsel to reserve argument for more significant and complex cases. Although court rules permit up to 30 minutes of argument time for each side, the courts are reluctant to grant even half that time in routine cases. At calendar call, the Presiding Justice often cajoles or demands reductions in the time requested for particular cases.

In recent years, the Appellate Division has become adept at meting out informal sanctions for what it views as indiscriminate or excessive zeal. Justices in both departments will peremptorily "thank" an attorney midway through her scheduled argument, remind her that they have read the briefs, and move on to her adversary or the next case. In 1986, AD2 adopted a policy of placing at the end of the day's calendar all attorneys reserving more than 15 minutes of argument time. Such practices encourage counsel to exercise a selectivity and discrimination that may not always be in the client's best interest.

Although the pressure to limit oral argument is applied to civil and criminal appeals alike, its effect on the latter is more striking: In 1980, 57 percent of AD2 criminal appeals were submitted rather than argued,[43] compared with 42 percent of civil appeals; in 1985, the submission rate had gone up to 62 percent for criminal cases, 47 percent for civil.[44] We have no way of knowing whether this difference is due to greater judicial pressure to submit criminal appeals, to counsel's own perception that criminal cases have less merit, or to lower accountability to clients in criminal cases.

CONCLUSION

Appellate defenders in New York face a first-level court with expansive review powers but with a historical, statutory, and administrative predisposition against exercising them to reverse criminal convictions supported by strong prosecution evidence. These review powers impose a tremendous responsibility on the court, since they require the examination of every record for unpreserved errors and substantial injustice. Skilled appellate representation is a mixed blessing for such a court: while it eases the judicial burden of review by assuring the court that no stone has been left unturned and that the strongest issues are being addressed, it also requires the court to devote more attention than it might prefer to routine cases.

This strain is amplified in New York by the high volume of cases coming before the Appellate Division and the absence of any formal screening mechanisms to limit adversary briefing and argument in routine cases. The tension between the court's expansive powers and its conservative disposition, and between its need for zealous appellate representation and its desire for selectivity, make the job of appellate counsel as difficult and important as in any American jurisdiction.

NOTES

1. Carrington, Meador, and Rosenberg, *Justice on Appeal* (1976): 2–3, divide appellate function into error review and institutional review, the latter encompassing both the regulation of lower-level functions and the refinement of legal rules.

2. To the extent that challenges to evidentiary rulings involve claims of police and prosecutorial misconduct, the second and third forms of error correction will overlap.

3. See generally Knight, *Criminal Appeals* (London: Stevens, 1978); Orfield, *Criminal Appeals in America* (Boston: Little, Brown, 1939).

4. See Orfield, *Criminal Appeals in America*, 77–91; Louis, "Allocating Adjudicative Decision making Authority Between the Trial and Appellate Levels," *North Carolina Law Review* 64 (1986): 993; Godbold, "Fact-finding By the Appellate Courts: An Available and Appropriate Power," *Cumberland Law Review* 12 (1982): 365, 383–89.

5. See Orfield, *Criminal Appeals in America*; Godbold, "Fact-finding by the Appellate Courts."

6. This restriction overlaps with the second when it involves the trial attorney's failure to make an "offer of proof"—a record of the facts he expected to establish with the evidence the court declined to take. Without such an offer on the record, the appellate court may have to obtain that information itself.

7. This restriction is usually regarded as a matter of "standing," not prejudice, but the two requirements are closely connected. I will treat the former as an aspect of the latter for present purposes, although that involves some oversimplification.

8. See Hopkins, "The Role of An Intermediate Appellate Court," *Brooklyn Law Review* 41 (1975): 459.

9. Ibid. 468–71.

10. The limitation on reviewing unpreserved errors may also have had a practical origin. In civil cases, there would often have been no record of the ruling or other event complained of unless the trial attorney "took an exception." Clearly, this practical necessity for objecting disappeared with the advent of modern stenography.

11. Orfield, *Criminal Appeals in America*, 77. An alternative method of appeals gradually evolved in civil cases, allowing the attorney to preserve his objection to a ruling by the judge during the course of the trial by an "exception," which he would put in writing and the judge would sign and seal. The appellate court would then review this "bill of exceptions" along with the formal record. This practice, however, was never extended to criminal cases.

12. In *The Riddle of Harmless Error* (Columbus, Ohio: Ohio State University Press, 1970): 85, Traynor cites one reversal based on the indictment's failure to state that the offense was against the "peace and dignity" of the state, rather than merely its "peace"; another was based on the indictment's failure to specify the means by which the defendant allegedly drowned the victim.

13. "The Criminal Appeal" in Carpentier, ed., *Counsel on Appeal* (New York: McGraw-Hill, 1968): 7–8.

14. McCrate et al., *Appellate Justice in New York*, 23.

15. Ibid. 25–26.

16. Ibid. 26.

17. Kavanaugh, "Improvement of Administration of Criminal Justice by Exercise of Judicial Power," *A.B.A. Journal* 11 (1925): 217, 222.

18. 328 U.S. 750, 759.

19. Davies, "Affirmed: A Study of Criminal Appeals and Decision-Making Norms in a California Court of Appeal," *American Bar Foundation Research Journal* 82 (1982): 543, 601.

20. Friedman and Percival, *The Roots of Justice* (Chapel Hill: University of North Carolina Press, 1981).

21. 386 U.S. 18. Note, *People v. Crimmins:* The New Prejudice Rule," *Albany Law Review* 40 (1976): 405, 408–11.

22. Traynor, *The Riddle of Harmless Error*, 19. Traynor nevertheless favored a harmless error standard that would have tolerated at least some errors of the latter class.

23. 367 U.S. 643.

24. Traynor disagreed, asserting that the defendant "is entitled not to a trial free of all possible error, but to a trial free of harmful error," *The Riddle of Harmless Error*, 20. This seems to confuse the defendant's rights with his remedies. The defendant is entitled to have all his rights respected, even if there may be no remedy for some violations. To the extent that a trial court error violates his rights or ratifies an earlier violation, the defendant will have a grievance, whether or not the state is willing to redress it. The alternative would be to claim that the defendant had a second-order, "appellate," right to have some but not all of his first-order rights respected.

25. The rule may also blunt the review of lower court rulings, since "judicial economy" will often dictate that the court determine if an alleged error is harmless before considering it on the merits, thereby sparing itself a substantive determination in many cases.

26. See Fischhoff, "Hindsight ≠ Foresight: The Effects of Outcome Knowledge on Judgments Under Uncertainty," *Journal of Experimental Psychology: Human Perception and Performance* 1 (1975): 288; Fischhoff and Beyth, "I Knew It Would Happen: Remembered Probabilities of Once-Future Things," *Organizational Behavior and Human Performance* 13 (1975): 1; Teitelbaum et al. found that attorneys and judges differed widely among themselves in assessing the prejudicial impact on a jury of a wide range of inadmissable evidence, but consistently estimated less prejudice than the lay people likely to serve on such juries. "Evaluating the Prejudicial Effect of Evidence: Can Judges Identify the Impact of Improper Evidence on Juries?" *Wisconsin Law Review* (1983): 1147.

27. Davies, "Affirmed," 569. It should be noted that in some of these cases, the court may not have been applying the *Chapman* standard for constitutional error but the more permissive California standard for finding nonconstitutional error harmless.

28. 26 N.Y. 2d 319.

29. Criminal Procedure Law (CPL) 450.10.

30. CPL 470.15 (1); 440.10,.20. If the trial court denies his motion to vacate judgement, the defendant may then seek leave to appeal that ruling along with the conviction itself. The Appellate Division, however, is only required to hear the direct appeal.

31. CPL 470.15 (3); 470.05 (2).

32. CPL 470.15 (3).

33. CPL 470.15 (3); 470.15 (6) (a).

34. 76 AD 2d 665.

35. CPL 470.15 (6) (b). Even the length of a plea-bargained sentence is subject to review—a 1984 legislative curtailment of this right was voided by the Court of Appeals as an unconstitutional restriction on the powers of the Appellate Division.

36. CPL 710.70 (2).

37. Botler, DeVita, Kallas, Ruane, and Weisbrot, "Project. The Appellate Division of the Supreme Court of New York: An Empirical Study of Its Powers and Functions as an Intermediate State Court," *Fordham Law Review* 47 (1978): 929, 984–85.

38. McCrate et al., *Appellate Justice in New York*, 55–57.

39. Botler et al., "The Appellate Division," 1018.

40. Appellate Division, Second Department, Annual Statistical Reports.

41. New York State Judicial Conference, Annual Reports.

42. The only exception is the *optional* procedure in AD2 for expedited sentence appeals in motion form, New York Court Rules and Regulations 670.17 (i).

43. This percentage excludes excessive-sentence motions, for which AD2 does not permit oral argument.

44. New York State Judicial Conference, Annual Reports.

3

Indigent Appellate Defense in New York City

Before *Douglas v. California*, almost all states relied on private counsel assigned on an ad hoc basis to handle the indigent appeals the court deemed worthy of legal assistance. Following *Douglas*, the states utilized three different means of supplying appellate counsel to the increasing number of indigents appealing their convictions. Many continued to rely on private counsel; often the same attorney who represented the defendant at the trial level was expected to handle the appeal. Other states set up appellate units within their public defender offices. Still others created state-level appellate defender offices, independent of city or county level trial defenders.

Like many American jurisdictions, particularly those in large urban areas, New York City has adopted a "mixed" system of indigent trial and appellate defense, in which the caseload is divided between an institutional defender and a panel of private attorneys. A single defender cannot handle the entire indigent caseload because of conflicts of interest: inconsistent duties or interests which may adversely affect her representation of the client. Two of the most common sources of conflict in a criminal setting are the attorney's representation of a codefendant and the client's complaints about the attorney.[1] Since conflicts are inevitable, a second defense entity is necessary in any system that does not rely exclusively on private assigned counsel.

A 1982 Justice Department survey found that 80 percent of the nation's indigent population was served by such mixed systems. Institutional defenders predominated in urban areas, serving 43 of the 50 largest counties in the United States.[2] The survey found, however, that the defenders themselves were handling a diminishing share of the caseload within mixed systems, "mainly because of the increasingly strict definition of conflicts of interest and limits on the number of cases the . . . defender is able to handle."[3]

The arrangements for indigent appellate defense involve a further variable: the relationship between the trial and appellate defenders. A 1987 survey divided state appellate defense systems into four categories: appellate units in statewide public defender systems (16 states), independent statewide appellate defense systems (11), local systems operating under state legislative restrictions (7), and local option systems constrained only by constitutional guidelines (16).[4] New York State falls into the third category: it requires each county (and county-encompassing city) to develop an indigent defendant plan but gives it the choice of a public defender, a private nonprofit defender, or a bar-sponsored assigned counsel system.[5]

The job of representing indigent defendants before the Appellate Division is handled by two defense organizations in New York City: the Criminal Appeals Bureau (CAB) of the Legal Aid Society (LAS) and the panel of certified private practitioners maintained by each department. Under the state's authorizing statute, Article 18b of the County Law,[6] New York City adopted an Assigned Counsel Plan in 1966 which made LAS, a private nonprofit organization, the city's primary defender.[7] The plan established panels of certified private attorneys in each department to take conflict cases. It recognized CAB, the appellate unit of LAS, as the city's primary appellate defender, and it set up separate "18b" appellate panels for conflict cases.

Under the LAS contract with the city, CAB is required to handle the state appeals of all indigent defendants convicted in the five counties comprising New York City, except those presenting a conflict of interest, which are assigned to the 18b appellate panel in the appropriate department.

The 18b trial and appellate panels replaced the informal rolls of private attorneys on which the courts had relied before the adoption of the Assigned Counsel Plan. The plan assumed that the panel's screening procedures would weed out the worst of the courthouse regulars while removing the stigma which had discouraged established members of the bar from undertaking indigent representation. The plan's authors envisioned a panel comprised of successful practitioners doing occasional indigent defense work, not full-time indigent defenders supported solely or principally by panel representation.[8]

The plan provides much fuller support for the city's institutional defenders than for its assigned defenders. LAS attorneys receive salaries fixed by contract with the Society; the city is expected to provide funds sufficient to maintain "parity" with assistant district attorneys at the same level of experience. In contrast, the compensation of the 18b panel is fixed by state statute. While state funding usually means higher rates of compensation than county funding, the rates set by New York State have been lower than those set by many rural counties in other jurisdictions.[9] In 1966, the rate was \$15 an hour for in-court work and \$10 an hour for out-of-court work; by 1984, it had only risen to \$25/\$15, respectively, with a maximum fee, or cap, of \$750, waivable only by a showing of special circumstances. The disparity was particularly great on appeals, where almost all work is out of court; until 1985, appellate panel members were compensated at an effective rate of $15 an hour.[10]

There has been a corresponding differential in the nonmonetary resources provided for the two defenders. LAS receives funding for office overhead, a large supervisory staff, and comprehensive support services. In contrast, 18b panel members are not reimbursed for their rent, secretaries, or routine office expenses, and receive no training or supervisory services except for optional refresher courses. The trial and appellate panels in each department are administered by a single lawyer with a small staff.[11]

This disparity in resources has a crucial dual significance for our research: first, it gives rise to chronic deficiencies in the provision of defense services on appeal, and second, it presents an opportunity to study the impact of differential funding and organization on the performance of the appellate defenders. That comparison is complicated, however, by the de facto control over the assignment process exercised by the Legal Aid Society, which as we will see in Chapter 6, may skew the distribution of cases to the two defenders.[12]

WILLIAM HELLERSTEIN AND THE EVOLUTION OF CAB

Like LAS itself, CAB was not a creation of the Assigned Counsel Plan but a significant institutional player at the time the plan was adopted. The Bureau was established by LAS in 1961, with a single attorney, "to cope with the obvious need for appellate representation of indigent defendants."[13] In 1963, it won its first case before the Supreme Court, the landmark decision of *Fay v. Noia*. In 1966, CAB represented one of the successful defendants in the *Miranda* cluster of cases.[14]

Under the energetic leadership of William Hellerstein, attorney-in-charge from 1969 to 1985, the CAB grew in size, organizational autonomy, and reputation. By 1976, it had a staff of 62 attorneys. In 1979, it became an independent bureau within the Legal Aid Society, no longer under even the formal authority of the Criminal Defense Division (CDD).

CAB represented the usually victorious defendant in a number of important Warren Court and early Burger Court decisions: *Sibron v. New York* (1969),[15] restricting the newly recognized police authority to stop and frisk; *McMann v. Richardson* (1970),[16] upholding the waiver of Fifth Amendment rights by guilty plea and spurring the New York legislature to preserve those rights by statute; *Baldwin v. New York* (1970),[17] imposing the right to jury trial for misdemeanors with a maximum penalty exceeding six months; and *In Re Winship* (1970),[18] holding that the due process clause required a "reasonable doubt" standard for criminal convictions.[19]

While such Supreme Court cases enhanced CAB's reputation, they comprised a minute, and wholly discretionary, portion of its work—the LAS contract with the city required CAB to represent indigent defendants no further than their first state appeal. CAB's reputation for quality, however, extended to its routine work of representing indigents on their state appeals. A 1985 City Bar Association report praised CAB's "long tradition of providing first class representation to its clients" and "its reputation in the courts and among the bar."[20] This carefully nurtured reputation served CAB well, ensuring its continued growth and high level of funding despite significant problems in delay and case management.

The source of many of CAB's subsequent problems lay in the fact that it had a contractual obligation to take all nonconflict cases, but had no contractual provision linking case volume with staff size. Unlike other institutional defenders, LAS neither had, nor sought, caseload caps to limit the number of cases it could be assigned.[21] As a result, CAB's staff increases and temporary reductions in assignments had to be arranged on an ad hoc basis through negotiations with the judiciary and the city. In obtaining these modifications, CAB's strongest argument was often its incapacity to handle its existing caseload.

A second limitation on CAB's effectiveness lay in its narrow conception of its role. Hellerstein and the organization he created had a strong but highly circumscribed view of appellate representation, which emphasized the aggressive pursuit of legal issues but downplayed client contact and collaboration with the Criminal Defense Division (CDD). Thus, while the LAS contract required CAB to represent defendants only in their direct state appeals, CAB also pursued federal habeas actions in cases where such a collateral attack seemed very promising and sought certiorari to the U.S. Supreme Court in exceptional cases with major unresolved issues.[22]

At the same time, CAB discouraged its attorneys from visiting their clients or involving themselves in their prison grievances.[23] Until the mid–1980s, CAB also made no provision for collaboration between its staff and CDD on undecided cases at the trial level and on trial court motions to set aside the verdict. As a result of these policies, CAB attorneys were almost as likely to be found in federal court as in state prisons or trial parts. This narrow but intensive approach to appellate representation frequently led CAB to exceed its contractual obligations but discouraged it from challenging or circumventing the restrictions on the scope and function of appellate review discussed in the last chapter.

In his desire to preserve CAB's quality and autonomy, Hellerstein encouraged the delegation of "ancillary" functions to other units: the LAS Law Advisory Bureau provided updates and backup research for CDD, and Hellerstein's own Prisoner's Rights Project handled inmate litigation. Under Hellerstein, CAB representation was largely confined to direct and collateral attacks on the conviction. While his emphasis on appellate specialization allowed CAB attorneys to develop formidable legal expertise and creative briefing strategies, it also cut them off from the very parts of the criminal justice system that suffered from appellate neglect, limiting their opportunity to discover and challenge significant abuses occurring in the "gate house."

THE CRISIS IN THE CITY'S TRIAL DEFENSE SYSTEM AND ITS IMPLICATIONS FOR APPEALS

In a 1986 report, the New York City Bar Association documented a serious and protracted breakdown in the Assigned Counsel Plan at the trial level. It found two striking departures from the plan's expectations: (1) CDD was disqualifying itself from a far higher proportion of cases than the plan anticipated; and (2) the 18b panels were consistently failing to provide minimally adequate representation, a failure exacerbated by the increasing share of the indigent caseload they were receiving.[24]

Relying on the McConville and Mirsky study of indigent trial defense in New York County,[25] the report found that as of 1986, the 18b panel was being assigned a majority of indigent cases rather than the small fraction anticipated in the plan, that the panel's active membership was far too small to adequately handle this caseload and was declining in proportion to the number of assignments, that a substantial percentage of its swollen caseload was handled by a core of high-volume "courthouse regulars," and most disturbingly, that in a large majority of cases, the panel attorney failed "to perform the basic lawyering tasks which are essential to effective representation in criminal cases," such as client interviews and pretrial discovery.[26]

The 1966 plan appears to have rested on two mistaken assumptions: that the number of conflict cases would be relatively small, and that established members of the private bar would be willing to take these conflict cases at a very modest level of compensation. It is now clear that the plan's drafters significantly underestimated the volume of cases and the proportion of conflicts, while overestimating the willingness of the private bar to provide a form of partially subsidized pro bono representation that did not generate favorable publicity or tax benefits. McConville and Mirsky, whose own study appeared two years later, concluded that the shift in the trial caseload was more a matter of design than accident. The city and the courts depended on the cheap, high volume representation provided by courthouse regulars and eagerly accommodated the Legal Aid Society's efforts to divert a growing share of the caseload to the 18b panels.[27]

The Assigned Counsel Plan has clearly experienced some of the same problems on the appellate level. In the two decades since the plan's adoption, it became clear that the appellate panels were handling a far higher share of the caseload than originally anticipated and that much of this work was being done by a small number of attorneys supporting themselves solely or principally through panel work. The plan's drafters had estimated that the appellate panels in both departments would be required to handle no more than 500 cases yearly.[28] This estimate was quickly exceeded, and now appears to have been almost recklessly optimistic. In 1986, the AD1 panel alone handled 1,600 appeals, with a backlog of several hundred more.[29]

This disparity cannot be attributed entirely to the increasing volume of criminal appeals: while AD1 criminal appeals increased 200 percent to 300 percent during this twenty year period, the number of cases assigned to the AD1 panel exceeded the plan's estimate by over 600 percent. According to the statistics collected in a 1985 New York City Bar Association report, the panel was briefing almost 33 percent of all indigent appeals by the early 1980s, a far higher percentage than the plan anticipated.[30] It is not clear how much of this disparity was due to a higher incidence of conflict than the plan anticipated, and how much to an overly rigid interpretation of the conflict rules by CAB and the failure of CAB to accept all nonconflict cases. I will address this question in Chapters 6 and 8, with a close examination of CAB conflicts practices.

The second striking departure from the plan's assumptions was in the background of the panel's active practioners. Even without systematic data collection, it was clear that many assigned appeals were still being handled by the same kind of courthouse regulars that had flourished before the plan's adoption. Mirsky and McConville have shown the continuing dominance of such regulars at the trial level,[31] and it is unlikely that the appellate panel, with many of the same members, had a radically different pattern of case assignment.

Despite these superficial similarities between the fate of the plan at the trial and appellate levels, the appellate courts may have not had the same incentives as their trial counterparts to encourage the diversion of the caseload to the 18b panels. The kind of intensive appellate representation promised by CAB can save as well as consume judicial resources: the more thorough, accurate, and self-contained the brief, the less time the court staff has to spend researching the record. For similar reasons, the more perfunctory representation associated with the 18b panels may tax the resources of a conscientious court, whose staff must search the record for unbriefed issues and omitted facts. Appellate judges are also unlikely to develop the loyalty and indebtedness that some trial judges may feel towards some courthouse regulars for "being there when they need them" to take over cases in the arraignment or calendar parts.

Regardless of the courts' interests, the caseload shift at the trial level may have *forced* a shift at the appellate level as well. To the extent that CDD attorneys were getting relieved of cases through exaggerated or spurious claims of conflict or aggrieving their clients by neglect, they effectively precluded CAB representation under the conflict rules. Thus, CDD case-shedding and client-management practices may have significantly reduced CAB's share of the appellate caseload. We explore this possibility in detail in Chapter 6 and its implications for reforming appellate defense services in Chapter 9.

THE PLAN'S SECOND DECADE AND THE CRISIS OF APPELLATE DELAY

By the late 1970s, it had become clear that the plan as implemented was not adequate for the steadily growing number of criminal appeals. Despite a number of increases in staff size after 1976, the CAB backlog of unbriefed cases continued to increase. The appellate panel was simply not large enough to provide representation for the increasing number of cases it was being assigned. The greater the backlog of unbriefed cases, the longer the indigent defendant had to wait to get his appeal before the court.[32]

By the early 1980s, the problem of appellate delay had reached crisis proportions. In 1982, a ten-week LAS strike swelled the CAB backlog and increased the flow of cases to an already overburdened panel. In 1983, the two departments adopted different measures to alleviate the growing CAB backlog. In AD2, the court stopped assigning CAB to cases in which the defendant had not been represented by LAS at the trial level. This "moratorium" on non-LAS cases lasted for 18 months. In AD1, the Presiding Justice asked for volunteers to help eliminate the CAB backlog, soliciting the attorneys in large corporate law firms to take unbriefed cases on a strictly pro bono basis.[33]

As its backlog grew, CAB experienced considerable pressure from the courts to increase its productivity. While it remained officially committed to thorough research and close supervision, it adopted a quota system in the late 1970s, under which every staff attorney was required to complete 14 "substantive"—trial and hearing—appeals a year.[34] Some of the staff attorneys opposed the quota as overly rigid and as reflecting an inappropriate emphasis on output over quality. Nevertheless, it had become a fixture of CAB employment by the mid–1980s.

The growing backlog of cases forced CAB attorneys to make difficult choices about the priority of their cases. Their general commitment to representing defendants on a first-come, first-served basis came into conflict with a strong desire to brief the most promising cases as quickly as possible: the better a client's chances of reversal, the less acceptable it seemed to delay his appeal, particularly if he was incarcerated. CAB's commitment to equal zeal was compromised by the increasingly long delays to which its attorneys often felt compelled to subject their weaker cases.

Despite the internal strains, CAB managed to parlay the backlog crisis to its advantage. Hellerstein's aggressive lobbying convinced the city, still threatening to replace LAS with a public defender, to fund major staff increases for CAB. Between 1983 and 1985, CAB staff size grew almost 33 percent. CAB also established control of the AD1 volunteer program, determining which cases would be assigned to volunteers, appearing as co-counsel on all volunteer briefs, and supervising those briefs as it saw fit.[35] The volunteer program succeeded in substantially reducing the CAB backlog without reducing CAB control of the case assignment process.

During this critical two-year period, there were no significant changes in the structure or funding of the 18b appellate panel. Through most of 1985, panel members continued to be paid $15 an hour for the bulk of their work, with a statutory cap of $750 that the court was rarely willing to waive. Both panels continued to be administered by long-serving political appointees with a reputation for cronyism and an aversion to reform.

In 1985, a New York City Bar Association Report examined the continuing crisis of delay and backlog in indigent appeals. It found that the average time between the appointment of counsel and the filing of a brief was about 14 months, longer than the prison terms of many defendants whose convictions were ultimately reversed or modified. The report recognized that much of the problem was systemic: "The appeals process is prehistoric, its capital structure, staffing and equipment, Dickensian. Haphazard management permeates a process which can only euphemistically be described as a system."[36]

Still, the report found that a significant share of the delay was attributable to the productivity of the appellate defenders. In 1983, CAB had taken an average of 13 months to file a brief in cases with a complete record. Panel attorneys were faster, averaging less than 9 months (only a month more than retained counsel), but there were simply not enough of them to handle the large share of cases assigned to the panel. The shortage of 18b attorneys meant that defendants rejected by CAB often had to wait months for substitute counsel.[37]

The report was also critical of CAB case management, noting that clear conflicts often went undetected for months after assignment. Despite CAB's limited case-handling capacity and inefficient case-processing, however, the report opposed any change in its role as the primary appellate defender or any compromise in its quality of representation. The report noted that in the previous two years, CAB had already cut its brief-filing time by almost 50 percent through staff increases and improved staff productivity.[38]

While it criticized their case management, the report also recognized that both appellate defenders presently lacked the capacity to handle the increased volume of cases they were receiving, let alone to eliminate their backlogs. It illustrated the inadequacy of existing compensation with a striking comparison: while the representation of a client with a 500 to 750 page trial transcript was estimated to require about three weeks of work, an 18b attorney working eight hours a day at $25 an hour would reach the statutory cap of $750 in six days. As the report concluded, "[i]t is little wonder that there is a scarcity of lawyers willing to take assignments on appeal."[39]

The report recommended that rates for all 18b work be increased, that appellate work be compensated at the same rate as in-court trial work, and that waivers on the statutory cap be readily granted. It also recommended that all attorneys on the trial panel be required to submit one brief yearly, and it urged the continuation of the volunteer attorney program. The report's most radical proposal was for the creation of a state appellate defender, which would serve as a backup to CAB in New York City. The report did not indicate if this "mid-range" defender would be limited to the conflict cases that CAB was barred from handling, or whether it would take nonconflict cases from CAB as well.[40]

In the two years following the report's publication, the city and state governments increased funding for both CAB and the appellate panel, but made no attempt to change the organization of indigent appellate defense or the rules governing case assignment. The city continued to fund the growth of the CAB staff, which peaked at 105 attorneys (excluding supervisors) in the fall of 1985. In late 1985, the state raised the rate of compensation for panel attorneys to $40 an hour for in-court and $25 an hour for out-of-court work, and raised the statutory cap to $1250. Most appellate work continued to be compensated at the lower out-of-court rate. In July, 1987, however, the state raised the rate for all appellate work to $40 an hour, finally establishing a rough parity with trial work.[41]

These changes improved the "delivery" of CAB representation but failed to increase the intake of the 18b panel. By the end of 1985, CAB had dramatically improved its filing time and found itself with an unprecedented shortage of cases. It began to send its attorneys on year-long rotations into the beleaguered CDD, and its staff size declined to 85 by the fall of 1987.

During this same period, the case-handling capacity of the appellate panels may have actually declined. The 1985 pay hike failed to attract enough attorneys to offset the attrition caused by age, upward professional mobility, and, ironically, the forced removal of several of the panel's most prolific members. The new panel administrators appointed in both departments in 1986 received no additional funding for training or supervision.

As the 18b backlog grew, the Presiding Justice of AD1 again issued a call for volunteers.[42] This 1986 campaign yielded only half the 1983 turnout, perhaps because the established bar was less willing to work under 18b than CAB auspices or perhaps because it felt that it had already "done its share" and preferred other, more rewarding, forms of pro bono activity.

As of early October 1987, 300 jailed defendants were still awaiting the assignment of appellate counsel in AD1 alone.[43] While it is difficult to assess if the 1987 rate hike attracted a significant number of qualified practioners to the appellate panels, the early returns were not encouraging. In response to the continuing backlog, the Chief Judge of the Court of Appeals finally joined with the City Bar Association in calling for a mid-range appellate defender.[44]

In the face of this backlog and the growing consensus for an institutional back-up defender, the AD1 18b administrator proposed the creation of an Appellate Defender Office, financed by 18b compensation but functioning as a mid-range defender. Under the terms of the spring 1988 plan, the office would be set up as a not-for-profit corporation with a board consisting of retired Appellate Division justices, a representative of the AD1 presiding justice, and the AD1 18b administrator.[45] The bulk of its briefing would be done by five recent law school graduates, who would bill 2,000 hours a year and receive $17.50 an hour. The remaining $22.50 of the 18b hourly fee would be "skimmed off," contributing to office overhead and the salaries of the three supervising attorneys.

The office would be expected to produce roughly 200 briefs a year, enough to eliminate most of the 18b backlog immediately, and gradually to reduce the city's dependence on the 18b appellate panel. Under the proposal, it would take only conflict cases, leaving the CAB caseload untouched. Chapter 9 reviews the design and implementation of this ingenious hybrid scheme, which began operation in September 1988.

CONCLUSION: THE COMPARATIVE RESOURCES OF THE TWO APPELLATE DEFENDERS DURING THE STUDY PERIOD

The empirical study presented in Part II will compare the two defenders during the period when their disparity in resources was greatest: from fall 1980 to fall 1985. Throughout this period, members of the 18b appellate panel were paid $15 for their out-of-court work. A panel member billing 35 hours a week, 48 weeks a year, would have received about $25,000 a year to cover salary, benefits, rent, secretarial and office expenses—$2,000 less than the 1985 starting salary for a bar-certified CAB attorney with no prior experience, who would also have received generous benefits and complete secretarial services while paying nothing for rent or office expenses.

This disparity between the two defenders in legal resources was equally great. The 18b attorney commencing his representation would receive nothing but a bare record and often an incomplete one. In contrast, a CAB attorney would receive a case that had already been screened for missing minutes; if it had been a CDD case at the trial level, she would also receive the complete trial file, including the trial attorney's motions, notes, and client correspondence. The client would already have been contacted by the Managing Attorney's office with an explanation of the appellate process and a questionnaire about the case.

While the 18b attorney would typically be a solo practioner, working alone, the CAB attorney would have a large number of experienced colleagues willing to review critical portions of the transcript and discuss possible issues. She would have the use of an excellent law library and a brief bank through which she could compare her colleagues' treatment of similar issues. Her brief would be thoroughly reviewed and edited by a supervising attorney; if she were still on probation, her supervisor would also review the transcript. Finally, she could call on the assistance of staff investigators and paralegals for any detective work or archival research the case might require.[46]

This disparity in resources raises some of the questions about the quality and impact of indigent appellate representation addressed in Part II: Do the disparate resources of the defenders make a difference in the quality of representation they provide? If so, does that difference affect the dispositions obtained by the defenders or the quality of review their cases receive? Chapter 4 will compare the briefs submitted by the defenders in comparable cases to assess the quality of representation they provide. Chapters 5 and 6 will examine the dispositions obtained by the defenders, to see if they mirror the qualitative differences we have found and can plausibly be attributed to them. Finally, Chapter 7 will analyze the grounds for appellate reversal and explore the ways in which skilled appellate advocacy can increase the odds of favorable action.

APPENDIX: THE PROCESS FOR FILING AN INDIGENT APPEAL AND ASSIGNING COUNSEL IN NEW YORK CITY

This appendix describes the steps involved in the appeal of a New York state felony conviction, from the imposition of sentence in state supreme court to the rendering of a decision in the Appellate Division. A familiarity with these steps, set down by statute, court rule, and unofficial practice, is helpful in understanding the crisis of backlog and delay described earlier in this chapter and the assignment practices of CAB, analyzed in Chapters 6 and 8.[47] The reader already familiar with New York appellate procedure can skip ahead to Part II.

The Preliminary Stages of an Indigent Criminal Appeal

Preserving the Right to Appeal and Requesting Assigned Counsel. Immediately after the judge imposes sentence, the court clerk informs a convicted defendant of his right to appeal his conviction and have an attorney appointed if he cannot afford one. The clerk hands him a form explaining, in English and Spanish, the procedure for securing an attorney and filing the appeal. His trial attorney is expected to explain the form and the procedure.

The first step for any convicted defendant, indigent or not, is to file a notice of appeal with the appeals bureau of the trial court. His trial attorney is required by court rule to advise him in writing of his right to appeal and to file his notice for him if he so desires. The State Department of Correctional Services also keeps a supply of forms at its reception centers. According to court clerks, almost all defendants, whether convicted by trial or plea, file this notice. Although the notice must be filed within 30 days of sentencing, late notices are routinely accepted by the Appellate Division.

The notice of appeal preserves the defendant's right to appeal by letting the trial court know that he is contesting its judgment, but it does not set the appeal in motion. After the notice has been filed, the paths of the indigent and nonindigent defendant diverge. The latter merely hires an attorney, often the same one who represented him at trial, to prepare his appeal. The retained attorney purchases the record from the court reporter at a market rate which varies with the speed of transcription; he files a brief sometime after receiving his fee. There are no legal deadlines for filing a private appeal. A conscientious retained attorney will tell his client if his appeal has little or no merit, and some attorneys offer paying clients an initial consultation, appraising the prospects of the appeal before undertaking to brief it.

For the indigent defendant, the process is more complex. To initiate an appeal, he must file a poor person application with the Appellate Division, seeking assignment of counsel and a free transcript. There is no time limit for filing, but AD1 clerks estimate that about 25 percent of eligible trial defendants and a far higher percentage of plea defendants never follow through on their notice of appeal. While it is not surprising that a large percentage of plea defendants choose not to challenge their convictions, the attrition rate for trial defendants, who face no practical risk in appealing their contested convictions, can only be attributed to ignorance, inertia, or resignation.

Poor person applications are rarely opposed by the district attorney and are routinely granted without judicial inquiry into the defendant's actual finances. There is a de facto presumption of indigence for defendants assigned counsel at the trial level. Even when the defendant had retained counsel below, his application will rarely be opposed unless his claims of indigence are clearly belied by the evidence or background information in his case, for example, if he paid his five- or six-figure bail in cash or was convicted of large-scale drug sales.

If the poor person application is unopposed and an attorney is available to take the case (see next section), the order of assignment will be granted within a month. That order instructs the appellate bureau of the Supreme Court to assemble the record and obtain any missing minutes. The Appellate Division will not order the record produced until it grants the motion to assign counsel, and it will not grant that motion until it has an attorney to accept the assignment.

Once the assignment order is issued, the law allows little more than seven more months to "perfect the appeal": the reporter has 90 days to prepare the transcript once it has been ordered by the appeals bureau, and assigned counsel has 120 days to submit the brief once he receives the full record. Because the appeals clerks are slow to order the transcripts, the reporters slow to produce them, and the attorneys rarely able to meet their filing deadlines, the process actually takes much longer, an average of 14 months in 1985.

The Assignment of Counsel. Because of a chronic shortage of private counsel to handle the cases in which CAB is disqualified because of a "conflict-of-interest" (see Chapters 3 and 8), it matters a great deal to the indigent defendant whether CAB accepts him as a client. The denial of CAB representation can add months and sometimes years to the defendant's appeal. As Part II of this report reveals, it may also reduce his chances of favorable action. For these reasons, it is important to take a close look at the assignment process.

The CAB Client Selection Process. Every two weeks, the assignment clerk of each department draws up a master list of all defendants who have submitted poor person applications. The clerk gives CAB's Managing Attorney's office two weeks to screen the cases for conflicts.[48] The Managing Attorney "checks off" without explanation the defendants it finds ineligible. The court almost always accepts CAB conflict claims made at this stage.

Defendants found ineligible by CAB are assigned directly to an 18b panel attorney as soon as one is available. The panel, however, gets a majority of its clients at a later stage, since most CAB conflicts are revealed after the initial assignment has been made: in the course of reviewing the transcript, corresponding with the client, or examining his trial attorney's file. The discovery may occur months or even years after the client has been assigned to CAB.[49]

Once it accepts a client, CAB can only be relieved by motion. The motion must specify a ground for relief, but the majority are submitted in letters which merely list the defendants for whom substitute counsel is sought under three or four conflict categories. These motions are rarely opposed and routinely granted. Their denial usually reflects some cumulative dissatisfaction with CAB conflicts practice, such as its onetime policy of rejecting any client who expressed dissatisfaction with his Legal Aid representation.

The longer it takes for CAB to discover a conflict, the longer the defendant must wait to perfect his appeal. The delay in discovering conflicts is exacerbated by the shortage of 18b appellate attorneys. The defendant relieved of CAB representation months after his initial assignment must often wait additional months for a panel attorney to become available to take his case.[50]

The defendants most likely to experience severe delay are those with codefendants already represented by CAB. Since the state provides only one copy of the transcript for the defense, regardless of how many defendants are appealing, the attorney representing the codefendant of a CAB client must either arrange to copy the minutes from CAB or wait for the disposition of the CAB case. Although CAB will make the minutes available for copying, and even copy short records free of charge, most panel attorneys do not go to the trouble of obtaining a copy.

The Later Stages of Appellate Representation

Once he has been assigned, the appellate attorney's first task is to make contact with his client, to ensure that he still wishes to pursue his appeal and is aware of any risks involved in doing so. Because of the practical risk in challenging a plea of guilty to a reduced charge, CAB attorneys will not brief such appeals without the written consent of their clients. There is no established practice for 18b attorneys, and it may be that many never contact their clients about potential risks.

CAB attorneys will also try to obtain their clients' withdrawal in hopeless plea cases before filing *Anders* briefs. Since 18b attorneys are compensated at the same rate for *Anders* briefs as other work, it is doubtful that many of them urge a preemptive withdrawal by their clients. While CAB has a strict policy of not filing *Anders* briefs in trial cases, my survey found several cases in which 18b attorneys had filed successful *Anders* briefs in trial appeals.

Once the decision has been made to pursue the appeal, the attorney's principal work consists in reviewing the transcript for possible issues, obtaining missing minutes, and researching and writing a brief which presents the case for reversal or other favorable action in a format prescribed by court rules: a preliminary statement, a statement of fact, and argument consisting of one or more points with appropriate headings, and a conclusion requesting specific relief. AD1 sets a limit of 70 pages for appellants' briefs, waivable only by motion: AD2 has no page limit.

While the law gives appellate counsel only 120 days from his receipt of the record to file the brief, this period is usually extended by stipulation or motion with the district attorney's consent. Unopposed applications are routinely granted by the courts, unless the case is particularly old or has been repeatedly postponed, or unless other special circumstances require expedited briefing. Cases that are neither filed nor "enlarged" in this manner are placed on the courts' dismissal calendar, subject to the threatened sanction unless filed by a specified date.

Once the defense brief has been filed, the district attorney has 15 days to file a response brief. Again, this period is routinely extended by stipulation or unopposed motion, except in special circumstances. The defense has a week after the response brief is filed to submit a reply brief, which is generally employed only to contest factual allegations or respond to new legal claims. Surrebuttal briefs are not permitted.

If the defendant is dissatisfied with his attorney's brief or simply wishes to supplement it with his own complaints, he can seek leave from the court to file a *pro se* supplemental brief. Permission is almost always granted if the application is made soon after the attorney's brief is filed. The filing of a *pro se* brief delays the proceeding considerably, since the single circulating copy of the transcript must be sent to the defendant, often before the district attorney has had a chance to review it. The district attorney will sometimes file a consolidated response to the main and supplemental briefs, will sometimes respond separately to the *pro se* brief, and will sometimes decline to dignify it with a response.

Once all the briefs have been filed, the court will set a specific date for the argument or submission of the case, placing it on the calendar for a particular term. The defense must reserve argument time when it files the brief, but it is always free to reduce its time request or to submit the case. The district attorney will rarely argue a defense appeal unless the defense does.

The court has no deadlines for deciding a case once it has been argued or submitted. Unanimous affirmances with no opinion or a brief memorandum are usually announced within two or three weeks in AD1 and within a month in AD2. Reversals and affirmances with signed opinions and dissents take several months to a year. The defendant has thirty days to seek leave to appeal an unsatisfactory decision to the Court of Appeals; assigned counsel is required to file the leave application in all cases where the defendant wishes to appeal further and the Court of Appeals has the power to hear the case.

NOTES

1. I will discuss the conflict rules in Chapters 6 and 8.

2. Bureau of Justice Statistics Special Report, *Criminal Defense Systems: A National Survey* (Washington, D.C.: Government Printing Office, 1984). The report also found that systems relying exclusively on assigned counsel served 60 percent of all *counties* nationally, predominating in rural and sparsely inhabited areas.

3. Ibid.

4. Levine, *Indigent Appellate Defense: A Review of State Systems* (Report to the Michigan Supreme Court, Lansing, Mich., 1987).

5. County Law 18a,b. Unlike most "qualified local systems," New York compensates its private assigned defenders at rates set by state statute, not county officials.

6. Sec. 722.

7. For a sketch of the plan's provisions and history, see Association of the Bar, City of New York, Committee on Criminal Advocacy, *A System in Crisis. The*

Assigned Counsel Plan in New York: An Evaluation and Recommendations for Change (1986): 10–16.

8. See McConville and Mirsky, "Criminal Defense of the Poor in New York City," *New York University Review of Law and Social Change* 15 (1987): 581, 641–43, 715.

9. See report to Michigan Supreme Court.

10. The inadequacy of these rates is suggested by a 1987 decision of the Kansas Supreme Court, holding that compensation at $30 an hour constituted an unconstitutional taking of the services of an attorney compelled to take court assignments. *State ex. rel. Stephen v. Smith*, 242 Kan 336. The court noted that an attorney's overhead typically reached or exceeded $30 an hour. The expenses of a New York City attorney are considerably higher.

11. Association of the Bar, *A System in Crisis*, 31–34.

12. The Michigan report noted "a trend toward reducing judicial involvement in the selection of assigned counsel . . . more advanced in the assignment of appellate counsel," 13. The control of assignments has generally shifted to the appellate defenders' offices: the study noted that 9 of the 16 statewide public defenders were "involved in the operation of coordinated assigned counsel systems for handling conflicts and overload," 6. What is unusual about the system in New York City is that it gives the indigent defender de facto control of the diversion of cases to the assigned counsel panel, but no responsibility for selecting panel members, assigning them appropriate cases, and overseeing their work. Critics like McConville and Mirsky have argued that this division of responsibility between the Legal Aid Society and the courts permits wholesale "case-shedding" by the institutional defender while depriving the panel of meaningful oversight.

13. Hellerstein, "Criminal Appeals Work in the Supreme Court," *Legal Aid News* 2, no. 2 (July 1976): 4.

14. Ibid.

15. 392 U.S. 40.

16. 379 U.S. 759.

17. 399 U.S.66.

18. 397 U.S. 358.

19. Hellerstein, "Criminal Appeals Work," 4–5.

20. The Association of the Bar, City of New York, Committee on Criminal Advocacy, *The Crisis in Indigent Appeals in the First and Second Departments* (1985): 25.

21. See *A System in Crisis*, 73–75.

22. The number of such cases has declined substantially with the increasing conservatism of the federal courts and the growing independence of the New York Court of Appeals.

23. See CAB, *Practice Manual* (1985 ed.).

24. *A System in Crisis*, 18–31.

25. Circulated in draft in 1985.

26. *A System in Crisis*, 28–31.

27. McConville and Mirsky, "Defense of the Poor," 894–902.

28. See Frey, "Appellate Division in Backlog Crisis," *Manhattan Lawyer* 1 (October 6–12, 1987): 1, 42.

29. Ibid.; Administrator, Assigned Counsel Plan, Appellate Division, First De-

partment, *Report to Office of Court Administration for Year January 1986–December 1987.*

30. *The Crisis in Indigent Appeals*, 22–24.

31. McConville and Mirsky, "Criminal Defense of the Poor," 715–45.

32. *The Crisis in Indigent Appeals*, 26.

33. Ibid. 23–26.

34. By national standards, this quota was fairly low. A CAB attorney who met her quota and also did the 6 or 7 plea appeals would be at the lower end of the spectrum for appellate defenders nationally. A survey of state appellate defenders found Illinois and California at one end, with average annual caseloads of 19.5 and 24 briefs, respectively, and Washington and South Carolina on the other, with 38 and 45, respectively. Hall, "A Means of Providing Effective Appellate Assistance," *The Defender* (1987): 20–21.

35. Conversation with Judge Michael Gross, former CAB supervising attorney in charge of volunteer program.

36. *The Crisis in Indigent Appeals*, 2.

37. *The Crisis in Indigent Appeals*, 23–26.

38. While CAB had long required its staff attorneys to produce 14 "substantive" (trial, hearing, or novel plea) briefs a year, that quota was not strictly enforced until the early 1980s.

39. *The Crisis in Indigent Appeals*, 29.

40. Ibid. 40–41.

41. See Frey "Appellate Division in Backlog Crisis," 42.

42. Ibid. 1.

43. Ibid. 1.

44. See "Courts Approve Public Appellate Defender Plan," *New York Law Journal*, 10 (1988): 1.

45. Draft proposal prepared by First Department 18b Administrator.

46. The background of the two appellate attorneys was likely to be different as well. The 18b attorney would have qualified for panel work simply by submitting a number of references and sometimes, but not always, being interviewed by a member of the screening panel. The CAB attorney would have been one of five applicants competing for the same spot, selected after an initial application and a series of interviews. The 18b attorney might have been alumnus of CAB or a District Attorney's appeals bureau, but was more likely to have spent his career as a solo practioner. The CAB attorney was likely have graduated from a good law school within the past several years.

47. The statutory rules governing criminal appellate procedure are contained in CPL Article 460; the rules for the First and Second Department in New York Court Rules and Regulations (NYCRR) Sections 600 and 670, respectively.

48. In AD2, the list includes only defendants convicted in the three New York City counties.

49. The 1985 City Bar Association report on appellate delay, discussed in the next chapter, urged an expedited procedure for conflict spotting by CAB, and some reforms, to be discussed later, have been instituted in the past year.

50. In one respect, the defendant relieved of CAB representation is better off than the defendant initially rejected by CAB: he already has a transcript on the way. The attorney eventually assigned to his case can begin work almost immediately, while

the attorney eventually assigned to a "checked off" defendant must wait for the minutes to be transcribed. To reduce this hardship, the AD1 panel has begun to enlist attorneys to serve as nominal or "dummy" counsel for checked off defendants, so that the court will have a name to put on the assignment order and the minutes can be obtained. In the months it takes to prepare the minutes, it is hoped that a real attorney can be found.

Part II

AN EMPIRICAL STUDY OF THE PERFORMANCE OF NEW YORK CITY'S TWO APPELLATE DEFENDERS

The following four chapters report the findings of an empirical study of the quality, results, and systemic impact of indigent appellate representation in New York City. It examines how the city's two appellate defenders performed under the constraints of criminal appellate adjudication in the 1980s: the relatively settled state of the criminal law, the limitations on the scope of appellate review, and the judicial perception that most indigent appeals have little or no merit. In evaluating the performance of two defenders with widely disparate resources and reputations, the study was designed to assess the impact of assigned appellate counsel in the review of criminal convictions.

The narrower question addressed by the study is whether New York City's arrangements for indigent appellate defense give some convicted indigents a better chance of success than others simply because of the unequal skill of the appellate defenders to whom they are assigned. The study first confirms the existence of significant qualitative differences between the two defenders through an evaluation of a small matched sample of briefs. It then analyzes the outcomes obtained by the two defenders in a much larger sample of cases, finding differences in outcome that correspond to the rated differences in quality. Finally, it considers an alternative explanation for the observed outcome differences based on the possibility that the two defenders are assigned appeals of differing merit. While that possibility cannot be ruled out, it cannot account for the specific outcome differences between the two defenders.

The broader question addressed by the study is the role played by assigned appellate counsel in furthering the basic goals of criminal appellate review: the correction of errors, the regulation of the lower-level functionaries in the criminal justice system, and the clarification and refinement of the law. Even if skilled appellate representation increases the odds of success for the individual defendant, it is not clear whether, or how, it enhances the regulatory functions of appellate review. Here, the evidence is necessarily more suggestive. A detailed analysis of the grounds for favorable action in the disposition sample reveals that few reversals are based on "technicalities," but even fewer on systemic abuses or unresolved issues: most involve a fortuitous conjunction of significant procedural or evidentiary error and significant weaknesses in the prosecution case. The analysis suggests, but cannot establish, that skilled advocacy plays an important role in procuring these reversals, by revealing often subtle or obscure errors and sensitizing the court to their prejudicial impact.

THE PLAUSIBILITY OF AN ATTORNEY EFFECT ON APPELLATE DISPOSITIONS

Appellate judges themselves disagree on the extent to which the quality of advocacy influences their decisions. In an informal survey, Thomas Marvell found that:

> most [judges] acknowledged that a good argument or brief probably does help one's cause. On the other hand, a number...said that there is no or extremely little impact, mainly because the judges know the law or do their own research.... In fact, quite a number of judges said that they did not really know whether the quality of an advocate's presentation affected the outcome, though they usually hazarded a guess anyway.[1]

On the one hand, most judges have confidence in the "robustness" of judicial review: the ability of the court to reach the same result regardless of the disparate skill of the opposing advocates. This confidence was recently expressed by the District of Columbia Court of Appeals in *Watson v. United States* (1987):

> [I]t is the unusual appeal whose outcome depends upon exceptional skill of counsel, because even a poor appellate argument is met with incisive consideration by the appellate court, where deliberation and review are undertaken to the extent necessary for considered decision.[2]

A similar view was taken by Justice Brennan, dissenting in *Jones v. Barnes*, who accused the majority of "overstat[ing] the lawyer's role in an appeal":

> While excellent presentation of issues...certainly serves the client's best interest, I do not share the Court's implicit pessimism about appellate judges' ability to recognize a meritorious argument.... Especially at the appellate level, I believe that for

the most part good claims will be vindicated and bad claims rejected, with truly skillful advocacy making a difference only in a handful of cases.[3]

At the same time, a belief in the importance of skilled advocacy seems to underlie many judicial complaints about the quality of routine appellate briefing. These complaints would seem exaggerated or peevish unless they were animated by a conviction that the skill of the advocate could influence the outcome of close cases. It is easier to acknowledge an attorney effect across a large number of cases, however, than to recognize it in a particular case.

Although there is some judicial recognition of an attorney effect on appellate dispositions, there is reason to doubt that judges can fully appreciate the impact of skilled advocacy in their own cases. For one thing, it is uncomfortable for judges concerned about fairness and autonomy to concede that their own decisions may depend on the skill of the attorneys before them. As Justice Brennan asserted in *Barnes*, "if the quality of justice in this country really depended on nice gradations in lawyers' rhetorical skills, we could no longer call it 'justice.' "[4]

Equally important, it may be difficult or impossible for appellate judges to *discern* the effect of advocacy in a particular case. As one of the judges interviewed by Marvell pointed out: "[with] a good attorney—like a real artist—the artistry doesn't show.... If he's doing a real good job, you don't think you're being conned."[5] The advocate's impact is further obscured by the fact that judges and clerks generally read the briefs before the records (if they read the records at all), and that prior exposure will indelibly effect what they "see" in the case. Most errors, however subtle, will seem obvious once they are pointed out, and even the most honest and self-conscious judge is likely to underestimate counsel's role in their discovery.

Empirical research on the impact of appellate advocacy is virtually nonexistent. Conducting an informal study, Marvell found that attorneys from better law schools tended to win more often, though he did not observe an effect for any other index of attorney quality. In those cases where Marvell himself found a significant imbalance in the quality of the opposing briefs, he found that the attorney doing the better job won three-fourths of the time, and almost always when the imbalance was great. He concluded that "on the whole, there is a strong possibility that the adversary system operates substantially in favor of lawyers who do a better job."[6]

Yet these informal observations must be set against the large body of research on trial-level representation, which finds that counsel type has little effect on case outcome (measured by frequency of conviction, grade of conviction, type and length of sentence), when other relevant factors like offense type and prior record are controlled for.[7] In a recent survey of two- and three-way comparisons of public defenders, assigned counsel, and retained counsel, Floyd Feeny found the evidence for an attorney effect on trial-level dispositions to be equivocal at best.[8]

If trial counsel has little demonstrable impact on outcome, appellate counsel might be expected to have even less. As the dissent in *Douglas v. California* (1963) insisted, the assistance of counsel may be less critical on appeal than before conviction.[9] Because appellate attorneys argue from a frozen record, fully available to the court, they may have less potential to hurt or help their clients.

Several considerations, however, limit the relevance of the trial-level findings for attorney effects at the appellate level. First, none of the studies cited by Feeny appear to have measured the quality of representation provided by the different types of counsel. There may have been little qualitative difference in the jurisdictions studied, especially after offense type was controlled for. Second, the standardization of plea bargaining in the 1970s may have had a dampening effect on the impact of attorney skill. Many of the studies reviewed by Feeny lumped plea and trial dispositions together, and the considerable effect of attorney skill on trials may have been swamped by its negligible impact on pleas.

Finally, there may be greater variations in *prosecutorial* effort and skill at the trial level than at the appellate level. Although prosecutors have at least as much opportunity on appeal as at trial to match their adversary's performance (since they get to see the appellant's brief before responding), they may have less incentive to do so, given the high baseline odds of affirmance. As a result, they may respond in the same boilerplate fashion to defense briefs of widely varying quality.[10] Adversary confrontation at the trial level may be more interactive and thus more likely to neutralize differences in the skill and zeal of defense counsel.

Even if variations in attorney skill will have a stronger or more discernible effect on appeal than at trial, superior advocacy will likely affect the outcome in only a small proportion of cases. As Kalven and Zeisel first pointed out in their classic study of jury trials, most cases are clear.[11] The most skillful advocate can rarely make a silk purse out of a sow's ear, and even the most inept advocate cannot obscure truly glaring errors. It is only in cases where, to quote *Douglas v. California* (1963), "the record is unclear or the errors hidden," and in those where the issues are novel or close, that attorney skill is likely to make a difference.[12]

Because skilled advocacy may only affect a minority of close, ambiguous, and novel cases, an empirical investigation of attorney influence will require the detection of very subtle influences. Even if significant differences in quality are established, their impact on the court may be poorly reflected in overall statistics, because the affirmance rate will be so high. The influence of skilled advocacy may be greatest in cases virtually impossible to identify in advance: those where the law is uncertain, disputed, or ambiguous; where the issues are not fully developed at the trial; and where the evidence looks deceptively strong. Clearly, a large part of the challenge is in knowing where such cases are likely to be found.

OUTLINE OF THE STUDY

Chapter 4 presents an evaluation, by eight retired appellate judges, of 32 paired CAB/18b briefs submitted in 1984 and 1985 for jointly tried codefendants. The evaluation compares the thoroughness and skill of the two defenders in handling appeals that arise from very similar factual and legal backgrounds. Given the enormous disparity in resources between the two defenders, described in Part I, it was expected that CAB would do appreciably better than 18b; in fact CAB briefs were rated modestly but consistently higher than their 18b counterparts. The judges' comparison of the briefs revealed other important differences between the work of the two defenders: the 18b briefs failed to raise meritorious issues far more often than the CAB briefs, and, in two of the three cases receiving favorable action, only CAB had fully briefed the winning issue.

Chapter 5 presents the results of an analysis of criminal appellate dispositions in the First and Second Departments from 1980 to 1985, the years in which the disparity in resources between the two defenders was greatest. It confirms the general impression of criminal appeals presented in Part I: the great majority of convictions are affirmed, mostly without opinion. At the same time, it reveals that CAB achieved significantly better results than the 18b panel in both departments, particularly in areas where skilled advocacy was likely to make a difference: in trial appeals generally, and in particular types of dispositions such as new trials, interest-of-justice reversals, and findings of harmless error. While retained counsel did consistently better than both assigned defenders, the gap between CAB and retained counsel was far narrower for trial than for plea appeals. Taken together, Chapters 4 and 5 suggest that a defendant was more likely to prevail on appeal if he was assigned to CAB, because of its superior representation.

Chapter 6 considers an alternative explanation for the outcome differences found in Chapter 5: that a defendant was more likely to be assigned to CAB if he had a better chance of prevailing on appeal. It is possible that CAB achieved better outcomes than 18b simply because it obtained more meritorious cases, either deliberately, through a policy of merit selection, or inadvertently, by the operation of the conflict-of-interest rules. A "spot audit" of CAB assignment practices offers no support for the first possibility, but an analysis of CAB's own records leaves open the second: that a neutral application of the conflicts rules gave CAB better-than-average cases.

Although the examination of CAB assignment practices does not rule out the possibility that a superior caseload enhanced CAB's performance, the differences in case merit arising from the assignment process cannot account for the magnitude and specific character of the outcome differences found in Chapter 5. Thus, the study concludes that CAB obtained better results than the 18b panel at least in part because it provided better representation.

Chapter 7 analyzes the grounds for reversal in the disposition sample, exploring the possible impact of defense advocacy on appellate decision-making in a system where 84 percent of all convictions are affirmed. It finds that most reversals and modifications involved factual determinations by the appellate court about the sufficiency or strength of the evidence, determinations which skilled representation may well influence. The successful appellate attorney appears to function more as an advocate than a technician, highlighting weaknesses in the prosecution case and sensitizing the court to the prejudicial impact of fairly simple and routine errors. Thus, the analysis Chapter 7 suggests that the outcome differences found in Chapter 5 may well result from the qualitative differences revealed in Chapter 4, and more generally, that skilled advocacy continues to play an important role in criminal appellate review a quarter century after *Douglas*.

NOTES

1. Marvell, *Appellate Courts and Lawyers: Information Gathering in the Adversary System* (Westport, Conn.: Greenwood Press, 1978): 37–39.

2. 536 A.2d 1056.

3. Brennan went on to concede, however, that this "handful" of cases "may include many cases that shape the law," 463 U.S. at 762. Brennan's opinion for the majority in *Evitts v. Lucey*, 469 U.S. 387 (1985), reaffirmed the importance of skillful advocacy in recognizing a constitutional right to the effective assistance of appellate counsel. *Evitts* itself, however, did not involve "nice gradations . . . in rhetorical skill" but the failure to satisfy a basic procedural prerequisite for filing an appeal.

4. 463 U.S. at 762.

5. Marvell, *Appellate Courts and Lawyers*, 38.

6. Marvell, *Appellate Courses and Lawyers*, 40. In criminal appellate advocacy, the effect may not be so striking, since it is only the skill of the defense advocate that is subject to wide variation—the Appeals Bureaus within each District Attorney's office turn out briefs of very similar tone and quality. In criminal appeals, there is likely to be a greater disparity between defense briefs than between prosecution briefs in different cases.

7. The pattern of results is familiar in recent social research on causal relationships, from the deterrence of criminal sanctions to the effects of welfare programs. Initial studies generally showed a strong effect for the attorney-type on type and severity of sanction. Later research, using statistical techniques to take account of the contribution of other factors correlated with attorney-type, such as prior record and offense-type, found little or no independent attorney effect. See D. Willison, "The Effects of Counsel on the Severity of Sentence: A Statistical Assessment," *Justice Systems Journal* 9 (1984): 87, 88.

8. Feeny, "Public Defenders, Assigned Counsel, Retained Counsel: Does the

Type of Criminal Defense Counsel Matter?" (paper prepared for American Society of Criminology Annual Meeting, Reno, Nevada, November 11, 1989).

9. 372 U.S. 353.

10. An argument could be made that *prosecutorial* skill matters less on appeal, where the presumption of innocence is replaced by a presumption of regularity in the trial-court proceedings.

11. *The American Jury* (Boston: Little, Brown, 1966).

12. 372 U.S. 353 at 358.

4

A Qualitative Evaluation of New York City's Appellate Defenders

This chapter assesses the quality of representation provided by New York City's appellate defenders. Its objectives are to determine (1) whether the disparity in resources between the two defenders is reflected in a corresponding difference in quality and (2) whether the quality of representation differs in ways that could affect appellate dispositions. It reports the findings of a study employing retired New York appellate judges to compare the briefs submitted by the two defenders in the appeals of jointly tried co-defendants. The study finds striking and consistent differences in rated quality and reveals significant deficiencies in 18b briefing in over a quarter of the sampled cases. Moreover, the differences it finds clearly have the potential to affect the outcome in close cases.

THE STANDARD OF COMPARISON

To assess the quality of representation provided by the two defenders, I arranged an evaluation of the briefs they submitted in closely comparable cases. The brief itself provides a fairly complete basis for assessing appellate representation, since it is the primary, and often the only, communication between the attorney and the appellate court.[1] Because the quality of a brief is largely evident on its face, particularly to someone familiar with the law, a reliable evaluation can usually be made without recourse to the trial record: the record is not necessary to judge the clarity of the writing, the cogency of the argument, or the proper use of legal authorities. The response brief filed by the district attorney provides a critical check on distortions and omissions in the defendants' briefs.[2]

To afford as fair and close a comparison as possible, I used the briefs submitted for trial codefendants convicted of the same offense. These brief-pairs almost always had a common factual background and at least one shared or overlapping issue, so that the rater could see how CAB and panel attorneys handled similar facts and law. A comparison of the two briefs revealed the skill with which the two defenders argued the same issues, and the care with which they selected and presented issues. The codefendant's brief also provided a partial substitute for the transcript, since it might reveal the failure of the one attorney to raise a strong issue applicable to both defendants.

Moreover, the use of codefendant briefs assured that most of the appeals being compared would not differ too widely in underlying merit. The mere fact that both defendants went to trial made it unlikely that there were major weaknesses in the evidence against either of them, since such evidentiary problems usually result in an acceptable plea offer.[3] The fact that the defendants were *jointly* tried also suggested that their cases lacked the large disparities in proof or culpability which would have warranted separate trials. Such disparities were even less likely in light of their joint conviction.[4]

To obtain a sufficient number of cases, it was necessary to use virtually all the 1980–1985 codefendant trial appeals from both departments for which briefs could be obtained.[5] Given the operation of the conflict rules, this meant that CAB always represented the CDD defendant when there was one, while 18b represented the panel defendant. (If a conflict of interest barred CAB from representing the CDD codefendant, CAB could not take either defendant). The factual information in the briefs, especially the prosecution brief, provided a ready check on the possibility that the CAB defendant was less culpable or heavily implicated.[6]

To ensure that the outcome differences found in the disposition survey could be attributed to the qualitative differences that turned up in the brief-evaluation, I limited the evaluation to briefs that were filed within the survey period. A concerted search of the two Departments yielded only 33 appropriate brief-pairs, 22 from AD1, all filed in 1984 or 1985, and 11 from AD2, all but one from 1984 and 1985.[7] (Most of the AD2 brief pairs came from consolidated appeals, while more than half of the AD1 pairs did not.) The brief sample was thus skewed toward AD1 and toward the later end of the survey period.

THE JUDGES AND THE EVALUATION PROCESS

I sought a measure of quality that captured the primary virtue of appellate advocacy—not mere eloquence, clarity or logical rigor, but the ability to engage and persuade appellate judges. At the same time, I did not want to operationalize "quality" entirely in terms of judicial reaction—to define a good brief simply as one that pleased an appellate judge. To balance the need for an appropriate audience and an objective evaluation, I selected raters who shared the background and orientation of sitting appellate judges, while structuring their evaluation with a carefully designed rating instrument.

The Evaluation Panel

To evaluate the briefs-pairs, I recruited a panel of retired New York appellate judges.[8] I obtained suggestions from the CAB attorney in charge, the AD1 18b administrator, a number of other appellate attorneys, as well as the judges initially contacted. I eventually contacted almost every retired New York appellate judge still in residence and good health; eight agreed to serve on the panel. Of these, four had served on AD1, three on AD1, and one AD3 and one on the New York Court of Appeals. All the Appellate Division justices had retired within the past five years; the Court of Appeals judge a number of years earlier.[9]

Because of the small number of judges and their busy schedules—over half the panel members still practiced full time—it was only possible to have each brief read by one judge. This limitation did not affect the reliability of the evaluation. Because the judges themselves were, for purposes of this evaluation, the ultimate arbiters of quality (and may have had irreducibly different criteria of quality), the issue of inter-rater reliability did not arise—a high level of agreement was desirable but not necessary.

Nevertheless, I adopted two procedures to ensure a minimum level of consistency in evaluation. First, I asked the judges to complete a 25-item evaluation form, discussed in the next subsection, before rating the brief. Second, I had all the judges evaluate a single "test" set of briefs, to ensure that they understood the instructions and evaluation form and to assess the divergence in their evaluations. Finally, I analyzed the ratings by judge, to see if there were any appreciable differences in their appraisal of CAB and 18b briefs.

As soon as a judge agreed to take part, he was sent the test briefs, and then as many other brief-pairs, up to five, as he was willing to take. Four judges took five brief-pairs, one took four pairs, three took three pairs, and one completed only two. The brief-pairs were not sent in any particular order; frequently, only one or two were available at a given time. An attempt was made, however, to give each judge at least one brief-pair from each department.

The packets sent to the judges consisted of the two codefendants briefs, with all indications of attorney affiliation removed, the response brief or briefs filed by the district attorney, and any reply briefs filed by the defendants.[10] The judges were instructed to rate only the defendants' briefs, but to read all the briefs before rating any of them.

The Evaluation Instrument

I sought a measure of quality which would capture both the minimum standards for appellate briefing and the qualities that make a brief persuasive. Although the competence of appellate representation is not usually assessed by the "checklist" approach employed by the American Bar Association for trial defense, it is clear that a minimally effective brief must have several features: it must raise the strongest issues presented by the record, including any issue with "a reasonable probability" of achieving favorable action;[11] it must summarize the procedural history and the evidence relevant to the issues it raises; and it must apply the law to the facts. Additionally, it must avoid raising blatantly frivolous issues or introducing matters not on the record.

Beyond these minimum standards, an appellate brief should have all the virtues of persuasive writing generally—clear organization, forceful arguments, felicitous prose, correct syntax and spelling—as well as some specialized ones—engaging headnotes, accurate citations, appropriate format. The rating form I developed contained a fairly exhaustive checklist of the necessary, desirable, detrimental, and improper features of an appellate brief.

In developing the rating instrument, I used two existing brief-evaluation forms as models—the AD1 form for 18b briefs, developed by the panel administrator, and the form employed by the administrator of the First District Appellate Project in California to rank the skill level of assigned counsel. I circulated a draft of my own form, longer and more comprehensive than the two models, to the CAB attorney-in-charge, the AD1 18b administrator, and an NYU Law School professor with an active practice in criminal appeals. I incorporated several of their suggestions and made some minor modifications after receiving back the evaluations from the test briefs.

The questions in the form were almost all in yes/no format, so that they could be completed fairly quickly.[12] The judges were encouraged to make additional comments. At the end of the form, the judges were asked to give an overall evaluation of the brief on a five-point, descriptive scale: 1 = poor, 2 = fair, 3 = average, 4 = very good and 5 = excellent.[13] The scale permitted judges to give intermediate rankings, and several did.

The questions preceding the overall rating served three purposes. First, they provided a great deal of additional information and judgments about the briefs. Second, they structured the judges' evaluations: although I could not and did not want to impose a fixed weighting on all the enumerated factors, completion of the form ensured that the judge had at least briefly considered all of these factors before giving his overall rating. Third, the responses to the questions could be compared with the final evaluations, to determine the contribution each made to the overall rating. I have included the evaluation form at the end of this chapter.

The Test Briefs

I selected one brief-pair for a "pretest," to see if there were any problems with the rating instrument and to compared the ratings given by the panel members on a single set of briefs. I chose a pair of briefs that impressed me as fairly similar and fairly ordinary, on the assumption that such a pair was more likely to reveal differences among judges than a conspicuously good, bad, or uneven pair.

I did not intend to use this pretest as a measure of inter-rater reliability: reliability is only an issue to the extent that the raters are assumed to be making fallible judgments of an independent, objective quality. For purposes of this evaluation, I wanted to treat the individual judge as the arbiter of brief-quality, not as a fallible observer. There was, of course, the possibility of irreconcilable differences of taste and legal opinion among the judges;[14] if their differences were too great, it would simply make it less likely that a clear "winner" would emerge in the pooled ratings of quality.

In the case selected, both defendants had been convicted of manslaughter for stabbing the victim during a racial brawl involving several other participants. The CAB defendant was seen by a friend of the 18b defendant threatening and later stabbing the victim; the 18b defendant was seen stabbing the victim by a policy officer arriving on the scene. The transcribed testimony of two or three other eyewitnesses, none apparently implicating the defendants, had been lost; the Appellate Division had previously refused to order a reconstruction hearing. The briefs raised three substantially identical issues: reasonable doubt as a matter of law, the failure to reconstruct the missing minutes, and the length of the sentences imposed. While the second issue was the only solid one, it required the court to reverse a recent ruling, a rare but not unprecedented event. In addition, the 18b brief argued that the charge on accessorial liability was erroneous, an unpreserved issue.

Both briefs received ratings ranging from 2 to 4, with two judges rating the CAB brief higher than the 18b brief, two rating the 18b brief higher, and four giving them the same rating (although one of these four described the CAB brief as better). The CAB brief was said by one judge to be "perfunctory" and too "sparse" by two others; the 18b brief was felt to be "overstated" by one.

The judges differed sharply in their appraisal of the charge issue raised by the 18b brief. Two judges (among the most recently retired) found the issue frivolous, and a third implied that it might be. On the other hand, two judges (among the longest retired) faulted the CAB brief for missing

Table 4–1
Ratings of CAB and 18b Codefendant Briefs by Retired Appellate Judges

	Overall	AD1	AD2
CAB	3.64	3.44	4.35
18B	2.47	2.60	2.00
Difference	1.17	0.84	2.36

5 - Point Scale:

5 = Excellent
4 = Very Good
3 = Average
2 = Fair
1 = Poor

the issue. Thus, the response to the test briefs revealed differences between the judges in substance as well as taste. These differences revealed that we had selected a panel with a healthy breadth of opinion, but they also made it less likely that we would obtain a consensus on the superior advocate, particularly if the judges disagreed about matters on which CAB and 18b briefs typically differed.

THE RESULTS

Overall Evaluations of the Briefs

The mean scores for the CAB and 18b briefs were 3.64 and 2.46, respectively: a "very-good minus" (B−) for CAB and a "fair plus" (D+) for 18b (Table 4–1). The principal dependent variable in the brief-evaluation was not the average ratings of the briefs, however, but the difference between each pair of codefendant briefs: the numerical rating of the CAB brief less the rating of the 18b brief. The mean difference between the CAB and 18b briefs was 1.17 points. Despite the small number of briefs involved, the overall difference was highly significant,[15] as was the difference in each department.[16]

An explanation of the statistical significance of this fairly modest difference in a small sample may be found in the consistency with which the CAB brief was rated higher than its 18b counterpart. Among the 32 brief-pairs, the CAB brief was rated higher in 21, the briefs were given the same rating in 8, and the 18b brief was rated higher in only 3. The CAB brief was given the highest possible rating in 5 cases, the 18b brief in none; the 18b brief was given the lowest possible rating in 9 cases, the CAB brief in none.

Despite the differences in legal and stylistic judgment revealed in the evaluations of the test briefs, the judges were consistent in their general preference for CAB briefs. Every judge gave the CAB brief a higher rating than the 18b brief in a majority of the cases in which he rated them unequally. Mean difference scores by judge ranged from 2.6 to .33, but all favored CAB.[17]

Descriptive Evaluations of the Codefendant Briefs

An examination of the evaluations completed by the judges reinforced the impression of CAB superiority and 18b deficiency, and suggested that the differences between the two defenders may not have been fully reflected in the overall ratings.

In eight of the cases, one quarter of the sample, the judge felt that the 18b brief had missed a viable issue, with no apparent tactical reason. In five of these cases, the judge further noted that the CAB brief for the codefendant had raised at least one of the missed issues (in one case, three such issues); in another, the 18b attorney had filed an *Anders* brief for a trial appeal which presented a number of meritorious issues. In contrast, there was only one case in which the judge found that the CAB brief had missed a meritorious issue. That issue had also been missed by the 18b brief (and the CAB but not the 18b brief had raised a closely related issue).

The 18b briefs were not only found to miss more meritorious issues but to raise more frivolous ones. The judges found frivolous issues in seven 18b briefs (and one judge found an argument for a viable issue "preposterous" in another) but in only two CAB briefs. Thus, it was apparent that CAB briefs did not avoid missing issues by indiscriminately raising all possible issues, regardless of merit. At the same time, CAB appears to have discovered issues more often than 18b: the judges noted unpreserved issues in eight CAB briefs but in only four 18b briefs.

In light of the judges' disagreement about the merit of raised and bypassed issues in the test briefs, it is clear that any single judgment of merit or frivolity must be regarded as a matter of opinion, possibly a debatable one. For this very reason, the results on the other briefs demonstrate a strong consensus on CAB superiority: judges with widely varying standards of merit and frivolity found far more missed and frivolous issues in the (unidentified) 18b briefs. The consistent differences we obtained would have been equally impressive if we had viewed the divergent responses to the test-brief as evidence of unreliability rather than disagreement. Unless the qualitative differences between the two defenders were quite large, we would not have expected them to be reflected in the ratings given by unreliable observers, and the probability of obtaining our rating differences by chance from unreliable observers is extremely small.[18]

The evaluations also suggested that the disparity in quality between CAB and 18b briefs may have been narrowed by the inclination of some 18b attorneys to paraphrase or borrow large portions of the CAB brief. Two of the judges felt that 18b briefs had incorporated substantial portions of the codefendant's brief. A third noted that the two briefs were virtually identical, word for word, without speculating about the direction in which the borrowing had occurred. In no case did a judge suspect that a CAB brief had borrowed from its 18b counterpart. Since CAB gets the record first in codefendant appeals, and usually files its brief first, there is a strong prior probability that any borrowing was done by the 18b attorney.[19]

Concerning the quality of argument and factual presentation in the briefs, the differences were consistent, though not as striking. The argument or supporting facts were found to be seriously incomplete in six 18b briefs and one CAB brief. The argument or factual presentation was found to be significantly confused in four 18b briefs and three CAB briefs. On the positive side, 18b briefs were found to raise complex issues in three cases, CAB in only one. CAB briefs were found to raise "novel" issues in two cases and "subtle" issues in another, while no 18b brief was credited with a novel or subtle issue.[20]

A Note on Oral Argument

In about half of the AD1 cases and several of the AD2 cases, it was possible to ascertain whether both of the codefendant briefs were argued or submitted. In four of the known cases, both attorneys submitted their briefs; in two, both argued them. In seven cases, the CAB attorney argued the appeal, while the 18b attorney submitted; in only one did the 18b attorney argue while the CAB attorney submitted.

The Outcomes of the Sampled Cases

Based on the results of the disposition survey described in Chapter 5 (which was completed before the brief-evaluation), I expected to find most of the sampled cases affirmed. I also expected to find little or no difference in the outcomes of the paired 18b and CAB cases, regardless of differences in quality. For one thing, the strength of the evidence in the paired cases was quite similar, and the probability of finding a winning issue in one case but not the other seemed quite low.

Moreover, is not necessary to raise an issue *on appeal* to benefit from its favorable resolution. If the court finds that an error was committed against a defendant, he is entitled to the appropriate relief whether or not his *appellate* attorney raised the issue. (This must be distinguished from the requirement that the defendant's *trial* attorney make a timely objection in order to preserve the issue.) If a defendant can benefit from the skill of a codefendant's attorney in a joint appeal, he can also suffer from her incompetence in a prior appeal. Once the court has ruled against one defendant on the same or a similar issue, it will almost never rule in favor of the other, even if that defendant would have prevailed on a clean slate: it is difficult for the court to reappraise an issue on which it has already made up its mind, and awkward for it to rule inconsistently in successive cases presenting a similar or identical issue.[21]

If the differences in quality revealed by the brief-evaluation affect case outcomes, it is likely to be in single-defendant appeals, where assigned counsel is left to his own devices, and his client's fate is not affected by the performance of any other assigned attorney. Thus, we would expect the disparity in skill between CAB and 18b attorneys to affect the outcome in appeals where there was no codefendant, where the codefendant was not appealing, or where he was appealing from a separate trial or a different disposition, for example, a plea to a reduced charge. Such single-defendant appeals constitute a large majority of 18b cases—in Chapter 6, we estimate that only 50 to 55 percent of the 18b appeals arise from cases with jointly indicted defendants, and that only a fraction of those end up in joint trials.[22]

In 27 of the 32 cases for which dispositions were known, 22 ended up with affirmances for both defendants, five with an opinion. Of these five, four were from AD2. The one from AD1 had a dissent and was subsequently reversed by the New York Court of Appeals. In one case, the 18b client, but not the CAB client, won a modification; in another, the CAB defendant, but not the 18b defendant, obtained a reversal.[23]

Finally, three of the cases ended with some favorable action for both defendants. An examination of the opinions in these cases revealed only one in which both attorneys had fully briefed the winning issue. In another, a remand had been granted for a hearing on the "independent source" for a suggestive identification; while both briefs attacked the identification as suggestive, only CAB argued the lack of evidence on independent source and requested a remand as an alternative to reversal. In the third case, only CAB fully briefed the issue on which reversal was based—the failure to establish an intent to kill where one of three robbers wounded a bystander with an accidental or warning shot. The 18b brief raised the issue summarily, merely asserting the absence of any "statements or situations" which would shed light on the intent with which the shot was fired.

It is, of course, impossible to know if the court would have reached the same results in these particular cases without the guidance of the CAB brief. We do not know if the winning arguments were obvious from the record or whether the court checks the record carefully for unbriefed or partially briefed issues. It is clear, though, that the court will not always spot issues which escape the attention of the defendant's attorney. Given the frequency with which 18b attorneys missed meritorious issues, it is likely that CAB wins some cases that 18b would lose, and that 18b loses some cases that CAB would win.

Was One Codefendant More Culpable or Heavily Implicated?

As a check on the possibility that the trial codefendants represented by one appellate defender were less heavily implicated or culpable than those represented by the other—a difference that might have affected the quality of the briefs or the judicial ratings of quality—I reviewed the prosecution briefs in eight of the sampled brief-pairs.[24] These briefs presumably displayed the state's evidence in the best possible light and the defendants in the worst.[25] I looked only for clear disparities in evidence and culpability: were there more eyewitnesses, or types of evidence, against one defendant; was only one defendant alleged to have used a weapon or injured the victim?[26]

The 18b defendant was more heavily implicated in three cases, the CAB defendant in two and there was no clear difference in the other three cases. The differences I found were not great. The most disparate pairs were an 18b defendant identified by two eyewitnesses and a CAB defendant by only one; an 18b defendant identified by a police witness and a CAB defendant identified by a civilian with possibly adverse interests; and a CAB defendant found with a knife and the victim's checkbook after being identified and arrested with the 18b defendant.

The CAB defendant was at least marginally more culpable in four cases, the 18b defendant in one, and there was no clear difference in culpability in the remaining three cases. Again, the differences were not great: in one case, the CAB defendant was the only one alleged to have had a weapon; in another, the CAB defendant was slightly more likely to have fired a shot that caused minor injury; in two other cases, one defendant initiated the verbal hostilities that led to violence.

It is clear from this subsample that the 18b defendants were generally not more heavily implicated or culpable than their CAB codefendants. As noted above, no systematic differences were expected, since gross disparities between arraigned codefendants in strength of evidence or culpability were likely to be "cashed out" in differing plea bargains. These findings leave little doubt that the differences in quality found in the brief-evaluation did not arise from differences in the codefendants' cases.[27]

Case Merit as a Factor Obscuring Differences in Quality

In the last section, I ruled out the possibility that differences in culpability and evidence strength contributed to the differences in rated quality; here, I consider the contrasting possibility that the weak issues and strong evidence which burdened *both* appeals limited the judges' appreciation of the skill with which they were presented. Better cases will not only elicit better advocacy but facilitate its appreciation. An interesting case with a significant chance of reversal may inspire an attorney's best efforts, while a losing and routing case is more likely to evoke a perfunctory response. Moreover, even the most disciplined judge may sometimes find his evaluation of the brief affected by his judgment about the case—it may be easier to appreciate a brief which makes forceful arguments on strong issues than one which makes a silk purse out of a sow's ear and easier to condemn a brief that does a poor job on a strong case than a marginal one.

Although I did not ask the judges to rate the underlying merit of the cases, it was apparent from their responses that many of the cases, CAB and 18b alike, were "sure losers." One judge described a fairly typical case-pair as "another of the many cases which illustrate that the practice of permitting the defendant to appeal without cost to him results in a clogging of appellate calendars with appeals utterly without merit."

Two judges conceded that they might have had difficulty in fully appreciating the quality of the briefs in weak cases; a third recognized that the quality of the briefs in such cases might not have fully reflected the attorneys' abilities. One 18b and two CAB attorneys were praised for doing "exceptionally well" or "the best possible job" in bad cases, but each received only a "4," not a "5," for these heroic efforts. To the extent that judgments of case merit influenced the appraisal of the briefs, they would have reduced both the overall ratings and the disparity between CAB and 18b, pulling the evaluation of both briefs toward a low common denominator.

The Representativeness of the Sampled Briefs

The possibility remains that in selecting a type of appeal that lent itself to comparison, I had also chosen a type that was not representative of the work done by one or both defenders: that poorer 18b or better CAB attorneys were assigned to these cases, or that the 18b or CAB attorneys assigned to these appeals did poorer or better work on these appeals than they did on others. On closer inspection, this turns out to be a more realistic possibility for 18b than CAB.

CAB claims to assign cases to its attorneys on the basis of availability and to make no exception for codefendant cases. While CAB does attempt to give particularly long and complex cases to more experienced attorneys, the sample cases were fairly short and the judges found very few to be complex. CAB also has a policy of trying to file first in codefendant cases, to avoid a prior unfavorable resolution of the 18b case—a policy that might favor assigning such cases to experienced attorneys. In fact, however, the sampled CAB briefs were not written by particularly experienced attorneys: only two were authored by supervisors, and only one by a staff attorney with more than four years at CAB at the time the brief was filed.

The 18b attorneys included in the brief evaluation, and the quality of their work, may have been less representative. The 18b rotation system should theoretically ensure that the assignment of codefendant cases is no different than the assignment of other cases. Nevertheless, it is clear that high-volume, low-quality panel members might prefer appeals with jointly tried codefendants, especially consolidated appeals, since they could often rely on the CAB brief to do much of the advocacy.[28] Their capacity to satisfy that preference would be severely limited, however, since the decision to consolidate codefendant appeals is often made long after those appeals are assigned.

If codefendants' appeals do not attract less zealous panel attorneys, they may nevertheless encourage less zealous briefing by the attorneys to whom they are assigned. Even a generally conscientious attorney might be tempted to rely on the work done by his CAB counterpart. The poor and sometimes derivative quality o the 18b briefs in these appeals might be uncharacteristic of 18b representation: in the large majority of cases, where the 18b attorney is left to his own devices, he may brief the appeal more carefully and exhaustively.

While this explanation for the poor quality of the sampled 18b briefs cannot be ruled out, it ignores the fact that many of the briefs' authors may not even have known about the existence of a CAB codefendant, let alone about the status of his appeal. While the trial minutes reveal if there are any jointly indicted or tried codefendants, the record received by the 18b attorney will generally contain no information on codefendants' appeals. As I discovered in my own research, it often takes a concerted effort to obtain this information from court records.

Although some of the 18b attorneys in the sample had obviously read the CAB brief for the codefendant, since they referred to or borrowed from it, most of them probably had not. Many of the attorneys with separate appeals may not even have known that a codefendant was appealing, let alone that his brief adequately covered the most important issues for both defendants. Moreover, while attorneys with consolidated appeals were more likely to have seen and relied on the codefendant's brief, it is doubtful that an attorney too lazy or inattentive to paraphrase a meritorious argument for his client would take the trouble to write one from scratch in a case where he was on his own. Thus, there is little reason to suspect that the quality of the sampled 18b briefs was unrepresentative of the general quality of the 18b appellate work.[29]

CONCLUSION

The brief-evaluation presents a contrast between the consistently adequate, often superior, representation provided by CAB, and the uneven but generally weak representation provided by the appellate panel. CAB briefs were rated significantly higher than 18b briefs in both departments and by all eight retired appellate judges. The numerical differences between the two defenders were reinforced by descriptive findings revealing serious deficiencies in almost half of the 18b briefs.

A quarter of the 18b briefs in the sample, but only one of the CAB briefs, were judged to have missed meritorious issues. Almost a quarter of the 18b briefs, but only two CAB briefs, were judged to have raised frivolous issues. In contrast, CAB briefs raised unpreserved issues twice as often as 18b briefs. The qualitative differences found by the judges could not be attributed to differences between the codefendants in strength of evidence or culpability, and the low merit of most of the cases may actually have obscured differences in quality between the two defenders.

The outcome-determining potential of these qualitative differences can be seen in two of the three cases in which both codefendants received favorable action. In one of those cases, the relief was based on an issue raised by the CAB brief alone; in another, the winning issue was briefed by CAB and merely adopted by 18b. While the court might have discovered the first of these issues by itself, and the 18b attorney might have raised the second on his own initiative, it is quite possible that the winning issue would have been overlooked in both cases, and the conviction affirmed, if the 18b brief had been submitted alone.

To summarize, this chapter has revealed statistically significant differences in the quality of representation provided by the two appellate defenders. The descriptive evaluations indicate that the differences between the two defenders are substantial, affecting basic aspects of appellate briefing. While almost all CAB attorneys and many 18b attorneys appear to provide at least minimally competent representation, a large share of 18b briefs fall below a minimum standard of competence, failing to raise important issues or provide a coherent statement of facts. An examination of the cases in which both defendants won favorable action suggests these differences, particularly in raising meritorious issues, may affect the outcome of close cases.

APPENDIX: RATING INSTRUMENT FOR BRIEF EVALUATION

People v. ______________ Defendant #

BRIEF EVALUATION FORM

Please answer all questions with a Y, N or NA (not applicable). Use the space at the end of the form for general comments and requested explanations.

Was this a complete case factually?________ legally?_________

(1) Does the statement of facts:
  a) give a complete and coherent account of the case?______
  b) emphasize facts favorable to the defendant and his claims without distorting the record? _______

(2) Does the argument:
  a) miss available issues with no apparent tactical reason? ____ (please specify, and note if the other defendant raises this issue)
  b) raise any frivolous issues? ______ (please specify)
  c) Raise any partly or fully unpreserved issues? ______ (please specify)
  d) raise any novel _____ subtle ______ or complex _____ issues? (Please specify)
  e) run distinct issues together in the same point or raise the same issue in different points? _____
  f) raise any issue applicable only to the codefendant or on which this defendant otherwise lacks standing? _____ (please specify)

(3) Are the arguments on the individual points:
  a) clear? _____ well-organized? _____ forceful? _____ terse? _____
  b) accurate _____ effective _____ in their use of authority?
  c) incomplete, omitting necessary parts of the argument (e.g. harmless error analysis, interest-of-justice review for unpreserved error)? _____ (please specify)
  d) overbroad, claiming more than necessary? _____
  e) connected, wherever possible, to weaknesses in the prosecution case? _____

(4) Are the point headings concise, accurate and engaging? _____

(5) Is the writing fluent? _____the tone appropriate? _____ the grammar and spelling generally correct? _____

(6) Is the appearance of the brief neat and professional? _____

(7) Do significant parts of the brief appear to be borrowed or adapted from the codefendant's brief? _____ (please specify)

(8) If a reply brief was filed, was its quality significantly different form the main brief's? _____ (please explain)

How would you rate the brief(s) overall? (Mark scale)

POOR —— FAIR —— AVERAGE —— GOOD —— EXCELLENT

COMMENTS:

NOTES

1. While some writers on appellate advocacy stress the importance of oral argument, other experienced practitioners doubt that it makes much of a difference even in close cases. See Stern, *Appellate Practice in The United States* (Washington, D.C.: Bureau of National Affairs, 1981): 358–60. In most appellate courts, a bench memo on the case has already been prepared before argument, which provides the court with a review of the facts and contentions and a presumptive decision. Even if oral argument makes a difference in some close cases, there is probably a high correlation between good briefing and good argument. While attorneys skilled in written advocacy may vary widely in their oral presentations, attorneys arguing from poorly researched and structured briefs are unlikely to be very persuasive.

Moreover, many briefs are simply not argued at all. AD2 prohibits argument of excessive sentence motions, and both departments encourage the submission—the nonargument—of routine plea and trial appeals. In my sample of codefendant briefs, over half the cases for which information was available were submitted. Generally, the stronger the case and the more zealous the attorney, the more likely the appeal is to be argued. Thus, even if I had been able to appraise oral arguments, I would have been reviewing an unrepresentative sample of cases and attorneys.

2. In only one of the 65 brief-evaluations I describe later in this chapter did a judge state that he felt unable to assess the validity of an argument because he could not consult the record.

3. See Mather, *Plea Bargaining or Trial? The Process of Criminal Case Disposition* (Lexington, Mass.: D.C. Heath, 1979): 60–63.

4. The fact of joint trial also significantly reduced the appellate impact of any disparities in trial representation. Objections by one trial attorney on matters affecting both defendants may be adopted by the codefendant's attorney even if he would not have made them himself, and they are "flagged" for the codefendant's *appellate* attorney, at least for interest-of-justice review. Moreover, unless the defendants had sharply conflicting strategies or faced very dissimilar evidence, both unlikely in a joint trial, the skill of one attorney is casting doubt on the prosecution case would redound to the benefit of the codefendant.

5. I had originally hoped to use a particular group of codefendant cases, assigned to the two defenders by a more or less random process. When two jointly tried codefendants are both represented by 18b attorneys at trial, CAB will (with minor exceptions discussed in Chapter 6) take the first to be granted poor person relief. This assignment procedure is not truly random, since the first codefendant to be granted poor person relief will usually (though not always) be the first to have requested it. Nevertheless, the procedure should eliminate any systematic differences between codefendants due to culpability, strength of evidence, or quality of trial representation. Unfortunately, there were simply not enough of these pairs for a meaningful comparison; I was able to locate less than five over as many years.

Even without this restriction, it proved surprisingly difficult to find an adequate number of jointly tried indigent codefendants with completed appeals. The First Department keeps a register of all criminal appeals, which lists codefendants' appeals together even when they were heard separately. It also has a space on its defendant file cards for codefendants. The Second Department, however, has neither a register nor any file card notation for codefendants—the only way to locate codefendants in AD2 is through its decision logs, which indicate only those codefendants with consolidated appeals—about a third of all codefendant appeals. There were also problems in locating the briefs of identified codefendant pairs. I had wanted to draw briefs from the entire period covered by the disposition survey, late 1980 to late 1985, but this was not feasible. Both departments began saving briefs on microfiche in 1984; AD1 discarded its earlier briefs, while AD2 preserves them in bound volumes difficult to transport or photocopy from.

6. This possibility was raised by the McConville and Mirsky report, which showed that CDD attorneys in New York County engaged in a systematic practice of selecting the least culpable or heavily implicated defendant at arraignment, McConville and Mirsky, "Criminal Defense of the Poor," 818–36.

7. One of these cases was a prosecution appeal; another was an appeal from a joint plea.

8. Several researchers have used judges or other legal professionals to make expert judgments: McConville and Baldwin had a retired police official and a retired law clerk review the adequacy of policy information to support an indictment. *Courts, Prosecution and Conviction* (Oxford: Clarendon Press, 1981); D. E. Rosenthal had judges assess the adequacy of personal injury settlements. *Lawyer and Client: Who's in Charge?* (New York: Russell Sage Foundation, 1974).

9. Four of the retired judges had been regarded as liberal in matters of criminal law and procedure, three as conservative, and one as middle-of-the-road.

10. An attentive rater might have been able to recognize the CAB briefs by noting their common format and similarities in style, but it would have required a close comparison of the different brief-pairs. Of course, judges might have assumed that the better brief came from CAB, based on the reputations of the two defenders (and their own experience with them), but in that case the judgment about affiliation would not have influenced the evaluation of the briefs, but vice-versa. In fact, in the two cases where raters made comments about the affiliation of the attorney, they were mistaken.

11. In *Watson v. United States*, 536 A.2d 1056 (1987), the court held that appellate ineffectiveness would be established if "counsel failed to raise an available issue which, of factually supported, would create the reasonable probability of reversal."

12. To avoid a response bias, questions for which "yes" was the favorable response were interspersed with questions for which "no" was.

13. The verbal labels on the scale were chosen as familiar evaluative terms, but their use resulted in a scale of uneven intervals; for example, the perceived difference between "very good" and average may have been considerably greater than between "average" and "fair." While the judges might have given different numerical ratings on a scale with equal verbal intervals, the differences between intervals did not affect the validity of the results: for the kind of statistical analysis I used, an ordinal scale can be treated like an integer scale.

14. Although some legal philosophers believe there is a correct resolution of every legal issue, this does not mean that there will always be a correct answer to the question of whether an incorrect legal claim is frivolous or meritorious.

15. $T=4.30$, $p=.0002$. The significance tests in this chapter use the T-Test procedure, Statistical Analysis Systems, Cary, N.C.

16. AD1: $T=2.91$, $p=.0076$; AD2: $T=4.53$, $p=.004$

17. An additional indication of the general consistency of the judges, at least in the severity with which they judged the briefs, may be found in their minimum, maximum, and mean ratings: six judges had minimum ratings of 1, one of 1.5, and one of 2; three judges had maximum ratings of 5, five of 4; mean ratings ranged from 3.5 to 2.6. These variations may reflect differences in the overall quality of the 4–10 defense briefs given to each of the judges; they certainly do not suggest major disparities in the judges' standards of quality.

18. If, to take an extreme view, we regarded judicial ratings of quality as truly random over the five-point rating scale, then we would have expected the overall ratings of CAB and 18b briefs to be about the same, just as if there were no qualitative differences between the two groups. The *p*-value for the difference test ($p<.0002$) indicates that the overall difference we actually obtained would have come about by such a chance process only one time in 5,000. Admittedly, no tests of statistical significance were performed for judgments of missed and frivolous issues, and we cannot have the same confidence in them that we have in the overall ratings.

19. Several 18b briefs also contained wholesale "incorporation clauses," adopting all points in the CAB brief consistent with its own. Others adopted specific arguments. None of the eight CAB briefs I examined closely contained such clauses.

20. I used the terms "novel," "subtle" and "complex" in the evaluation form without defining them, trusting the judges to recognize these qualities when they saw them.

21. The first defendant can always move for reargument, but he can expect little assistance from the attorney who missed the winning issue or argument in the first place, and the court will not reopen his case on its own initiative.

22. Unfortunately, it is also in such cases that we would expect to find some differences in underlying merit of CAB and 18b cases (see Chapter 6).

23. I was unable to locate the opinions for these two cases.

24. Six of the eight cases were in the first batch sent out to the judges; the remaining two were chosen simply because the briefs were handy. Five were from AD1, three from AD2.

25. I relied exclusively on the prosecution briefs because the differential quality of the defense briefs might contribute to, as well as reflect, apparent differences in evidence strength and culpability—better appellate briefs might *make* the defendant *seem* less heavily implicated and culpable.

26. I did not compare the prior records of the codefendants. Even if their records might have influenced their trial and appellate dispositions, they would not have affected either the quality of the briefs written on their behalf or the judicial perceptions of brief quality.

27. Greater disparities would be expected where only one codefendant went to trial, however, so that these findings do not provide a check on a general "merit confound" for appellate performance.

28. A check on this possibility could be provided by reviewing the control cards on the panel attorneys represented in the brief evaluation, to see if they were an unusually active and veteran group.

29. There is, however, some suggestive evidence that 18b briefing may be better in circumstances where the attorney has no access to the brief submitted by CAB for a codefendant. In 9 of the 32 paired cases, the 18b appeal had been heard first,

so that the attorney probably had no opportunity to see the CAB brief before submitting his own. (I say "probably" because in some of these cases, the CAB brief may have been filed first, but the appeal delayed for the filing of a *pro se* supplemental brief by the defendant.) While these paired cases had an average difference score about the same as the overall average (1.16 vs. 1.17), they also included two of the three pairs in which the 18b brief had been rated *higher* than the CAB brief, and none of the cases in which the 18b brief was found to have missed a meritorious issue. In contrast, the 15 consolidated appeals, where 18b access to the CAB brief may have been greatest, had an average difference score (1.6) appreciably higher than the overall average, had no pairs in which the 18b brief was rated higher, and included six of the eight cases in which the 18b brief had been found to have missed a meritorious issue. This last finding, the most striking, has a more plausible explanation: appeals may get consolidated just because they present similar or overlapping issues, a fact which makes the omission of a meritorious issue by one defendant particularly conspicuous.

5

Criminal Appellate Dispositions in New York City, 1980–1985

This chapter examines the performance of New York City's appellate defenders through an analysis of First and Second Department dispositions from 1980 to 1985. It reveals small but statistically significant differences in the outcomes obtained by the two defenders during a period when the vast majority of appealed convictions were affirmed without opinion. These differences are generally consistent with the qualitative differences found in the previous chapter. The pattern of results revealed in the disposition survey suggests, though it cannot establish, that skilled advocacy increases the likelihood of favorable action on appeal.

THE NATURE AND SCOPE OF THE SURVEY

To survey the results obtained by the two appellate defenders, I drew a random sample of 2,000 First and Second Department decisions from West's *New York Supplement*, which reports all final Appellate Division decisions. The sample covered a five-year period, from the fall of 1980 to the fall of 1985, during which over 14,000 criminal appellate cases were decided in the two departments.

Prior to this survey, there were no available statistics on the outcomes of criminal cases in the Appellate Division. The Second Department (AD2) and the State Office of Court Administration both keep cumulative records of *all* appellate dispositions, but the former cannot, and the latter will not, provide a separate breakdown for criminal cases.[1] The First Department (AD1) keeps no statistics at all. Further, it is not possible to track the performance of the two defenders through their own records. The 18b panels in both departments keep no disposition records whatsoever, and CAB has complete records for assignments only since 1984.

The only complete record of criminal appellate dispositions is contained in the official New York case reports and in West's *New York Supplement* (NYS), both of which publish all decisions on completed criminal appeals.[2] Neither source, however, provides information on conviction type (trial or plea) or on attorney affiliation (CAB or 18b) for most of the appeals that are affirmed without opinion. West's was chosen because it provided this information more often.

Once the sample of criminal dispositions was obtained, it was necessary to track down the missing information on case and attorney type from the Appellate Division files. Both departments maintain defendant cards in alphabetical order, which give the attorney, the chronology of the appeal, and the disposition. AD1 cards also record the conviction type, while AD2 cards only indicate whether the appeal challenged the conviction (the "judgment") or just the length of the sentence (using the special AD2 excessive sentence motion).[3]

The Survey Period

I chose a five-year period in order to detect stable patterns and significant trends in the performance of the two defenders. The period ended with the latest bound volume of the NYS available at the time, containing cases decided in the early fall of 1985. The survey thus covered the period during which the disparity in resources between the two defense entities was greatest, ending just as the CAB staff reached its maximum size and the 18b panel received the first rate increase in its 20-year history. While the survey obviously could not assess the impact of the 1985 and 1987 rate increases, its results indicate that the prior level of compensation may well have had a severely adverse effect on the panel's performance.

THE CONTENTS OF THE SURVEY

The Independent Variables: Department, County, Attorney, Conviction Type and Time Period

For each of the cases selected from the *New York Supplement*, the survey coded the appellate department, the county of conviction, the type of appeal (trial/plea in AD1; judgment/sentence in AD2), and the type of attorney (CAB, 18b, or retained).[4] Appellate department was a critical variable for two reasons: First, the two departments are distinct courts, with different traditions, policies, and positions on the law, as well as the power to resolve similar cases quite differently on the facts or in the interest of justice. Second, the 18b panels in the two departments are also distinct entities, with different administrators and only a small number of overlapping members.[5]

The county of conviction is also a significant variable, not only because it determines the department which hears the appeal, but because the judges and prosecutors in the different counties may differ widely in the frequency with which they commit reversible errors. The type of appeal has obvious importance: trial appeals would be expected to result in favorable action more often than plea appeals, because they involve a far wider range of potential errors and issues.[6] If the two defenders handled different proportions of trial and plea appeals, that alone could explain an overall difference in their outcomes, since trial appeals are likely to succeed more often.

Trial appeals are not only more likely to succeed than plea appeals, but are more likely to hinge on attorney skill. Under current New York law, a plea will almost always be affirmed unless there is something obviously wrong on its face.[7] The fate of a close trial appeal, in contrast, will often depend on the way the court weighs the magnitude of the error against the strength of the state's evidence, a balance which skillful advocacy may tip. This is particularly likely to be true of appeals resulting in a new trial rather than an outright dismissal, since dismissals are more likely to be automatic, for example, when the evidence is legally insufficient or the prosecution untimely. Thus, success in trial appeals, particularly in obtaining new trials, is more likely to reflect superior advocacy than success in plea appeals.

The survey included retained as well as assigned cases for two reasons: first, to present a breakdown of *all* criminal appellate dispositions, which would reveal the overall rate of affirmance and the proportion of cases handled by assigned counsel; second, to compare the performance of assigned and retained counsel. Retained counsel have a number of possible advantages: fewer violent crimes, more sympathetic clients, and greater possibilities for error in more complex cases. Their most significant advantage, however, is self-selection: as noted in Chapter 1, it is widely believed that defendants will be less likely to appeal a hopeless case if they have to pay their lawyer than if he is provided free of charge. If one of the assigned defenders obtained better results than retained counsel, it would almost certainly be due to greater skill, not better cases.

Finally, the *New York Supplement* volume in which the decision appeared served as a surrogate time variable (West's reports cases approximately in the order they are decided). The 60 *New York Supplement* volumes used in the survey were divided into four 15-volume "quarters," covering about 13–15 months of decisions apiece. Each quarter was thus a little less than a year and a quarter, and in the remainder of the analysis, I will refer to the survey's four quarters rather than its five years.

A number of significant developments had occurred during the survey period which may have affected the performance of the two defenders: the backlog crisis, the growth of the CAB staff, the Legal Aid strike, and the partial CAB moratorium in AD2. There may also have been changes in the composition of the appellate courts, in the practices of the police, prosecutors, and trial courts, and in criminal law doctrine which affected the probability of successfully challenging a conviction. If these developments affected the performance of the two appellate defenders, then the outcomes obtained by one or both would vary by quarter.

The Dependent Variable: The Classification of Outcomes

Outcome coding was designed to measure two distinct, though not independent, dimensions of appellate performance: practical success and issue resolution. The first concerns the bottom line—what did the outcome mean to the client? Did it leave him better off, and, if so, in what way? The second concerns a broader range of appellate success—did the court write an opinion, reach an unpreserved issue, find the trial court in error? The two measures of success are obviously related, since the court will almost always write an opinion and make an explicit finding of error when it reverses, but only infrequently when it affirms. Nevertheless, the second measure may capture differences in judicial response that are not apparent from the first measure.

Practical Success. The dispositions were coded to distinguish the different forms of favorable action, from a reversal and dismissal, which unconditionally frees the defendant and precludes his reprosecution, to the dismissal of a lesser included count, which does not alter the defendant's record, sentence, or parole eligibility in any way. Between these two extremes lies a range of partial victories: a reversal and new trial,[8] whose practical significance depends on the surviving evidence and the difficulties of reprosecution; the dismissal of the top count, which reduces the defendant's sentence and improves his record; a simple "time cut," which reduces the defendant's sentence without improving his record; and the dismissal or reversal of a concurrent or lesser nonincluded count, whose benefits to the defendant are slight and collateral. Somewhere within or slightly outside this spectrum are remands without reversal, which return the case to the trial court for further factual findings and give the client some possibility of reversal, however slight.

Another category of dispositions did not fit into this spectrum at all: the granting of an *Anders* motion, which simultaneously relieves the attorney and affirms the conviction. The anomaly arises from the nature of *Anders* relief itself: it is obviously a defeat for the client, but it is also a vindication of his attorney's judgment that the appeal lacked merit. The frequency with which *Anders* motions are requested and granted is of great interest, but *Anders* relief was not counted as a win or loss because of its ambiguous nature.

After the outcomes were coded, they were placed into larger groupings for purposes of statistical analysis. Two different definitions of "favorable action" were used, the first including, the second excluding, dismissals of concurrent and lesser counts. The second reflected the viewpoint of the self-interested client (Holmes's "bad" appellant), concerned only with the time he would have to serve and the record he would carry with him.

Issue Resolution. There are two important reasons for coding judicial response to the issues raised in the appeal even when those responses had no practical consequences for the defendant. First, the resolution of issues is of interest to the system as a whole. An appeal may be "successful" in clarifying the rights of the defendant or the restrictions on the police, even if the clarification does not lead to reversal, either because the court finds no error or finds the errors harmless or unpreserved. The attorney who brings about the clarification has achieved a useful result for the system if not for his client.

Second, and more important from a client-oriented perspective, a narrow measure of outcome success may overlook or understate the actual benefits of skilled advocacy to the clients in a small but significant number of close and difficult cases. The impact of superior lawyering might well be lost or obscured in a simple tally of wins and losses. As noted in Chapter 1, most criminal appeals will be clear from the outset—a large majority of sure losers and a very small number of sure winners.

In clear cases, differences in advocacy will at most affect the style, not the substance, of the disposition, for example, by inducing the court to comment on the defendant's position, rather than ignore it in a terse or silent affirmance. While such expressions of interest and partial agreement might be small consolation to the client, they would reveal an attorney influence on the court that might well affect the outcome in close, ambiguous, and novel cases, even if such cases were too infrequent to yield statistically significant outcome differences.

Thus, the survey coded not only the bottom line—affirmance, reversal, or modification—but other significant aspects of the decision: whether or not there was an opinion, a dissent, or a discussion of the issues raised by the appellant. For any case in which the court made a determination on one or more issues ("reached the merits"), the coding indicated whether it found an error, whether it found the issue preserved, and whether it found the error, if any, harmless. The coding distinguished between a case where the court found "any errors" harmless, thereby declining to discuss them; a case in which the court denied that there was an error but declared that any error would have been harmless, making a determination against the defendant; and a case in which the court recognized an error but found it harmless, agreeing with the defendant on the issue but not on its consequences for his conviction. Although all three convictions are "affirmed," in the latter two appeals, the court has resolved an issue raised by the defendant, in the last case in his favor. In a study of the impact of appellate advocacy, these are important differences.[9]

THE RESULTS OF THE ANALYSIS

Of the 2,000 cases initially selected, almost 25 percent were AD2 cases from counties outside New York City. These were eliminated from the sample, as were the small number of motion and habeas decisions. The 62 prosecution appeals were analyzed separately and are discussed in a separate section. The remaining 1410 defense appeals constitute the sample for the following analysis.

The Independent Variables: Who Appeals in New York City, From What Do They Appeal, To What Department, Who Represents Them?

1. Almost 90 percent of all decided appeals came from indigent defendants, of whom CAB represented less than 60 percent.

Fifty-one percent of the defendants were represented by CAB, 36 percent by the 18b panel and 10 percent by private counsel (Figure 5–1). (The remaining 3 percent were volunteers supervised by CAB and non-CAB attorneys who could not be classified further.) Two facts are noteworthy: an overwhelming majority of criminal appellants are indigent, and CAB handles a far smaller share of indigent appeals than the 1966 City Bar Association Plan contemplated.

2. The First Department decides the majority of New York City criminal appeals.

57.5 percent of the decisions in the sample came from AD1; 42.5 percent from AD2 (Figure 5–2). Since the 33–50 percent of AD2 criminal dispositions that came from outside the city were excluded, it is clear that AD2 has a much larger criminal caseload than AD1.

About a third of the dispositions came from New York County. Kings County provided 26 percent, Bronx, 22.6 percent, Queens 12.6 percent and Richmond was a distant fifth with 2 percent.[10]

3. The 18b panel was the plurality defender in AD2.

In AD1, 51 percent of the defendants were represented by CAB, 31 percent by 18b and 9 percent by retained counsel. In AD2, the percentages were 41 percent, 43 percent and 12 percent, respectively. Thus, during the sample period, the backup appellate defender in AD2 was handling a larger share

Figure 5–1
NYC Criminal Appeals by Attorney

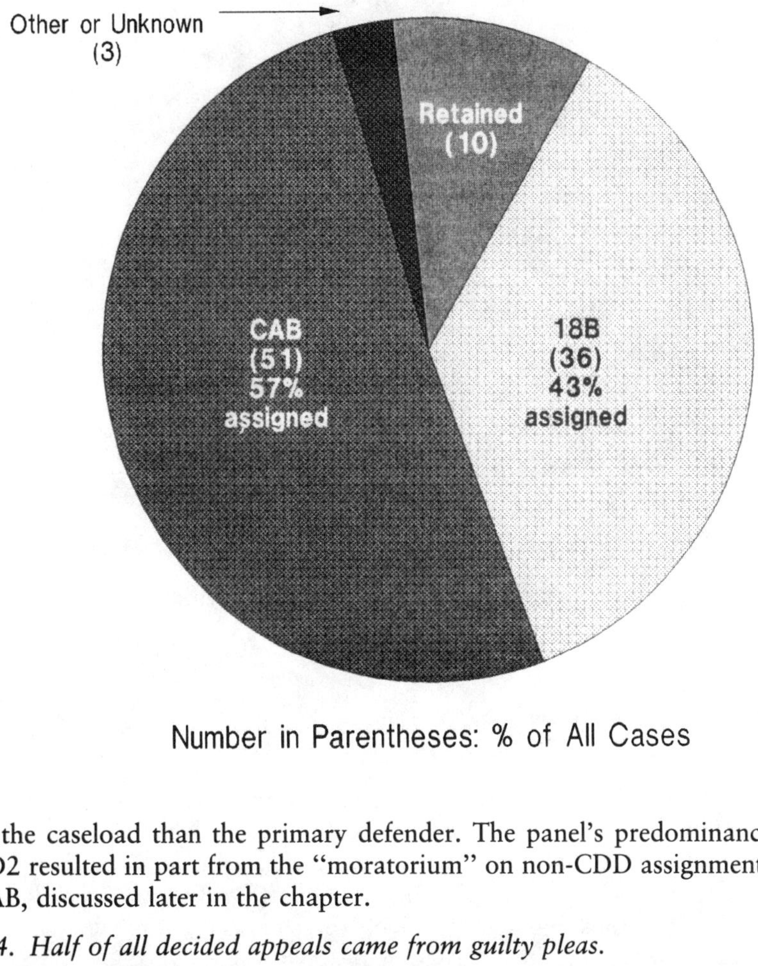

of the caseload than the primary defender. The panel's predominance in AD2 resulted in part from the "moratorium" on non-CDD assignments to CAB, discussed later in the chapter.

4. *Half of all decided appeals came from guilty pleas.*

Forty-one percent of the appeals were from trial convictions; 34 percent from plea convictions (Figure 5–3). The latter includes AD2 sentence motions, which comprised 9 percent of the sampled cases. In 15 percent of the cases, almost all from AD2, it was not possible to tell if the judgment appealed from was a trial or plea. These 15 percent were almost all affirmed without opinion, which was not surprising, since almost all published opinions report the conviction type.[11] The remaining 2 percent were appeals from other trial court orders, such as the denial of a 440.10 motion to vacate judgment.

The mix of known trial and plea appeals is about the same for the two

Figure 5–2
NYC Criminal Appeals by Department

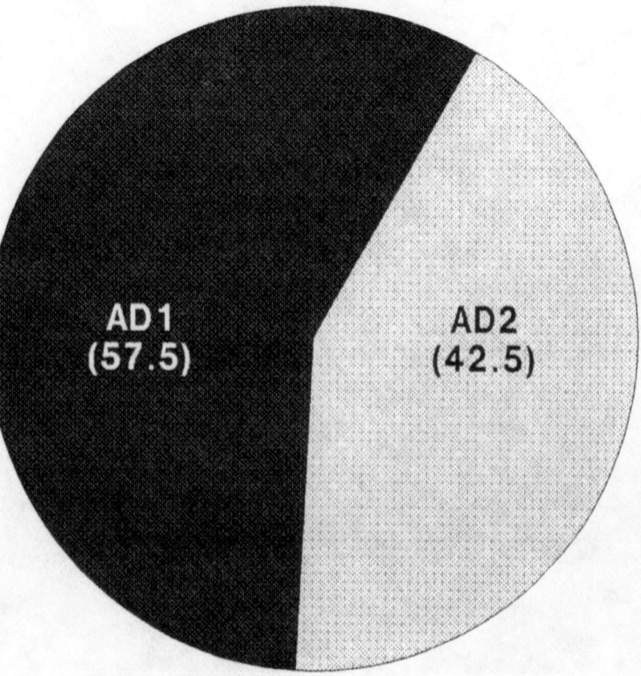

Number in Parentheses: % of All Cases

defenders. In AD1, where fairly complete information was available, 46.5 percent of CAB cases and 50 percent of 18b cases were trials. In contrast, over 63 percent of all retained cases were plea appeals. Since there is no reason to believe that a higher percentage of retained cases are resolved by plea, this difference has two possible explanations: (1) both indigent and nonindigent defendants exercise some selectivity about appealing pleas, but the former exercise far less selectivity than the former about appealing trials; or (2) indigent defendants are considerably more selective than nonindigent defendants about appealing pleas.

The first is clearly the more plausible explanation. It is unlikely that defendants with a "free ride" are more selective about appealing pleas than defendants who must pay for their appeals. Moreover, the difference between the success rates for retained and assigned counsel is greater for plea than for trial appeals (see next section), which hardly suggests that paying defendants are less selective than indigent defendants about pleas. It is more likely that indigent defendants are much less selective about appealing trials

Figure 5–3
NYC Criminal Appeals by Conviction/Appeal Type

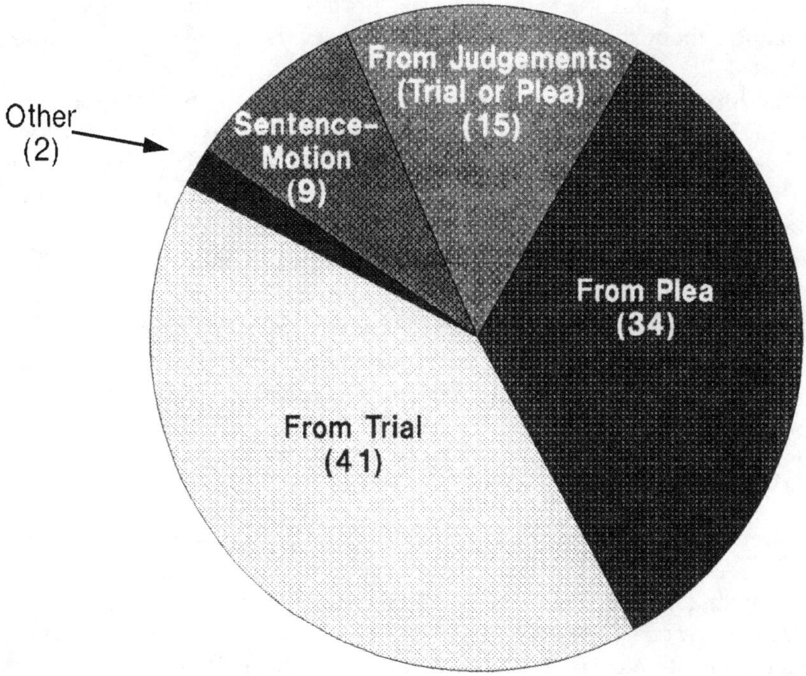

than paying defendants, giving the former a higher proportion of trial appeals.

5. *The number of decided appeals has been increasing.*

The number of decided cases increased slightly over the first three quarters (approximately the first four years), and then went up about 20 percent from the third to the fourth quarter, between the late spring of 1983 and the early fall of 1985:

Percentage of Total Dispositions in Survey

First Quarter	21.8
Second Quarter	22.9
Third Quarter	25.6
Fourth Quarter	29.7

The proportion of appeals decided by the two departments remained about the same through the first three quarters. In the fourth, however, AD2 decisions increased considerably more than AD1 decisions, approximately 27 percent vs. 8 percent. The proportion of trial to plea appeals remained about the same across the four quarters, as did the proportion of CAB to 18b cases. Decisions in all these categories increased substantially in the fourth quarter. Thus, neither the strike nor the partial moratorium on AD2 assignments appears to have affected the overall proportion of decided cases handled by CAB. The number of retained cases, however, actually dropped in the fourth quarter, after holding steady in the first three. This indicates that the general increase in decided cases in the last 12–15 months of the survey period resulted entirely from an increase in indigent appeals.

The Dependant Variable: Dispositions as a Function of Department, Conviction Type and Attorney Type

1. The great majority of appealed convictions were affirmed.

Overall, 83.9 percent of all New York City appeals were affirmed (Figure 5–4).[12] Another 4.74 percent were affirmed on counsel's *Anders* motion, and the remainder received favorable action (FA) of some kind: 4.08 percent resulted in new trials, 1.6 percent in the dismissal of the indictment, 2.6 percent in a modification of some kind, 2 percent in a sentence reduction, and .7 percent in a remand to the trial court. The overall FA rate declined 50 percent from the first quarter to the fourth, from 12.67 percent to 6.27 percent. The largest drop occurred between the third and fourth quarter.

2. AD2 took favorable action far more often than AD1.

AD2 took favorable action in 18.2 percent of defense appeals, AD1 in 6.05 percent (Figure 5–5). This difference is highly significant.[13] The higher rate in AD2 may reflect the court's greater willingness to find prejudicial error. It may also be that Kings, Queens, and Richmond judges and prosecutors are more error prone or recalcitrant than their New York and Bronx counterparts, or less adept at insulating their conduct from review.[14]

3. Trial appeals received favorable action far more often than plea appeals.

Defendants obtained favorable action in 19 percent of known trial appeals but in only 7.75 percent of known plea appeals.[15] These percentages are higher than the FA rates for *all* pleas and trials: since the conviction type was only known in AD2 when there was an opinion, the subset of cases

Figure 5–4
Overall NYC Criminal Appellate Dispositions

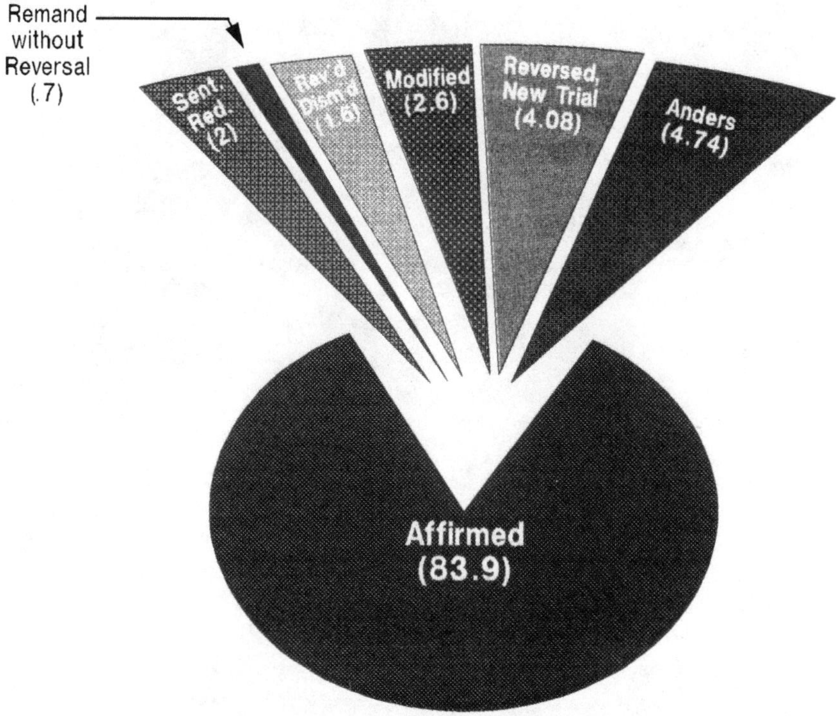

with known conviction types excluded the large number of pre–1984 AD2 cases affirmed without opinion. It is possible to estimate the FA rate for all trials and pleas by randomly assigning unknown AD2 cases to trial and plea categories.[16] Using the ratio of trials to pleas affirmed without opinion in AD1—27/23—this reassignment yielded an overall FA rate of 16.08 percent for trials and 6.94 percent for pleas.[17]

4. CAB obtained favorable action significantly more often than the 18b panels, but significantly less often than retained counsel.

CAB defendants got FA more often than 18b defendants: 11.82 percent vs. 7.91 percent, but less often than those represented by retained counsel: 17.88 percent. These differences are significant,[18] as are the differences between CAB and 18b analyzed separately.[19] In specific outcome categories,

Figure 5–5
Favorable Action by Department

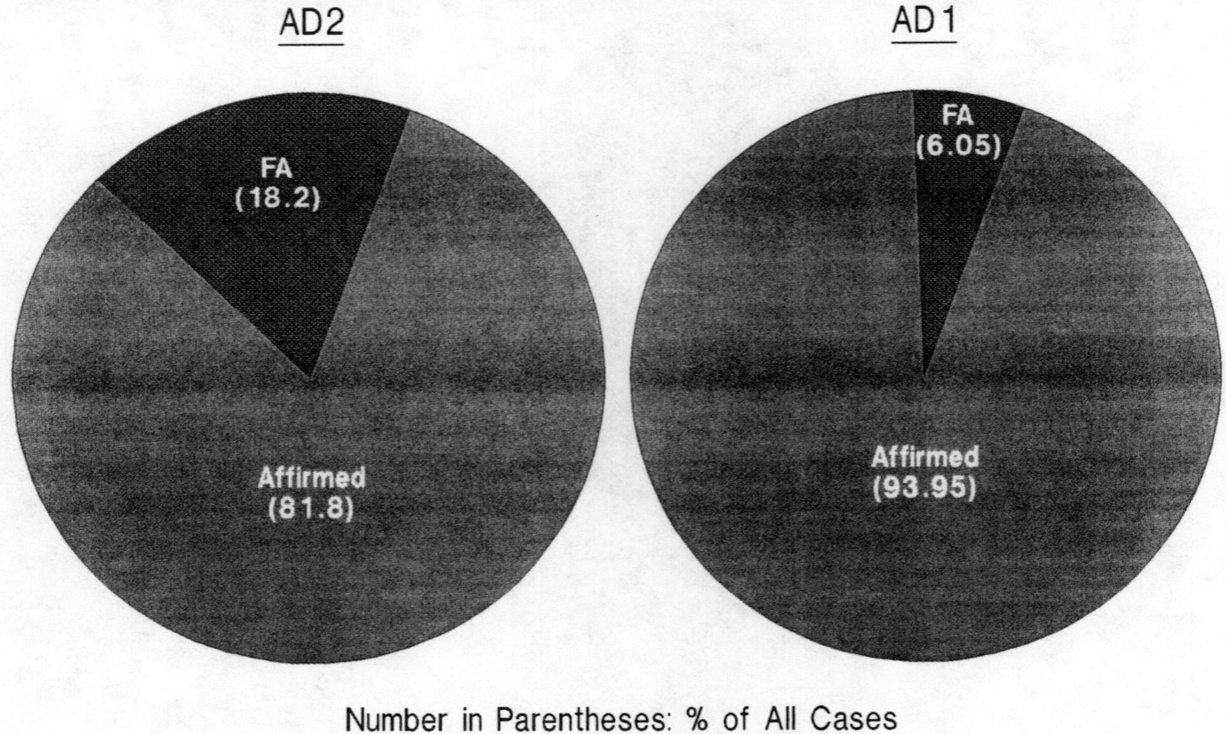

the difference between CAB and 18b was greatest for new trials, 4.37 percent vs. 1.61 percent, compared with 9.79 percent for retained cases; and for sentence reductions, 2.68 percent vs. 1 percent, with 2.1 percent for retained cases. For dismissals, however, the rates for CAB and 18b were the same, 1.41 percent, compared with 3.5 percent for retained cases. The 18b panel obtained *Anders* affirmances more than twice as often as CAB, 8 percent vs. 3.5 percent.[20]

The fact that the disparity between CAB and 18b is greatest for new trials and sentence reductions may reflect the fact that these forms of relief are more dependent on skilled advocacy than are dismissals and modifications. The determinations involved in dismissing the indictment or a particular count are usually fairly mechanical, albeit complex, for example, whether there was evidence on the value of the stolen property, or whether the prosecutor exceeded the 120-day limit. In contrast, the determinations involved in granting a new trial typically involve balancing and estimation, for example, whether the prejudicial impact of the evidence so far exceeded it probative value that the judge abused his discretion in admitting it, whether court's reasonable doubt instruction was burden-shifting, or whether the error was harmless. These are the "judgment calls" which a skilled marshalling of the facts might well influence. Sentence appeals may depend on the attorney's skill in making an apparently recalcitrant and dangerous offender appear sinned against as well as sinning.

On the other hand, CAB's greater success in obtaining new trials and sentence reductions may merely indicate that its clients are less heavily implicated or culpable than their 18b counterparts, making them more eligible for these forms of relief. We will address this possibility in Chapter 6, where we examine the effect of the assignment process on the client population of the two defenders.

The overall FA rate actually overstates the comparative performance of 18b, since over 50 percent of 18b cases but only 37.5 percent of CAB cases came from AD2, which has a substantially higher FA rate than AD1. The higher rate of FA enjoyed by CAB cannot be attributed to a higher proportion of trial appeals, since CAB appealed a slightly lower proportion of trials than 18b. The difference between the two defenders becomes even more striking when we examine trial appeals separately.

5. The outcome differences between the two defenders are substantially greater for trial than plea appeals.

CAB achieved a considerably higher FA rate for trials than 18b, 15.45 percent vs. 7.02 percent.[21] Once again, retained counsel did better than CAB, with 21 percent. This pattern of results differs in one interesting respect from that found for overall FA: for trial FA, the absolute and relative differences were greater between 18b and CAB than between CAB and retained counsel; the reverse was true for overall FA. As this contrast between overall and trial FA suggests, a quite different pattern of results is found for plea than trial appeals (excluding AD2 excessive motions): 18b does very slightly better than CAB, 5.08 percent vs. 4.84 percent, while retained counsel does far better than either, with 20.45 percent.

The CAB's edge over 18b in trial FA is slightly greater in AD1 than AD2, while the difference between CAB and retained counsel is about the same. In AD1, the rates are 5.90 percent for CAB, 1.83 percent for 18b and 9.86 percent for retained counsel; in AD2, the rates are 17.17 percent, 10.17 percent and 27.1 percent, respectively.

The large difference in plea FA between retained and assigned counsel is less likely than the smaller difference in trial FA to reflect disparate skill, since New York pleas are largely immune to appellate challenge, however skilled. When pleas are vacated, it is usually for obvious irregularities.[22] The difference also cannot be explained merely by self-selection, since indigent defendants are clearly more selective about appealing pleas than trials, and retained counsel have a higher proportion of plea to trial appeals than assigned counsel. Rather, the difference may result from the information available to the defendant in deciding whether to appeal his plea: paying defendants may get far better advice from their own trial attorney or an appellate "consultant" on whether a plea challenge stands any chance of success, and whether its success will do them any practical good. Moreover, a retained attorney may hesitate to recommend an appellate challenge to a plea she has negotiated, and the client's own involvement in the negotiations may make him more reluctant to challenge it.

There are also a number of possible explanations for the fact that CAB does better than 18b in trial but not plea appeals: there is less room for skilled advocacy to influence the outcome of a plea than a trial, CAB may devote less effort to pleas, CAB may lose some of its more meritorious pleas because of its policy of sending "risk letters" to plea defendants with viable issues (discussed in Chapter 6), or CAB may start with more meritorious trials but not more meritorious pleas.

For AD2 sentence motions, 18b appears to do significantly better than CAB or retained counsel, getting time-cuts in 9.52 percent of its cases (2/21) vs. 3.52 percent for CAB (3/85) and 0 percent for retained counsel (0/12). The number of sentence motions in the sample was small, however, and these differences are not statistically significant. This finding also appears inconsistent with the fact that CAB obtains "time-cuts" more often than 18b in full appeals.[23]

Several striking results emerge when pleas and trials are separately analyzed by department (Table 5–1): Not *one* of the 113 18b trial appeals in AD1 received FA, while the trial rates for CAB and retained counsel were 6.76 percent and 11.11 percent, respectively. In AD2, CAB's FA rate for trials was almost as high as that of retained counsel, 31.40 percent vs. 33.33 percent, respectively, both over twice the 18b rate of 13.91 percent. The

Table 5–1
Favorable Action by Department, Attorney, and Appeal Type

	AD1			AD2			
	CAB	18B	Retained	CAB	18B	Retained	Row
Trial Appeals (inc. 54% of unknown judgements)	6.76	0	11.11	31.40	13.91	33.33	13.17
Plea Appeals (inc. 46% of unknown judgements)	4.76	4.12	8.33	5.26	6.00	35.00	6.53
Sentence Motions	--	--	--	3.52	9.52	0	5.0
Column	5.90	1.83	9.86	17.70	10.17	27.54	

Number in Cell: % of Cases Receiving FA

differences in trial outcomes between the two defenders were highly significant in AD1 and marginally significant in AD2.[24] Finally, retained counsel got FA on pleas *seven times* more often in AD2 than CAB and 18b, 35 percent vs. 5.26 percent and 6 percent, respectively.

6. CAB obtained interest-of-justice reversals more often than 18b but less often than retained counsel; AD2 was responsible for almost all the decisions involving explicit interest-of-justice review.

Attorney influence is particularly likely to be felt in interest-of-justice reversals, where the court acts in an entirely discretionary manner to rectify an unpreserved error. There were only 45 cases in the sample in which the court reversed in whole or part in the interest of justice or affirmed on the merits of an unpreserved issue.[25] All but 3 of the 20 interest-of-justice reversals came from AD2, as did all 25 of the interest-of-justice affirmances—cases where the court reached the merits of an unpreserved issue, and either found no error or error of insufficient magnitude to warrant reversal. All but 4 of the reversals came from trials; 15 of the affirmances from pleas.

For interest-of-justice reversals, the differences reported earlier for general trial FA were amplified: IJ reversals comprised 1.6 percent of CAB dispositions, .4 percent of 18b dispositions, and 5 percent of retained cases. Although the proportion of reversals was quite small, these differences were highly significant, as were the differences between 18b and CAB analyzed separately. Interest-of-justice reversal rates for trials ran 3 percent, .9 percent and 5 percent, respectively. The high rate for retained counsel is surprising, since an attorney retained for both the trial and appeal is unlikely to spot his own omissions and call attention to them on appeal. It may be that most retained appeals are handled by new attorneys.

A strikingly different pattern emerged for interest-of-justice affirmances: 20 were 18b cases, 5 were CAB. I examined 13 of the 18b affirmances and discovered that all involved unpreserved challenges to the voluntariness or completeness of the plea, which the court found to lack merit. None raised what appeared to be, on cursory inspection, viable issues under New York law. Eight of these IJ affirmances came from a single attorney.

7. *Most convictions were affirmed without opinion, and the court "reached the merits" in less than a quarter of all cases.*

The courts affirmed without opinion in 73 percent of all cases and addressed one or more issues in only 21.5 percent. The difference between the departments was striking: AD1 reached the merits in less than 8 percent of its cases, AD2 in more than 40 percent. The difference between the departments is partly attributable to AD2's practice, starting in late 1984 or early 1985, of writing something in every case.

8. *CAB obtained written opinions less frequently than 18b or retained counsel, opinions addressing the merits as often, and the findings of harmless error more often.*

While CAB received FA significantly more often than 18b, it elicited judicial comment *less* often (Table 5–2). There was a memo, opinion, or dissent in 22.5 percent of CAB cases, 31.5 percent of 18b cases, and 35 percent of retained cases. This difference was due largely to a lower rate of CAB affirmance-with-opinion: 9 percent of all CAB dispositions vs. 19.5 percent for both 18b and retained counsel. There are a number of possible explanations: losing CAB briefs and issues may be less interesting to the court, either because of their content or their manner of presentation; 18b and private briefs may be addressed more often in losing cases because they can be dismissed more summarily; or opinions in losing cases may simply be a sop thrown more often to private than institutional counsel.

Only the last explanation seems compatible with the fact that the court "reached the merits" slightly *more* often for CAB than 18b, 21.5 percent vs. 18.5 percent, (although in 33.5 percent of retained cases): the court responded substantively to CAB at least as often as to 18b. Moreover, the court made explicit findings of harmless error—reaching the merits but declining to reverse—more often for CAB than 18b or retained counsel: 1.6

Table 5–2
Opinions, Dissents, and Other Issue-Resolution by Attorney

	Memo. Opinion or Dissent	Affir-mances with Opinion	Reached Merits	Error, Found Harmless	IJ Reversals	IJ Trial Reversals	IJ Affirm-ances
CAB	22.5	9	21.5	1.6	1.6	3.0	.7
18B	31.5	19.5	18.5	.8	.4	.9	3.0
Retained	35.	19.5	33.5	.7	5.0	5.0	0

Number in Cell: % of All Cases Receiving Indicated Treatment

percent, 0.8 percent and 0.7 percent, respectively. Although these figures are obviously quite small and the differences are not statistically significant, they suggest that CAB succeeds more often in getting the court to resolve issues that it could dispose of more economically by simply finding that "any errors were harmless."

Changes in the FA Rates of CAB and 18b in the Two Departments during the Survey Period

Some insight into the outcome differences between CAB and 18b is yielded by tracking the FA rates of the two defenders in both departments across the survey period (Table 5–3). An examination of attorney and department FA by quarter reveals two trends: (1) AD1 FA started low and declined gradually, going from 6.78 percent in the first quarter to 4.29 percent in the fourth, while AD2 FA started fairly high and declined substantially, going from 22.03 percent to 9.84 percent. The biggest drop in AD2 came between the third and fourth quarter, from 18.06 percent to 9.84 percent. (2) CAB's FA rate declined slightly, from 12.92 percent in the first quarter to 9.90 percent in the fourth, while 18b's rate declined substantially, from 12.86 percent to 5.07 percent.[26] Thus, while the FA rates for CAB and 18b were about the same in the first quarter of the survey, the 18b rate had dropped to just over half the CAB rate by the last quarter.[27]

Since individual CAB attorneys are assigned cases from the two depart-

Table 5–3
Case-Volume and Favorable Action by Department over Time

	AD1		AD2		Overall	
	# Cases	% FA	# Cases	% FA	# Cases	% FA
First Quarter F'80– W'82	174	6.32	118	22.03	292	12.67
Second Quarter W'82–Sp.'83	187	4.81	121	17.36	308	9.74
Third Quarter Sp.'83–Su'84	200	5.50	144	18.06	344	10.76
Fourth Quarter Su'84–F'85	216	3.24	183	9.84	399	6.27

Table 5–4
Attorney FA and Case-Share by Department over Time

	AD1						AD2					
	CAB		18B		Ret.		CAB		18B		Ret.	
	% FA	Cases	% FA	Cases	% FA	Cases	% FA	Cases	% FA	Cases	% FA	Cases
First Quarter	8.0	58.5	0	26.9	14.3	12.3	23.1	44.1	18.4	41.5	21.4	11.9
Second Quarter	6.9	55.8	1.6	33.7	5.9	9.4	10.2	40.5	18.4	40.5	30.4	19.0
Third Quarter	5.5	58.2	1.8	30.2	14.3	11.1	25.8	46.5	5.6	38.0	26.3	13.3
Fourth Quarter	3.9	65.3	3.6	27.6	0	6.5	11.8	41.5	3.5	47.0	26.7	8.2

ments on a more or less random basis, the explanation for the divergent trends in AD1 and AD2 must lie in the two departments or the two appellate panels (Table 5–4). It is possible that the 18b panel in AD1 was steadily improving in AD1 while its AD2 counterpart was steadily declining, but this is highly unlikely, given common problems of poor screening and low compensation during the survey period. A more plausible explanation involves AD2's response to the case backlog created by the Legal Aid strike, which ended in December 1982, toward the end of the second quarter. Beginning in the late spring of 1983, AD2 permitted CAB to decline all appeals from non-CDD cases: not only conflict cases, but homicides and other nonconflict cases assigned to 18b below, and all appeals from retained cases. This "moratorium" was lifted in early 1985.

It might be suspected that the sharp drop in 18b FA in AD2 resulted from the transfer of these declined cases, which swamped the panel with large numbers of low-merit 18b trial-level appeals[28] while permitting CAB to maintain its performance with fewer and better cases. The problem with this explanation lies in the timing of the moratorium: allowing 14 months between assignment and decision,[29] cases reassigned by the moratorium would not have been decided until the summer of 1984 at the earliest, at the beginning of the last quarter.[30] This estimate is borne out by the ratio of 18b to CAB decisions in AD2, which held at 1/1 for the first two quarters, dropped to 9/11 in the third, and only rose in the fourth, to 43/38. The drop in 18b FA in AD2 occurred between the second and third quarters, however, effectively ruling out the moratorium as an explanation.

Two other explanations focus on changes in AD2, since that department was responsible for almost all the overall decline in FA during the survey period. It may be that AD2 entered a more conservative phase in the final quarter of the survey period, less inclined to grant FA. This change may have placed greater demands on the attorneys before it, which CAB was able to meet while 18b was not. It is also possible that as the number of active 18b members in AD2 declined, a small group of marginal practitioners were providing inadequate representation for an increasing share of the caseload. The attrition rate for qualified practitioners may simply have been lower in AD1. Both possibilities are consistent with the disposition data, but they remain quite speculative.

Prosecution Appeals

1. Prosecution appeals won almost as often as defense appeals lost, but less frequently against retained than assigned counsel.

The prosecution won on appeal about 80 percent of the time in both departments (Table 5–5). Of the 56 People's appeals with known outcomes, CAB won 4 and lost 20, 18b won 1 and lost 4, and retained counsel won

Table 5–5
Prosecution Appeals

	Affirmed	Reversed
CAB	16.7% (4)	83.3% (20)
18B	20% (1)	80% (4)
Retained	27.8% (5)	72% (13)
TOTAL	20.8% (10)	79.2% (38)

5 and lost 13. While the difference in the success rate of government and defense appeals is certainly striking, it does not necessarily reflect a pro-prosecution bias in the Appellate Division. A study of state supreme court reversals over the past hundred years concluded that government agencies are among the most selective appellate litigants, and owe their high success rate to their accuracy in gauging the appellate prospects of their cases.[31]

2. Retained counsel had a much higher share of prosecution than defense appeals, the 18b panels a much lower share.

The share of prosecution appeals handled by retained counsel was almost three times their share of defense appeals. One reason may be that retained trial counsel obtained questionable breaks for their clients more often than assigned counsel. In contrast, the share of prosecution appeals handled by the 18b panels was a third their share of defense appeals. One reason may be that the 18b trial attorneys whose cases would go to the 18b appellate panel get questionable breaks for their clients considerably less often than either retained or CDD attorneys; another reason may be that CDD clients rarely complain about attorneys who have won them questionable relief, so that one major source of conflict in CAB representation will rarely arise in prosecution appeals.

Although the number of cases is small and the difference in success rates is not statistically significant, retained counsel certainly seem to do better than assigned. *This* difference cannot be attributed to self-selection—it is the District Attorney who chooses which cases to appeal—and may reflect the superior quality of retained counsel. There are, however, other plausible explanations: It may be that appellate judges are more sympathetic to paying, usually middle-class clients, a bias that would also help to explain the superior performance of retained counsel in defense appeals. Arguments from social class are double-edged, though: if appellate courts are more likely to be sympathetic to paying clients, trial courts may not only give them more frequent breaks, but more questionable ones.

A final alternative would attribute the edge enjoyed by retained appellate counsel to the superior performance of retained trial counsel: to the creation of a better record, better researched motions, and more convincing arguments. This would also help to account for the performance of retained counsel on defense appeals. If the quality of trial counsel had a large effect on appellate outcomes, it might also help to account for the differences between CAB and 18b, a possibility explored in Chapter 6.

NEW YORK'S CRIMINAL APPELLATE DISPOSITIONS IN NATIONAL PERSPECTIVE

Since this study was conducted, Chapper and Hanson completed a survey of criminal appellate dispositions during the same time period in five jurisdictions: four state intermediate appellate courts and one state supreme court.[32] The overall picture was much the same as in New York City: affirmance was the norm for defense appeals, reversal the norms for prosecution appeals. The affirmance rates for defense appeals in the four intermediate appellate courts surveyed ranged from 79 percent to 82 percent; the reversal rates for prosecution appeals ranged from 40 percent to 73 percent.[33] Although these rates are high, the contrast is less extreme than in New York, where 80 percent of prosecution appeals were reversed and 84 percent of defense appeals were affirmed—88.6 percent if *Anders* affirmances are counted.

In several other respects, the pattern of dispositions in the five-court survey differed sharply from the pattern in New York. Chapper and Hanson found only 247 plea appeals among the 1,747 cases they sampled, roughly 14 percent of the total. This is less than a third the share in New York, where an estimated 43 percent of all criminal appeals came from pleas. Chapper and Hanson's states presumably had about the same proportion of plea convictions as New York, so the difference is likely to have resulted from legislative restrictions on plea appeals or greater self-selection by plea defendants.

There was a corresponding difference in the success rate for plea appeals: the overall rate in Chapper and Hanson's five courts was 16.6 percent, almost three times as high as New York City's rate of 6.5 percent and almost as high as the 21 percent success rate for *trial* appeals in the five courts.[34] In contrast, the success rate for New York City trial appeals was 13.2 percent, almost two-thirds as high as in Chapper and Hanson's courts. The differential success rates for pleas thus appears to account for most, though not all, of the difference in the overall affirmance rates.

Finally, Chapper and Hanson found "virtually no difference in outcome by counsel type: all are within one-half percentage point of the five-court average."[35] They did find that retained counsel and public defenders were slightly but significantly more likely to "win big" than appointed counsel, an overall pattern similar to New York's."[36] In New York, however, this pattern was found in *trial* but not plea appeals, while in Chapper and Hanson's courts, it was found in *nontrial* but not trial appeals.[37] The absence of strong and readily interpretable attorney effects in Chapper and Hanson's survey is not surprising, since the composition of the three attorney groups and the distribution of cases among them varied widely across the states surveyed.[38]

CONCLUSION

The overall pattern of criminal appellate dispositions in New York City is similar to that found in other jurisdictions: the vast majority of convictions are affirmed. Despite the high overall affirmance rate, there are consistent, statistically significant differences in the results obtained by the two defenders. These differences are striking just because the overall rate of favorable action is so low.

CAB obtains better outcomes than 18b in almost every area where its superior advocacy might be expected to make a difference—overall, in trials, in new-trial reversals, in sentence reductions, in IJ reversals and in findings of harmless error. The differences in overall outcomes, in trials, and in IJ reversals are statistically significant in each department separately and in the two taken together; the differences in the other two categories are not significant, but the pattern of outcomes is so similar as to make a chance explanation highly improbable. The 18b panel surpassed CAB in only three areas: sentence reductions in AD2, opinions, and findings of "no error" on unpreserved issues. The defenders did about the same on all other measures of success and impact.

The fact that CAB did better than 18b in trials but not in pleas is certainly consistent with a qualitative explanation for overall outcome differences—superior advocacy would be *expected* to make more of a difference in trial appeals. CAB also did better than 18b in obtaining new trial and "time-cuts," consistent with our expectation that superior advocacy would make more of a difference in obtaining those forms of relief than outright dismissals. CAB superiority in interest-of-justice reversals further suggests that CAB's overall superiority does not rest on better preserved records, although it does not rule out weaker evidence or less culpable defendants as confounding factors.

Additional support for a qualitative evaluation of outcome differences comes from a comparison of CAB with retained cases. While retained counsel does considerably better than CAB overall, the gap is narrower for trials; in AD2, CAB's trial FA is almost as high as retained counsel's. Much of the difference between retained counsel and CAB is clearly due to self-selection by paying clients. The impact of self-selection is revealed in the findings for plea appeals, where paying clients appeal comparatively less often than indigent clients and win comparatively more often. While paying clients may be particularly selective in appealing pleas, they are also likely to be more selective than indigent clients in appealing trials. Although the performance of retained counsel in prosecution appeals suggests that quality as well as selectivity contributes to their success, the fact that CAB trial FA in AD2 almost matches that of retained counsel may suggest that CAB sometimes makes up in quality what it lacks in client selectivity.[39]

Nevertheless, there is an alternative explanation for CAB's performance: In most of the areas where CAB does better than 18b, CAB clients may be more eligible for relief than their 18b counterparts. The assignment process may permit CAB to select cases with stronger issues, or it may inadvertently assign CAB to less culpable or heavily implicated defendants. In either case, the resulting "merit bias" would give CAB an advantage in trial appeals and in forms of relief requiring a finding of harmful error. While such merit bias could not account for all of CAB's comparative successes or for the specific pattern of outcome differences between the two defenders, it must be carefully assessed in gauging the impact of attorney skill on appellate outcomes. We turn to this assessment in Chapter 6.

NOTES

1. The Office of Court Administration research director, Richard Ross, refused to permit his programmers to sort OCA's appellate disposition statistics into criminal and civil cases, although he had been informed by his programmers that the "sort" procedure I requested would have been simple and quick to execute. Mr. Ross did express a willingness to allow a New York University programmer to sort the data, but we decided that the expense of employing a programmer unfamiliar with the OCA system for such a limited purpose was too great, and chose to rely exclusively on our own disposition survey.

2. The Appellate Division file cards, while fairly complete, provide insufficient information on the dispositions themselves. Moreover, drawing the sample from these card files would have presented enormous practical difficulties.

3. There is only a partial overlap between these categories. AD2 only permits sentence motions from pleas. On the other hand, a substantial number of judgment appeals may also arise from pleas. While a plea-defendant may face the theoretical risk of a higher sentence in challenging his conviction, the practical risk may be negligible, and New York affords him a wider range of challenges than most jurisdictions. The AD2 "judgment" appeals were assigned to trial and plea categories for purposes of statistical analysis.

4. For most AD1 cases, the offense type was also coded.

5. Under the Bar Association plan, an attorney is permitted to belong to only one panel, but exceptions are made because of the chronic shortage of attorneys in both departments.

6. Trial representation is also an important variable, for two reasons: first, better trial attorneys may leave better records, with more preserved errors and more effective challenges to the state's case; second, better and more selective trial attorneys may not only win more often, but lose more closely, leaving more "near misses" to appeal. Unfortunately, the Appellate Division records contained no information on trial-level representation. CAB's own records do contain this information, which I will discuss in Chapter 6 as part of my analysis of the CAB defendant file.

7. See Chapter 1.

8. A reversal and new trial may be granted a plea or trial appeal. "New trial" does not imply that there was or will be a trial, merely that the conviction is thrown out but the indictment preserved.

9. The outcome coding also indicated if the court's determination was informative. A conclusory holding that "appellant's contentions are without merit" does not even identify those contentions, let alone explain why they were mistaken. There is little more information conveyed in the lengthier conclusion that "under the circumstances found by the trial court, the police were justified in frisking appellant." Without the record or briefs to reveal those circumstances, the decision has no precedential value.

10. An additional 2.5 percent were from AD1, but could not be classified by county.

11. The sample included a number of appeals from rejected 440.10 motions (motions to set aside the verdict) that had not been consolidated with a direct appeal from the judgment, but these discretionary appeals were less than 1 percent of all decided cases.

12. Unless otherwise indicated, this section uses the broader definition of favorable action (FA) discussed above, which includes all modifications of judgment favorable to the defendant, regardless of practical consequences, from dismissal of the indictment to dismissal of a lesser included count.

13. $p = .000$. All the significance tests reported in this chapter use the ANOVA procedure, Statistical Analysis Systems, Cary, N.C.

14. Within the two departments, there are some interesting outcome differences by county. While Manhattan and Bronx appeals have the same low rate of new trials (about 1.25 percent), Bronx indictments are dismissed more than twice as often as Manhattan indictments (1.88 percent versus .064 percent), although both the numbers and the percentages are very small. The differences are more striking in AD2, with 6.58 percent of Brooklyn appeals getting new trials, 9.55 percent of Queens appeals, and 14.29 percent of Staten Island appeals, more than twice Brooklyn's percentage. Also 19.27 percent of Brooklyn *trial* appeals result in new trials, 26.79 percent of Queens trial appeals, and 44.44 percent of Staten Island trial appeals, again more than twice Brooklyn's percentage. (This last figure must be treated with caution, however, since it is based on only nine Staten Island trial appeals.)

15. $p = .000$. There are appreciably more technical, "paper" wins in trials than in pleas, 2.91 percent versus .41 percent. I suspect that this is simply because such

wins usually involve the correction of multiple count convictions, and it is quite likely that a far higher portion of trial than plea convictions have multiple counts.

16. This can be done using the RANUNI procedure, Statistical Analysis Systems, which randomly assigns cases having one value of a variable to other values by any ratio specified.

17. I obtained virtually the same results when I reassigned cases by the ratio that would yield the same proportion of trials to pleas in AD2 as in AD1—3:2.

18. $p = .033$.

19. $p = .033$. The outcome differences for attorney type are also found with the narrower definition of FA, which excludes such purely technical victories as the dismissal of a lesser included count. With this narrower definition, the FA rates were 10.07 percent for CAB, 6.15 percent for 18b, and 18.57 percent for retained counsel. CAB and 18b won strictly paper victories in 1.75 percent of all case, retained counsel in .71 percent.

20. The survey did not included the denial of *Anders* motions, since such denials would preserve the appeal for full briefing and would not be coded as final dispositions.

21. The results reported in the remainder of this chapter use the narrow definition of FA unless otherwise indicated. The results are based on the random assignment of unknown "judgment" cases in AD2 to trial and plea categories, using a 27/23 ratio. Since almost all the reassigned cases are affirmances, the effect of the reassignment is to lower the artificially high FA rates for known trials and pleas in AD2. Since 18b had almost twice as many of these unknown cases as CAB, the higher the percentage of such cases shifting to the trial category, the worse 18b's comparative success rate on trial appeals. To present the findings in the light most favorable to 18b, I picked the lower of the two plausible ratios, 27/23.

22. See Chapter 1.

23. It may also be that 18b attorneys are more likely than CAB attorneys to file a sentence motion rather than a full plea appeal when the sentence issue is strong and other issues weak, but this is sheer speculation.

24. $p = .066$.

25. The initial coding found only 13 cases in which the court had made an explicit finding of unpreserved error, and several of these were affirmances. While CAB and retained counsel obtained such findings in a higher proportion of cases than 18b, the differences were not significant. To obtain a fuller measure of interest-of-justice review, I coded all reversals and modifications in the sample (except sentence reductions) in which the court stated that it was acting in the interest of justice. This recoding revealed 13 cases in which the court reversed or modified a conviction "in the interest of justice" without explicitly finding an unpreserved error. These were apparently cases in which the error was only partially or inadequately preserved or the court was otherwise acting in a purely discretionary manner. These cases were combined with those in which the court had explicitly made a finding of unpreserved error and reversed or modified; all were counted as interest-of-justice reversals.

26. The number of retained cases in each quarter was so small, particularly by department, that even a descriptive analysis of its trends would not have been meaningful. In AD1, for example, retained counsel had 21, 17, 21, and 13 cases in the four strata; its corresponding FA rate was 14.29 percent, 5.88 percent, 14.29 percent, and 0 percent.

27. In AD2, the FA rate for CAB fluctuated considerably by quarter, going from 23.08 percent to 10.20 percent to 25.76 percent to 11.84 percent, while 18b experienced a sudden drop between the second and third quarter (as did AD2), going from 18.37 percent to 18.37 percent to 5.56 percent to 3.49 percent. In contrast, CAB and 18b appear to have *converged* in AD1, with CAB FA steadily descending, from 8 percent to 6.93 percent to 5.45 percent to 3.85 percent, while 18b FA steadily ascended from 0 percent to 1.64 percent to 1.75 percent to 3.64 percent, matching CAB FA in the last quarter.

28. See Chapter 6 for a discussion of why 18b trial appeals may have low average merit.

29. This is the average time between assignment and brief-filing reported by the Association of the Bar, City of New York, Committee on Criminal Advocacy, in *The Crisis in Indigent Appeals in the First and Second Departments* (1985): 23–29.

30. *New York Supplement* 479, the first volume in the fourth quarter, reports cases from June through September 1984.

31. Note "Courting Reversal: The Supervisory Role of the State Supreme Courts," *Yale Law Journal* 87 (1978): 1191, 1205–07.

32. Chapper and Hanson, *Understanding Criminal Reversals*, (Williamsburg, Va.: National Center for State Courts, 1989). The courts surveyed were the California Court of Appeal, Third District (Sacramento); the Colorado Court of Appeals; the Appellate Court of Illinois, Fourth District (Springfield); the Maryland Court of Special Appeals; and the Rhode Island Supreme Court. The first four are intermediate appellate courts in two-tier appellate systems; the last the only general appellate court in a one-tier system. Chapper and Hanson analyzed *all* criminal appeals decided on the merits within a set time frame in each jurisdiction: 1983 in Sacramento and Springfield, 1985 in Colorado and Maryland, and 1983–1984 in Rhode Island.

33. The one state supreme court in the survey had far more balanced dispositions: the affirmance rate for defense appeals was 71 percent; the reversal rate for prosecution appeals was 25 percent.

34. The selectivity exercised by plea defendants in Chapper and Hanson's courts is suggested by the low frequency and frequent success with which they challenged the voluntariness or procedural validity of their pleas: that issue was raised only 28 times, and was successful almost 15 percent of the time it was raised. Another indication of the relationship between selectivity and success in plea appeals is the apparently strong positive correlation, within the five jurisdictions studied by Hanson and Chapper, between the ratio of nontrial to trial appeals and success rate of nontrial appeals. It should be noted, however, that pleas constituted only about 60 percent of nontrial proceedings, with parole revocations the second largest category.

35. Chapper and Hanson, *Understanding Criminal Reversals*, 21.

36. Chapper and Hanson divide appellate victories into "big wins"—new trials and dismissals—and "little wins"—sentences reductions, remands without reversal, and charge modifications, including such paper victories as the dismissal of a lesser concurrent count. The two categories together correspond to the broad definition of favorable action used in this chapter.

37. Letter to author from J. Chapper, August 15, 1989. In Chapper and Hanson's trial appeals, retained counsel "win big" slightly but insignificantly more often than public defenders and appointed counsel, while appointed counsel "win little" more

than the other two attorney groups. Appointed counsel, however, "win little" more often than retained counsel or public defenders in nontrial appeals. In New York nontrial appeals, retained counsel do far better than either indigent defender.

38. The size of Chapper and Hanson's sample was not large enough to permit a state-by-state analysis of attorney effects.

39. The fact that the gap is not as narrow in AD1 trial appeals might reflect the fact that the retained appellate counsel is significantly better in AD1 than AD2.

6

Selection Bias and the Assignment Process: An Alternative Explanation for Outcome Differences Between the Defenders

INTRODUCTION

This chapter examines whether the superior performance of CAB on trial appeals can be attributed in whole or part to a difference in the merit of the trials assigned to the two defenders. The results of the brief-evaluation offered only one possible explanation of CAB's superior performance, and not necessarily a complete one. While the observed outcomes differences between CAB and 18b are consistent with the rated differences in quality, the latter are not dramatic, and a causal link between quality and outcome has not been directly established. Because of this uncertainty, it is important to consider alternative explanations for CAB's superior performance. One obvious possibility is that CAB starts with more winnable, or "meritorious," cases.

The possibility of such "merit bias" would not arise if cases were assigned to the two defenders on a random basis. We know from Chapter 3, however, that they are not: all cases are supposed to be accepted by CAB unless they present a conflict of interest, and CAB makes the initial, and usually the final, determination of whether a conflict exists. There are two ways in which this assignment process might favor CAB: CAB could exploit its de facto control of the process to obtain better cases, by bending or disregarding the conflict rules, or the operation of the conflict rules could itself leave CAB with better cases. I refer to these, respectively, as deliberate and inadvertent bias.

In the sections that follow, I will describe how I evaluated these alternative hypotheses. I examined the possibility of deliberate merit bias through a spot audit of CAB "taking" practices for two overlapping six-month periods in 1986 and 1987. The audit found no trace of the irregularities that would suggest deliberate manipulation of the assignment process. At the same time, it revealed that some of the conflict determinations made by CAB are highly discretionary, permitting conscious or unconscious partiality in a small but possibly significant number of cases.

The examination of inadvertent bias was more complicated. Based on the spot audit and CAB's own records, I estimated the proportion of different types of conflict claimed by CAB, and then examined whether the more prevalent types of conflict were likely to be found in weaker cases. While the analysis of its internal records confirmed the impression that CAB does not engage in deliberate merit selection, it also supported the possibility that the operation of the conflict rules may rid CAB of some of its less winnable trial appeals.

Specifically, I found (1) that CAB itself did better on CDD than 18b trials, and (2) that a high proportion of the "CDD-relieved" defendants assigned to 18b on appeal were repeat offenders who went to trial and received heavy sentences. These findings, together with McConville and Mirsky's observations of CDD selection practices,[1] lead me to conclude that merit bias cannot be ruled out as one source of the outcome differences between CAB and 18b trial appeals. While the possibility of such bias exists, however, it cannot fully explain the magnitude and pattern of the observed outcome differences. Superior advocacy by CAB is almost certainly responsible for some, if not all, of these differences.

The Official CAB Conflict Rules

The investigation of merit bias must begin with a review of CAB's official conflict rules. These are the rules which CAB would have to bend or disregard to engage in deliberate merit selection, and whose impartial application may leave CAB with better cases. According to its stated policy, CAB will ordinarily seek to be relieved of cases in which:

1. A codefendant was represented by CDD below or by LAS in some other proceeding.
2. A codefendant has already been assigned to CAB.
3. CDD represented the defendant beyond arraignment and was relieved by the trial court.
4. The defendant has publicly expressed dissatisfaction with his CDD representation, e.g., in a motion to be relieved.
5. The CDD trial file or client correspondence reveal strong, persistent dissatisfaction with CDD.
6. A nonfrivolous argument could be made that the defendant received ineffective representation by CDD.

7. The defendant has already challenged or could challenge the validity of a predicate conviction with CDD counsel.
8. The client has expressed strong dissatisfaction with CAB.
9. LAS represented a prosecution witness.[2]

On their face, these rules appear clear, mechanical, and neutral with respect to case merit. The possibility of deliberate merit selection depends on the extent to which they can be manipulated by CAB to obtain more winnable trial appeals; the possibility of inadvertent merit bias depends on the extent to which the conflicts defined by these rules are associated with less winnable trial appeals.

The distinction between deliberate and inadvertent merit selection is important for methodological purposes, since it determines the kind of inquiry we make—into the accuracy of CAB conflicts claims or into the merit of conflict cases. At the same time, the distinction is somewhat misleading. The bias which results from CAB's impartial application of the conflict rules may well perpetuate deliberate merit selection by CDD, and calling the end result "inadvertent" ignores CAB's place in the larger system of case-processing.

Thus, if CDD deliberately chooses the *less* culpable or heavily implicated defendant, as McConville and Mirsky found in New York County, the impartial application of the conflict rules will pass that defendant on to CAB, and will preclude CAB representation of his *more* culpable or heavily implicated codefendant.[3] Similarly, if CDD attorneys are often relieved in "dead bang" cases because of their low appearance rate or their client's refusal to accept a "reasonable" plea offer, as McConville and Mirsky suggest, a mechanical application of the conflict rules may assign the defendant to the 18b appellate panel.[4] In both cases, the application of facially neutral rules serves to limit LAS representation to more "deserving" defendants. The transmission of CDD bias to CAB through these rules could be regarded as an integral part of an LAS policy of selectivity. In isolating deliberate and inadvertent CAB bias for research purposes, it is important not to lose sight of this broader institutional perspective.[5]

Deliberate Merit Selection

CAB has two strong motives for holding on to the most winnable indigent trial appeals: to do good and to look good. In a system of appellate review with virtually no "sure winners," the better advocate could maximize its effectiveness by taking the strongest cases: while there are almost no appeals strong enough to "win themselves," even the best advocate can do nothing for the vast majority of "sure losers." In maximizing its effectiveness, CAB would also be enhancing its appearance—selecting stronger cases would give CAB a higher "batting average." Indeed, even a handful of "wins" could make an appreciable difference in its comparative success rate.

While it would clearly be tempting for CAB to pick the better trial appeals, it might not be feasible for it to do so. In order to implement a merit selection policy, CAB would have to (1) identify strong cases which its conflicts rules, properly applied, would bar it from taking, or identify weak cases which its conflict rules, properly applied, would require it to take; and (2) bend the conflict rules so as to keep the former and/or shed the latter. It seems very unlikely that CAB could engage in either the necessary case-screening or rule manipulation on a systematic basis.

While CAB could improve its overall performance simply by taking more trial appeals and fewer plea appeals, its superior performance *within* the trial category could only be explained by a much closer screening process. In order to gauge the merit of a trial appeal, CAB would need to review the transcript, interview trial counsel, or rely on background characteristics of the case. Even the crudest case evaluation would require information that was not immediately available at the time of assignment. Delaying that evaluation would involve significant costs. The longer it took to assess the merit of a trial appeal, the harder it would be to prevail on a motion to be relieved.

Moreover, the attempt to reject cases without conflicts or retain cases with conflicts could have potentially embarrassing consequences for CAB. A false claim of conflict would involve a fraud on the court and a violation of the LAS contract with the city, while the failure to be relieved in a conflict case might involve a breach of the Code of Professional Responsibility. Since many conflicts, such as those involving the representation of codefendants, will be easy to confirm or disconfirm, CAB would be exposing itself to the constant possibility of censure by pursuing a merit selection policy for all trial appeals.

This general skepticism about the possibility of merit selection needs to be qualified, however, since there are some trial appeals whose merit can be readily assessed by CAB and some conflict rules that CAB has wide latitude in applying. Merit assessment is facilitated in CDD cases by the availability of a trial file containing a form on which the CDD attorney notes any possible issues for appeal and any possible sources of conflict. By ordering the trial file, the CAB Managing Attorney's office can obtain a preliminary appraisal of the merits (though rarely within the two-week deadline for responding to the poor person list). If it wished to be relieved, it would usually be able to contrive a conflict using information from the trial file.

There are two ways in which the application of the conflict rules gives CAB considerable discretion. First, CAB can decide when privately expressed dissatisfaction is sufficiently sharp and persistent to call for reassignment. On the one hand, a dissatisfied client with a meritorious case can often be mollified. Unless the defendant actually demands substitute counsel or claims ineffectiveness, CAB can proceed in the face of unreconciled differences. On the other hand, a client with an obviously nonmeritorious case can be dropped at the slightest sign of dissatisfaction. Additionally, CAB has considerable discretion in deciding whether client complaints about CDD have any legal substance. While CAB's official policy is to get relieved whenever a nonfrivolous ineffectiveness claim could be made against CDD, "frivolity" and "ineffectiveness" are vague enough concepts to leave a great deal of room for merit-based partiality.

The second area of discretion which CAB enjoys in applying the conflict rules is in soliciting client waiver. Disciplinary Rule 5–105(c) of the Code of Professional Responsibility allows an attorney to seek waiver (at least in codefendant cases) when she determines that she can "adequately represent" the conflicting interests. Clearly, this standard allows CAB to seek waiver selectively, and would provide a convenient screen for merit-based selection. The flexibility that CAB enjoys in construing the conflict rules is illustrated by the fact that its policies on client dissatisfaction and waiver shifted considerably between 1985 and 1987 without any formal change in its official rules.[6]

In practice, CAB discretion is still broader, because the courts are usually willing to grant its unopposed relief motions without independent inquiry. While this reflex approval might end abruptly if CAB were found to be making highly exaggerated conflict claims, the risk of exposure has been fairly low in a system where the courts never had, until the 18b backlog crisis, a strong motive to scrutinize those claims. As noted earlier, the risk of concealing conflicts would be somewhat greater. Frequent CAB representation of unconsenting codefendants would be obvious, while clients with unappeased grievances against CDD or CAB might well bring them to the court's attention in a motion for substitute counsel, a *pro se* brief, or a collateral attack following affirmance.

In conclusion, it would be difficult and risky for CAB to engage in systematic merit selection for trial appeals. While such merit selection is unlikely, however, it cannot be dismissed without looking at the accuracy of the conflict claims actually made by CAB. An examination of those claims will also permit a partial assessment of CAB relief practice in the one area where merit selection seems feasible—in appeals from CDD trials with dissatisfied clients.

THE SPOT AUDIT

To assess the factual accuracy of CAB conflicts claims, I examined (1) all CAB "check-off" letters for the AD1 poor person calendar between April and November 1986 and (2) all CAB relief motions to AD1 between September 1986 and February 1987.[7] The check-off letters listed the defendants who present conflicts of interest but not the specific conflict; the relief motions listed the defendants who fall into specific conflict categories, for example, "CDD represented codefendant below."[8]

In checking these claims, I was looking for the kind of irregularities that would suggest a deliberate attempt to hold on to better cases or get rid of worse ones. If all or almost all the conflict claims were accurate, the question would not even arise. If there were a significant number of inaccuracies, it would be necessary to examine the cases in which they occurred. By its very nature, an audit of this sort could only provide a check on "false positives"—mistaken or unconfirmable claims of conflict. It could not rule out the possibility of "false negatives"—meritorious cases with actual conflict improperly retained by CAB. My analysis of the CAB defendant file, described later in the chapter, provided a partial check on such cases.

I analyzed all relief motions from AD1, but attempted to verify the accuracy of conflicts claims only in New York County, where information necessary to verify those claims was readily available. While the frequency with which different kinds of conflict are claimed by CAB may vary somewhat by department or county, the accuracy of those claims should not.[9] I used the Supreme Court's computerized records to verify as many claims as I could, examined the trial files for those I could not, and presented those claims still unconfirmed or apparently disconfirmed to the CAB Managing Attorney's office for explanation.

It was simpler to check the accuracy of relief motions than check-offs, since the former but not the latter specified a particular type of conflict.[10] For check-offs, it was necessary to consider all possible grounds for relief that CAB might have discovered in the two-week period it had to respond to the poor person list, including, but not limited to, the sources of conflicts usually revealed in the court file: CDD codefendants and CDD relief after arraignment. Because other types of conflict might sometimes be spotted at this early stage, such as CAB representation of a codefendant, it was impossible to disconfirm a check-off conclusively on the basis of the court file alone.

Check-offs

Of the 67 New York County check-offs examined, the Supreme Court's records revealed a valid ground for relief under CAB policy in all but 16. In 5 of these 16 cases, I could not locate the court file so I did not pursue the matter further. I submitted the remaining 11 to the CAB Managing Attorney's office. In 9 of these, CAB's computerized record revealed a basis for relief clearly within the stated conflicts rules. Typically, the records revealed a CDD codefendant on the same or a consolidated indictment. In one or two of these cases, I had not turned up the codefendant's name in the court files; in the others, I had not been able to determine his representation.

Only two of the check-off cases were questionable. In one, a CDD lawyer had, at the judge's request, stood in for the defendant's indisposed private attorney at sentencing. In the other, the CAB paralegal appeared to have marked down the wrong codefendant as the CDD client. This clerical error is unlikely to have been deliberate: a letter in the court file from one of the jurors praised the CDD lawyer and condemned 18b counsel, hardly a reason for CAB to reject the CDD case.

Although all the claims of CDD trial relief were confirmed, the files rarely revealed any actual conflict between the defendant and his CDD attorney.[11] Typically, the court file merely indicated the dates on which CDD counsel was assigned and relieved. CAB paralegals explained that in the absence of any specific indication of conflict, they usually reject cases where CDD was relieved more than two weeks after arraignment. The longer CDD holds onto a case, the less likely it is to be relieved in the absence of conflict, and the two-week cutoff reflects a rough estimate of the point at which CDD relief is likely to have resulted from a conflict.

Motions

Of the 52 motions in letter form, I verified 40 through court records.[12] Of the remaining 12, eight involved claims that CAB had been previously assigned to a codefendant, a claim particularly difficult to check through court files. CAB records showed that in three of these cases, the other codefendant has in fact been assigned first, that in three, the codefendant was assigned the same day but received an earlier file number (that is, was "processed" sooner) and in one case, that the codefendant was assigned later but had his record available at an earlier date.[13] The Managing Attorney provided convincing verification for the four other relief claims.

A final group of 26 claims, arising from individual motions filed by the CAB Managing Attorney between August and December of 1986, involved client dissatisfaction with CDD representation.[14] I made no attempt to assess the accuracy of these motions, since it seemed highly unlikely that CAB would fabricate these often lengthy and vehement complaints. I did examine the types of complaints reported, to see if they were serious enough to warrant relief.

All these motions appeared to involve serious if not intractable dissatisfaction, and in at least half, the defendant had already made his complaints public. Five of the 26 motions I examined involved claims by the defendant that he had been coerced or misled into a plea by CDD counsel; eight involved claims that the CDD attorney had betrayed, abandoned, or seriously neglected the defendant; six involved sharp tactical or personal conflicts between the defendant and his CDD attorney; and five involved claims of deficient investigation or general ineffectiveness.[15] The remaining two involved challenges to a predicate plea negotiated by CDD counsel. In at least 12 of the 26 cases, the defendant had apparently made his dissatisfaction a matter of public record, in a trial or appellate court motion for reassignment, or in a transcribed colloquy or outburst.

These complaints may justify CAB's efforts to be relieved, but they do not paint a very attractive picture of CDD trial representation. Admittedly, they must be taken with a grain of salt: motions for substitute counsel are often used as a delaying tactic, and convicted defendants are notorious Monday-morning quarterbacks. Nevertheless, many of the complaints conform too closely to the familiar realities of trial practice to disregard completely. Nor can we attribute these complaints to a handful of malcontented clients or neglectful attorneys—my analysis of the CAB defendant file, discussed later in the chapter, reveals that CAB was relieved of more than a *third* of all CDD trials in 1984–1985. Although many of the underlying complaints may have been minor, and many more baseless, CDD appears to have been alienating a large share of its clients.[16]

A final source for reassignments are the relief motions filed by individual CAB attorneys. The Managing Attorney keeps no record of these cases, but they are screened by a committee of supervising attorneys. Committee members estimate that no more than 25 of these motions are filed yearly. Of these, about two-thirds involve possible CDD trial ineffectiveness or deficiencies in CDD-counseled pleas. The remainder involve belated or belatedly discovered client complaints, which are sometimes found in the ineffectiveness cases as well. Committee members acknowledge that in the occasional case where the ineffectiveness issue is weak and there are other, much stronger issues, the client will be invited to forgo the ineffectiveness claim to permit continued CAB representation.

In conclusion, the audit of CAB conflict claims did not reveal a significant number of errors, let alone a suspicious pattern of irregularities. This audit provided only a partial check on deliberate merit selection, however, since it did not rule out "false negatives"—meritorious conflict cases improperly retained by CAB. CAB supervisors acknowledge that considerations of merit influence them in borderline cases, and it is also possible that perceived merit affects the *recognition* of borderline conflict in the first place. It is also quite likely that perceived merit affects the persistence with which CAB attorneys seek waiver from clients with potential conflicts.

MERIT BIAS FROM THE OPERATION OF THE CONFLICT RULES

Even if CAB adhered scrupulously to its own conflicts policy, its application would leave, it with better cases if the conflicts it identified were found with disproportionate frequency in weaker, less winnable cases. Some of the specific rules listed above have no conceivable relation to case merit. For example, LAS representation of a prosecution witness (#9), or CAB assignment to a codefendant (#2), have no significance for the prospects of the appeal. The adequacy of CDD representation on a *prior* cases (#7) will also have little or no bearing on the merits of the appeal in most cases. While clients may become dissatisfied with CAB (#8) because of unrealistic expectations for hopeless appeals, CAB rarely gets rid of their cases—they do not really present a conflict of interest, and the court will usually appease the client by letting him file a supplemental brief.

All other conflict situations arise from CDD involvement in the defendant's present case: CDD represented a codefendant (#1) or was relieved by the trial court (#3), the client was dissatisfied with CDD (#4,5) or the CAB attorney thinks a nonfrivolous claim could be made that CDD was ineffective (#6).[17] In all these circumstances, the conflict may be more apparent than real: CDD may have been relieved simply to "move the case," client complaints may be insubstantial and long-appeased, and the errors supporting a "nonfrivolous" claim of CDD ineffectiveness may be fairly minor. Nevertheless, these cases may still be weaker, on average, than the cases retained by CAB.

In particular, the operation of CAB's conflict rules may give the 18b appellate panel some of the less promising trial appeals. The panel will get those CDD trials in which CAB had doubts about the quality of representation, and those 18b trials in which the defendant was passed over or shed by CDD because he was too heavily implicated, culpable, or intransigent. Moreover, to the extent that the panel gets a disproportionate share of 18b trials, for whatever reasons, it may be handicapped by poorly preserved records and largely uncontested prosecution cases.

Dissatisfied Clients and Possible Ineffectiveness

Even if most client complaints are insubstantial and most instances of arguable ineffectiveness are marginal, it is still likely that the average level of representation is higher in cases without these conflicts than in cases with them—truly skillful and zealous representation is unlikely to provoke complaints or smack of ineffectiveness. Better representation, in turn, will yield stronger appeals. First, by raising timely and appropriate objections, trial counsel will preserve issues for review and bring them to the attention of appellate counsel. Second, by challenging the prosecution evidence and presenting a coherent defense, counsel will make the People's case seem less "airtight." The weaker that case appears, the more likely the appellate court will be to consider unpreserved issues "in the interest of justice" and the less likely it will be to find harmless the errors it does consider.

Poor representation, in contrast, will often present the appellate court with largely unpreserved errors against a backdrop of apparently overwhelming evidence. This major handicap is hardly compensated by the possibility of a strong ineffectiveness claim. First, the mere failure to object, however devastating on appeal, has never been found to constitute trial ineffectiveness. Second, ineffectiveness claims, however substantial, are almost never successful (see Chapter 7), in part because the need to show prejudice insulates ineffectiveness from appellate review—the poorer the representation, the more hopeless the case will look. Thus, to the extent that CAB gets relieved of cases with substandard CDD representation, it will give away CDD trial appeals that are less winnable on average than those it keeps.

CDD Codefendants and CDD Postarraignment Relief

An even stronger connection between conflict and merit may be present in cases where CDD did *not* represent the defendant at trial, either because it represented a codefendant (#1) or because it was relieved by the trial judge after arraignment (#3). In almost all these cases, the defendant will have been represented by a member of the 18b felony panel. These cases may make less winnable appeals for two reasons:

(1) CDD may have been assigned to a codefendant or relieved following arraignment just because the defendant was strongly implicated, highly culpable or unwilling to accept a "reasonable" plea offer. McConville and Mirsky found that CDD in New York County had an established practice of taking the least culpable or heavily implicated codefendant.[18] If this practice is not limited to Manhattan, then a significant number of the defendants assigned to the 18b appellate panel may have been passed over by CDD just because they were more heavily implicated or culpable than a codefendant. When these disfavored defendants go to trial, lose, and appeal their convictions, they will be represented by the 18b panel.

Moreover, McConville and Mirsky's field observations suggest that one common reason why CDD attorneys get relieved is that they are reluctant to try "dead bang" cases—cases where the evidence is too strong for either an attractive plea offer or a plausible trial defense. The CDD-relieved category includes cases in which CDD was replaced as a direct or indirect consequence of the weakness of the case: for example, where the client refused to accept a "reasonable" plea offer or the attorney failed to appear on several adjourn dates. If these cases are ultimately tried by 18b counsel, they will go to the 18b appellate panel following the defendant's almost inevitable conviction. Thus, some of the defendants assigned to the appellate panel will have been rejected by CDD because of their relative "weight" or shed by CDD because of their recalcitrance, and their appeals may well have lower average merit than the CDD trials kept by CAB.

(2) Regardless of the reasons for assignment, CDD attorneys may do a far better job than their 18b counterparts in excluding and discrediting prosecution evidence, in developing a plausible defense theory, and in preserving errors by specific and timely objection, thereby leaving better records

Figure 6–1
New York County Overall

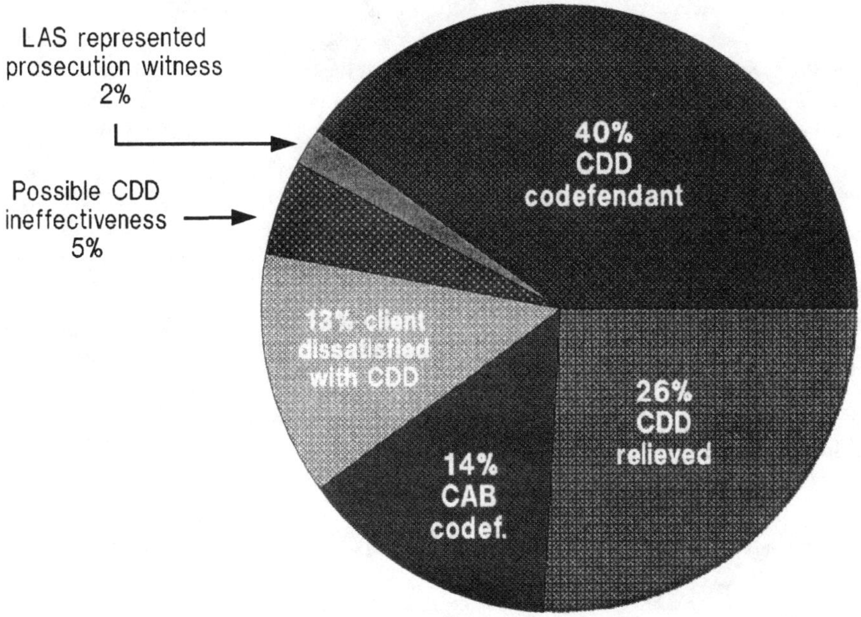

for appeal. In contrast, the gross deficiencies in 18b preparation and motion practice found by McConville and Mirsky may often lead to convictions that are virtually immune to reversal. A large proportion of viable suppression, speedy trial, and other pretrial issues may be waived by 18b counsel, and a large proportion of serious trial errors left unpreserved.

Thus, it is possible that the impartial application of the conflict rule leaves CAB with better cases than the appellate panel. In order to explore the possibility of a merit bias empirically, I analyzed the proportion of cases rejected by CAB under the different conflict rules. Because a significant proportion were in fact assigned under rules that have a significant potential for bias, I then examined ways of testing for actual bias. The measures I employed indicate that CDD selection practices and trial performance may indeed have resulted in CAB receiving trial appeals with slightly higher average merit than the 18b appellate panel.

The Types of Conflict Leading to 18b Substitution

Figure 6–1 shows the estimated breakdown of conflict types for all cases rejected by CAB in New York County in 1986. These estimates are based on the projected 1986 total of check-offs and relief motions in each category—the spot audit only covered eight months of check-offs and six months of relief motions.[19] While these estimates are very rough, they clearly reveal the *potential* for merit bias. The three grounds for relief that may have a significant negative correlation with merit—CDD codefendants, CDD relieved, and possible CDD ineffectiveness—are the first, second, and fifth most common grounds for relief, respectively, together accounting for over 70 percent of all the cases rejected by CAB. In contrast, the two clearly innocuous grounds—CAB codefendants and LAS prosecution witnesses—account for only 16 percent of the rejected cases.[20]

Moreover, only the client dissatisfaction and possible ineffectiveness cases, a mere 18 percent of the total, involve CDD trial level representation (and not the best); most of the remaining 82 percent of the cases going to the 18b appellate panel, and well over 95 percent of the checked-off cases, will have the handicaps of 18b trial representation. Clearly, the rules under which cases are actually assigned to the panel may, on average, select appeals of lesser merit.

Still, the significance of these findings for our purposes is limited by the fact that the spot audit covered assignments two years after the disposition survey. It is possible that the pattern of reassignments changed in the interim, and that the potential for bias had not been as great at the time of the survey. Fortunately, I was able to examine this possibility through CAB's own records.

The Analysis of the CAB Defendant File

A partial picture of CAB taking practice at the time of the disposition survey is provided by CAB's computerized defendant file. That file contains information on the background characteristics and disposition of all cases initially assigned to CAB: the attorney type at trial level; the record type—trial, plea with hearing, or simple plea; the department and county; whether (but not why) CAB was relieved; and the appellate disposition of the cases CAB retained.[21] The file included relief motion but not check-off cases, since the latter are never assigned to CAB.

The file included some but not all of the cases in the population sampled by the disposition survey: it contained all 1984 and later assignments, most 1983 assignments, some 1982 assignments, but very few assignments from earlier years. With the assistance of CAB paralegals, I coded and analyzed a printout of recorded assignments from November 1982 to November 1985.

By analyzing this file, it was possible to compare some of the critical characteristics of the cases CAB rejected and retained, particularly the attorney type and conviction type. It was also possible to compare CAB's own performance on cases with different characteristics—did it get favorable

Table 6–1
Estimated Case Characteristics for CAB and 18b, 1983–1985 Assignments

% of CAB cases in this cell/ % of 18B cases in this cell

Trial-level Attorney

Conviction/Record Type:	CDD	Trial 18B	Retained
Trial	16.5 / 21.8	17.4 / 23.1	5.0 / 6.1
Hearing	4.7 / 3.8	5.0 / 3.4	1.4 / 0.2
Plea	22.6 / 24.2	20.5 / 12.5	7.0 / 4.5

action in trial appeals more often than in plea appeals, and in CDD trials more often than in 18b trials?

The results of this analysis were inconclusive, but largely confirmed the impression left by the spot audit: while CAB appears to make no systematic effort to retain better cases, the operation of the conflict rules and the case-taking practices of CDD may have left CAB with cases of higher average merit than those assigned to the 18b panel. Moreover, CAB appeared to get better results with cases possessing the characteristics associated with higher merit.

"False Negatives." While the defendant file did not reveal a single instance in which CDD had represented more than one codefendant, it did include a number of cases in which CDD had been relieved for 18b or retained counsel. While many CDD-relieved cases appear to involve no actual conflict, the retention of some but not others might suggest an attempt to hold onto better cases. A more innocent explanation is suggested, however, by the outcome of the CDD-relieved trials which CAB kept—it received favorable action on only 1 of 29, far less often than for any other trial category. It is more likely that these were cases in which CDD was relieved soon enough after arraignment to avoid a presumption of conflict.

Types of Cases Retained and Rejected by CAB. Table 6–1 shows the number and proportion of cases retained and rejected by CAB, by attorney type and record type. It is apparent from this table that CAB kept a higher proportion of pleas and hearings than trials, and that the 18b panel received a higher proportion of trials than CAB retained. Even more surprising, CAB rejected almost as high a proportion of CDD trials as 18b trials. Overall, CAB rejected slightly *more* CDD than non-CDD cases. This hardly appears to reflect a policy of systematic merit selection. It does indicate, however, that CAB was rejecting a far higher proportion of CDD trials during the period covered by the disposition survey than it was during the later period covered by the spot audit.[22]

Despite the high proportion of CDD trials reassigned to the 18b panel, there can be little doubt that a substantial majority of the panel's appeals, including trial appeals, did not involve CDD representation. This is because the cases checked off the poor person list by CAB (not recorded in the defendant file) would have almost all been non-CDD cases. Virtually all the check-offs examined in the spot audit involved CDD codefendants or CDD trial relief, and the practice in these two areas was essentially the same during the earlier period covered by the disposition survey—no inquiry was made into the facts of the individual case and waiver was never solicited (see Chapter 8).

Attorney Type and Favorable Action. Because the 18b appellate panel was almost certainly assigned a higher proportion of non-CDD trials than CAB retained during the period of the disposition survey, it is important to examine the effect of trial attorney type on case outcome. Since the 18b panels keep no records comparable to the CDD defendant file, this can only be done indirectly, by examining the outcomes of the CDD and non-CDD cases retained by CAB.[23] If CDD trial appeals have greater merit because of superior performance by CDD counsel, they should receive favorable action more often than non-CDD trial appeals.

More frequent success on CDD than non-CDD trial appeals would support, a fortiori, the possibility of significant merit bias. The 18b panel will not only get a smaller proportion of CDD cases, but some of the less promising ones—those CAB rejects because of possible CDD ineffectiveness and client dissatisfaction. The panel will clearly not receive a compensating advantage in the quality of its non-CDD cases—a plurality of the non-CDD defendants assigned to the panel will have had CDD codefendants and may have been passed over by CDD counsel just because they were the more culpable or heavily implicated.[24] By the same token, if CAB did no better on CDD than non-CDD trials, it will not eliminate the possibility of merit bias, since it would still be possible that CAB kept better CDD or non-CDD cases than it rejected.

As Table 6–2 indicates, CAB appears to do better on CDD trials than non-CDD trials, although the magnitude of the difference depends on the kind of analysis that is used.[25] This difference may reflect superior CDD trial practice, but also greater CDD selectivity. If CDD routinely picks the

Table 6–2
Favorable Action in CAB Trial Appeals as a Function of Trial-Level Attorney

Number in Cell: % of Cases Receiving FA

Type of Analysis:[1]	CDD	Trial 18B	Retained	NLA[2]
1) Redistributing unknown/ 18b/ Retained cases by unknown ratio 2) Redistributing miscoded "LAB" cases by known CDD/LAB ratio	12.7%	11.9%	8.5%	--
1) Analyzing unknown 18b/ Ret. cases separately 2) Excluding all miscoded "LAB" cases	15%	10%	7.7%	16%
1) Analyzing unknown 18b/ Ret. cases separately 2) Excluding all cases coded by erring paralegal	14.6%	9%	9.8%	14.75%

1) See Chapter Notes for Explanation
2) Not Legal Aid

better codefendant, and codefendants are no worse as a group than single defendants, then CAB will inherit slightly less culpable and heavily implicated defendants on average from CDD than from 18b trial counsel.[26] This possibility, however, is hard to reconcile with the fact that appeals from retained counsel fared even worse than appeals from 18b counsel: Selectivity is unlikely to play a role in explaining that difference, since CDD rarely has its pick of defendants who can afford to retain counsel. While the difference between CDD and non-CDD cases is not dramatic, it does suggest that merit bias cannot be ruled out as one source of the superior results obtained by CAB in the disposition sample.

Withdrawals by CAB Clients. The analysis of CAB's defendant file effectively ruled out another possible source for its superior performance—a policy of encouraging clients with less promising appeals to withdraw, which would serve to induce the kind of self-selection practiced by paying clients. CAB obtained withdrawals and dismissals in only 30 of the 584 trials it retained. This rate of withdrawal is simply too low to significantly affect the merit of its trial appeals.[27]

The Fate of CDD-Relieved Cases. I conducted one further check on the possibility of merit bias by examining the ultimate trial-level disposition of cases which CAB had rejected because of CDD postarraignment relief. If this relief category contained, as I suspected, a disproportionate number of serious, "dead bang" trial losers, it should be reflected in court records showing a high rate of trials for these cases and heavy sentences.

To test this prediction, I tracked the defendants in all of the New York County motions claiming CDD-relief as a conflict, and half of the New York County check-offs for which CDD-relief was the only apparent conflict. There were 10 cases in the former category and 15 in the latter, for a total of 25. In 14, or 56 percent of these cases, the defendant went to trial, compared with only 43 percent for all cases initially assigned to CAB (and entered in the CAB defendant file). Of these 14, 9 were convicted of the top count. The CDD-relieved defendants also received fairly heavy sentences: 4 of the 25 got life maximums, another 5 received 15 years or more, and 14 received some kind of enhanced sentences, which almost always indicates prior felony convictions.

Although a precise comparison is not possible—I did not have a paired group of cases lacking this specific kind of conflict—it is clear that the defendants relieved of CDD representation went to trial more often than the average appellant, and it is probable that they were convicted of more serious offenses and more likely to have been predicate offenders. Given their background, the likely strength of the evidence they faced, and the sentences they received, it is reasonable to suppose that they had even less chance of favorable action on appeal than the average indigent defendant convicted of a felony in New York.

CONCLUSION

While CAB does not appear to engage in systematic merit selection, the discretion it enjoys in resolving borderline conflicts may result in some merit-based partiality. More important, there are three ways in which the impartial application of the conflict rules may give CAB more winnable trial appeals on average than the 18b panel: (1) by giving CAB a higher proportion of CDD cases, which appear from CAB records to do somewhat better on appeal; (2) by giving 18b poorer CDD cases—those in which the defendant or the CAB attorney was dissatisfied with CDD performance; and (3) by giving 18b poorer non-CDD cases—those where CDD was relieved after arraignment, possibly because of the recalcitrance of a heavily implicated defendant, and those where CDD represented a codefendant, possibly because he was less culpable or heavily implicated.

My discussion of these possibilities has relied on generalizations about the CDD trial practices found by McConville and Mirsky in New York County and plausible but largely unproven assumptions about the quality of CDD and 18b trial representation and the impact of trial representation on appellate prospects. While I have found some evidence that merit bias actually occurs, the evidence is inconclusive and the effects fairly small.

It is clear that merit bias cannot provide a complete explanation of superior CAB outcomes. In particular, CAB's success in obtaining interest-of-justice reversals cannot easily be explained by better trial-level representation, since these are precisely the cases in which the court reversed *despite* the absence of an adequate objection. Still, an interest-of-justice reversal is more likely for a sympathetic or weakly implicated defendant, and CDD assignment practices may leave CAB with a preponderance of such defendants. But CAB retention of less heavily implicated or better represented defendants could not explain CAB preponderance in cases where the court recognized error but found it harmless—cases where the court declined to reverse just because the evidence against the defendant was overwhelming.[28]

Thus, a bias in the selection process may account for some, but certainly not all, of the variance in the performance of the two defenders. It is quite likely CAB would achieve superior results even if cases were randomly assigned, and that any given appellant has slightly greater odds of favorable action with CAB representation. At the same time, this chapter has revealed fragmentary but consistent evidence of a merit bias arising from CDD selection practices and trial performance. The transmission of this bias through the operation of the conflict rules maintains LAS representation of the "deserving poor"—those defendants with limited culpability or tenuous links to the crime. While this selection bias cannot fully account for the outcome differences found in the disposition survey—the focus of this chapter—it raises troublesome questions about the allocation of criminal defense resources, to which we will return in Part III.

NOTES

1. McConville and Mirsky, "Criminal Defense of the Poor In New York City," *New York University Review of Law and Social Change* 15 (1987): 581, 818–54.

2. This list is derived from the CAB *Practice Manual* (1985 ed.) and other CAB materials.

3. McConville and Mirsky, "Criminal Defense of the Poor," 817–36.

4. Ibid., 842.

5. I am grateful to Chet Mirsky for helping me keep this perspective in sight while focusing on narrower methodological concerns.

6. This shift is discussed later in this chapter and in Chapter 8.

7. I also examined a letter-motion from February 1986, the only one saved from the first half of 1986. This gave me a total of six letter-motions, since I did not have one for December 1986.

8. Until quite recently, neither CAB nor the AD1 assignment clerk saved CAB relief requests for more than a few months. I used the earliest records available, which involved 1985 and 1986 assignments. The audit thus covered a later period than the disposition survey, whose 1985 dispositions would have arisen from 1983 and 1984 assignments. While CAB conflicts policy changed appreciably in the interim, the 1986 profile offers a baseline from which earlier practice can be estimated.

Moreover, there is no reason to suspect that the *accuracy* of CAB claims improved or declined between the survey and the spot audit.

Few of the motions and none of the letters indicated whether the appeal was from a trial or plea. Had I found significant numbers of false or unverifiable claims, I would have attempted to ascertain which type of conviction they came from.

9. CAB uses the same paralegals to check court files in all five counties, and it would have no apparent reason to be more accurate in some than others. While the record-keeping may well be more accurate or complete in some counties, any resulting variations in the accuracy of CAB claims would not be (directly) attributable to CAB or reflect its manipulation of the conflicts rules. Moreover, neither department had subjected conflict claims to very close scrutiny at the time of the audit, so CAB had no incentive to be more careful in one than the other.

10. While CAB might move to be relieved for an invalid reason when a valid reason existed, such relief, though ultimately correct, would still involve a misrepresentation to the court.

11. Some of the cases in which CDD was relieved after arraignment were also cases in which CDD had been assigned to a codefendant. It is not clear if CDD representation of a codefendant was not known at arraignment, or whether CDD held onto the case past arraignment for other reasons, such as the unavailability of 18b counsel. In any event, I coded these cases as "CDD codefendant," since that was undoubtedly the reason for CDD getting relieved in most or all of them.

12. This figure excludes the three cases in which it was claimed that LAS had represented a prosecution witness, since I had no means of independently verifying these claims.

13. The Managing Attorney explained that in cases where a prior assignment to a codefendant is belatedly discovered, CAB generally keeps the first defendant to receive a complete record, even if he was not the first to be assigned. While this may be a reasonable policy, it is somewhat misleading to claim in the relief motion that the defendant to be kept was "previously assigned" to CAB.

14. This figure includes seven motions to AD2.

15. Thirteen of these motions arose from pleas, 11 from trials; in two, the conviction type was not indicated.

16. As I discuss later in this chapter and in Chapter 8, CAB's threshold for moving to be relieved in cases of client dissatisfaction was much lower in 1984–1985 than thereafter.

17. Client dissatisfaction will often be apparent well before CAB has a chance to review the record, and CAB will not wait for the record before seeking relief in cases where the client's complaints are particularly vehement. Because CAB sometimes gets relieved without independently assessing the validity of the client's complaints, an unknown percentage of dissatisfaction cases will also be possible ineffectiveness cases.

18. McConville and Mirsky, "Criminal Defense of the Poor," 817–36.

19. Figures 6–2 and 6–3 present separate breakdowns of the conflicts claimed in CAB check-offs and relief motions in New York County. In comparing the figures, two features are striking. First, there are a number of conflicts which are rarely picked up at the check-off stage: client dissatisfaction not resulting in CDD relief, prior CAB assignment to a non-CDD codefendant, LAS representation of a prosecution witness, and possible CDD ineffectiveness. Second, while a large number of

Figure 6–2
New York County Check-offs

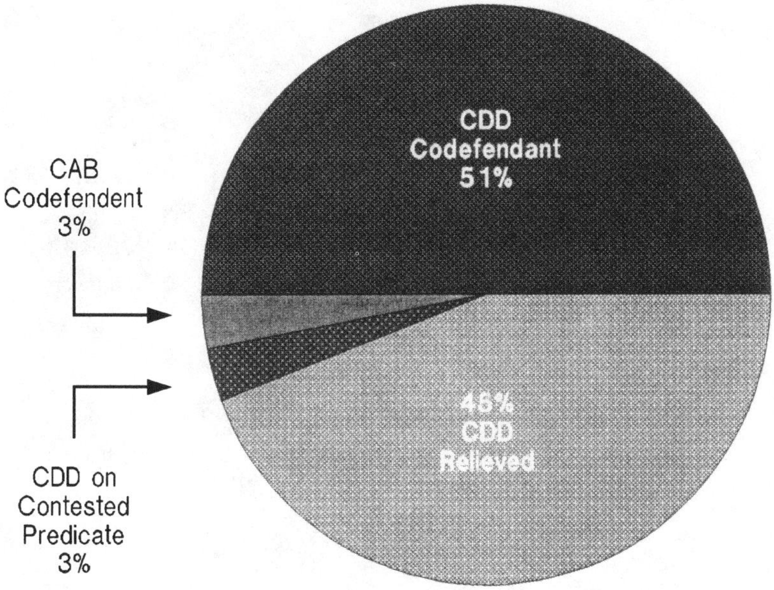

the remaining conflicts—CDD codefendants and CDD-relieved—are spotted at the check-off stage, almost as many are not: more than half the codefendant cases and more than a third of the CDD-relieved cases were not spotted until after assignment. The CAB Managing Attorney attributes this to missing and incomplete court files, although it is possible that some of these conflicts are overlooked by CAB paralegals.

20. This figure may be even lower if some of the CAB codefendants were also CDD codefendants.

21. The file does indicate if CAB was relieved because of conflict or because the defendant obtained private counsel, but it does not indicate the specific kind of conflict.

22. In contrast, the spot audit showed only 30 percent of all relief motions in 1986 arising from CDD cases (client dissatisfaction and possible ineffectiveness). The most likely explanation for the dramatic reduction in CDD reassignments is that CAB had, in the two intervening years, been making an increasing effort to mollify clients dissatisfied with CDD representation, rather than treating the first expression of discontent as an irreconcilable difference. The extent to which CAB was able to cut back its CDD reassignments suggests that a large proportion of client complaints resulted from misunderstanding and irritation, rather than from serious CDD lapses requiring relief on ineffectiveness grounds. It is also possible, of course, that CDD was giving its clients less to complain about during the period covered by the spot audit.

23. I have been treating non-CDD trials as if they all involved 18b trial repre-

Figure 6–3
New York County Motions

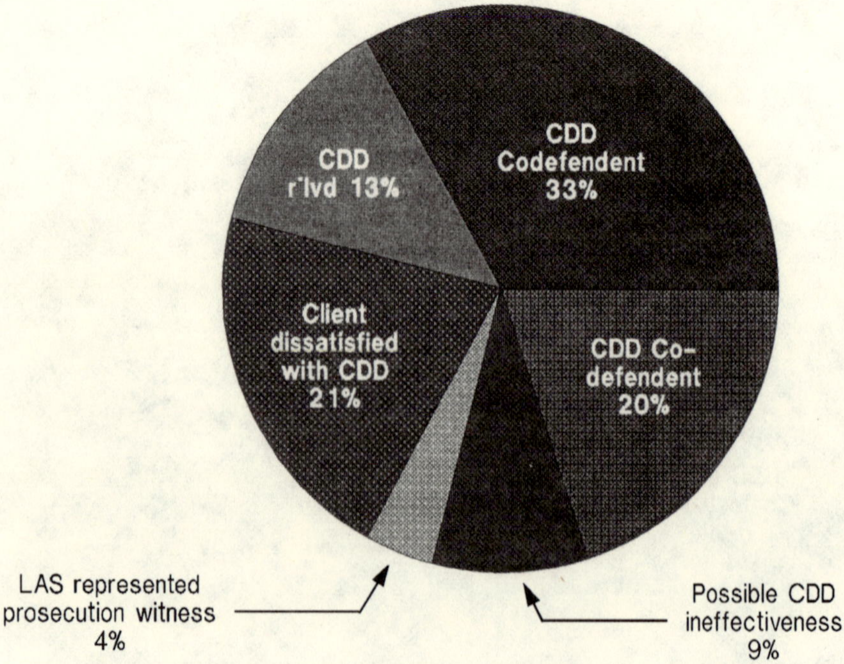

sentation. In fact, about 20 percent were private trials. Since all these privately represented defendants were found indigent on appeal, they were probably not able to afford very high quality trial representation. This impression is supported by the fact that CAB does no better on these private trials than on 18b trials, while it does appreciably better on CDD trials (see Table 6–2).

24. See McConville and Mirsky, "Criminal Defense of the Poor," 818–36. It is still possible that the *panel's* CDD cases are no better than its 18b cases, since the CDD cases assigned to the panel may be much worse than those kept by CAB. This would merely locate the merit bias in the differential merit of the CDD cases assigned to the two defenders rather than in their differing proportions of CDD and 18b cases.

25. One of the CAB paralegals who coded the printout mistakenly gave the same label to cases with CDD representation and with CDD-relieved. Unfortunately, the cases could not be recoded, since the coding sheets were not indexed to the printout. I analyzed the data in several ways to correct for this error: randomly assigning the mislabeled cases to CDD and CDD-relieved categories according to their frequency in the rest of the printout (about 17/1 for CDD/CDD-relieved), eliminating all the miscoded cases, and eliminating all the cases coded by the erring paralegal.

The first procedure should have had a negligible effect on the results for CDD cases, since almost all the miscoded cases would in fact have been CDD. The last "cleanest" procedure should not have affected the overall results, since the coders had divided up the alphabetically ordered file more or less randomly. Unfortunately, since the miscoded cases contained disproportionately few wins, their redistribution had the effect of lowering, and their elimination of raising, the success rate on CDD cases and thereby increasing the difference between CDD and non-CDD cases.

A second issue concerned the treatment of non-CDD cases in which it was not known whether counsel had been assigned or retained. Since these unknown non-CDD cases got favorable action more frequently than either known 18b or known retained cases, their redistribution to the 18b and retained categories improved the performance of non-CDD cases, although not as much as the elimination of the miscoded cases improved CDD performance.

Table 6–1 shows three of the six possible ways in which the data could have been analyzed (three for the miscoded cases × two for the unknown non-CDD cases): redistributing both the unknown non-CDD cases and the miscoded cases, redistributing the unknown non-CDD cases but eliminating either the miscoded CDD cases or all the cases coded by the erring paralegal. None of these analyses changes the basic picture reported in the text: that CAB does at least slightly better with CDD than non-CDD cases.

26. This does not imply that all or most CDD cases inherited by CAB will involve multiple defendants, or that all 18b cases it inherits will involve single defendants.

27. In contrast, CAB obtained withdrawals in 394 of its 921 pleas and hearings. Almost half as many pleas and hearings were withdrawn as briefed: 54 to 101 for hearings, 221 to 408 for pleas. This high rate of withdrawal undoubtedly reflects the CAB practice of soliciting withdrawal by plea defendants with no viable issues and from plea and hearing defendants unwilling to risk a higher sentence on remand. It is unlikely that this high rate of withdrawal helps CAB's performance in those areas. Hopeless plea cases would almost always end up as *Anders* briefs (separately coded in the disposition survey) if they were not withdrawn. The high rate of withdrawal in risky cases, usually pleas with hearings, may actually have *hurt* CAB's performance, by removing cases identified as having meritorious issues. Almost every CAB attorney has had a good hearing case "get away" because the defendant chose to withdraw.

It is doubtful that many 18b attorneys point out the risks in plea and hearing challenges—they have an economic interest in going ahead with the appeal, and their standard instructional materials do not even mention "risk letters." Of course, CAB attorneys may downplay the risks in writing to clients with really strong issues, in their desire to raise those issues. As in the case of client dissatisfaction, this may lead to some merit selection at the margins.

28. Moreover, the quality of CAB briefs does not appear to depend on the merit of its cases—CAB was rated consistently higher in the brief evaluation, although its codefendants appeared on appeal to be no less culpable or heavily implicated than their 18b counterparts.

7

The Character of Appellate Intervention in Criminal Cases and the Role of Appellate Advocacy

This chapter examines the grounds for favorable action in the Appellate Division through an analysis of the reversals and modifications found in the disposition sample. The analysis focuses on appellate decision-making, but it has important implications for appellate advocacy. By examining the kinds of error that actually lead the courts to reverse or modify convictions, it helps us to assess the role of the successful appellate attorney in routine first-level appeals: does she function mainly as a technician, finding loopholes and subtle procedural errors, or mainly as an advocate, trying to convince the court that her client suffered a grave injustice? The analysis also explores the significance of favorable action for the criminal justice system: does it increase the safeguards against the conviction of innocent defendants, address systematic abuses in investigation and prosecution, clarify important ambiguities in the law, or merely catch the occasional error produced by a basically sound system in the prosecution of "obviously guilty" defendants?

These are pressing questions, raised by the discussion in Part I and left unresolved by the empirical analysis of the last three chapters. In Chapter 1, I argued that the recognition of a universal right to appellate counsel and the outward success of the due process revolution had decreased the proportion of cases in which skilled advocacy made a difference to the outcome. At the same time, I suggested that the declining merit of the average criminal appeal placed a premium on skilled advocacy, to overcome an increasingly strong presumption of regularity in the trial-level proceedings. In the last three chapters, we observed a likely connection between superior advocacy and better outcomes but were unable to rule out the confounding effect of case merit. An analysis of the grounds for favorable action will help to clarify the impact of skilled advocacy, by revealing whether appeals are won on the basis of issues whose discovery or effective presentation is likely to depend on the skill of appellate counsel.

The analysis undertaken in this chapter confirms both the modest role of appellate review in routine cases and the continuing importance of zealous advocacy for the individual defendant. On the one hand, few reversals and modifications involved in the resolution of novel or important issues, or the explicit vindication of apparently innocent defendants, while a large number rested on technical issues, particularly the sufficiency of proof on aggravating elements and the necessity of charging lesser offenses (charge-downs). The courts made relatively few findings of pretrial misconduct and rarely confronted some of the most serious problems in contemporary criminal adjudication: unreliable identifications, coercive guilty pleas, and ineffective trial counsel.

Despite their caution and inertia, however, the courts appeared sensitive to the possibility of serious injustice in individual cases, and it was here that zealous advocacy may have played a critical role. The decision to intervene was rarely a mechanical one: two-thirds of all reversals and modifications had been subject to harmless error analysis, and a large share of the cases involving the sufficiency of the evidence or the submission of lesser offenses also involved close factual determinations. In some areas, the courts showed a surprising willingness to seize on minor legal errors in the face of factual doubts or serious inequities. While the courts were unsympathetic with efforts to find a needle of error in a haystack of incriminating evidence, they sometimes grasped at straws when their own sense of injustice was aroused by serious misconduct or the specter of a wrongful conviction.

THE CHARACTER OF FAVORABLE ACTION IN THE APPELLATE DIVISION

I examined all cases from the disposition sample in which the court granted significant relief to the defendant—reversing his entire conviction, eliminating the top count, reducing or otherwise favorably modifying his sentence.[1] I did not include remands to the trial court for further findings or the elimination of lesser and concurrent counts. Altogether, I analyzed 114 reversals and modifications of the conviction, and 25 sentence reductions and modifications. Additionally, I analyzed all 16 cases in which the court affirmed on a finding of harmless error.

This analysis revealed the frequency with which errors were found, but not the frequency with which they were raised. I did not examine defense briefs in the sampled cases, and my information on the issues raised came entirely from the court's opinions, which were only issued for reversals, modifications, and a small fraction of affirmances.[2] Thus, I cannot be certain whether the court ignored a particular issue or was rarely given the opportunity to review it. Nevertheless, the brief evaluation in Chapter 4 indicated that CAB was fairly thorough in raising meritorious issues. If its attorneys failed to raise issues supported by the record, it is probably because they judged their odds of success to be vanishingly small.

I classified the grounds for favorable action into 14 error categories. While the classification was somewhat ad hoc, it relied on the court's own description of its reasons for granting favorable action. I noted the attorney type in every case, but the number of cases in each error category was too small for a statistical comparison of the grounds on which the different attorneys obtained favorable action. There were a few categories in which one type of attorney was heavily overrepresented relative to its overall share of reversals, and these are discussed in the text or footnotes.

REVERSALS AND MODIFICATIONS OF CONVICTIONS

Table 7–1 presents a breakdown of the grounds for reversal and modification. I counted all cases in which the type of error was cited as a ground for intervention, even if it was not the exclusive or principal ground. (For this reason, the total number of reasons in the table exceeds the number of reversals and modifications, and the percentage total exceeds 100%).

Significant Features of the Sample

The picture that emerges from this analysis is of a reviewing court reluctant to reexamine the mainstays of criminal prosecution—guilty pleas and eyewitness identification. The Appellate Division found only 4 of the roughly 800 pleas in the sample to be involuntary. It held the performance of trial counsel ineffective only once. It never found eyewitness evidence too unreliable to sustain a conviction. There were indications, however, that the court was receptive to the possibility of serious injustice. It appeared particularly sensitive to the kinds of procedural error which typically occur in eyewitness cases, and it sometimes reversed weak eyewitness cases on grounds that seemed thin and even pretextual.

Few Cases Made or Clarified Law. Only 11 of the 114 reversals or modifications involved issues that could be regarded as novel or decisions that could be regarded as clarifying the laws.[3] Of these, most were relatively minor refinements of existing doctrine: for example, the recently established rule that an already represented defendant can only waive his right to counsel in counsel's presence was held not to be satisfied by a station house phone call to an associate of the defendant's attorney. The single case of truly broad significance was a Second Department decision holding that in cases where identity was disputed, the jury must be instructed to subject the identification evidence "to the same searching scrutiny used for the alibi."

Table 7–1
Grounds for Favorable Action: New York

Reason for Favorable Action	# and % of Favorable Action	
1) Legally insufficient evidence	(22) 19%	
a) actus reus		(5) 4%
b) mens rea		(3) 3%
c) Complicity		(3) 3%
d) Aggrav/technical		(11) 10%
2) Erroneous admission of evidence	(19) 17%	
a) ID bolstering		(5) 4%
b) Other		(14) 12%
3) Erroneous jury instructions	(18) 16%	
a) ID/alibi		(8) 7%
b) Other		(10) 9%
4) Prosecutorial misconduct	(17) 15%	
a) Summation		(8) 7%
b) Cross-examination		(7) 6%
c) Pretrial		(2) 2%
5) Judicial intrusion or mismanagement	(9) 8%	
6) Errors in submitting lesser offenses and alternative defenses	(9) 8%	
7) Improper search and seizure	(7) 6%	
a) Stop & frisk		(4) 4%
b) Other		(3) 3%
8) Involuntary pleas	(4) 4%	
a) Sentence misrepresentation		(3) 3%
b) Protest; failure to inquire		(1) 1%
9) Police interrogation/counsel	(3) 3%	
10) Improper joinder of defendants or offenses	(3) 3%	
11) Improper ID procedures	(3) 3%	
a) pretrial		(2) 2%
b) trial		(1) 1%
12) Speedy trial violations	(2) 2%	
a) statutory		(1) 1%
b) constitutional		(1) 1%
13) Ineffective counsel	(1) 1%	
14) Double jeopardy	(1) 1%	

This case, discussed later in the chapter, was cited in at least four of the sample's other reversals.

Few Cases Involved Questions about Basic Liability. Although insufficient evidence was the single most frequent ground for favorable action, only six or seven of the sufficiency reversals involved a question of the defendant's factual guilt (including one of the complicity cases in which the court found no criminal intent)—whether he actually committed a crime or whether a crime was actually committed. Of these, three were strictly circumstantial cases in which the court found that the evidence did not exclude the defendant's innocence "to a moral certainty." In contrast, there was not a single case in which the court found that eyewitness identification testimony was incredible or that a verdict based on such testimony was against the weight of the evidence. I examine this contrast below in discussing the appellate review of identification issues.

Four of the six basic sufficiency reversals were obtained by retained counsel. If this is not merely a fluke, it may reflect a closer scrutiny of the evidence in retained cases by counsel or the courts. It is not clear, however, why the disparity in the review received by retained and assigned cases should be greater for sufficiency claims than for other sources of error. It may be that retained appellate counsel are particularly attuned to meritorious sufficiency issues because they, or their associates, have aggressively litigated those issues at trial. Again, however, it is not clear why this should be true of sufficiency more than other trial issues. It is also possible that retained cases are more likely to have evidentiary gaps because of their greater complexity. This is unlikely, however, since insufficient evidence of aggravating and technical elements is found in proportionately more assigned than retained cases.[4]

A Significant Proportion of Cases Involved Technical Issues. The remaining sufficiency cases all involved aggravating elements, such as the value of property or the magnitude of physical injury. While some of these issues had an important bearing on the defendant's culpability, such as his intent to kill rather than merely injure, most involved less important gradations or elements of proof—for example, the degree of impairment necessary to establish physical injury under the assault statutes—or inadvertent failures of proof on uncontested elements—for example, the value of a stolen car. The relatively large number of cases may be attributable to the complexity of New York's penal law, which typically requires proof of a large number of narrowly defined elements.

This statutory complexity may also have been responsible for many errors involving the improper submission or failure to submit a lesser included offense to the jury. In these cases, the threshold issue is whether the lesser offense is "included" in the greater—whether its elements are a (proper) subset of those in the greater offense.[5] The fact that intelligent judges occasionally get this wrong is hardly a serious failing in the criminal justice system, and the resulting errors, though often requiring reversal, do not involve what most laymen would consider substantial injustice.

Many possible technical errors are conspicuously absent or infrequent. While the New York speedy trial (or, more accurately, prosecutorial readiness) statute requires both controversial allocations of responsibility for delay and complex numerical computations, it accounted for only one reversal in the disposition sample. This may be due in part to the consequences of finding unreadiness: automatic dismissal without the possibility of reprosecution.

Of the 14 cases involving insufficient evidence on aggravating, technical, or mental elements, ten were CAB appeals, two were 18b, and two were retained. The small number of retained appeals in this area suggests that retained counsel do not owe their disproportionate number of "basic sufficiency" reversals to greater statutory complexity in the charged offenses. CAB preponderance in this area may result from the greater familiarity of CAB attorneys with the minutiae of the Penal Law, from their ability and inclination to methodically check the proof in each case, element by element.

Comparatively Few Cases Involved Pretrial Issues. Sixty-five percent of all reversals and modifications arose from errors and improprieties committed during the course of the trial. A large majority of these—42 percent of all cases—involved legal errors by the trial court: mistaken evidentiary rulings and instructions, and errors in the submission of defenses and lesser offenses. The remaining 23 percent involved misconduct by the prosecutor or the court: inflammatory summations, improper cross-examination, refusals to grant reasonable continuances, and excessive judicial intrusion into the examination of witnesses or the attorney-client relationship.[6] In contrast, only 17 percent of the cases involved claims of pretrial misconduct by police or prosecutors: improper searches, seizures and interrogations, suggestive identification procedures, failure to make required disclosures to the defense, and failure to be ready for trial. The court found police searches improper in only seven cases, police interrogations in only three, and pretrial identifications in only two.

Several factors may explain the preponderance of trial over pretrial issues. First, it may be easier for the appellate court to evaluate fully transcribed trial error and misbehavior than police or pretrial prosecutorial misconduct: while it can assess the former for itself, relying only on the accuracy of the court reporter, it must rely on allegations made in testimony and affidavits to assess the latter. Second, trial judges may be better at monitoring pretrial than trial conduct, particularly when the latter involves interactions in which they are directly involved. Decisions concerning pretrial misconduct are often made after a hearing and full briefing, while decisions on trial conduct, the admission of evidence, and jury instructions, particularly supplemental ones, are often made extemporaneously.

Third, appellate judges may be more disposed to find trial misconduct because it rarely requires the dismissal of the indictment or the exclusion of critical prosecution evidence. For example, in cases involving mistaken evidentiary rulings, the challenged evidence is usually far less central to the prosecution case than the evidence challenged in pretrial suppression hearings, whose loss often precludes reprosecution. Pretrial suppression often results in the release of "obviously guilty" and dangerous offenders, and that specter may raise the judicial threshold for finding error. Additionally, trial errors and improprieties are often found in combination. For example, while improper summations were cited as a basis for reversal eight times, they never constituted the sole or even principle reason for reversal.

There is an interesting contrast between CAB and retained counsel in reversals involving prosecutorial misconduct. The only two reversals for pretrial misconduct, both involving *Brady* violations (failure to disclose exculpatory evidence), came from retained appeals, while all seven reversals citing presummation trial misconduct, usually in cross-examination, came from CAB appeals. It may be that retained appellate counsel had greater knowledge of nondisclosure or that retained trial counsel engaged in more extensive pretrial discovery, while CAB attorneys were more closely attuned to transcribed trial misconduct.

Few Cases Directly Confronted Systemic Problems of Coercive Plea-Bargains, Unreliable Identifications, and Ineffective Assistance. The "neglect of the gate house" was suggested by the small number of cases involving pretrial misconduct. Such misconduct may escape close appellate scrutiny because it is not fully apparent from the record; because it is insulated from review by appeals-conscious police, prosecutors, and judges; or because the appellate courts defer heavily to the trial judge in this area. It is unlikely to result from defense quiescence: while the disposition survey did not reveal the frequency with which defendants raised issues of pretrial misconduct, the brief evaluation sample and my own experience as an appellate attorney suggest that such issues are raised quite frequently and vigorously.

As noted above, the court found pretrial identification procedures to be fatally suggestive in only two cases, one involving a totally gratuitous show-up. As I will discuss below, the court's inactivity in this area may not have reflected a confidence in the pretrial identification process, but the absence of a procedural foothold for intervention. The court found ineffective assistance in only one case. The circumstances suggest the kind of showing necessary to overcome the presumption of competence: the attorney had presented a detailed alibi defense for the wrong day.

Judicial restraint was even more striking in the review of guilty pleas. Although almost half of the defense appeals in the disposition sample came from guilty pleas, the Appellate Division vacated only four pleas as involuntary.[7] Of these, three involved a broken or misunderstood promise: in two cases, the trial court imposed a sentence higher than promised without giving the defendant the option of withdrawing required by *People v. Selikoff* (1974);[8] in the other, defense counsel made the unusual admission that he had understated the maximum sentence to the defendant. The final plea reversal involved a defendant who protested his innocence at sentencing; the court failed to make the inquiry required by *People v. Serrano* (1973).[9] To those familiar with plea bargaining, these cases are distinguished less by their coercive or deceptive character than by the players' departure from a script that would have insulated them from critical review.[10]

Most Favorable Action Was Subject to Harmless Error Analysis or Other Factual Review. Approximately 66 percent of the reversals and modifications were subject to harmless error analysis—the court was required to determine not only that error had occurred, but that there was some possibility that the error might have affected the outcome.[11] This figure includes trials with pretrial suppression errors as well as most errors which occurred in the course of trial, with three exceptions: violations of the right to a public trial (closing part of the proceedings to all or part of the public), to be present at trial (trying the defendant in absentia), and to be tried on an indictment (submission of nonincluded offenses), all of which required automatic reversal. A significant number of other cases also involved close factual determinations, even if they did not require the court to "weigh" the evidence: those assessing the magnitude of physical injury, those reviewing the adequacy of strictly circumstantial evidence, and, more generally, those considering what inferences could reasonably be drawn from a given body of evidence.

The three most common areas requiring harmless error analysis were evidentiary rulings, charge errors, and prosecutorial misconduct, respectively the second, third, and fourth most frequent grounds for favorable action. The evidentiary errors were often technical—for example, several involved the failure to lay an adequate foundation for physical or scientific evidence—and the court usually devoted more attention to the errors themselves than to their impact on the case. At least four evidentiary cases, however, were explicitly concerned with the balancing of prejudice against probative value and thus involved factual analysis at two levels—the imbalance in the evidence and the harm done by admitting it. In the case of one type of evidentiary violation, the bolstering of identification testimony, the real issue was almost always, as I discuss later, the weakness of the evidence.

The weakness of the prosecution case also played a critical role in most of the cases involving charge issues. That role was perhaps most obvious in the three reversals based on a biased judicial summary (marshalling) of the evidence, but it was not far from the surface in the cases involving instructions on the reasonable doubt standard, justification, and other defenses. In only one case, involving the omission of any instruction on the presumption of innocence, did the court bypass the question of harmless error.

The third most common subject for harmless error analysis was prosecutorial misconduct. As noted above, these errors by themselves rarely led to favorable action. Other errors were given greater emphasis by the court in all eight of the inflammatory summation cases[12] and in two of the six improper questioning cases. Still, the court devoted a fair amount of discussion to these improprieties, since it was engaged in chastisement as well as simple error correction.

Not surprisingly, these were also the three areas in which the court found errors to be harmless. Prosecutorial misconduct was the most frequent category, with ten findings of harmless error. There were also four findings of harmless charge errors, and only one finding of harmless evidentiary error.

The preponderance of prosecutorial harmless error is not surprising, since appellate judges may feel obliged to condemn particularly egregious instances of prosecutorial misconduct even when they feel constrained to affirm the conviction. Additionally, prosecutors may sometimes act with less restraint in such "airtight" cases, having little reason to fear reversal. The desire to publicly condemn such defiant misconduct will sometimes overcome the court's general inclination to dispose of harmless errors with a silent affirmance.

Most Sentence Reversals and Modifications Involved Discretionary Reductions, Not the Correction of Technical Errors. Of the 25 sentence reversals and modifications I examined, 18 were discretionary reductions, made "in the interest of justice" by the Appellate Division. Eleven of these were simple "time cuts"—reductions in the defendant's prison sentence within the statutory range. In three of these cases, the court cited mitigating circumstances in reducing long homicide terms: the defendant was 18 years old with no prior record (20–life to 15–life); the defendant was an "outstanding youth" with no prior record convicted of killing another youth who squirted him with a fire extinguisher (8⅓–25 to 5–15); the defendant, a burglar, was trapped by the homeowner and killed him in the ensuing struggle. The two remaining time-cuts were discretionary drug resentences, more responsive to the harshness of the law than the circumstances of the offenders. None of these circumstances, as described in the courts' terse opinions, seem particularly unusual or compelling, an impression which suggests that sentence appeals do not "win themselves," but depend heavily on advocacy.

In the other discretionary sentence reductions, the court substituted a noncustodial for a jail sentence (2), replaced a consecutive with a concurrent sentence (2), granted youthful offender status (1), and eliminated additional conditions—a 90-day payment deadline in a restitutionary case and a fine-or-extra-year provision on a 25–life term.

In the remaining seven cases, the court corrected a legal error in sentencing adverse to the defendant. In three cases, it vacated predicate or persistent felony adjudications which were based on invalid predicate offenses or an improper compounding of predicate offenses—perhaps the most technical type of sentencing error. In another case, it corrected a mistaken sentence-enhancing offense classification. The court found one sentence to be higher than the statutory limit and reduced it to the maximum authorized term; it reduced another sentence to the minimum authorized term, as the parties below had apparently intended. In a final case, the court restored the bargained-for sentence, which had been raised by the judge after the defendant failed to appear at sentencing.

Considering the complexity of the New York penalty scheme, it is surprising that there were so few detected sentencing errors. While there were twice as many discretionary modifications of legally correct sentences, they represented a tiny fraction of the appeals in the sample which requested sentence reductions. It appears that New York trial judges have largely mastered a complex sentencing scheme, and that the Appellate Division uses its sentence review power, like its other discretionary powers, quite sparingly. Favorable action on sentences, as on convictions, less often involves the correction of technical errors than the alleviation of perceived injustice, an activity in which zealous advocacy may play a significant role.

The Appellate Review of Eyewitness Identification

The potential importance of skilled advocacy in rectifying fundamental injustice is perhaps most apparent in the cases finding improper identification charges and the bolstering of identification testimony. The Appellate Division reversed ten convictions because of an improper identification or alibi charge, five because of improper identification testimony, but only two because of the suggestiveness of an out-of-court identification and only one because of the impropriety of an in-court procedure. The court never reversed a conviction on the ground that the identification evidence was too unreliable.

Taken together, these cases suggest that appellate judges are sensitive to the unreliability of eyewitness identification, but unwilling to reverse without procedural error. Under New York law, as jurors in identification cases are often instructed, "the identification of the defendant as the perpetrator by a single eyewitness is legally sufficient to support his conviction."[13] While the legal sufficiency of eyewitness identification evidence does not prevent the court from finding such evidence incredible as a matter of law or against the weight of the evidence, the courts are extremely reluctant to do so, apparently because they feel that it would usurp the jury's fact-finding function.

In contrast, the judges express no hesitation about reviewing the sufficiency of the evidence in circumstantial cases. According to the standard formulation, there is legally insufficient evidence to convict in a case where the inferences that can reasonably be drawn from the evidence are equally consistent with innocence as guilt, but not in a case in which most but not all of the disinterested bystanders deny the defendant's identity. This distinction between eyewitness and circumstantial cases is questionable, but the courts are strongly committed to it.[14]

Despite its circumspection, the Appellate Division appears to be troubled by weak identification cases. It is particularly sensitive to the kinds of procedural error which typically occur in eyewitness cases. The two most common forms of error are inadequate or imbalanced instructions on identification and alibi evidence and third-party bolstering of identification testimony. These errors occur with sufficient frequency to give the court a procedural excuse—a fairly thin one in the cases of bolstering—to reverse the most troublesome convictions without appearing to override the jury and without precluding retrial.

The disposition sample included perhaps the most important identification charge case to emerge from the Second Department this decade, *People v. Daniels*. *Daniels* is a striking case for several reasons: it involved the conviction and ultimate vindication of an innocent man, it illustrates the outcome determinative impact of zealous representation in a single case, and it reflects the court's recurring efforts to erect procedural safeguards against the vagaries of eyewitness identification without challenging the jury's factfinding prerogatives or the standard operating procedures of the police.

Charles Daniels, a gainfully employed 35-year-old man with no prior record, was convicted of attempted second-degree murder on the testimony of a ten-year-old, emotionally handicapped neighbor who claimed to have seen Daniels throw a baby off a nearby roof. His identification of Daniels as the man on the roof was not only contradicted by his first and subsequent reports of the incident, but by the testimony of several respectable witnesses who claimed to have been with, or seen, Daniels throughout the time that the incident was likely to have taken place. The jury, however, took less than four hours to convict Daniels.

On appeal, the court asked the obvious question: "In the face of such seemingly persuasive testimony, as opposed to the somewhat questionable identification testimony . . . how did the jury return a verdict of guilty?" Its answer was not very reassuring. The jury could only have found that Daniels had an opportunity to commit the crime by disregarding the testimony of the four alibi witnesses. "Even though it may be difficult to accept such a conclusion upon the record of uncontradicted testimony in this case, the jury was well within its rights in rejecting such testimony." The court was unwilling to usurp the jury's factfinding prerogative, however badly it had been exercised.

The court, however, subjected the jury instructions to very close scrutiny, insisting that they were a critical safeguard against a mistaken conviction in a weak identification case. Fortunately for Daniels, the court found that safeguard fatally defective:

> Because of its persuasive power and inherent unreliability, eyewitness identification is always fraught with peril but when, as here, it is suspect, it is frightening indeed. Under such circumstances, the prosecution case rests on a most slender and shaky reed . . . a situation demanding the utmost caution . . . in which harmless error is anathema. . . . A reading of the court's charge on identification makes it clear that it was fundamentally flawed.

The court claimed that the instructions had misled the jury about the real infirmities in the prosecution case. First, the charge had made the "ultimate question" for the jury the *truthfulness* of the witnesses testimony:

A reading of the record makes it clear that what was at issue was *not* whether young Simms was telling the *truth*, but whether or not he was *mistaken*. This is the situation found in many, if not most, pure identification cases. The eyewitnesses are usually firmly convinced that they *are* telling the truth. . . . Bitter experience tells us, however, that the real issue is whether or not the witness is mistaken—however honest or truthful that mistake might be.

Second, in a case where "the facts surrounding the identification of the perpetrator were so unusual, complex, and confusing as to require careful and prudent judicial guidance," the jury received only "a thin, sparse, and inadequate identification charge." Finally, "not only was there no direction to subject the identification test to the same searching scrutiny used for the alibi, but also the court neglected to charge that the prosecution must disprove the alibi defense beyond a reasonable doubt."

None of these charge errors had been objected to, but the court reversed in the interest of justice. While we can only speculate, the role of appellate counsel may well have been decisive. Although the court certainly would have been troubled by the case, however effectively it was presented on appeal, it would not have reversed without finding the charge errors. It might not have found those errors or fully appreciated their magnitude without forceful advocacy by appellate counsel. The impact of counsel is even more apparent in the sequel: CAB turned the case over to CDD, whose investigators found the actual perpetrator and obtained the dismissal of all charges against Daniels.

Following *Daniels*, AD2 reversed scores of convictions, most supported by much stronger evidence, for the failure to give an adequate or balanced identification charge (as noted above, four other identification charge cases in our sample cited *Daniels*).[15] The trial courts eventually learned to use acceptable language, and, according to the CAB attorneys who monitor AD2, "*Daniels*" reversals had dropped sharply by 1985.

While the end result in *Daniels* was gratifying, it was too fortuitous for comfort. Daniels's vindication, like his conviction, rested on a slender reed—the bad identification charge given by the trial court. Jury instructions can certainly affect the outcome, but it is hard to believe that *this* jury, which disregarded a clear preponderance of exculpatory evidence, would have acquitted Daniels even if it had been properly instructed. In the end, Daniels was probably better off with a "thin, sparse, and inadequate" identification charge than he would have been with a barely adequate one.

The fundamental error in *Daniels* was not the charge but the verdict—no matter how the jury was instructed, Daniels should never have been convicted on the unreliable evidence offered at his trial. By deferring to a clearly mistaken jury verdict and resolving the case on the narrowest possible grounds, *Daniels* gave the trial court a formula for immunizing convictions based on similarly unreliable evidence from reversal. The instructions required by *Daniels* may have reduced the frequency of mistaken convictions in eyewitnesses cases, but they certainly did not eliminate them—even the *Daniels* court did not claim that a well-instructed jury would never convict an innocent man on unreliable evidence. The problem of mistaken identifications remains, now better insulated from appellate review.

The second area of frequent court intervention in troublesome eyewitness cases involves the prohibition on bolstering—third party references to an admissable out-of-court identification. The prohibition arises from a common law ban on all references to out-of-court identification, subject in New York to a narrow exception for testimony by the person who made the identification. Although the law is fairly settled, its violation is pervasive, occurring whenever a police officer mentions the results as well as the circumstances of a pretrial identification procedure. Even the suggestion of an intervening identification in the testimony that an officer "spoke with the complainant, then arrested the suspect" is held to constitute "inferential bolstering." If the mere juxtaposition of a complaint and an arrest involves bolstering, so, arguably, does the simple fact of a courtroom accusation by a purported eyewitness.

Bolstering is generally as harmless as it is pervasive. It is hard to see the prejudice in an officer's passing mention that a witness made an identification when the witness has just testified to that very identification at great length. The claim that such a brief reminder provides illusory corroboration for the eyewitness, the argument made in the leading case of *People v. Trowbridge*, is simply not convincing, even to the appellate attorneys who routinely invoke the *Trowbridge* rule.[16]

The real value of that rule, and the critical role of appellate counsel in invoking it, can be seen in its application in two of the sample cases. In one, the defendant had been identified by only one of three eyewitnesses, a witness who identified a man already in state prison as a coperpetrator. In the other, the complainant's identification was fully and credibly contradicted by an apparently disinterested bystander. In both cases, the court conceded that the evidence was legally sufficient despite its manifest weakness, and then went on to reverse on the basis of, respectively, an officer's oblique reference to the defendant's selection in a photo array and the "inferential" bolstering contained in the officer's brief arrest narrative.

In the latter case, a dissenting justice complained that "this case simply has nothing to do with the evils of improper bolstering."[17] In a sense, this could be said about almost all *Trowbridge* reversals. What they have "to do with" is the unreliability of eyewitness identification, and their value is in giving the court a procedural straw to grasp at when that evidence is too unreliable for comfort. Obviously, counsel may play a critical role in inducing the court's discomfort and in spotting what is often a slight and subtle testimonial error. In this connection, it is interesting to note that all four *Trowbridge* reversals in our sample were CAB cases. *Trowbridge* itself was a CAB case, and CAB attorneys are trained to look for bolstering errors that a vigilant attorney might easily overlook. Its success in this area may thus reflect less on the skill of individual attorneys than the advantages of pooled experience.

Although *Trowbridge* reversals seem more pretextual than reversals based on inadequate or imbalanced identification charges, they do not give the trial courts the same opportunity to insulate doubtful convictions from appellate review. A trial judge can avoid a *Daniels* reversal simply by reciting the identification charge recommended by the *Daniels* court and incorporated in the New York State Criminal Jury instructions. In contrast, no mechanical formula is proof against a *Trowbridge* error. Just because bolstering is subtle and pervasive, it can slip into the best-managed trials, leaving a foothold for appellate intervention.

Even more clearly than charge errors, however, which may actually contribute to an unjust result, *Trowbridge* violations illustrate the disturbing fortuity of a system of appellate review oriented toward procedural error. In examining doubtful jury convictions and their resistance to appellate review, Baldwin and McConville (1979) concluded that "from the defendant's point of view, the pity was that there had not been . . . a procedural irregularity or misdirection by the trial judge. . . . These defendants were for the purposes of appeal at a disadvantage precisely because their trials had been conducted properly and fairly."[18]

NEW YORK'S CRIMINAL REVERSALS IN NATIONAL PERSPECTIVE

The Chapper and Hanson survey of appellate dispositions, described in Chapter 5, analyzed the grounds for reversal and modification in four state intermediate appellate courts and one state supreme court.[19] Table 7–2, adapted from their findings, shows the percentage of reversals and modifications attributable in whole or part to different kinds of error.[20] These results are remarkably similar to our findings in New York, considering the varying powers of the courts and the differences in overall dispositions noted in Chapter 5. There was the same preponderance of trial errors, and the same paucity of issues concerning systemic problems in plea bargaining, effective assistance of counsel, and police misconduct.

As in New York, a majority of reversals in the five surveyed states arose from errors committed during trial, in the admission of evidence, in jury instructions and jury verdicts, and in a variety of procedural and "housekeeping" rulings. Relatively few reversals involved pretrial misconduct in searching, seizing, interrogating, or conducting identifications—about 10 percent in both jurisdictions. Few reversals were based on what are perhaps the two most common sources of injustice to indigent criminal defendants:

Table 7–2
Grounds for Favorable Action: National

Issue	Percentage of All Error Associated with the Issue
Admission/exclusion of evidence	20.6
Instructions	13.5
Procedural or discretionary ruling	13.1
Sufficiency of evidence	12.0
Merger of offenses	10.5
Suppression of evidence, statements, or identification	10.5
Ineffective assistance/waiver of counsel	6.0
Other constitutional claims (double jeopardy, speedy trial)	4.9
Jury selection or deliberation	3.4
Statutory interp. or application	2.2
Plea Voluntariness	2.2
Prosecutorial misconduct	1.1
	100%
	N=267

coercive or otherwise involuntary guilty pleas—4 percent in New York and 2.2 percent in the surveyed states—and ineffective assistance—less than 6 percent in the surveyed states and 1 percent in New York. A somewhat smaller percentage of reversals were subject to harmless error analysis in the surveyed states—about 50 percent, compared to 66 percent in New York.[21]

A similar preponderance of trial over pretrial error was found in Texas, where Gellis (1985) analyzed all criminal reversals from the first and second tier criminal appellate courts during part of 1983.[22] The single most common ground for reversal was charge error, cited in 90 cases and deemed "fundamental" in 44 of those. The second largest category was insufficient or no evidence, found in 61 cases.[23] Evidentiary errors, including suppression errors, were cited in 30 cases, prosecutorial misconduct in 22, and faulty indictments or informations in 21. Although in Texas the proportion of charge reversals is comparatively high, and that of evidentiary errors comparatively low, the state's pattern of reversals shares one critical feature with New York's and Chapper and Hanson's jurisdictions: the overwhelming majority of reversals are based on errors occurring during trial, committed on the record. Texas was no more demanding than her sister jurisdictions in reviewing counsel's performance: only three reversals were based on ineffectiveness grounds.[24]

CONCLUSION: THE IMPORTANCE OF APPELLATE ADVOCACY AND THE LIMITATIONS OF APPELLATE REVIEW

The picture of appellate review that emerges from this analysis is of a reviewing court convinced of the basic soundness of trial-level adjudication but receptive to the possibility of serious misconduct, error, and injustice in individual cases. If this is not the (perhaps mythic) activist court of the Warren Court era, aggressively enlarging defendants' rights and challenging the routine practices of the police and prosecutors, it is also not the complacent rubber stamp described by Thomas Davies, which sees its basic function as affirming the trial court's decision.

On the one hand, the court entertained few serious challenges to the basic way of doing business in the precinct houses and trial courts. It rarely looked beneath the usually smooth surface of plea colloquies, rarely held the performance of trial counsel to be ineffective, and never found eyewitness evidence too unreliable to sustain a conviction. This passivity is disturbing, since two decades of criminal justice research have given us strong reason to believe that many facially valid pleas are foisted on resigned, cynical, or confused defendants, that many trial attorneys fail to perform the most elementary tasks of criminal defense, and that many properly elicited identifications are highly unreliable, if not mistaken.

At the same time, this analysis of favorable action challenges the picture of appellate review as a mechanical search for technical error and confirms the critical role that zealous advocacy continues to play in correcting serious injustice in particular cases. Few cases in the disposition sample involved narrow errors with automatic relief; most involved the kind of judgment and balancing in which advocacy may play a critical role. In granting favorable action, the court was more often moved by a sense of substantial injustice than constrained by a clearcut error. Nevertheless, the court usually required a specific procedural or evidentiary error to reverse as a foothold for intervention. Like the legal rules seized on by Kalven and Zeisel's juries, these errors "liberated" the court to act on its sense of basic equity and fairness.

The preponderance of cases involving close factual analysis confirmed the continuing importance of skilled advocacy in raising doubts about the prosecution case, in suggesting alternative ways to view the evidence, and in making the defendant appear sinned against as well as sinning. Thus, despite the severe limits on appellate review and the increasingly technical nature of trial court error, appellate advocacy still appeared to have a significant role to play in rectifying individual injustices.

Perhaps the most critical function of the skilled advocate is to supply the court with a narrow, facially appropriate reason for what it wants to do on instinct; to provide an indirect means of rectifying or alleviating serious injustices that it is unable or unwilling to confront directly. We saw how appellate counsel might perform this function in cases involving suspect eyewitness identifications and where the court was willing to seize on fairly minor procedural errors to overturn the convictions of possible innocent defendants. The exploitation of fortuitous error is no substitute for the searching review of every conviction for accuracy and fairness, but it is better than nothing at all. Thus, zealous appellate advocacy appears to play an important role in a highly circumscribed system of appellate review.

NOTES

1. This corresponds to the narrow definition of favorable action used in Chapter 5.
2. While the court kept microfiche copies of all briefs, the volume of cases I was analyzing—almost 2,000 over a five year period—did not permit me to review the issues they raised or assess the strength of the evidence against the defendant.
3. In his study of California's First District Court of Appeals, Davies estimated that only 3 percent of all cases decided presented issues of first impression. "Affirmed: A Study of Criminal Appeals and Decision-Making Norms in a California Court of Appeals," *American Bar Foundation Research Journal* 82 (1982): 543, 588. One would expect the proportion of reversals and modifications presenting such issues to be significantly higher.
4. Of course, it may be that retained cases are more likely to be found wanting because they involve longer and more complex chains of inference, not because they have more, or more obscure, elements.
5. While I excluded all cases in which the court's intervention was merely technical—where it dismissed a lesser or a concurrent count—the errors in these cases were quite similar to those where the court improperly failed to submit a lesser included offense, had submitted a nonincluded offense, or had accepted an inconsistent verdict, as well as some of those involving insufficient evidence on aggravating or technical elements. All these errors involve confusion about the logical relationship of offenses in a complex statutory penal scheme.
6. The classification of a trial issue as one involving error or misconduct was not always clear-cut. When a prosecutor conducts, over defense protest, an unorthodox courtroom identification, it could be regarded as misconduct on the part of the prosecutor, for conducting a suggestive identification, or error by the court, for permitting the identification to take place. The refusal to grant a continuance could be regarded as a legal error in weighing need against inconvenience, or as poor trial management. I classified both as misconduct, the former because it was akin to police suggestiveness, the latter because it smacked of impatience more than improper judicial balancing. Obviously, these classifications were to some extent arbitrary.
7. This excludes the plea convictions vacated on the basis of a suppression issue raised in a hearing.
8. 35 N.Y. 2d 227.
9. 33 N.Y. 2d 623.
10. A study of the fate of reversed federal convictions subject to reprosecution revealed that 30 percent resulted in guilty or nolo pleas to the same or a lesser count.

Roper and Melone, "Does Procedural Due Process Make a Difference?" *Judicature* 63 (1981): 136, 139. The study did not reveal, however, what percentage of these had been guilty pleas to begin with.

11. The degree of probability depends on whether the error is of constitutional dimensions. If it is, it requires reversal unless it is found to be harmless beyond a reasonable doubt, *Chapman v. California* 386 U.S. 18 (1967); if not, it requires reversal unless the evidence was overwhelming and there was no substantial possibility that the error affected the outcome, *People v. Crimmins* 26 N.Y. 2d 319 (1970). The practical difference between these standards is hard to assess, particularly since the *Crimmins* standard is notoriously difficult to understand and apply.

12. It should be noted that all of these summation reversals were CAB cases.

13. See Leventhal, *Charges to the Jury and Requests to Charge in a Criminal Case: New York* (Deerfield, Ill.: Callahan, 1988 rev.). This language is not included, however, in the model charge on identification in the official New York *Criminal Jury Instructions*.

14. The court is substituting its own judgment for that of the jury in both types of cases, and it simply begs the question to claim without explanation that the adequacy of circumstantial evidence is a matter of sufficiency, while the adequacy of eyewitness identification is only a matter of weight. The distinction behind these labels seems to be that eyewitness cases rest, in a way that circumstantial cases do not, on the reliability of testifying witnesses, which is the "special province" of the jury. But while the jury may be in a far better position than the reviewing court to judge the *credibility* of eyewitnesses, they are in no better position to judge their *accuracy*, which is what most cases of disputed identity are about. The reviewing court may well be in a stronger position to second-guess the jury on the accuracy of sincere identifications than it is on the strength of circumstantial inferences.

While the court is no more expert than an intelligent jury at evaluating the logical strength of competing inferences in a circumstantial case, it knows far more than the average jury knows or could be made to know about the "vagaries of eyewitness identification." A decade of research has shown that the jurors' exposure to the actual eyewitness testimony will more likely confuse than sharpen their assessment of reliability. It is hard to avoid the suspicion that the court's self-restraint in eyewitness cases is influenced by the sheer volume of such cases and their vulnerability. There is no comparable danger in strictly circumstantial cases—such cases are as rare in state criminal prosecutions as eyewitness cases are common—so the court can override the jury without opening the floodgates.

15. Although the Court of Appeals held in *People v. Whalen*, 59 N.Y. 2d 273 (1983) that an expansive identification charge was desirable but not necessary, the Second Department continued to demand greater detail; see *People v. Boneparte* 98 AD 2d 772 (1983).

16. While all the *Trowbridge* reversals in the sample were CAB cases, a number of CAB attorneys have informally expressed skepticism about the rationale for the *Trowbridge* rule.

17. *People v. Brown*, 91 AD2d 639 (2d Dept. 1982).

18. Baldwin and McConville, *Jury Trials* (Oxford: Clarendon Press, 1979).

19. Chapper and Hanson, *Understanding Criminal Reversals*, (Williamsburg, Va.: National Center for State Courts, 1989).

20. The figure N = 267 gives the number of errors found, not the number of

reversals and modifications, which was somewhat smaller (since multiple errors were often found), nor the number of errors *claimed*, which was, of course, much larger.

21. The only striking difference between the national and the New York findings was in the proportion of reversible errors based on prosecutorial misconduct—15 percent in New York, only 1 percent in Chapper and Hanson's courts.

22. Gellis, "Reasons for Case Reversal in Texas: An Analysis," *St. Mary's Law Journal* 16 (1985): 299.

23. Errors in statutory and case law interpretation were next, found in 58 cases (most of which may have been from the higher court).

24. Davies's analysis of California reversals and modifications in 1974 also presents some interesting similarities and contrasts with our findings for New York City. "Affirmed: A Study of Criminal Appeals and Decision-Making Norms in a California Court of Appeal," *American Bar Foundation Research Journal* 82 (1982): 543, 613–19. It confirms the general impression of caution and inertia in the review of criminal convictions. In almost all the appeals that ended in reversal or modification, the errors either required automatic reversal or were reinforced by significant doubts about the defendant's guilt. As in New York, trial errors concerning evidence, instructions, and prosecutorial misconduct accounted for a large proportion of reversals and modifications; these were also the errors most often found harmless. In both states, a large majority of reversals were based on errors committed during trial.

There were three notable differences in the grounds for appellate intervention. While the California court never found the evidence legally insufficient, the largest single category of reversals in New York was insufficient evidence, albeit usually on technical or aggravating elements. This may reflect the greater complexity of New York penal statutes, based in large part on the Model Penal Code, or the indirect effect of the Appellate Division's factual review powers, which may have caused it to pay closer attention to gaps in the evidence.

A second striking contrast is the far greater proportion of California reversals based on police misconduct in searching and interrogating—20 percent versus 7 percent. In Chapter 1, I suggested that appellate court regulation of police misconduct has been impaired by the increased appeals consciousness of the police and by their ability to discourage appellate scrutiny by making a record indicating formal compliance with the requirements imposed on them. The New York police may simply have been better at investigating or testifying by 1980–85 than their California counterparts were in 1974, or the New York courts may have been less interested in scrutinizing their conduct. The relative inattention of the Appellate Division to search issues is particularly disturbing because of the Court of Appeals's retreat from this area under the "mixed question" doctrine, which precludes its review of most issues in which legal and factual determinations commingle.

Finally, Davies found that almost all reversals in California involved cases with serious procedural errors and significant weaknesses in the prosecution evidence. In New York, in contrast, there were two areas in which the appellate courts sometimes reversed in the absence of serious procedural error: where the evidence was legally insufficient, and where the evidence of the defendant's identity was highly suspect.

Part III

THE CONTINUING CHALLENGE OF CRIMINAL APPELLATE REPRESENTATION: IMPROVING QUALITY, CONSERVING RESOURCES, AND BROADENING IMPACT

Part III addresses three critical issues raised by the preceding research and analysis: how to improve the quality of indigent appellate representation in conflict cases, how to conserve appellate resources for more meritorious cases without compromising the attorney's duty of zealous advocacy, and how to increase the role of appellate representation in correcting concealed errors and systematic injustices. The first issue is raised by the poor quality of 18b appellate representation in a large proportion of conflict cases; the second by judicial impatience with the low merit of criminal appeals and by the high rate of affirmance without opinion; the third by the inability or reluctance of appellate courts to directly confront major sources of injustice in criminal adjudication.

The problem of quality may be the most tractable: while present levels of funding are not adequate to ensure high-quality representation for all defendants wishing to appeal, a significant improvement in quality can probably be achieved without massive increases in appellate funding and perhaps without a basic reorganization of the system for providing appellate defense services. Moreover, a significant relaxation in the conflicts policy of the institutional defender could significantly reduce the share of the caseload assigned to substitute counsel. The prospects for conserving and targeting appellate resources are less encouraging: there is an unavoidable tradeoff between reliability and economy in making allocation decisions in an adversary system. The present system of appellate review, however, might benefit from measures to enlarge the record in routine appeals and to expand the scope of appellate factfinding.

Chapters 8 and 9 present complimentary approaches to improving the representation of the large minority of indigent defendants in New York City now assigned to the 18b appellate panel: increasing the share of cases rejected by the primary defender and upgrading the quality of substitute counsel. The first approach requires a significant change in the law and policy governing conflicts of interest on the appellate level. The second approach involves a variety of nonexclusive options for reform, whose appraisal is complicated by the need to consider the relationship between appellate and trial defense.

Chapter 8 considers the first approach, organizationally simple but doctrinally complex. It argues for a significant relaxation of the conflicts rules, which would require CAB to represent a large share of the indigent defendants it now rejects. The first part of the chapter develops an analysis of conflicts of interest in the criminal appellate setting, which the second part applies in reviewing CAB's evolving conflicts policy. Readers may safely skim the first part of the chapter if they are more interested in policy reforms than in their doctrinal underpinnings.

Chapter 9 considers a variety of organizational changes to improve the quality of representation in conflicts cases, from the "divorce" of the primary trial and appellate defenders to the creation of a "mid-range" appellate defender. The chapter addresses issues of national importance in the organization of appellate defense services, but focuses on New York City, whose problems are at once representative and idiosyncratic. It reviews two ongoing experiments in upgraded representation, the California appellate projects and Appellate Defender Office in New York's First Department. I am cautiously optimistic about several possibilities for reform, but find too many tradeoffs and uncertainties to give my unqualified endorsement to any one.

Chapter 10 examines measures to "screen" criminal appeals to focus judicial attention on the closest and most significant cases. It argues that attempts to conserve appellate resources for more "deserving" cases inevitably create more problems than they solve, compromising the advocate's role, sacrificing reliability, or increasing the complexity of appellate litigation. It concludes somewhat pessimistically that New York's system of unrestricted appellate review, despite its strain and tedium, is as fair and reliable as any existing or proposed "tracking" system.

Chapter 11 explores several ways of altering the conventional roles of appellate judges and lawyers to improve the oversight of criminal justice for indigent defendants. It considers the possible benefits and costs in empowering appellate courts to receive new evidence, in increasing collaboration between trial and appellate counsel to enlarge the record and generate test cases, and in involving the convicted defendant in the review process.

Finally, it proposes an expanded role for appellate defenders, which casts them not only as advocates for indigent defendants but as monitors of the trial-level participants. Like the preceding chapter, it concludes on a conservative note, reaffirming the importance of the traditional functions of the indigent appellate defender.

8

Conflicts of Interest and Indigent Appellate Defense

This chapter examines the source and justification of the conflicts rules under which CAB disqualifies itself from representing over 40 percent of all indigent criminal appellants. In Chapter 6, we found that the factual basis for CAB conflicts claims was largely accurate. Here, we examine the legal basis for these claims: the argument that it would violate the professional duties of CAB or its individual attorneys to represent the defendant under these circumstances. Given the delay and the risk of inferior representation which reassignment to 18b entails, it is important to consider (1) whether the restrictions on CAB representation imposed by the American Bar Association's Code of Professional Responsibility (CPR) are reasonable, and (2) whether CAB's conflicts policy is dictated by those restrictions.

My thesis is that the official conflict rules are unduly restrictive, that CAB's conflicts policy is even more so, and that even without significant organizational changes, CAB could provide fully adequate, unimpaired representation for a large share of the convicted defendants it now declines to represent. I will begin by reviewing the official rules on conflicts of interest and the case law and literature on conflicts in criminal representation. I will distinguish three risks in the representation of potentially conflicting interests: impaired judgment and performance, adverse impact on the fact finder, and the appearance of impropriety. All three risks arise in the joint representation of codefendants and other related clients at the trial level.

I will argue that these risks are relatively minor when clients with potentially conflicting interests are represented by different attorneys within an appellate defender's office. First, even when a single attorney represents such clients on appeal, the risks from actual "adversity" will be more limited, foreseeable, and manageable than at trial, although significant enough to discourage joint representation. Second, those risks are greatly attenuated by the division of labor within the defender's office. Finally, the risks that do exist in these circumstances are no greater than those faced by unrelated defendants represented before the same court by the appellate defender, whose interests are made adverse by their competition for judicial intervention. If it is permissible to subject unrelated defendants to these risks, there is no principled basis for barring multiple representation when the adversity between defendants falls into one of the traditional conflicts categories.

The courts of several jurisdictions, including New York, have recognized that the dangers of representing clients with potentially adverse interests are more limited and tractable for an institutional defender than for a private law firm or solo practioner, and at least one court has recognized that the risks from actual adversity are less severe on appeal than at trial. Several related factors, however, have constrained judicial approval of liberal conflicts and waiver policies: an insistence on treating the defender organization itself, and not its individual attorneys, as the unit of analysis for conflicts purposes; a concern that the representation of clients with adverse interests will create an appearance of impropriety that cannot be dispelled by client consent; a belief that the indigent client lacks a constitutional interest in choice of counsel; and doubts that the indigent's choice between possibly impaired and probably incompetent representation can be regarded as voluntary. The New York courts in particular have displayed a striking ambivalence about the possibility of avoiding and waiving conflicts of interests in institutional defense.

In the second part of the chapter, I will examine CAB's own conflicts policies in light of these constraints, pointing out the respects in which they are more restrictive than even the most conservative interpretation of the CPR's conflicts rules would require. I will argue that these restrictive rules can only be justified by CAB's administrative convenience, and that its convenience is outweighed by the significant costs borne by clients reassigned to 18b counsel. There are, however, some conflicts for which CAB cannot adopt a more liberal policy, particularly those arising from the possible ineffectiveness of CDD trial counsel.

I will conclude that even under a conservative interpretation of the CPR conflict rules, CAB could represent a significant share of the indigent appellants it now rejects, although it might have to incur considerable administrative costs to do so. There are, however, two significant barriers to a broader liberalization. First, the New York courts and Bar Association have applied the conflict rules in a very rigid and mechanical way to institutional defenders. Second, in the areas of possible ineffectiveness and intractable client grievances, CAB must be relieved even under the most liberal interpretation of the conflict rules.

CONFLICTS OF INTEREST IN THE CODE OF PROFESSIONAL RESPONSIBILITY

Disciplinary Rule 5–101(A) of the CPR prohibits a lawyer from accepting employment if her own economic or personal interests are likely to effect "the exercise of [her] professional judgment on behalf of a client." D.R. 5–105(A) requires a lawyer to "decline proffered employment if the exercise of [her] independent professional judgment in behalf of the client will be or is likely to be adversely affected . . . or if it [the employment] would be likely to involve [her] in representing different interests."[1] D.R. 5–105(C), however, permits a lawyer to represent multiple clients in the situations covered by D.R. 5–105(A) "if it is obvious that [the lawyer] can adequately represent the interests of each and if each consents to the representation after full disclosure of the possible effects of such representation on the exercise of [her] independent professional judgment." Finally, the CPR's ninth Canon of Professional Ethics commands lawyers to "avoid even the appearance of impropriety."

These rules are generally understood to enforce two of the basic duties owed by counsel to her client in an adversary system: loyalty and confidentiality. The lawyer is prohibited from representing conflicting interests, or from representing a client whose interests conflict with his own, because of the danger that the conflict may (1) prevent the lawyer from representing the client with the single-minded zeal that her role requires, violating his duty of loyalty, and (2) tempt her to "misappropriate" her client's secrets, violating her duty to confidentiality. Although the notion of a "conflict-of-interest" is central to legal ethics, however, its definition is complex, ambiguous, and widely misunderstood.

The Definition of a Conflict of Interest

Justice Marshall observed in *Cuyler v. Sullivan* (1980) that the term "conflict of interest" was "often used and little defined."[2] He summarized the conventional view as follows:

> There is a possibility of conflict . . . if the interests of the defendants may diverge at some point so as to place the attorney under inconsistent duties. There is an actual . . . conflict of interests if, during the course of the representation, the defendants' interests do diverge with respect to a material factual or legal issue or to a course of action.

There appear to be two distinct elements in Marshall's definition of an actual conflict of interest: (1) divergent or adverse interests—(to oversimplify) what is best for one client is not best for the other and (2) inconsistent duties—as a result of these divergent interests, the lawyer's duties to one client require her to act in a way which violates her duties to the other. These elements are not really distinct, however, since clients will not have divergent interests in the intended sense unless the attorney has inconsistent duties.[3] The lawyer has a duty to serve the interests of her clients, and a conflict will arise whenever the interests of one require her to act against the interests of the other. The lawyer will act against the client's interests not only when she actually harms them, but whenever the risk of harm to the client clearly exceeds the prospective benefit.

Much of the conflicts literature has focused on the distinction between actual and potential conflicts: on determining how likely it is that the interests of one client will require acts that are adverse to the other's interests, and on the questions of how, when, and by whom that determination should be made.[4] There are good reasons for this emphasis: the distinction may be critical in defining an "appearance of impropriety" and in restricting the scope of client waiver.[5] Less attention has been paid, however, to the distinctions among actual conflicts, impaired representation, and actual prejudice, distinctions that may be as important in deciding whether conflicts can be tolerated by the court or waived by the client.

An attorney whose duty to one defendant requires her to act against the interests of the other will have an *actual conflict*, but that conflict may not result in *impaired representation*: she may represent each defendant as zealously and skillfully as a separate attorney. To illustrate the distinction with an extreme example, imagine an attorney who represents two defendants at a joint trial in which both testify to having been unwitting participants in a robbery conceived by the other. While this obvious conflict may impair her representation of one or both, for example, she may forego any cross-examination of their mutually incriminating testimony, it need not do so, for example, she may subject each defendant to a blistering cross-examination on behalf of the other. If so, her representation of each defendant will damage the other just because it is unimpaired, and neither will receive poorer representation as a result of their adverse interests.[6]

Still, either defendant may suffer *actual prejudice* from his unimpaired representation: He may be worse off than he would have been with a separate attorney, not because of how the attorney performed, but because of the impact of her joint representation on the fact finder. Thus, the jurors may be more likely to find the inconsistencies in the defendants' stories discrediting to both just because they were elicited by a single attorney. Or the jurors may assume that the attorney really believes one defendant and not the other, and draw inferences adverse to one defendant from comparisons of the attorney's demeanor towards the two, comparisons they would not have made if each defendant had a different attorney. In both cases, the attorney will have provided unimpaired representation, viewed in isolation from its effects on the fact finder, but at least one client will have been prejudiced by their joint representation.[7]

It is also possible, conversely, for one or both clients to suffer impaired representation without prejudice. This will be the case whenever their attorney's ineptitude or bad judgment has no harmful consequences or consequences that are on balance beneficial. Thus, imagine that in the trial described in the last paragraph, the attorney is so enervated by her role reversals that she delivers rambling, inaudible summations for both defendants. It may be that each defendant actually benefits more by having a weak argument made for his codefendant than he loses by having a weak argument made for himself. If so, both defendants are better off for their joint, impaired representation than they would have been with separate, unimpaired representation.[8] Representation can also be impaired without prejudice in cases so hopeless that the attorney's skill and zeal could make no difference—if such cases exist.

Lower courts sometimes confuse actual conflict with impaired representation and prejudice. The confusion is understandable, since inconsistent duties often lead to impaired performance and prejudice, while impaired performance may be symptomatic of conflict.[9] Moreover, a conflict in criminal representation does not require reversal under the Sixth Amendment unless it can be shown to have impaired the attorney's performance—although it is not necessary to show actual prejudice.[10] Nevertheless, it is critical for my purposes to define "actual conflict" strictly in terms of adverse interests and inconsistent duties, because my claim will be that an institutional appellate defender can represent actually conflicting interests *without* impairment or prejudice.

The Appearance of Impropriety and the Possibilities for Waiver

Two distinct, but related, concerns appear to underlie the CPR's broad restrictions on representing clients with adverse interests. The first is that even a conscientious attorney may not be able to resist the subtle and often subliminal effects of divided loyalties on her professional judgment. The code's main concern is not that the attorney will deliberately shortchange one client for the sake of another—though this can certainly happen—but that her judgment of what is best for one will be distorted by her desire to promote the other's interests or reconcile their interests.

If the attorney could trust her own judgment about the risks posed by adverse interests, there would be no need for a blanket disqualification rule. If she found her clients' interests adverse, she could decide for herself whether she would be able to represent each client as effectively as a zealous attorney with no conflict, and continue her joint representation if there was no significant threat of impaired performance or prejudicial impact. Those threats, however, may be very difficult to appreciate: it may well be easier for an attorney to recognize adverse interests than to gauge their prejudicial impact, especially on her own performance. In imposing a blanket disqualification rule, the CPR protects the attorney, and her clients, against her fallible judgment and professional hubris.

The second concern is that even if the attorney can exercise unimpaired judgment, her representation of clients with adverse interests will still create the "appearance of impropriety." Representation may appear improper to the client, the court, or the public either because they do not believe that the attorney can actually exercise unimpaired judgment, or because, even if they believe she can, they simply find it "inappropriate" for a single attorney to represent conflicting interests.[11] The distinction between a lack of confidence and a feeling of impropriety, blurred by the CPR, will become significant in considering the division of labor in an institutional defender's office, which can reduce the both the actual and apparent risk of impairment, but not necessarily the feeling of impropriety, in representing clients with adverse interests.

There is a related ambiguity in the CPR's provision for waiver. On alternative readings, D.R. 5–105(C) may permit clients with "different interests" to consent to representation by the same attorney (1) only if the attorney concludes that those interests are not adverse, (2) only if the attorney is confident that even if those interests are adverse, her "independent professional judgment" will not be impaired, or (3) only if the attorney is confident that she can provide each client with minimally adequate (though possibly impaired) representation.

The CPR does not clearly favor any one of these positions,[12] and the determination of which is correct depends on whether, under D.R. 5–105(C), it can ever be "*obvious* that [the attorney] can adequately represent" clients even if their interests actually diverge, or even if they not only diverge, but threaten the attorney's "independent professional judgment." The requirement that the adequacy of representation be "obvious" may suggest that waiver is only permitted when it will not create the appearance of impropriety, not that appearance can be overridden by client consent.

It is not clear whether the CPR's presumption of impaired judgment is rebuttable, or whether the threat of impairment is waivable by the client. The first interpretation of 5–105(C) suggests a negative answer to both questions, since it limits waiver to circumstances where there is no adversity; the second suggests a negative answer to the latter question, since it limits waiver to circumstances where there is no impairment. If either interpretation is correct, it seems odd that the only danger the attorney must disclose to the client is one that either does not arise or that he has already ruled out—the risk of impaired judgment.

The third, most expansive interpretation requires no more than minimal competence for "adequate" representation and permits the informed client to choose the lesser of two evils. He can continue to be represented by a highly skilled attorney whose judgment, even impaired by conflict, is likely to be considerably better than that of substitute counsel.[13] Although courts sometimes appear to accept this expansive view in theory, they are, as we will see, quite reluctant to accept client waiver of possible impairment in practice, particularly when the attorney facing the conflict has been assigned rather than retained.[14]

Conflicts of Interest in Criminal Representation

In the context of criminal representation, the CPR's conflicts and waiver provisions must be applied in conformity with the defendant's Sixth Amendment right to counsel, which has been construed by the Supreme Court to include both a right to the effective assistance of counsel and a qualified "right" to counsel of choice. In *Glasser v. U.S.* (1942) the U.S. Supreme Court held that the representation of conflicting interests in a criminal trial will sometimes, but not always, deny the defendant the right to the effective assistance of counsel, though that right, like others of constitutional dimension, is subject to waiver.[15] While the Court has never recognized an unqualified right to counsel of choice, lower federal courts recognize a strong presumption against interfering with the defendant's choice of counsel.

In an influential article, John Geer proposed a per se ban on the representation of criminal codefendants, the principal type of conflict of interest in criminal trials.[16] He argued that, for a single attorney, the temptations to compromise the interests of a codefendant in plea bargaining and trial strategy were too pervasive and subtle to be ruled out in advance, so that waiver was prohibited under the CPR: "Given the manifold circumstances under which a defense attorney's professional trial judgment may be impaired... it would seem that it could never be *obvious* that a defense attorney could adequately represent the interests of codefendants in criminal case."[17] Moreover, even a knowing waiver would not eliminate the threat that the lawyer's divided loyalties would undermine the integrity of criminal adjudication: "the lawyer's professional duty to the courts and the administration of justice remains unfulfilled whether or not he obtains the consent of his clients."

While the Supreme Court in *Cuyler* acknowledged that "a possible conflict of interest inheres in almost every instance of multiple representation," it refused to adopt a per se ban on the trial representation of codefendants by a single attorney. The court recognized that multiple trial representation was frequently harmless and often beneficial, even when the defendants had some adverse interests. While it urged close scrutiny by the trial judge, the Court recognized the possibility of knowing and intelligent waiver.

In the next two sections, I will examine whether the risks of multiple representation emphasized by Geer and recognized by the Supreme Court apply on the appellate level. I will conclude that the risks of joint representation are limited but still significant for a single appellate attorney. Those risks are negligible, however, for different appellate attorneys within the same appellate defenders office.[18]

WHAT RISKS ARE INVOLVED IN THE APPELLATE REPRESENTATION OF CODEFENDANTS AND OTHER CLIENTS WITH RECOGNIZED ADVERSE INTERESTS?

The two generally recognized sources of appellate conflicts of interest are the (1) the adverse interests of codefendants and other related defendants, such as a defendant and the principal witness against him in a previous trial, and (2) the adverse interests of the defendant and his attorney, when the attorney or an affiliate represented the defendant in a related proceeding. In this section, I will focus on the first source of conflict, because it accounts for a large majority of the cases from which an institutional defender must disqualify itself, and because it has been the subject of most of the case law and commentary in the area. In reviewing CAB conflicts policy at the end of the chapter, I will discuss the distinct problems raised by conflicts between attorney and client, which may pose a more serious and less tractable threat to zealous and effective appellate representation.

A single fact limits the risks posed by adverse interests in criminal appellate representation: the main work of an appellate attorney consists in fashioning the strongest possible arguments from a frozen record. Because the record is frozen, a criminal appellate attorney rarely faces the kind of strategic and tactical choices that might be compromised by divided loyalties: There are no decisions about the admission of evidence or testimony which could help one client at the other's expense. Unlike in civil cases, there are no preappeal negotiations that might tempt her to make a deal for one client harmful to the other.

Moreover, the general ban on using off-the-record information virtually eliminates the problem of confidentiality on an appellate level. An appellate attorney rarely receives, and could rarely utilize, confidential information from a present or former client, and an appellate court will have no reason to suspect that the defendant's attorney made or failed to make an argument because he possessed confidential information.

Generally, then, an appeal has none of the contingencies which, at the trial level, determine if a potential conflict will become an actual one: for example, whether the prosecution will seek to introduce a piece of evidence harmful to one defendant but helpful to another. For this reason, I do not find it useful to distinguish possible from actual conflict at the appellate level. Once the appellate attorney has obtained a full record of the trial proceedings and has communicated with her clients, there will rarely be additional possibilities for conflict, only varying degrees of uncertainty about whether the most effective arguments for one client will be detrimental to the other.[19]

The difference in the risks posed by conflicts of interests at the trial and appellate levels has been recognized by the Supreme Court of Illinois. In *People v. Rogers* (1981), the Court held that

> appellate representation does not involve to the same extent the risk attending trial representation that confidential communications will be abused or that divided loyalty will interfere with an attorney's ability to develop a favorable trial record [citations omitted]. We believe that these critical distinctions dictate a standard less rigorous than the one applied to conflicts of interest in trial representation.[20]

Although the risks of impaired judgment and performance may be considerably more limited on appeal, however, they are great enough to discourage the simultaneous representation of codefendants and other related clients by a single attorney. Even on appeal, the interests of codefendants may be sharply adverse. It may be helpful to one defendant to claim that the other was more culpable or heavily implicated; that he was prejudiced by their joint trial or by the admission of the other's statements or property; that he was coerced, misled, or overborne, or that he received a comparatively harsh sentence. These adverse interests pose the familiar risks of impaired judgment by the attorney, prejudicial impact on the court, and improper appearances.

The primary risk in joint appellate representation is that a single attorney will fail to discern, appreciate, or effectively raise arguments that would help one client at the expense of another. Her judgments about what issues to raise and how to raise them are often subtle and easily swayed by a natural tendency to see her clients' interests as compatible. Even if she recognizes that a nonfrivolous argument could be made for one client that would be detrimental to the other, she may underestimate its potential benefits and decline to make it, or present it in a way that reduces its force as well as its prejudicial impact.[21] Her desire to reconcile her clients' interests may thus leave one or both defendants with less effective representation than he would have received from separate counsel.[22]

Even if the attorney's judgment is not impaired by adverse interests, the clients may still be prejudiced by their joint representation. While judges may recognize intellectually that a lawyer does not "vouch" for the arguments she makes for each client and that the same body of law and facts may support conflicting arguments, they may still have a subconscious tendency to discount both of the conflicting claims advanced by a single attorney.[23] Equally disturbing, they may try to "read" the attorney's judgment about the relative merit of the conflicting claims and rely on that judgment in their own decision-making. The client with the disfavored claim will be worse off than he would have been with separate representation, where the court would have been far less likely to impute a comparative judgment to his attorney.[24]

Finally, the representation of adverse interests by a single appellate attorney may create the appearance of impropriety. This appearance will rarely be as disturbing as at trial, because there is less reason to fear impairment, prejudice, or betrayal from the existence of adverse interests. In the relatively dispassionate setting of the appellate courtroom, it may also *seem* less disloyal to raise arguments for one client at the expense of another. Still, the appearance of disloyalty is only reduced, not eliminated. There is still something unseemly about an attorney disparaging his client's claims or arguing against his interests.

Thus, despite the circumscribed nature of appellate advocacy, the representation of codefendants and other related clients on appeal involves many of the same risks as joint representation on the trial level: impaired judgment by the attorney, distorted impact on the fact finder, and the appearance of impropriety. These risks create a strong presumption against joint representation by a single appellate attorney.

WHAT RISKS ARE PRESENT WHEN CLIENTS WITH ADVERSE INTERESTS ARE REPRESENTED BY DIFFERENT ATTORNEYS FROM THE SAME APPELLATE DEFENDER'S OFFICE?

The risks of impaired advocacy and diminished credibility are quite different when the "attorney" representing clients with adverse interests is a large institutional defender which assigns those clients to different lawyers. While the defender itself may technically face a conflict in representing clients with adverse interests, that conflict will not create inconsistent duties for the individual attorney as long as she can give her undivided loyalty to the client she represents. There will only be a conflict of interest *for her* if the defender's other commitments pose a threat to her representation: if her advocacy may be impaired, or her impact on the court diminished, by the fact that she is affiliated with an organization representing another client with adverse interests. If her effectiveness is not threatened, her affiliation is irrelevant for all practical purposes; at worst, it will create an exaggerated appearance of impropriety.

It is certainly possible that attorneys within the same office will feel some pressure to maintain consistency in the claims made for different clients and that judges will be adversely affected by inconsistencies. The risks of affiliation clearly depend on the size, structure, and policies of the institutional defender: the degree of centralization or coordination in its brief-supervision process, the extent to which its attorneys are aware of and involved in each other's cases, and the organization's commitment to providing zealous representation for every client. The risks also depend on the perceptions and attitudes of the reviewing court: how much attention it pays and weight it gives to the affiliation of the attorneys appearing before it.

Typically, the pressures for consistency within an institutional defender's office will be negligible. Even in a small and informal office, individual attorneys will concentrate on their own appeals, getting only occasional, haphazard exposure to their colleagues' cases. Most defender offices give their attorneys a great deal of autonomy and provide more incentives for competition than collusion. In a large or medium size office, even the supervisors will rarely know who the organization is representing, let alone how their cases are being argued. Most important, external pressure will rarely impair the *judgment* of the individual attorney—unlike an attorney personally representing clients with adverse interests, she will not be in danger of confusing or distorting those interests in her own mind. As long as she can clearly distinguish her client's interests from those of her colleagues' clients, she can rely on strong professional norms to resist compromising the former to accommodate the latter.

Moreover, appellate judges are less likely to be troubled by inconsistencies in arguments from the same office than from a single attorney. While the chief appellate defender will usually be the attorney of record for every case assigned to her office, the actual arguments will be made by different attorneys. The fact that the conflicting claims are raised by different attorneys should reduce any tendency the judges feel to discount them because of their inconsistency.

While affiliation poses some risk of impaired advocacy and reduced impact, that risk is no greater for codefendants and other clients with prior adverse interests than it is for unrelated clients whose adversity arises from the appeals process itself: from aspects of their cases or of the law that makes it advantageous for them to raise legally inconsistent arguments, from the nature of the relief they are seeking, which may be available in only limited supply, or from their common representation by a defender under judicial pressure to "screen" cases of differing merit. These circumstances give rise to actual conflicts: the interests of the clients diverge, imposing inconsistent duties on the defender and threatening the effectiveness of the assigned attorneys. There can be no principled basis for treating these conflicts differently than those arising among related clients.

Inconsistent Arguments

Hertz and Ogletree have discussed the adversity that arises among unrelated defendants who raise conflicting doctrinal claims.[25] They note that it is generally thought improper for an appellate defender to raise conflicting arguments before the same tribunal but not before different ones. This distinction may suggest a concern for reduced credibility—that a court hearing two conflicting arguments from the same defender may be inclined to discount them both—or a concern for directly adverse consequences—if the conflicting arguments are presented to different courts, they may rule differently, so the success of one client will not necessarily mean the failure of another.

The first concern may be somewhat exaggerated—the courts generally understand the adversary's role—while the second may be shortsighted—conflicting doctrinal decisions by different courts will eventually be reconciled by a higher court, at the expense of one client or the other. Nevertheless, these concerns are as valid for doctrinal conflicts as for recriminations among codefendants: if the court is not disturbed by joint representation in the former case, it should not be troubled by joint representation in the latter case. Clearly, this argument is double-edged, since it might be taken, as Hertz and Ogletree in fact take it, to favor greater restrictions on the advocacy of conflicting doctrinal claims by a single defender's office.[26]

The typical inconsistency faced by appellate attorneys from a large office is less abstract than the doctrinal conflicts described by Hertz and Ogletree but more general than a dispute between codefendants. For example, A argues that his client's prior conviction for prostitution should not have been admitted to impeach her because of its limited relevance for credibility; B, next on the calendar, attacks the credibility of a complaining witness because she was a prostitute. The fact that these positions may be logically reconcilable does not make their juxtaposition less awkward. Such small inconsistencies are inevitable when more than half of the criminal cases on a given day are argued by attorneys from a single office.

While most judges appreciate that an attorney must take positions inconsistent with those taken by her colleagues, and sometimes with her own positions in other cases, their very awareness of that fact may detract from the attorney's impact—it is hard to be persuaded by an argument while being reminded of the constraints under which it is made. Veteran trial attorneys insist that they can only persuade a jury if they themselves appear fully convinced, and judges are hardly immune from the tacit vouching of a skilled appellate attorney. Institutional attorneys will obviously be less successful at such vouching when they are presenting conflicting arguments back to back.

While any attorney appearing frequently before the same tribunal may find herself making inconsistent arguments, the attorneys working for an institutional defender will find themselves in this awkward position more often. Two other areas of potential conflict between unrelated defendants are even more specific to an institutional defender, since they arise largely because of the size and share of the court's criminal docket handled by that defender. These are (1) the tensions inherent in representing a large share of the clients seeking the same limited relief from the same court, and (2) the resulting judicial pressure on institutional attorneys to indicate the differing merit of their cases.

Limited Relief

The interests of unrelated clients will diverge whether all of them seek a result—a leave grant, a remand, or a reversal—that they cannot all obtain, whenever they are competing for a limited number of "prizes." The degree of adversity among the defender's clients will obviously depend on a number of factors: the share of the "contestants" a single defender represents, the ratio of contestants to prizes, and the extent to which the number of prizes is fixed or flexible. While the appellate courts are not legally restricted in the number of "prizes" they can bestow, there are a number of settings in which the success of one defendant marginally disadvantages the others.

Sometimes the constraint will be a matter of statutory definition—a majority of sentences within the legal limits cannot be disproportionately severe, and a finding that one client's sentence is excessive may raise the court's threshold, however slightly, for finding another's excessive. Sometimes, the constraint will be a matter of administrative convenience or necessity—the Court of Appeals lacks the time to hear more than a small fraction of criminal cases, and a leave grant in one may diminish, however slightly, the odds of a leave grant in another. The attorney seeking leave from a court that grants one of 20 leave applications is implicitly arguing that her case is worthier than the next 19, an awkward posture when her colleagues are making the same claim for 11 or 12 of the other 19 cases.[27]

Competition for limited relief will create inconsistent duties for the defender organization itself: the stronger the arguments it makes for any one client or group of clients, the more it reduces the chances of the others. If each attorney within the defender's office represents only a small number of defendants, however, the adversity among *her* clients will be truly de minimis; the important question is whether the defender's commitment to so many other clients seeking the same relief will prevent her from representing each of her own clients as zealously as an unaffiliated attorney, or make her advocacy for them less persuasive to the court.

The threat of reduced effectiveness in this setting is no different than it is for codefendants or other clients with preexisting adversities: the attorney may feel pressure to avoid inconsistent claims or may lose credibility in failing to do so. For example, a defender's office might pressure its attorneys to reserve excessive sentence arguments for exceptional or compelling cases, not because a weak argument would damage an ordinary case, which would be a legitimate consideration, but because a practice of claiming excessiveness in every case with a higher-than-minimum sentence might make the court less attentive to the small minority of grossly disproportionate sentences. Moreover, the office might be wrong in its policy but right in its perception—the courts really might begin to regard its excessive sentence arguments as pro forma.[28]

These risks are certainly as great as those faced in the appellate representation of antagonistic codefendants. There is an additional factor which exacerbates the danger: judicial pressure on the defender to "screen" its cases. While the court may have little interest in learning which of a pair of inconsistent claims the codefendants' attorney "really believes," it may feel a strong temptation to learn from the attorneys representing a large share of its criminal appellants which cases they find "truly meritorious."

Judicial Pressure to Screen Cases

In Chapter 1, we observed that appellate defenders representing a majority or large plurality of indigent defendants before an overburdened court may be subject to intense pressure to conserve judicial resources by indicating, through the length and tenor of their briefs and oral arguments, the cases that really warrant the court's close attention. The larger the share of the court's criminal docket handled by the defender, the greater the pressure to screen cases. A defender handling 66 percent of all criminal appeals, like CAB, can obviously perform a more valuable screening function than one handling 10 percent, like the California State Appellate Defender. The pressure to screen will be even greater where the assignment process itself reveals little or nothing about the merit of the appeal, as in New York, where cases are assigned on a more or less random basis.[29]

The demand for information on the relative merits of the appeal confronts the appellate defender with a kind of Sophie's Choice: to sacrifice the interests of many or most clients by implicitly denigrating the merits of their cases in order to win closer attention for a minority of strong cases, or to risk cursory review for all clients by refusing to assist the court. The harm in choosing the first course is not merely in the lost benefits of an oral argument or a longer brief, which may be negligible, but in the message to the court that the client's case is not worthy of its close attention.

The court's expectation of screening by an appellate defender changes the significance of its tactical choices. While the decision to submit rather than argue may do no harm to a weak or simple case where the court draws no inference from that decision, it may be severely prejudicial in a system where the court takes submission as a sign of slight merit. In such a system, an appellate defender committed to zealous advocacy may feel that it has to argue every case, just to avoid this adverse inference. Such "overrepresentation" may reduce the attention paid to the defender's cases by an overburdened court.

It is not clear how much of this pressure is actually felt by the individual attorney in the institutional defender's office. The evidence of such pressure adduced in Chapter 1 came from attorneys in policy-making positions, whose own response to judicial pressure may well have limited the extent to which it was brought to bear on individual attorneys. Despite the courts' frequently manifested impatience, William Hellerstein encouraged CAB staff attorneys to argue every trial appeal. That policy not only protected the attorneys from internal pressure to be selective, but relieved them of the burden of justifying to the court their decision to argue a particular case. But Hellerstein's uncompromising policy may well have resulted in more perfunctory treatment from a court which expected to find little merit in the average CAB oral argument.

The recognition of these adverse interests among unrelated criminal appellants provides a further reason for liberalizing the conflicts rules as they are applied to institutional defense organizations. If codefendants with conflicting interests cannot be represented by two attorneys simply because they work for the same defender, it is hard to see how *any* two defendants can be represented by an organization which obtains certain forms of relief for some clients only at the "expense" of others, and which faces judicial pressure to make tradeoffs among its clients. These "conflicts," like the more traditional ones, need to be analyzed from the perspective of the individual attorney, treating her institutional affiliation as but one factor capable of compromising her zeal. This has not been the analysis adopted by most courts, however, which have taken a far more mechanical approach to multiple representation by an institutional defender in traditional conflict settings.

THE JUDICIAL TREATMENT OF CONFLICTS WITHIN AN INSTITUTIONAL DEFENDER'S OFFICE

Most legal authorities treat a law firm as a single entity, and a public defender as a law firm, for conflicts purposes. A 1978 ABA Ethics Opinion held that a public defender was disqualified under the same circumstances as a private law firm, so that defendants with conflicting interests could not even be represented by different branch offices. The opinion blandly noted that a defendant who would have to be relieved under this rule "can be represented by other counsel." While some jurisdictions have been willing to apply a less stringent standard to institutional defenders than private law firms, only one, Illinois, has begun to analyze conflicts from the perspective of the individual attorney, treating her institutional affiliation as but one factor capable of compromising her loyalty to her clients.

New York was one of the first jurisdictions to recognize that institutional defenders like the Legal Aid Society (LAS) should *not* be treated the same as private firms for conflicts purposes. In *People v. Wilkins* (1971), the Court of Appeals stated:

> While . . . for the purposes of disqualification of counsel, knowledge of one member of a law firm will be imputed by inference to all members of that law firm . . . , we do not believe that the same rationale should apply to a large public defense organization like the Legal Aid Society. . . . In view of the nature of the organization

and the scope of its activities, we cannot presume that complete and full flow of "client" information between staff attorneys exists, in order to impute knowledge to each staff attorney within the office.[30]

Despite *Wilkins*' promise of a separate conflicts analysis for institutional defenders, lower court cases have limited its holding to its narrow, if fairly common, circumstances: the inadvertent successive representation of defendants with potentially adverse interests.[31] In the one recorded case in which the Legal Aid Society sought to maintain *simultaneous* representation of a juvenile and adult codefendant in different courts, the court distinguished *Wilkins* and required explicit waiver.[32]

Courts in other jurisdictions have taken up *Wilkins*'s dictum that an institutional defender must be treated differently than a private law firm for conflicts purposes. In *People v. Robinson* (1980),[33] the Illinois Supreme Court questioned *Wilkins*'s emphasis on the size of a defender organization but rejected a per se rule which would disqualify an institutional defender in conflict cases whenever a single attorney would be disqualified.[34] It argued that such a rule would often cause the very harm it was supposed to prevent:

> In many instances, the application of . . . a *per se* rule would require the appointment of counsel with virtually no experience in criminal matters, thus raising with justification, the competency of counsel. Balanced against this is the possibility, in most circumstances, that an experienced member of the public defender's staff might labor under a conflict of interest because another member . . . was so burdened.[35]

Robinson adopted a case-by-case approach, which required the court to determine whether there was actual conflict in the defender's representation of conflicting interests and whether, given existing institutional arrangements, the conflict created a threat of impaired representation. In *People v. Rogers* (1981)[36] and *People v. Jones* (1982),[37] the Illinois court applied this approach to *appellate* representation by an institutional defender, adopting, as we noted earlier, a "less rigorous" standard for determining the existence of actual conflict.[38]

Most recently, in *People v. Black* (1987), the Illinois Supreme Court found the branch offices of the State Appellate Defender sufficiently independent in policy, brief supervision, and promotion to permit them to represent codefendants with clearly conflicting interests and even to challenge the effectiveness of appellate attorneys in other branch offices.[39] While the court found the risk of impaired judgment too great to allow attorneys within any of the branch offices to represent conflicting interests, it simply transferred conflict cases to other offices.

Two features of the Illinois approach are noteworthy: First, the focus shifts from the organization to the individual attorney. The critical question is whether the attorney's zeal or effectiveness for a particular client may be impaired by her affiliation with other attorneys representing clients with adverse interests. If not, there is no need to be relieved and, apparently, no need to seek the client's consent for continued representation. Second, the costs of reassignment are taken into account in adopting a more flexible rule, but not on a case-by-case basis in determining if a conflict exists. As I argue in the next section, these case-specific costs may be more appropriately weighed by the client in deciding whether to waive a conflict.

SHOULD INDIGENT DEFENDANTS BE ABLE TO WAIVE CONFLICTS OF INTEREST INVOLVING AN INSTITUTIONAL DEFENDER?

Because the risks in representing adverse interests are quite limited on appeal, and greatly attenuated by the division of labor in an institutional defender's office, it is likely that many prospective clients would be willing to waive conflicts that did not directly threaten the loyalty or performance of their designated attorney. The risks that do exist are not only easy to anticipate, but simple to explain. The possibilities for rational waiver seem particularly strong in light of the costs of reassignment in delay and deficient representation.

Although there are a large number of cases rejecting the defendant's waiver of actual conflict or impaired representation, most involve concerns of little or no relevance to the indigent appellant. In one group of cases, the concern is that multiple representation would prejudice the prosecution, not the defendant;[40] in another, the question is whether the defendant was made aware, by counsel or the court, of the risks of multiple representation.[41]

Where the prosecution's interests are not directly threatened by multiple representation and the waiver is clearly knowing and voluntary, the court may be considerably more tolerant of potential conflict. Thus, the California Supreme Court has permitted a client to *retain* counsel despite a very strong possibility of impairment and a striking appearance of impropriety. In *Maxwell v. Superior Court* (1982),[42] the Court upheld a retainer contract which gave the lawyer the rights to the client's life story and which included a warning that these rights might give the attorney an economic interest in seeing the client sentenced to death.[43] The Court found that client's acceptance of this contract constituted a knowing and intelligent waiver. If the defendant can risk of a conflict between his own survival and his attorney's desire for publicity, he should certainly be able to waive potential conflicts of lesser magnitude.

A more significant barrier is the fact of indigence itself, which limits the defendant's choices and may thereby constrain his freedom to waive conflicts. The *Maxwell* court limited its holding to retained counsel and suggested that the options for waiver might be more limited when counsel was assigned. While it might seem that the choice of counsel made by an indigent defendant should be accorded the same weight as the choice made by an affluent defendant, the latter may be regarded as more voluntary.

First, the mere act of retaining counsel may suggest an affirmative willingness to risk conflict, not a mere acquiescence in the possibility. Second, a defendant with the resources to hire counsel will typically have more options than an indigent defendant forced to choose between possibly impaired and probably incompetent representation.[44] Ironically, then, the very inadequacy of private assigned representation may deprive the indigent defendant of the legal authority to decline it.

There are other, less perverse, reasons for discouraging waiver by indigent defendants with clearly adverse interests. First, the existence of adverse interests places the initially assigned attorney in an awkward position in advising the clients about their options. The attorney who concludes that there is no adversity in the interests of related clients can simply inform them that she sees nothing that could impair her representation. In denying the threat of impairment, she is implying nothing about the quality of representation she will provide (though she is vouching for her ability to make an unimpaired assessment of possible adversity).

In contrast, the attorney who concludes that she and her colleagues can adequately represent clients with adverse interests *despite* the threat of impairment is vouching for their capacity to exercise unimpaired judgment throughout the appeal. Moreover, full disclosure may require the attorney to inform her client of the risks of reassignment, which she can hardly do without evaluating the quality of substitute counsel.[45]

A second, closely related concern is that an attorney who has assured a wary or undecided client that she can adequately represent him despite her colleagues' representation of clients with adverse interests may "overcompensate" to prove that point, for example, by attacking the credibility or character of a codefendant when it is not in her client's interest to do so. Such "defensive lawyering" may be aggravated by the client's own continuing suspicions about the attorney's loyalty, or the attorney's fear of the client's recriminations in the likely event that the conviction is affirmed.

These concerns apply to affluent as well as indigent defendants—retained attorneys must also vouch for their capacity to avoid impairment and will also risk overcompensation and client recriminations. If affluent defendants are permitted to waive conflicts despite these risks, so should indigent defendants. Given the overall quality of substitute counsel and the usual delays in reassignment, waiver may, in general, be a considerably more attractive option for indigent than affluent defendants.

Moreover, the dangers of self-promotion, defensive lawyering, and client recrimination will rarely arise unless the defendants' interests are clearly adverse. The dangers in seeking waiver are negligible when two affiliated attorneys, working independently, have concluded that their clients' interests are *not* adverse; that neither will be most effectively served by arguments adverse to the other. The main problem with obtaining waiver in such cases is not ethical but administrative. As we will discuss in the next section, it is often expensive and time-consuming for an institutional defender to screen cases with related clients in this manner and to seek waiver if their interests do not appear adverse.

CAB POLICY ON CONFLICTS OF INTEREST

On their face, the official CAB conflict rules (reviewed in Chapter 6) reflect a conventional, if fairly strict, interpretation of the American Bar Association's conflict-of-interest standard, D.R. 5–105(A). Since the New York courts and American Bar Association have never endorsed the representation of clients with adverse interests by an institutional defender, it seems reasonable for CAB to take the most restrictive view of waiver and decline to represent related defendants unless it can assure itself that their interests are fully compatible.

Two features of CAB's conflicts policy, however, make it even more restrictive than the most conservative reading of the CPR would require: (1) its presumption of conflict from the mere fact that the LAS Criminal Defense Division (CDD) was relieved after arraignment, and (2) its refusal to seek waiver in order to represent coappellants and codefendants of CDD clients. These are very significant self-imposed restrictions on organizational representation, since the types of conflict they involve account for almost 80 percent of the cases which CAB declines to take: in New York County, 40 percent of the cases rejected by CAB involved CDD codefendants, 26 percent involved CDD trial relief, and 14 percent involved CAB representation of a coappellant.

Such a per se rule cannot be justified by even the most restrictive interpretation of the conflict rules, since there are certainly cases in which CAB can rule out any adversity in the interests of related defendants or in the relationship of LAS to a defendant relieved of CDD representation. However, a blanket disqualification rule may be justified on other grounds: Because the information needed to assess the potential for conflict in a particular case is generally not available until weeks or months after the initial assignment decision must be made, the code's conflict provisions must be applied mechanically if they are to be applied promptly. While speed and economy will not justify the breach of professional duties, they may provide a rationale for "overenforcing" such duties by using a strict, easily applicable per se rule. But speed and economy must be weighed against the costs of reassignment for the "false positives" rejected under such a rule. To assess the balance that CAB has struck, it is necessary to take a closer look at its specific rules and practices.

Codefendants

As I have argued, the principal risks in the appellate representation of defendants with adverse interests are greatly reduced when different attorneys represent the defendants and make no attempt to reconcile or coordinate their arguments. Nevertheless, New York has never explicitly approved the waiver of actual conflicts involving assigned counsel, so it is reasonable for CAB to decline to represent codefendants whose interests are clearly adverse.

Even on the most restrictive interpretation of waiver outlined above, however, the CPR permits the attorney to determine whether the interests of her clients are really adverse and to seek waiver if they are not. CAB's refusal to make a case-by-case determination can only be based on a fear that bias will impair even this threshold exercise of judgment or on a concern for the administrative costs involved in making the determination and obtaining the clients' consent.

The first reason has some abstract validity, because an attorney may tend to gloss over differences in the interests of her clients, particularly if they were not brought out at the trial level. But there is no reason to fear that separate attorneys in the institutional defenders office, initially working without consultation (and perhaps in ignorance of each others' assignments), would be any more likely to overlook adverse interests than unaffiliated attorneys. Moreover, the CPR permits even a single attorney to make the threshold determination that related clients do not have adverse interests and to seek waiver on that basis.

The second reason provides a much stronger basis for a per se rule for codefendants: the possibility of adverse interests cannot be adequately excluded without reviewing the transcript and considering the arguments for both clients. Given the high probability of finding some adversity or failing to obtain both clients' consent, the delay and administrative expense may be hard to justify. They might be justified, however, by the costs of reassignment: the certainty of a substantial delay and the likelihood of poor representation.

Although CAB has never actively sought waiver in codefendant cases, it began in 1986 to represent a handful of consenting codefendant pairs, where it has been persuaded by the defendants themselves, or by knowable third parties, that no prejudice could result. It is too soon to determine whether this portends a change in policy. At the present time, CAB will still not investigate codefendant conflict on its own initiative. If a change does occur, it may well be due to a recognition that the delay in obtaining waiver may be considerably shorter than the delay in obtaining substitute counsel, and perhaps by a belief that even impaired CAB advocacy is better than typical 18b representation.

Under the most restrictive version of the waiver rule, however, CAB would only be able to offer the option of joint representation to codefendants if it found that their interests were not adverse. Under the intermediate rule, it could solicit waiver from clients with clearly adverse interests if it could assure them that its effectiveness would not be impaired. Finally, under the most liberal view, it could offer waiver as long as it could provide minimally adequate representation and the clients were fully informed of the alternatives.

Ineffectiveness and Client Dissatisfaction with CDD Performance

CAB's affiliation with CDD introduces another possible source of conflict for its attorneys: the CAB attorney or the client may be dissatisfied with CDD trial representation. According to CAB policy, the CAB attorney must be relieved if she believes that a nonfrivolous argument could be made that trial counsel was ineffective, even if she thinks that the argument is too weak to be worth making. This policy has two components: (1) a refusal to permit a CAB attorney to argue that CDD was ineffective, and (2) a refusal to rely on the judgment of the CAB attorney that argument would not be worth making in the absence of conflict.

The first component is solidly grounded in conflicts law. Even courts willing to relax the restrictions on multiple representation by an institutional defender are reluctant to let one affiliated attorney attack the effectiveness of another.[46] The rationale for this distinction was articulated in a recent ethics opinion of the Kentucky Bar Association:

> Even though the rule against imputed disqualification is not always applied to lawyers in public agencies, there are sound reasons to apply it here. Lawyers in the same office have personal relationships and share an interest in the quality of legal work in the same office. These are interests that conflict with the client's interest in establishing that the lawyer erred.[47]

The affiliated attorney may understate the ineffectiveness claim to soften the criticism of a colleague with whom she may be personally acquainted, or she may overstate the claim to demonstrate her independence.[48] There may also be a striking appearance of impropriety in having an attorney argue the incompetence of a member of his own organization.

The second component of CAB ineffectiveness policy is harder to defend than the first. Even granting that the attorney's judgment is less reliable about his colleagues' performance than his clients' interests, the CAB rule still seems to place the threshold for impaired judgment in a fairly arbitrary location: while the CDD attorney can be trusted to determine if a possible argument for ineffectiveness is frivolous, she cannot be trusted to determine if a nonfrivolous argument is worth raising. Given the widely recognized vagueness in the notion of "frivolity," the second determination hardly seems more subjective or susceptible to bias than the first. CAB policy is particularly hard to justify when the ineffectiveness claim is very weak and there are much stronger issues that may not be raised as forcefully, if they are raised at all, by substitute counsel. While a sensible compromise would permit client waiver of marginal ineffectiveness claims, and this may be done in practice, the CPR makes no explicit provision for waiver in cases where the *attorney's* interests may conflict with his client's.

The appellate defender may have more latitude when the client reveals a legally insubstantial complaint against trial counsel. If, however, the client insists that the appellate defender be relieved because of his affiliation with trial counsel, continued representation is problematic: it would not only appear improper to represent a client against his will, but might also impair the attorney's zeal.[49] Although no court has recognized an absolute right to choice of counsel for indigent defendants, appellate counsel should certainly do nothing to restrict the defendant's freedom of choice.

The case for relief is less compelling when the client does not seek substitute appellate counsel. If he insists that he was misrepresented by trial counsel, however, it seems inappropriate for an affiliated appellate defender to continue representing him, particularly if he seeks to raise his grievance in a *pro se* brief. If he agrees not to raise the issue, either because he has been persuaded by his present attorney that it lacks merit or is simply willing to defer to her judgment, the case for relief is weaker: he has not waived the conflict, but eliminated it. The danger remains, however, that he has merely suppressed his discontent to accommodate his attorney and avoid a time-consuming reassignment.

CAB traditionally drew a sharp line between clients who went public with their discontent in a motion, letter, or transcribed outburst, and clients who merely complained in private. Obviously, the continued representation of the former would create a greater appearance of impropriety. Clients who complained privately were sometimes given the option of changing their minds, depending on the vehemence and persistence of their complaints. Until 1986, CAB would always seek to be relieved when the client had complained on the record, whatever his present attitude. Since there is no disloyalty in representing a now-reconciled client, the apparent impropriety can only lie in the suspicion that his earlier grievances may have been legitimate or that they were dropped only because of the threat of reassignment.

Since 1986, CAB policy towards discontented clients has undergone a significant shift. A much greater effort has been made to ascertain the source and strength of client complaints, to disabuse clients of obvious misconceptions, and to inform clients of their option to accept continued CAB representation. This more flexible policy has even been extended to publicly discontented clients. Starting in 1987, CAB no longer sought relief if the client's public complaints were made early in the proceeding, were not repeated, and did not involve a charge of ineffectiveness. This tilt towards reconciliation may have been motivated by a growing concern about the alternative of 18b representation, or by pressure from the Appellate Division, concerned about the high rate of CAB disqualification.

Clients Previously Represented by CDD

New York State's complicated provisions for increasing the sentences of repeat felony offenders has increased the frequency of conflicts arising from CDD representation by increasing the number of prior CDD activities relevant to the defendant's present sentence. In challenging the constitutionality of a predicate conviction, the client will often be impugning the performance of counsel, claiming that he did not receive effective assistance at his trial, that he was misled about the terms of a plea bargain or the range of possible sentences, or that he was forced to plead guilty because of the attorney's inadequate preparation or refusal to go to trial. If his attorney was from CDD, these amount to ineffectiveness claims against LAS.

The CAB attorney must be relieved if she finds such claims nonfrivolous, since she may otherwise have to challenge the effectiveness of a colleague. If the CAB attorney finds no fault with CDD counsel in the prior case, the situation will be similar to that of a client publicly dissatisfied with CDD representation in the present case. Since CAB no longer employs a per se rule for dissatisfied clients, the CAB attorney may seek reconciliation if the complaint was not too vehement.

Clients Relieved of CDD Representation

In over a quarter of all cases rejected by CAB, CDD was relieved after arraignment. In some of these cases, a conflict is obvious, for example, when CDD has been relieved on the client's own ineffectiveness motion or on the basis of his recorded complaints. Cases where the client retained counsel are more ambiguous: a preference for paid counsel need not imply a dissatisfaction with assigned counsel (though it is more likely to do so the greater the financial hardship in the substitution).

In the large majority of cases in which CDD is relieved, court records do not indicate why relief was granted: the trial file merely indicates that on some date between arraignment and conviction, a panel attorney was substituted. The reason may range from irreconcilable differences between the defendant and his CDD attorney, to the discovery of an antecedent conflict (e.g., prior CDD representation of a prosecution witness), to the judge's irritation at the CDD attorney for missed appearances on "adjourned dates." The McConville/Mirsky study on trial-level representation indicates that judges often substitute counsel as a means of "moving" sluggish cases; such "calendar-clearing" need not involve an actual or potential conflict.[50]

Discovering the actual reason for CDD relief would often be difficult and time-consuming, and sometimes impossible. The CDD case file, if one has been kept, may reveal nothing more than the court file, and the CDD attorney is unlikely to remember the grounds for relief unless the case involved a major confrontation with the judge or client. Even the defendant may have no idea of what brought on the substitution, and substitute counsel may never have bothered to find out. As a general rule, the earlier the substitution, the less likely it is to arise from a conflict. Very late substitutions (e.g., just before jury selection) are quite likely to indicate conflict.

Faced with uncertainty about the grounds for CDD relief and with only two or three weeks to decide whether to accept assignment, CAB has three options: (1) it can decline to represent any defendant relieved of CDD representation because of the possibility of conflict; (2) it can accept all such defendants if the trial file does not reveal a specific conflict and later seek to be relieved if further inquiries warrant; or (3) it can represent only those defendants whose CDD attorneys were relieved within a short time of arraignment, subject to further inquiry.

CAB has adopted the third option: its practice in the mid–1980s was to reject all defendants relieved of CDD representation more than two or three weeks after arraignment. There does not seem to be a precise cut-off point, and different CAB staff members may use different time periods. It is possible that CAB will shift toward the second option, particularly since the rejected client would rarely find a panel attorney in the time it would take CAB to make inquiries about the existence of an actual conflict.

Prior LAS Representation of a Prosecution Witness

As Chapter 6 revealed, in about 2 percent of all cases declined by CAB, LAS had once represented a prosecution witness. Considering the frequency with which prosecutors must rely on "turned" witnesses, the incidence of such representation is probably much higher than this figure would suggest. The appearance of impropriety in representing a defendant against whom a former client testified is greater than the actual threat to the duty of confidentiality owed the latter or the duty of loyalty owed the former, since neither duty will be compromised if simple precautions are taken.

The CAB attorney can avoid any actual prejudice simply by declining to obtain confidential information on the former client, information which (unlike in the case of a CDD codefendant) will have no direct bearing on the present case and could only have been used for impeachment purposes. The former client will suffer no harm from the fact that it is his former attorney who attacks his testimony (assuming it is even in the interest of the present client to do so) unless the court improperly gives greater credence to that attack; the present client cannot complain that his attorney failed to take advantage of material to which a substitute attorney would never have had access.[51]

Starting in 1986, CAB sought waiver in cases where, in the attorney's opinion, there was no reason to attack the prosecution witness, for example, when he testified on an undisputed matter, or when the only appropriate attack involved such transient factors as his opportunity to observe, which did not reflect adversely on the witness' character or suggest a breach of his confidence. As in client dissatisfaction cases, however, even this limited waiver policy is more restrictive than a liberal reading of the CPR would allow. There is no reason why a broadside attack on the witness' character and credibility would require the disclosure of confidences or even arouse suspicion that confidences were being exploited. On a more expansive view of waiver and the appearance of impropriety, the present client should be able to give his consent to continued representation under these circumstances, while the former client need not even be consulted as long as his confidences are not at risk.

CONCLUSION: THE CONSTRAINTS ON CAB CONFLICTS POLICY

This detailed examination of the evolving CAB conflicts rules has revealed that at the level of policy, if not in individual cases, CAB does take some account of the costs of reassignment to the client in deciding whether to seek relief. The poor quality and short supply of panel attorneys has played an acknowledged role in liberalizing CAB policy toward discontented clients, and in relaxing, however slightly, its per se rule on codefendants.

There are two connected barriers to a broader liberalization of CAB conflict rules. First, there are certain forms of conflict—those involving unreconciled clients and arguable CDD ineffectiveness—which require disqualification even under a liberal conflicts policy. Second, the New York courts have retreated from the earlier promise of a more realistic conflicts analysis for LAS and also appear to have taken a fairly restrictive view of waiver. In light of these judicial constraints, CAB is clearly justified in declining to represent codefendants unless it can rule out adverse interests. Making this determination on a case-by-case basis, however, would involve substantial delays in obtaining the necessary records and significant administrative costs in screening them for conflict.

Even under the more liberal Illinois approach to conflicts within an institutional defender, CAB is not presently set up to represent defendants with adverse interests, since the attorneys writing and supervising conflicts cases would not have the independence achieved in Illinois by the physical separation and functional autonomy of the Appellate Defender's branch offices. Moreover, the assignment of more codefendant appeals to CAB would not eliminate the problems of reassignment, only reduce the number of defendants affected by them. There will always be some conflicts which require disqualification, and adequate appellate representation for all defendants can only be assured by upgrading the availability and quality of substitute counsel. When that goal is achieved, the subject of criminal appellate conflicts will become largely academic, rather than the pressing concern it is in the present system. In the next chapter, we examine the proposals for achieving that goal.

NOTES

1. The CPR defines "differing interests" to "include every interest that will adversely affect the judgment or loyalty of a lawyer to a client, whether it is a conflicting, inconsistent, diverse, or other interest," a definition which makes it virtually synonymous with "adverse interests" as that term is used in the conflicts literature.

2. 446 U.S. 335.

3. Thus, if two brothers seek to contest a will leaving their father's estate to a charity, while fiercely disputing the division of the estate under the previous will, a single lawyer might not have inconsistent duties in challenging the latest will alone. If the validity and effect of the two wills had to be resolved in a single probate proceeding, however, the brothers' duties would be adverse and the attorney's duties inconsistent.

It might be argued that the first element of an actual conflict could be present without the second, although not vice-versa. Thus, two clients wishing to enter a single prize lottery would have adverse interests, since one's win would mean the other's loss, and the entry of each would marginally reduce the odds of the other being selected. The lawyer representing both, however, would arguably not have inconsistent duties if he was only required to file their entry forms and knew that the maximum number of entries would be reached whether or not he filed—perhaps the winner would only be selected at the point where a given number of entries were received. In these circumstances, the fulfillment of his duties to one would not affect the interests of the other.

This example would be better taken, however, as the limit case of an actual conflict that had no adverse consequences, a case in which it was certain from the outset that no prejudice could result from the lawyer's discharge of his formally conflicting duties.

4. The question of whether a conflict is actual or merely possible is inherently difficult, since actual conflicts themselves are defined, or should be defined, with reference to the probability of harming the client's interests. Thus, a particular action will be against the client's interests if it has too high a probability of harming those interests. An actual conflict will exist if the lawyer's duties to the other client require her to perform that action, a possible conflict if those duties *may* require her to. (Clearly, all circumstances present the possibility of conflict, and "possible conflict" is just elliptical for "a possibility of conflict high or salient enough to worry about.") If the client's interests are not harmed by the attorney's actions, it may be because

a conflict never arose or because, while it did arise, the actions taken against the client's interests did not have any harmful effects.

5. The denial of actual conflict in situations of potential conflict also presents the casuistical challenge of reconciling apparently conflicting duties.

6. To maintain a distinction between impairment and damage to the defendant's interests it is necessary to segregate the attorney's actions for each client. Otherwise, actions on behalf of client A which were damaging to client B would also constitute impaired representation of B; for example, the attorney would not only be harming A, but misrepresenting him, in delivering a summation for B which placed the blame on A. The distinction, however, is intuitively clear, although more in trial than negotiation settings. If the attorney is offered a deal highly favorable to B but not A, but contingent on acceptance by both, we could view him as accepting for B but declining for A, which would damage B's interest without impairing his representation, or simply as declining the offer, which would look like impaired representation from B's point of view.

7. Obviously, a defendant may be also prejudiced by impaired representation.

8. This will be so if the separate attorneys would not have been able to coordinate their summations in such a way as to benefit both clients more than they would benefit from mutual recriminations. In these circumstances, the defendants are involved in a prisoner's dilemma, in which joint representation is likely to produce better outcomes for both defendants than separate representation. If the single attorney is required to act for each client as she would if she were not representing the other, she may have to act in a manner that is not in either client's best interest.

9. As discussed earlier in this chapter, the inconsistent duties present in an actual conflict may not require the attorney to harm the interests of one client or the other, but merely to create an unacceptably high risk of harm.

10. As I read *Cuyler*, it implicitly recognizes this three-way distinction by requiring a showing of actual conflict and impaired performance but not of actual prejudice. Thus, an attorney who refused to deliver a closing argument for the more heavily implicated of her two codefendants would clearly have denied him the effective assistance of counsel under *Cuyler*, even if the evidence against him was so overwhelming that the most eloquent summation could not have led to an acquittal. *Cuyler* is silent, however, about the possibility of prejudice without impairment. It may be that the court would have regarded any adverse effect of joint representation on the fact finder as a form of impairment, even if it did not result from deficiencies in the attorney's skill and zeal.

11. A similar point was made with respect to the duty of confidentiality in civil representation in, "Disqualification of Counsel," *Columbia Law Review* 81 (1981): 199, 214 n.119: "Two . . . appearances of evil inhere in the case of simultaneous adverse representations. One . . . signals a potential actual evil, in this situation the misappropriation of client confidences. This can be eliminated by screening, which precludes the possibility of violating confidences. The second evil appearance cannot be so eliminated, that is, the evil perceived by all laymen as inherent in the situation; 'divided loyalty' comes close to describing this evil, but it is really nothing other than a gut feeling that one lawyer (or firm) must not represent opposing interests."

12. At least one state, however, has effectively taken the first position in holding that an actual conflict is not waivable, *People v. Hunt*, 219 Cal. Rptr. 726 (1985).

13. The client's authority to consent to representation despite the danger of impaired effectiveness depends on the source of the duties of loyalty and confidentiality. If these duties are imposed because of their instrumental value to the system in producing more accurate outcomes, then the client should not be allowed to consent to a significant risk of their violation—his interests are not the only ones at stake. If, on the other hand, the duties are imposed solely for his benefit, his power to relax them depends on the kind of relationship they arise from.

Thus, "Developments in the Law, Conflicts of Interest in the Legal Profession," *Harvard Law Review* 94 (1981): 1244, 1251–70, explores the implications for waiver of two contrasting views of the attorney-client relationship, the fiduciary and the contractual. In the former, the attorney's role is to serve as the client's professional alter ego, a role he cannot fill, or fill only schizophrenically, if he has divided loyalties. In the latter, he is constrained only by the hypothetical bargain he could have struck with an informed, fully rational client, a bargain which could take account of the fact that his impaired representation might be far better than unimpaired representation by another attorney. On the contractual but not the fiduciary view, the client can consent to significant compromises in his representation.

14. For state court holdings in criminal conflict cases, see Annotation, "Criminal Counsel—Conflicts of Interest," *ALR* 4th 18: 360, particularly sections 25–27 on client waiver.

15. 315 U.S. 60.

16. Geer, "Representation of Multiple Defendants: Conflicts of Interest and the Professional Responsibilities of the Defense Attorney," *Minnesota Law Review* 62 (1978): 120.

17. Geer, "Representation of Multiple Defendants," 155.

18. Geer himself conceded the possibility of fully adequate representation of multiple interests by an institutional defender, although he did not explore this possibility in an appellate setting.

19. It is, of course, possible to imagine circumstances where conflicting interests on appeal would impair the attorney's ability to advise her clients on critical strategic choices or compromise confidentiality; for example, the attorney must advise one of the two codefendants she represents about the risks involved in withdrawing his plea, when the other codefendant has revealed in strictest confidence that he will turn state's evidence if the case goes to trial. Such circumstances will obviously present a serious conflict of interest and require the attorney to extricate herself, as discretely as possible, from representing one or possibly both defendants. The point is that such conflicts are both rare and readily detectable; they can be dealt with on a case-by-case basis and should not shape the general conflicts policy of an appellate defender.

20. 428 N.E. 2d 547.

21. There is also the risk that the attorney will underestimate the prejudice to the other client in raising the argument, but this would merely make it more likely that she would raise the argument, and raise it forcefully. Unless the mere fact of joint representation magnifies the prejudicial impact of that argument, the client prejudiced by it does no worse than he would have if he and the codefendant had been represented by separate attorneys.

22. To illustrate the distinct ways in which clients' adverse interests may impair

the effectiveness of appellate counsel, consider the case of two jointly tried defendants convicted of armed robbery:

According to the prosecution, A entered the bodega with a handgun, ordered the clerk and two customers down on the floor, rifled their pockets, and repeatedly threatened to shoot them, while B entered the store and emptied the register. Only one of the three witnesses identified A in a lineup and in court, while none identified B; B, however, was told by the police that a witness had identified him; he responded that he had walked in on a robbery-in-progress and looted the unattended cash register. There was no other evidence.

Before trial, both attorneys moved for severance. B's attorney objected to the admission of his statement as involuntary, while A's attorney objected to the prejudicial effect on his client of B's description of the gunman's clothing and weapon, which matched the eyewitness description of A and was admitted against B to show a knowledge of detail inconsistent with the quick cameo appearance he claimed to have made. Both defendants received the maximum sentence for armed robbery, the judge citing A's terrifying conduct and B's extensive prior record.

On appeal, the two defendants will have a complex mix of compatible and adverse interests. Both will want to argue that it was error for the trial court to deny severance and both will challenge the admission of B's full statement. To that extent, their interests are compatible. The arguments they (should) employ to make these points, however, will reveal sharply adverse interests. Both will argue that the denial of severance was highly prejudicial just because the evidence against the other was so much more incriminating. While both will assail the admission of B's confession, A will argue that the circumstances in which it was given to the police made its inculpatory aspects highly credible, and therefore more prejudicial to A, while B will argue that those same circumstances made it involuntary and incredible, not only inadmissible but insufficient to convict.

The defendants may also have adverse interests in challenging their sentences. A's attorney will argue that A should not have received a sentence as long as that of the recidivist B; B's will argue that B should not have received as long a sentence as the armed and violent A. Because the convictions rest on fairly weak evidence and the sentences are extremely harsh, this may be a case in which skilled, zealous advocacy could make a difference to one or both clients.

These adverse interests may impair the attorney's representation in a number of ways. In focusing on the damage done to B by his joinder with A, she may ignore or understate the damage done to A by the admission of B's confession. More subtly, she may fail to argue in A's brief that B's confession was highly credible after arguing in B's brief that it was not. Or, rather than favoring one defendant over the other, she may consciously or unconsciously tailor her arguments for both clients to avoid the implication that either was more culpable or heavily implicated. I believe that each defendant would be best served by claiming that the other *was* more culpable and heavily implicated, but even if I am mistaken, it seems too risky to leave that judgment to an attorney whose commitment to both defendants makes it hard to discern and promote their possibly conflicting interests.

23. These contradictions vary in content from claims about the credibility of specific witnesses to case-specific instances of the doctrinal conflicts described by Hertz and Ogletree (note 25). In the hypothetical case, the attorney will, in pursuing what I believe to be the most effective strategy for both clients, embrace a number of "contradictory" positions: that the evidence against A was both weaker and

stronger than the evidence against B, that the inculpatory aspects of B's confession were credible and incredible, and that the judge gave both too much and too little weight to prior record compared with role in the present offense. If such "contradictions" do not reduce counsel's credibility, they may compromise her effectiveness in a different way: the court may look for signs that she "really accepts" one of the positions and be unduly swayed by her assumed preference.

24. An additional concern is that the attorney may damage one client's interests simply by advancing another's more effectively than would substitute counsel. If she would do a better job than substitute counsel for either defendant, then each is worse off than he would be if she were not representing the other. Thus, in the hypothetical case discussed above, B would be better off if A were assigned to an attorney who would not argue that A was prejudiced by his joinder with B, who gave such a transparently implausible account of his actions, or that A's minor record made him less culpable than B. If the codefendants could be regarded as facing a prisoner's dilemma (an appropriate quandary), B could complain that the attorney's pursuit of a competitive strategy for A reduced his odds of favorable action, since substitute 18b counsel would have been likely to pursue a "cooperative" strategy for A, to B's considerable advantage.

There are two problems with taking this kind of prejudice into account: First, it conditions the degree of prejudice on the assumed competence of substitute counsel: the worse the alternative, the more prejudice to both defendants in their joint representation. Second, it requires the attorney to decline to represent of one of the defendants precisely when it will do him the most harm—when the disparity between present and substitute counsel is greatest. Thus, this kind of prejudice does not seem to be an appropriate consideration in assessing the costs of joint representation.

25. "The Ethical Dilemmas of Public Defenders in Impact Litigation," *New York University Review of Law and Social Change* 14 (1989): 23.

26. "Ethical Dilemmas," 37–40.

27. Sometimes, the constraint will be a matter of policy—for example, the courts sometimes reverse to deter misconduct that would otherwise be immunized by the harmless error, such as the inflammatory summations which some prosecutors reserve for their strongest cases. The courts engage in this form of chastisement very sparingly, and individual attorneys in the defender's office are, in effect, competing to have the court "make an example" of their cases.

28. One judge on the brief-evaluation panel noted that CAB seemed to raise excessive sentence claims as a matter of course, and such an attitude might have made him more dismissive of strong as well as weak CAB sentencing arguments.

29. See Chapter 6. In California, by contrast, the Appellate Defender picks the most significant cases.

30. 28 NY 2d 53, 56.

31. *People v. Chambers*, 133 Misc. 2d 868 (Sup.Ct., Kings.Co. 1986) (LAS represented codefendant in prior, unrelated proceeding); *People v. Spencer*, 103 Misc.2d 259 (Sup.Ct., Kings.Co. 1979). (LAS had represented prospective state's witness in unrelated proceeding.)

32. *Matter of Bruce W.*, 114 Misc. 2d 91 (Family Ct., Queens Co. 1982). Surprisingly, in light of the very conservative position usually taken by LAS on conflicts, LAS was not only the unsuccessful respondent in *Bruce W.*, but the successful respondent in *Chambers* and *Spencer*, in all three cases seeking to continue repre-

senting defendants facing a potential conflict of interest. The opinion in *Bruce W.* noted that different divisions and offices of the Legal Aid Society seemed to have different conflicts policies.

33. 402 N.E. 2d 157

34. Alaska and New Jersey have also rejected a per se rule for institutional defenders, although, unlike Illinois, they have not developed guidelines for determining when multiple representation by a public defender is appropriate. See *People v. Flores*, 598 P 2d 893 (Alaska 1979); *People v. Bell*, 447 N.E. 2d 525 (N.J. 1982).

35. *People v. Robinson*, 402 N.E. 2d 157, 162 (1980).

36. 428 N.E. 2d 547.

37. 435 N.E. 2d 823.

38. One disturbing aspect of the approach taken in *Robinson*, *Rogers* and *Jones* is an casuistic tendency to find consistency in apparently conflicting positions, and a confusion between actual conflict and actual prejudice. The former is illustrated by the *Rogers* court's finding that no actual conflict was revealed by the codefendant's argument that his sentence was excessive in being as long as Rogers, "who was more culpable and also had a record of prior convictions." The court reasoned that this argument "in no way conceded the propriety of Rogers' sentence." The second tendency is suggested by the court's reasoning in *Jones*, where it found that the defendants' antagonistic claims as to who was in control of the heroin-filled apartment did not create an actual conflict, since Jones's claim on appeal was consistent with his trial testimony and he did not seek substitute appellate counsel until after the codefendant's appeal has been decided. The court's finding seems to involve a confusion of actual conflict, which merely requires a significant *ex ante* possibility that one client's success will diminish the other's chances—a possibility clearly present here—with an ex post appraisal of the damage done by joint representation, which apparently turned up little prejudice in this case.

Both casuistry and confusion may be present in *People v. Freeman*, decided with *Robinson*, in which the court found no actual conflict in a summation by Freeman's public defender arguing that a conviction of the *codefendant*, represented by a colleague, would be a "travesty of justice" and implicitly conceding that the evidence against Freeman was stronger, though inadequate. While the court may have been correct in finding that this argument was not necessarily harmful to Freeman and need not have been made to aid his codefendant, it is also clear that the emphasis on the disparate strength of the evidence invited a split verdict with little apparent benefit to Freeman. The mere possibility that Freeman's odds of reversal would be reduced by this contrast created an actual conflict of interest, even though a competent independent attorney for Freeman might conceivably have made the same argument.

The confusion underlying the court's findings in these cases is disconcerting, because a relaxation of the conflicts rules for public defenders requires a clear discrimination between actual conflict and its consequences, in impaired advocacy and diminished odds of success.

39. 507 N.E. 2d 1237.

40. In *Wheat v. U.S.*, 100 L.Ed. 140 (1988), the Supreme Court held that the trial judge had broad discretion to reject the defendant's waiver of potential conflicts. *Wheat* is typical of one group of waiver cases, which involve the disqualification of retained counsel by the trial judge on the prosecutor's motion, in the face of the

defendant's concededly knowing and voluntary waiver of any potential conflict. While the *Wheat* prosecution claimed that serious conflicts of interests might arise from the defendants representation by the same attorney, the dissent dismissed them as pretextual; even the trial judge conceded that the attorney was likely to have been highly effective for Wheat. While the *Wheat* majority found greater legitimacy in the government's stated concerns, it insisted that it needed to consider "not only the interests of the defendant by the institutional interests in the rendition of just verdicts." *Wheat v. U.S.*, 100 L.Ed. at 149.

The interests of the prosecution were more explicitly acknowledged in *People v. Hall*, 46 N.Y. 2d 873, 875 (1979), where the New York Court of Appeals upheld the disqualification of counsel over the defendant's strenuous protests in circumstances where continued representation "would very likely work unfair prejudice to the *prosecution* or to the defendant." (emphasis supplied). The "conflict" in *Hall*, the attorney's prior representation of the complaining witness, was clearly and unequivocally advantageous to the defendant, since the complainant had declined to make an identification out of "loyalty" to defense counsel.

41. See *American Law Reports*, 4th ed., 18: 360, secs. 25–27. The leading New York case on defendant waiver imposed a state constitutional duty on the trial judge to make a limited inquiry about the defendants understanding and acceptance of these risks. *People v. Gomberg*, 38 N.Y. 2d 307 (1975).

42. 639 P. 2d 248.

43. The contract also warranted, somewhat inconsistently, that the attorney would serve as a "reasonably competent... diligent, conscientious advocate."

44. This was clearly not the case in *Maxwell*, however, where the defendant was indigent and the contract gave the attorney some of the same incentives as a banned contingency fee. In fact, this was one of the principal points raised by the dissent—that *Maxwell*'s poverty forced a choice between indifferent representation by assigned counsel and more aggressive but compromised representation by a private attorney with divided loyalties. The dissent argued that a choice between these options could not be voluntary.

45. This problem of vouching for her own competence, and of assessing the competence of substitute counsel, may be less acute for retained counsel. For one thing, she has already vouched for her competence in holding herself out for employment—she may even have advertised her services. For another thing, her client is not choosing between her and an unknown alternative—he can often shop around for substitute counsel. Of course, it may be more awkward to advise a paying client on a specific attorney than an indigent client on the general quality of the assigned counsel panel.

46. See *People v. Thompson*, 447 N.E. 532 (Ill. 1986); *People v. Massie*, (Pa. 1982). Another Illinois opinion suggested that a conflict arising from possible ineffectiveness was not waivable. *People v. Robinson*, 410 N.E. 2d 121 (1980). In *People v. Black*, 507 N.E. 2d 1237 (1987), however, the court permitted an attorney from one branch office to argue the ineffectiveness of an attorney from another.

47. *Ethics Opinion* No. 321.

48. This is one area in which affiliation with a private defense organization may be more constraining than employment by a public defender—the former may have a greater interest in protecting itself from malpractice liability and bad publicity and may place stronger pressure on the attorney arguing ineffectiveness. The problem

with malpractice insurance is particularly acute, since most insurance contracts require a good faith effort by the insured to minimize damages, a duty that may well be breached when the organization's own employees help to establish the ineffectiveness claim on which a malpractice action is based. The difference between private and public defenders in this area may be disappearing, however, as courts begin to hold public defenders liable for malpractice.

49. Clients often become discontented with CAB representation for other reasons as well, most often with its pace, but sometimes with its substance. It is rare, however, for either type of dissatisfaction to lead to CAB getting relieved. CAB generally attempts to mollify impatient clients with apologies, explanations, and vague promises of due speed. Except in extreme cases, the court will not grant a motion for substitute counsel on grounds of delay, knowing it would be self-defeating, although the court will sometimes impose an earlier deadline on CAB.

Clients unhappy with the substance of CAB representation rarely complain about the issues that CAB does raise, but rather about the issues it does not. Even generally satisfied clients often insist on making points that the attorney regards as meritless or counterproductive. Many jailhouse lawyers seem to have a list of "essential" issues which they urge upon newly sentenced defendants, often in ignorance of the most basic details of their cases. Since the Supreme Court held in 1983 that effective assistance on appeal does *not* require counsel to raise all nonfrivolous issues the client requests, *Jones v. Barnes*, 463 U.S. 745 (1983), CAB attorneys have become increasingly firm in declining to raise issues they feel would detract from the brief, especially when those issues do not appear to originate with the client himself.

The courts almost always resolve disputes over unraised issues by the simple expedient of letting the client file a *pro se* supplemental brief, often ghosted by the same jailhouse lawyers who made them necessary. These briefs delay the proceedings considerably, since the client must be sent the record and the District Attorney will usually wait to respond to both briefs together. To the best of my knowledge, no CAB client has received favorable action on the strength of a point raised in the supplemental but not in the main brief.

50. McConville and Mirsky, "Criminal Defense of the Poor in New York City," *New York University Review of Law and Social Change* 15 (1987): 581, 817–36.

51. Because of the very limited potential for prejudice, it is not too disturbing that many instances of witness representation are never detected. No one in CAB takes the time to run the name of every witness in every case through the Legal Aid files to check for prior representation, and conflicts only come to light if the witness's representation is revealed in the record. Clearly, what the CAB attorney does not know cannot hurt the former client.

9

Improving the Quality of Indigent Appellate Representation in Conflict Cases

The evaluation of New York's appellate defenders in Part II suggested that an institutional defender like CAB could provide skilled representation for a majority of indigent appellants. Several findings, however, highlighted the need to upgrade the quality of representation in conflict cases: the poor evaluations of the sampled 18b briefs, the failure of many of those briefs to raise important issues, and the significantly lower rates of favorable action in 18b appeals. The measures taken to improve assigned appellate defense in California and Michigan, discussed later in this chapter, suggest that the quality of representation in conflict cases is a national problem.

In Chapter 8, we discussed a simple but controversial means of improving the quality of representation in conflict cases—relaxing the conflict rules or their administration so that the institutional defender could take a large share of the cases it now rejects. A significant modification in CAB conflicts policy could bring the proportion of cases requiring reassignment close to the level contemplated by the 1966 Assigned Counsel Plan, a share that could be handled by a much smaller and more select appellate panel. Unfortunately, as we saw, such a shift would require significant changes in a conflicts law that now prohibits a single defense organization from representing adverse interests. We also observed that CAB could increase its share of the caseload by checking codefendant and CDD-relieved cases for actual conflict and seeking client waiver when it was absent, but that such investigation would involve considerable delay and administrative costs.

In this section, we review proposals which do not involve a significant modification of the conflict rules, but rather changes in institutional arrangements to reduce the number of conflicts and improve the representation in conflict cases. We will begin with the most administratively simple but politically extreme: the "divorce" of appellate and trial defenders; of CAB from CDD and LAS. We then consider three proposals which maintain LAS as the primary appellate defender, variants of the City Bar Association proposals for improving trial-level representation.[1] Finally, we consider two hybrid forms of indigent appellate defense, one introduced in California, the other in New York.

AN INDEPENDENT APPELLATE DEFENDER

The simplest means of upgrading the quality of representation in New York would be to eliminate the principle source of conflict—CAB's affiliation with CDD. As we saw in Chapter 6, most of the conflicts which trigger CAB's replacement under current conflicts law involve its relationship with CDD: the estimated 40 percent in which a codefendant was represented by CDD, the 26 percent in which CDD was relieved after arraignment, the 13 percent in which the client had serious complaints about CDD representation, and the 5 percent in which CDD was arguably ineffective.

An unaffiliated defender could take all of these defendants without a conflict of interest, with the exception of those CDD defendants whose codefendants it was already representing. The unaffiliated defender would be barred only from representing more than one codefendant, as well as defendants who had been witnesses against present clients or against whom present clients had been witnesses. With a negligible number of defendants in the last two categories, an unaffiliated defender could represent almost all defendants who were not codefendants of its present clients.

The percentage of cases with ineligible defendants would be less than the 25 percent of all felony cases nationally with more than one defendant, since many of these codefendants are discharged or acquitted, or never appeal.[2] The percentage would probably be higher than the 7–9 percent of criminal appeals in AD1 in which more than one jointly convicted codefendant appeals, since an unknown percentage of separately convicted codefendants will appeal as well. Splitting the difference, we can estimate that an unaffiliated appellate defender operating under CAB's present conflicts rules would be disqualified from representing roughly 15 percent of all appealing codefendants—a *third* of the 43 percent share of the indigent appellate caseload assigned to the 18b panels between 1980 and 1985.

There would be two advantages to expanding CAB's clientele by disaffiliation. First, it would raise the average quality of representation for the almost 30 percent of indigent appellants now assigned to the 18b panel who would become eligible for CAB representation. Second, and possibly more important, it might facilitate the regulation of the trial defender. The careful review of client complaints by an independent appellate defender would provide an important check on the kind of case-shedding and client neglect found by McConville and Mirsky, even if it led to few successful ineffectiveness claims. However, as I argue in Chapter 11, an affiliated defender could also be an effective monitor, compensating for a lack of independence with greater access and informal oversight.

The primary drawback to the divorce of CAB and CDD is that it would limit the possibilities for collaboration between the two defenders, possibilities that were just starting to be explored in the mid–1980s. Appellate participation in the trial process might improve the quality of representation almost as much as appellate oversight. It would also extend the reach of appellate review into the gatehouse: the precincts, lockups, arraignment, and calendar parts that are now virtually immune to appellate scrutiny. An assessment of these prospects and of the costs of disaffiliation will have to wait until Chapter 11, where we examine the benefits of increased collaboration and the extent to which affiliation is necessary to enjoy them.

A quite distinct concern is that CAB's history of affiliation with LAS might make it a less objective or severe judge of CDD performance than it should be. Although there is no way to rule out this possibility, the history of corporate divestiture shows that far closer institutional relationships have evolved into competitive and adversary ones. Given the generally high quality of representation provided by CAB, it would be wasteful to replace it with a new organization, even if its affiliation with CDD had previously constrained its oversight of trial counsel.

THE CITY BAR ASSOCIATION OPTIONS FOR CONFLICT CASES ON APPEAL

The 1986 CBA report considered three proposed reforms for indigent trial defense in conflict cases: a private, independent mid-range defender (MRD) which would take an estimated 80 percent of the cases rejected by CDD; a Conflicts Unit within the Legal Aid Society, separated by a "Chinese Wall" from its primary trial-defense operations; and an upgraded 18b panel. The Report strongly favored the first alternative, since "an independent not-for-profit organization . . . enjoys the best chance of creating a countervailing force on behalf of the most despised and least powerful interest group in the system—poor people charged with crimes."[3]

The report insisted that "competition between the Legal Aid Society and the MRD should ultimately be good for both," and for the criminal justice system as a whole, as long as it was confined to quality, recruitment, and case management.[4] It feared that a Legal Aid Conflicts Unit, though legally and ethically feasible, "would be more of the same"—more irresponsible case-handling, bureaucratic inertia, and staff–management conflict.[5] It concluded that a revitalized 18b panel would cost far more than the other two alternatives if it was to assure the high quality representation it had thus far conspicuously failed to achieve.[6]

The same three options for mixed institutional and private defense are available at the appellate level: a two-tier system like the present one, with a single institutional defender and a backup panel of private attorneys; a modified two-tier system in which most conflicts are handled by a separate unit within the institutional defender's office; and a three-tier system, with an independent defender unit established to handle most conflict cases. The comparative advantages of these options, however, may be quite different at the appellate than the trial level.

A CAB Conflicts Unit

The City Bar Association report concluded that there would be "no insuperable constitutional or ethical barriers to setting up a Legal Aid Conflicts Unit" at the trial level.[7] The report argued that defendants' interests would be fully protected by the National Legal Aid and Public Defenders Association (NLADA) guidelines, which required safeguards to ensure vigorous representation and barred exchanges and transfers between the main and conflicts units. The report recognized, however, that no conflicts unit had actually received judicial approval, and that for some participants and observers, particularly defendants, such units might present "an abiding appearance of impropriety... especially if there seemed to be a special camaraderie among cocounsel, who, in formal terms, work for the same office."[8]

These countervailing concerns apply with far less force to an appellate conflicts unit. First, the possibilities for collusion and impairment are far more limited and readily controlled on appeal than at trial. The dangers of impaired advocacy and reduced impact in codefendant cases, discussed in Chapter 8, could be virtually eliminated by prohibiting attorneys and supervisors in the conflicts unit from coordinating their work with the main office. As long as attorneys in the main and conflicts units had independent supervisors of the same rank and were prohibited from collaboration or access to each other's files, there would be no practical risk in their representation of codefendants. There is no reason to fear that opposing claims would be understated by counsel or discounted by the court if they were advanced by such clearly segregated institutional units.

While there would still be some defendants and observers who would find an appearance of impropriety in such arrangements, the appellate process does not provide the same opportunity as a trial for a visible display of "special camaraderie" between affiliated attorneys.[9] Finally, the high court of at least one state, Illinois, has explicitly approved of the representation of codefendants with sharply adverse interests by different branches of the State Appellate Defender. The Illinois Supreme Court based its endorsement of such joint representation on a finding that the brief-supervision process for first-level appeals in each branch office was completely independent. If it is permissible for autonomous branches of a single appellate defender to represent codefendants without special safeguards, it is a fortiori acceptable for a specially constituted conflicts unit to do so.

An internal conflicts unit could take some but not all of the attorney-client conflict cases that could be handled by an unaffiliated appellate defender or an MRD. It is doubtful that such a unit could properly raise claims of CDD ineffectiveness or represent clients wishing to do so. As we discussed in Chapter 8, the common economic and professional interests of the appellate and trial attorneys would probably preclude such representation, at least in the absence of client waiver. Although the Illinois Supreme Court has permitted branches of the State Appellate Defender to raise claims against each other, such representation seems fraught with both the appearance of impropriety and the real danger of impaired advocacy.

A Mid-Range Defender

A mid-range defender would not have to be limited to conflict cases—it could be assigned a fixed percentage of all indigent appeals, of which conflict cases would only be a part. There is, however, another important limitation on its caseload. The City Bar Association Report urged that the caseloads of the primary and mid-range defender be restricted by "caseload caps"—strict, enforceable limits of the number of cases an attorney can take. The report insisted that such caps could not be subject to competitive bidding: "It would be unethical and counter-productive for the City to have defender organizations competing for funds by bidding to undertake a higher caseload cap.... Quality legal work should not be manipulated by quotas or subject to 'speed-ups' like work on an assembly line."[10]

Uniform caseload caps are as important on appeal as at trial. Particularly since the advent of the word processor, it is all too easy to manipulate or speed up the production of briefs to secure a competitive advantage. While a trial attorney cannot be in two parts at the same time, an appellate attorney could turn out two briefs with only the slightest marginal effort on the second. While there are obviously legitimate efficiencies in computer-assisted briefing, there is also a greater temptation to "standardize" client's briefs, at a serious cost to individual representation. Because the word processor makes it easier for an appellate attorney to satisfy the "facial" requirements of his assignment with an excessive caseload, the costs to the client of excessive commitments may be less visible.

Even with caseload caps, the competition between the MRD and the primary appellate defender would not necessarily be healthy for their clients. The division of the appellate caseload between two appellate defenders might lessen the judicial pressure on either one to perform a screening function, since neither could perform that function as efficiently as a single defender. But it is at least as likely that competition would intensify this pressure, especially if the court favored the defender exercising the greater discrimination in the presentation of its cases—requesting oral argument selectively, writing shorter briefs in routine cases, and indicating in other ways which cases were truly worthy of the court's attention. This danger would be amplified if one of the defenders enjoyed a closer relationship than the other with their common funding authority or with the courts. As I argue in evaluating the proposed AD1 Appellate Defender, there is a serious risk of favoritism and accommodation in the establishment of a mid-range appellate defender under judicial auspices.

An Upgraded 18b Appellate Panel

At the present time, a solo practitioner in New York is clearly handicapped by the lack of available resources for researching, supervising, and producing briefs. Nevertheless, we cannot be certain about the quality of representation provided by the 18b appellate panel in the late 1980s. While our study found significant deficiencies in the quality of work done by the panel, the briefs it examined were submitted in 1984 and 1985, at a time when panel members were still receiving $15 an hour for the bulk of their work. By mid–1987, the panel was receiving almost three times that amount, and this rate increase alone may have had a significant effect on the quality of its briefing.

The continuing case backlog, however, suggests otherwise: as of late 1987, it was still difficult to get private attorneys to take many of the indigent appeals rejected by CAB, let alone to provide high-quality representation. While it is possible that the attorneys already active on the panel upgraded the quality of their work, the rate increase is just as likely to have spurred a further increase in volume at the expense of quality.

The disappointing response of the private bar may reflect a reluctance on the part of many established lawyers to get involved in a stigmatized or disreputable form of representation. While the bar quickly answered the call to take up the CAB backlog in 1985, it barely responded to the equally urgent summons to reduce the 18b backlog in 1987. Wall Street lawyers may have grown tired of criminal appeals, but it is also quite possible that they preferred volunteering under CAB than 18b auspices. Less-established lawyers may have feared that the city would be slow and grudging about paying the modest compensation it was offering. Moreover, panel rules may discourage the type of collegial activity that many attorneys, particularly younger ones, would prefer.[11]

A final drawback to panel representation is the attorney's uncomfortable dependence on the court and a court-appointed administrator for compensation on a case-by-case basis. While the CAB attorney may incur the court's displeasure in representing each client with single-minded zeal, the 18b attorney is in a more awkward and vulnerable position: he must ask the court to pay him for work which the panel administrator regards as excessive. His request may be greeted with suspicion if most panel members put in considerably less time on routine cases—an administrator relying on panel norms may have difficulty believing that the attorney really worked as many hours as he billed.

The problem is more acute when the attorney's hours exceed the "cap"—the statutory limit on total compensation. The decision to lift the cap is discretionary, and the administrator and judges may hesitate to exercise their discretion in favor of an attorney they regard as overzealous. The threat is not so much that the administrator and courts will use the waiver in a coercive or punitive manner—in practice, they may give the attorney the benefit of the doubt—but that their complaints about long briefs and their obvious preference for brevity may have a "chilling effect" on attorney zeal.

The problem in New York has been especially severe since 1987, when the legislature raised the hourly rate but not the "cap." After June, 1987, an attorney needed to bill only 30 hours to exceed the $1,200 cap. If a panel attorney averaged only *half* the estimated 80 hours of a quota-making CAB attorney, he would require discretionary waiver in most of his cases. However fair and generous the administrator may be in these circumstances, an attorney will be hard pressed to maintain his independence and zeal when he must so often petition for discretionary compensation.

To examine the prospects of an upgraded system of assigned appellate representation, it is instructive to compare the appellate projects that have been set up in California in the mid–1980s with the mid-range appellate defender which began operation in AD1 in the Fall of 1988. Both experiments arose from increases in the caseload assigned to private counsel and from a perception that the previous arrangements for assigned appellate representation were inadequate. While both reflect a commitment to higher quality representation, the AD1 appellate defender may lack the financial wherewithal and institutional independence to sustain that commitment.

TWO HYBRID FORMS: CALIFORNIA REALITY AND NEW YORK DREAMING

The California Appellate Projects and the Limits of an Assigned Counsel System on Appeal

California's need for upgrading its assigned appellate bar arose from cutbacks in the size and funding of the State Appellate Defender, whose share of the appellate caseload declined from 40 percent to 10 percent in the early 1980s. The rate of compensation for assigned appeals in California was far higher than in New York throughout this period: $40 an hour in 1980, $50 an hour in 1984. Nevertheless, the California appellate judiciary found that "the quality of representation in these indigent appeals has been, quite frequently, substandard."[12]

Faced with briefs which failed to adequately summarize the record and missed important issues, the courts found themselves compelled, in a growing number of cases, "to undertake an exhaustive search of the record." The appellate judiciary came to view skilled appellate representation as a means of conserving their resources, and decided to contract with groups of veteran appellate attorneys "to provide assistance and supervision of the private attorneys appointed to supervise cases." First established in San Diego, Los Angeles, and San Francisco, such supervisory organizations have now been set up in all of California's Judicial Districts, staffed in large part by alumni of the State Appellate Defender.

In the First Judicial District, which covers San Francisco and 12 other counties, the supervision of the assigned appellate bar has been handled since 1986 by an Appellate Project. With a staff of nine attorneys, the project effectively controls the assignment and supervision of 85 percent of the indigent appellate caseload. It procures the minutes, corresponds with the defendants about prospective issues, matches attorneys and cases, and, in cases assigned to less experienced attorneys, prepares memoranda outlining possible issues. For purposes of matching, the project ranks attorneys by an evaluation of their writing samples, and it ranks cases by the length of sentence, the grade of crime, the length of the record, and the presence of novel or complex issues.

Two thirds of all assignments are on an "assisted" basis, requiring the attorney to submit his work to the project for often intensive supervision. A third of the assignments are "independent," with optional project supervision. The project staff keep about 5 percent of the appeals for themselves: those which have records already available, which must be briefed on an expedited basis, and which present particularly interesting issues.

The major problem in such a system of private appellate representation supervised by the court or a court proxy is the threat to counsel's autonomy. The private attorneys working under project auspices are paid on a case-by-case basis by the courts, and project supervision obviously has a potential for abuse. Supervisors may impose severe economies on "assisted" attorneys to satisfy cost-conscious courts and may enforce stylistic or doctrinal orthodoxies under the guise of maintaining quality.

The Director of the First District Appellate Project feels that the projects have generally been successful in avoiding both threats, although he concedes that their success depends on the cooperation of the court and the self-restraint of the project supervisors.[13] In the First District, the court rarely questions attorney billings that the project has approved. Such judicial cooperation depends, however, on the attitude of the court's research attorney, who acts as liaison with the project. Other districts have had less happy experiences with budget-minded courts, which contain costs by consistently awarding attorneys only two-thirds or one-half of what they bill.

In editing attorney briefs, project supervisors strive to respect stylistic and small doctrinal differences. They encourage the use of the court-approved appellate style, but will intervene only when they feel that the attorney is ineffective in her presentation of the appeal or in her failure to raise an important issue. In the former case, the project will move to be relieved from its joint assignment; in the latter, it will often seek leave to file a supplemental brief. While this informal policy of self-restraint seems adequate for the short-term, it should be reinforced by formal guidelines and by internal review of the project's use of its supervisory powers.

Another concern about the California Projects is that the relationship between supervisors and assigned attorneys is close enough to restrict the representation of codefendants and other related clients. The staff attorneys of the First District Project do not personally represent clients whose codefendants have been assigned to a private attorney under their supervision, but there may be a conflict of interest even in supervising the attorneys representing codefendants. The Illinois Supreme Court, the country's most liberal on appellate conflicts policy, regards supervisory autonomy as a critical factor in ensuring the vigorous representation of adverse interests. At the very least, the projects should establish guidelines requiring codefendant briefs to be supervised by different attorneys and prohibiting any attempt to coordinate their appeals. The First District Project avoids the problem by assigning only one codefendant to an "assisted" attorney; all the rest are assigned to independent counsel, whose briefs are not supervised by project staff.[14]

The California experiment in supervised assigned representation is apparently regarded as a success by its judicial sponsors. Initially established in the three largest jurisdictions, Appellate Projects had been set up in every Judicial District in the state by 1988. While their growing acceptance in California offers hope that the bulk of indigent appellate representation in other jurisdictions can be assumed by closely screened and supervised panels of private attorneys, the success of the experiment might be hard to replicate in New York.

The first barrier would be the cost. By New York standards, an appellate project is an expensive operation: not only are the assigned attorneys themselves compensated at a higher rate, but the court pays the supervisory organization several hundred thousand dollars a year for salaries and expenses. The City Bar Association Report expressed concern about the cost of panel representation at 1986 levels of compensation; an appellate panel upgraded along California lines would be considerably more expensive.

Quality appellate representation, however, is an expensive enterprise, and the state may have a constitutional obligation to provide the increase in funding necessary to achieve it. That increase could perhaps be made palatable to the legislature by pointing out that New York still lags behind jurisdictions where the average attorney earnings are far lower. The costs could be contained by decreasing the proportion of cases assigned to the panel, a reduction that could be achieved by requiring CAB to pursue an active waiver policy for codefendant and CDD-relieved cases without actual conflicts.

A second obstacle to the creation of a California-style appellate project in New York would be the likely resistance of the present 18b bar to greater supervision. Part of the reason that the California projects were able to impose such a high degree of supervision over private attorneys was they were distributing cases that had previously been assigned to the State Appellate Defender. A similar program in New York would assume control of a caseload which already "belonged" to the private bar, and its supervision of that caseload might be seen as an encroachment.

While a supervisory agency in New York City would almost certainly be resisted, an even graver danger is that it would be "captured" by the courts. We saw how some of the California Appellate Projects faced pressure from the courts to impose economies on appellate lawyers; an agency funded by the Appellate Division would likely face the same kind of pressure. If that agency enforced the kind of selective zeal the courts sometimes seem to desire, it would serve indigent appellants no better than an agency with the laissez faire attitude of previous 18b administrators.

The AD1 Appellate Defender: A Too Modest Proposal?

In the spring of 1988, the AD1 18b Administrator received the approval of the Presiding Justice to set up an Appellate Defender's Office. The organization is an ingenious hybrid, funded at 18b rates but functioning as a mid-range defender. This AD1 initiative reflects an admirable effort to reform an inadequate system without significantly increasing its costs. It is, however, based on highly optimistic forecasts of attorney output, and its success depends heavily on the cooperation of a judiciary and city administration not noted for their unqualified support of zealous indigent representation.

The office has been set up as a not-for-profit corporation, governed by a board of retired Appellate Division justices, members of the 18b Central Screening Committee, and the 18b administrator, sitting as proxy for the Presiding Justice. When it began operations in October 1988, the office consisted of two supervising attorneys and eight staff attorneys, whose salaries—$80,000 and 35,000, respectively—and office expenses were paid by the city from a fixed budget. Attorney salaries were based on the compensation, at 1987 rates, for ten panel attorneys working 40 hours a week, 50 weeks a year. The administration and overhead were, in effect, financed by "skimming off" more than half of the $40 an hour "billed" by each staff attorney, which would give them $80,000 a year as panel members.

The supervisors, experienced appellate attorneys, were expected to complete 15 briefs a year as well as training and overseeing the staff attorneys. Those attorneys, mostly recent law school graduates, were expected to produce 15–20 briefs a year. The office as a whole was thus expected to produce about 200 briefs a year, enough to eliminate the backlog that existed in the spring of 1988.

The economy of the proposed office is appealing, but its establishment raises several questions: (1) Does the funding mechanism set up for the organization conform to 18b rules? (2) Are the billable hours and briefing levels for supervisory and staff attorneys realistic? (3) Will the organization remain sufficiently independent of the judiciary to represent its clients with undivided loyalty, or will it be drawn into a destructive competition with CAB for more "efficient" appellate representation?

The answer to the first question is a definite "no." Under the rules in effect at the time the office was being set up, 18b compensation could only be paid for work already completed by permanently or provisionally certified members of the panel, not to a law firm. The Appellate Defender is funded by a fixed budget, and most of its briefs will be written by staff attorneys who are not even members of the bar, let alone certified for 18b representation. The salaries of the two supervisors, who are the attorneys of record for all clients, are based largely on work that neither they nor an eligible attorney has done. Moreover, the amount of money paid to the office for an average brief would be more than three times the $1,200 "cap." If each staff attorney completed 20 briefs and billed 2000 hours a year, his average billing would be 100 hours × 40 an hour = $4000. The Presiding Justice may waive the cap for regular panel appeals, but only in exceptional cases.

These departures from the 18b rules illustrate how the Appellate Defender's contract with the city diverges from the arrangements for panel representation under County Law 722(b) and the Assigned Counsel Plan for New York City. While the 18b rules do not govern the Defender's day-to-day operations, they may have an important bearing on its future. Panel rates and caps are the baseline for the Defender's budget, and its continued funding may be in jeopardy if it proves to be a more expensive or less productive enterprise than advertised.

The answer to the second question is "doubtful." Private law firms typically estimate that billable hours represent only two-thirds to three-fourths of the time an attorney must actually spend in the office. It is certainly optimistic to expect even highly motivated indigent defenders to work 60 hours a week, 50 weeks a year. The expected brief output is even less realistic. While a new staff attorney might be expected to produce 15 or 20 briefs a year, the attorneys training and supervising him could hardly be expected to do likewise.

CAB expects its own supervisors to produce five substantive briefs a year, and it is unlikely that the Appellate Defender's supervisors, however efficient and highly motivated, could do three times as many. Although the ratio of supervisors to staff attorneys would be higher in the proposed Appellate Defender's office, the average staff attorney, fresh from law school, would also require more supervision. The office would be doing very well if it produced 130 briefs a year, 20 for each staff attorney and 10 for each supervisor.

The third question is the most important, and the answer must be the most speculative. The most obviously threatening form of competition between the two defenders—for cases—could not arise immediately, since under the LAS contract with the city, the Appellate Defender could only receive cases that CAB had already rejected. A more insidious form of competition might arise, however, from judicial pressure for economy and selectivity in appellate representation.

As we noted in Chapters 1 and 8, appellate judges sometimes expect a high-volume appellate defender to perform a screening function, conserving judicial resources by indicating, through the tenor of its advocacy, the cases that are truly deserving of the court's attention. We observed that CAB had generally resisted this pressure, for example, by encouraging its attorneys to argue all trial appeals, so that the court would not draw an adverse inference from the failure to argue any one of them. Nevertheless, CAB has made some accommodations to "productivity," including the adoption of a briefing quota which some staff attorneys have seen as requiring "rush jobs" on weaker cases.

A second institutional defender might prove less resistant than CAB, particularly one, like the AD1 Appellate Defender, established under judicial auspices and governed by a board of trustees composed of present and retired judges and judicial administrators. Such sponsorship might well make the defender more receptive to judicial pressure than CAB and less committed to the often competing demands of zealous advocacy for every client.[15] If the AD1 Defender proved more accommodating, if, for example, it reserved oral argument for a minority of "truly significant" cases and filed *Anders* briefs in trial appeals with marginal issues, it would not only shortchange some of its own clients, but increase the pressure on CAB to do likewise. If CAB refused to make similar accommodations, a frustrated judiciary might well lobby for the Defender to take over some or all of the CAB caseload. The city might be quite receptive, given its frequent disputes with LAS and its recurrent threats of disestablishment.

It is possible, of course, that the Appellate Defender will resist judicial pressure at least as effectively as CAB, and compete only in quality, zeal, and recruitment. The initial signs are encouraging. The office began operations with two supervising attorneys, one a recent United States Supreme Court clerk and the other a former Legal Aid trial attorney and law professor. Before taking cases, these attorneys sought and received guarantees of autonomy from their judicial and municipal sponsors.[16] While they believe, and have assumed for budgetary purposes, that they and their fledgling staff attorneys will each be able to produce 15 to 20 briefs a year, they insist that they regard these output figures only as a rough "benchmark," not as a quota.

Both supervisors have expressed a strong commitment to "vertical" representation by individual staff attorneys, including client visits and, in appropriate cases, habeas and certiorari petitions. They are also committed to oral argument in any case "with an arguable issue," a commitment more qualified than William Hellerstein's but probably approximating CAB practice. They insist that they will resist any pressure by the courts or the city to economize on their representation. While they acknowledge that a shortfall in productivity would make their budget negotiations more difficult, they are optimistic that they can maintain and perhaps increase their funding without any compromise in their level of representation. If the Defender falls substantially short of its predicted output, however, it may have to adapt to survive, and yesterday's benchmark may become tomorrow's quota.

Obviously, the success of this experiment depends on the as-yet-untested resolution and political skill of the supervising attorneys, the quality and productivity of their staff, and the willingness of the city to pay the extra costs of high-quality appellate representation in conflicts cases. The office would benefit from institutional safeguards that it presently lacks. At the very least, the board of trustees should have no more than a single representative from the Appellate Division, and should maintain an arm's length relationship with the 18b administrator. A refusal to ensure the Defender's autonomy would suggest that its judicial sponsors regarded its independence as a vice, not a virtue.

CHOOSING AMONG THE ALTERNATIVES

It is difficult to choose among these competing proposals without taking account of concurrent reforms at the trial level. Significant reforms in CDD, for example, might weaken the case for CAB disaffiliation. If CDD took a larger share of indigent defendants and did a more effective job of maintaining "vertical" representation, an affiliated CAB would be able to handle a larger share of the caseload. A more aggressive and responsible CDD would also require less case-by-case monitoring and offer greater opportunities for appellate collaboration.

The advantages of a CAB conflicts unit or an appellate MRD would be increased by the creation of a similar unit at the trial level. The "isomorphism" of the trial and appellate defense systems would simplify the tracking of cases from trial to appeal and offer the opportunity for collaboration between each trial unit and its appellate counterpart. An appellate MRD would have an edge over a CAB conflicts unit in being able to handle complaints of CDD ineffectiveness.

The division of the trial caseload would also have a significant impact on the proportion of cases going to the 18b appellate panel and the difficulty of monitoring the quality of representation it provides. The smaller the share of appeals assigned to the panel, the easier the task of selecting and supervising panel members. No matter how large a share of the trial and appellate caseload were taken by the institutional defender(s), however, a residue of conflict cases would still have to be assigned to the private bar, and the quality of representation it provides would have to be closely monitored.

Although a California-style supervisory agency may be too ambitious for New York City, the state is not likely to improve the quality of representation in conflict cases without spending a great deal more than it now does for panel compensation and supervision. Given the economic realities of legal practice in New York City, it is doubtful that $40 an hour can pay for overhead, support staff, training, and supervision as well as through briefing. The state must be willing to raise the rates for 18b appellate work, or at least to provide reimbursement for routine office expenses. It should also provide more staffing for the 18b administrator, to allow it to exercise greater oversight of panel representation. Routine supervision of panel work is far more feasible on appeal than at trial, and even spot checks would be a considerable improvement over the complaint-based system of review in effect in the mid–1980s.

Overall, the most realistic and conservative route to improved representation in conflict cases may lie in a more flexible application of the conflict rules and a more aggressive waiver policy by CAB, which would allow it to retain a larger share of the appellate caseload. These changes in CAB conflicts practice should be coupled with a modest increase in the funding of the 18b panel and in the resources and authority of the 18b administrator, permitting tighter control over a smaller, more select appellate panel.

NOTES

1. Association of the Bar, City of New York, Committee on Criminal Advocacy, *A System in Crisis: The Assigned Counsel Plan in New York: An Evaluation and Recommendation for Change* (1986).

2. See Spangenberg, Smith, and Davis, *National Defense Systems Study: Final Report* (1984), 7.

3. *A System in Crisis*, 46.

4. Ibid., 47.

5. Ibid., 59.

6. Ibid., 67–68. The report evoked the expected responses from members and partisans of the existing defense organizations: that it whitewashed LAS or failed

to display sufficient confidence in its capacity for self-reform; that it unfairly maligned the 18b panel and underestimated the salutary effects of the 1985 rate increases. There was also a concern that the competition between CDD and MRD would inevitably become destructive, as the courts played off the two to achieve the most accommodating, least confrontational style of criminal defense.

7. Ibid., 57.

8. Ibid.

9. The question remains, however, of whether the representation of conflicting interests by different attorneys in the same organization still creates the appearance of impropriety. In resolving this issue, the ambiguity in the notion of "improper appearances" which we noted in Chapter 8 assumes critical importance: while a "Chinese Wall" may eliminate the practical risk of prejudice, it cannot eliminate the inherent awkwardness of representing conflicting interests. While it may be less awkward for a single organization to represent conflicting interests than a single attorney, the division of labor cannot entirely eliminate the troubling appearance of divided loyalties.

It might seem, however, that informed consent would dispel any lingering discomfort: even if defendants cannot waive a significant risk of impaired representation, as they can on the third view of waiver described in Chapter 8, they should certainly be able to waive any objection to the mere fact of divided loyalties, as they can on the second, moderate view of waiver. If the defendants are clearly protected from prejudice and are not themselves troubled by the outward appearance of disloyalty, it is hard to see what interests would be protected by prohibiting their joint representation.

10. Ibid., 74.

11. Law firms cannot receive 18b assignments, and while panel rules permit more than one attorney to receive compensation for a case, all must be panel members. No provision is made for permitting attorneys to each bill for the time they spend *together* on the case—a significant share of the work on a closely edited or supervised appeal. Finally, while 18b appellate lawyers do not have the same range of uncompensated or poorly compensated expenses as their trial counterparts, for example, they will rarely need investigators or experts, they lack the research services provided for CAB staff attorneys.

The City Bar Association Report, oriented towards trial defense, did not address the problems of the 18b appellate panel. The report recommended closer screening of panel applicants, more aggressive recruitment of LAS and District Attorney alumni, and prompter payment of vouchers, but concluded that routine supervision of 18b trial attorneys by panel staff would be prohibitively expensive and unnecessary; see *A System in Crisis*, 60–67. The report considered the possibility of a firm-retainer contract for arraignments (64–66), but did not examine the possibilities for joint ventures on appeal. More broadly, it did not address the structural problems facing independent practitioners on appeal.

12. This quotation and those in the next paragraph are taken from a letter sent by the First District Appellate Project to funding agencies, seeking a "bridge loan" to set up operations.

13. Conversation with Robert Calhoun, director of First District Appellate Project, June 10, 1988.

14. Clients complaints about "assisted" appellate representation would present

an even more difficult problem, since they would implicate the quality of supervision, but such grievances have yet to surface in the First District.

15. The initial proposal for the Appellate Defender submitted by the 18b administrator was hardly reassuring on this score. It called for 31 briefs a year from supervisors and 23 from new staff attorneys, a volume that would virtually preclude adequate attention to each case.

16. This paragraph and the next are based on a conversation with E. Joshua Rosenkranz and Ira Mickenberg, supervising attorneys for the Appellate Defender, held on October 7, 1988.

10

Enhancing the Impact of Criminal Appellate Representation: Conserving Appellate Resources for More Meritorious Cases

This chapter examines existing and proposed measures to conserve appellate resources for the most meritorious cases—meritorious in presenting significant errors, close issues, or significant opportunities for law articulation or institutional control. The desire to screen criminal appeals arises from the substantial increase in their volume and the apparent decline in their average merit over the past 25 years. It is a desire shared by most judges who hear criminal appeals and by many attorneys who brief them.

Unfortunately, screening is not desirable for everyone. Oakley and Thompson provide a succinct summary of its benefits and perceived risks:

> Abridgment of traditional methods of appellate adjudication in selected cases enables the court to maintain an acceptable net rate of disposition while continuing to offer traditional adjudicatory procedures in the remaining cases. But this compromise has not generally been conceived as advantageous to the litigants who receive the non-traditional treatment. The fear is that in appellate decision-making, as in most of life, acceleration entails a tradeoff between the goal of the quick and the risk of the dirty.[1]

We will review three forms of screening: measures to induce greater defendant selectivity in appealing, screening by defense counsel, and judicial screening mechanisms. All three approaches have drawbacks at least as serious as the tedium and expense of New York's present system of largely unrestricted appeals and full briefing: measures to induce defendant selectivity will discourage meritorious as well as marginal appeals, screening by assigned counsel violates the duty of loyalty as well as the equal protection clause, and judicial screening achieves economy at the expense of reliability. A detailed examination of several screening mechanisms raises doubts that significant savings in judicial resources can be achieved without violating equal protection or reducing the quality of appellate review.

MEASURES TO INDUCE SELECTIVITY BY INDIGENT DEFENDANTS

In Chapter 1, we discussed several schemes for giving indigent defendants the same incentives for not appealing as affluent defendants. Here, we will focus on the most generous and constitutionally sensitive of those schemes: the proposal of Carrington, et al. (1980) to pay indigent defendants the average cost of a criminal appeal if they do *not* appeal.[2] Carrington argues that this scheme is not only more generous but more efficient than those which merely penalized frivolous appeals, since payoffs would discourage merely weak and insubstantial appeals as well: many defendants would happily accept several thousand dollars to drop an appeal they had almost no chance of winning. In this section, we will consider whether such a payoff scheme would satisfy due process and equal protection, and whether it would be desirable as a matter of policy.

Would the Scheme Satisfy Due Process and Equal Protection?

Superficially, the scheme seems above constitutional reproach, since it appears to reward the indigent defendant for not appealing rather than punish him for appealing. As critics of the analogous argument for plea "discounts" have pointed out, however, the implicit norms which cause us to perceive an arrangement as rewarding one action rather than punishing its opposite may shift: if most defendants chose to take the money and hold their peace, the Carrington payoff would become the normal wages of conviction, which the defendant would forfeit by appealing. Even if the scheme came to seem punitive, however, it would not offend due process any more than the fees-for-services paid by nonindigent clients. Nevertheless, it may seem morally offensive for the state rather than the market to put a price tag on the defendant's exercise of an important right.

The Carrington scheme would also seem to afford the defendant fully equal protection, since unlike the nonindigent defendant, he could get a competent appellate lawyer without any out-of-pocket expense. There is one important respect, however, in which he would be worse off: he would frequently be unable to obtain competent legal advice on whether to appeal.[3] In contrast, the affluent defendant can pay for an appellate lawyer to review the record and advise him on the prospects for an appeal. Without the opportunity for consultation, the indigent defendant arguably cannot make a knowing waiver of his right to a counseled appeal.

If the Carrington payoff scheme were adopted, then, it should be supplemented by free, nonbinding appellate consultation for any indigent defendant who desired it. While this would place the indigent at an advantage, since nonindigent defendants would still have to pay for consultation, the "free ride" would be much shorter than it is now.[4] Such consultations would be valuable to the system as well as the defendant, increasing the odds that meritorious appeals would be pursued and marginal ones dropped.

There is another way in which the Carrington payoff might be thought to deny equal protection, though not in a strictly constitutional sense: it might give poor defendants a greater incentive than affluent ones to forego their appeals: receiving a few thousand dollars means a lot more to the former than losing that amount means to the latter. The "average cost of an appeal" may be a sum large enough to tempt a poor defendant to drop a truly meritorious appeal.

This objection is similar to that raised against cash welfare payments, in favor of payments in-kind. It appears to reflect a paternalistic concern that poor defendants in need of "appellate treatment" will forego it if they are given the option of taking cash, since their poverty makes the dollar cost of an appeal more valuable to them than to affluent defendants. While the disparity in value could be reduced by paying indigent defendants *less* than the cost of a private appeal for not appealing, the question remains of whether, as a matter of social policy, it is desirable to offer them even this smaller temptation.

Should We Rely on Self-Selection by Indigent Defendants to Conserve Appellate Resources?

No incentive scheme, however ingenious, could hope to give defendants an interest in raising all and only those issues which are worth the court's time to resolve. Well-advised defendants will often have good reason to waive important issues and press marginal ones: A defendant with marginal issues and a life sentence might have little use for the payoff and reasonably prefer a chance of freedom, however slight; a defendant with a short sentence and major issues likely to be resolved against him might reasonably prefer a payoff to a published affirmance. This kind of tension is inevitable in a system which relies on private litigants to enforce public policy; the question is whether we want to alter private incentives in the proposed manner.

We know far too little about the perceptions of convicted indigents to even guess the comparative impact of a uniform payoff on the submission of meritorious and marginal appeals.[5] We do know that administrators more concerned with volume than merit are almost certain to neglect the risk of discouraging meritorious appeals, particularly since a drop in marginal appeals will be far more obvious than a reduction in deserving ones. Given our concern about the integrity of criminal adjudication, we should be far more concerned about the latter—it may be preferable to suffer twenty hopeless appeals than to discourage one meritorious issue from being raised. The discounts offered for guilty pleas already give defendants a powerful incentive to waive significant claims, and we should be very hesitant to offer them further temptation.

Of course, the widespread use of plea bargaining might be seen as undercutting the opposition to payoffs: If we bribe defendants to waive the adjudication of basic legal and factual issues with plea discounts, why not encourage them to waive the appellate review of those issues by offering payoffs?[6] The short answer is that plea bargaining is (or is generally thought to be) a grim necessity in a system that would be overwhelmed by the need to try even a significant fraction of the cases now disposed of by plea. There is no similar necessity for inducing defendants to waive the appellate review of their convictions.

It might also be objected that *non*indigent defendants face the same temptation to forego their appeals. If the cost of retained counsel discourages meritorious appeals, then perhaps that cost should also be borne by the state. But the state arguably has a greater interest in assuring adequate appellate review for indigent defendants. They may be far more likely than their affluent counterparts to have been victims of ineffective assistance, police misconduct, and prosecutorial overreaching, and far less likely to be aware of their legitimate grievances.

SCREENING BY THE APPELLATE COUNSEL

In this section, we will consider the role that assigned counsel can constitutionally play in the screening process. There is an obvious and tempting economy in having counsel decide which cases warrant full briefing, oral argument, and "conferencing" by judicial panels, and which cases can be resolved by expedited procedures. (I will use "expedited procedures" and "fast-tracking" interchangeably to refer to procedures which dispense with one or more of these three features of regular appellate adjudication.) Although attorney screening seems inconsistent with the duty of undivided loyalty, it is not necessarily unconstitutional. The Burger and Rehnquist courts have not interpreted the equal protection clause to require full adversary representation for indigent defendants, only those aspects of adversary representation which contribute to the odds of a successful outcome. Thus, the poor defendant has no right to a "meaningful relationship" with counsel, *Morris v. Slappy* (1983),[7] nor, as we have seen, to counsel committed to serving the defendant's own lawful ends, *Jones v. Barnes* (1983).[8]

If there was no reason to believe that fast-tracking reduced the odds of favorable action, screening by assigned counsel would merely create the appearance of impropriety.[9] If, however, there is any prejudice to the defendant in attorney-screening, it will offend equal protection almost as much as the outright denial of counsel before *Douglas v. California* (1963).[10] The "rich man" will not be subject to attorney screening, since he can purchase full briefing and oral argument in any nonfrivolous case, and there will always be rich men willing to do so if it increases their odds of favorable action. Unless the freedom of private appellate counsel is severely curtailed, assigned counsel cannot perform a screening function detrimental to their clients, nor assist the court in performing that function.

There are three distinct reasons why attorney screening may reduce the odds of favorable action for some defendants. First, judicial inattention to fast-tracked cases may itself reduce the odds of favorable action those cases would have enjoyed with full briefing and oral argument. Second, judges may give even less attention to cases relegated to fast-tracking by the defendant's own attorney than to cases they themselves, or their staff, have decided to fast-track. Finally, the attorney's involvement in the screening process may reduce her motivation or opportunity to find concealed error—the very basis for the assignment of counsel under *Douglas*.

It is difficult to demonstrate the adverse effect of fast-tracking because it is hard to separate out the accuracy of the screening process from the effect of the screening decision.[11] If the system correctly selected weak cases for expedited review, we would expect much higher affirmance rates in the fast track even if the tracking decision had no effect on the odds of reversal. To tease out the effect of fast-tracking itself, we would have to compare the fate of cases assigned without regard to their assessed merit to regular and fast-tracks.

Surprisingly, this has been done. Jerry Goldman has conducted one experiment and discovered a second, "natural" experiment in which significant numbers of cases were assigned to regular and fast tracks without regard to assessed merit.[12] In the California First District, unscreened cases were randomly assigned to argument or no-argument tracks; those assigned to the no-argument track were affirmed significantly more often. In the Ninth Circuit of the Federal Court of Appeals, cases already selected for fast-tracking were divided arbitrarily between the circuit's argument and screening panels; those sent to the screening panel were affirmed slightly but insignificantly more often, with significantly fewer published opinions.[13]

Even without statistical evidence, we would have strong reason to suspect that the decision to fast-track a case would reduce its odds of favorable action. Appellate courts generally operate with a presumption—a very strong one in criminal cases—that the trial court outcome is correct. In light of that presumption, the decision to fast-track a case may reduce the odds of favorable action in two ways. First, the tracking *procedure* may deny the case the attention needed to overcome that presumption. Second, the tracking *decision* may strengthen the presumption, since the classification of a criminal case as "routine" is tantamount to a preliminary judgment that the presumption is valid: appellate judges know better than anyone that a case with potentially reversible error is not routine.[14]

The presumption of correctness is strengthened still further when the attorney herself makes the fast-tracking decision. Even judges inclined to second-guess their clerks and colleagues on the value of full briefing might see no reason to question the attorney's own determination that it was not necessary. The very factors which make the attorney so useful for screening appeals—her familiarity with the case and her predisposition to find error—may encourage the court to draw a highly adverse inference from her decision to fast-track a case.

Finally, the attorney expected to make a preliminary assessment of the merits, significance, or complexity of her cases may fail to discover errors and complications she might have found if she began not merely with a predisposition to find error, but with an unqualified commitment to full adversary briefing and argument. As William Simon notes, "responsibilities to third parties, the public or norms of merit would require her to entertain hypotheses about the ultimate merit of the client's claim early in the proceeding, potentially blinding her to considerations favorable to her client she might otherwise have perceived."[15] Even if the attorney's judgment were not impaired, she might not have received enough exposure to the case to make a reliable judgment on its merits. While the attorney may be able to make a more accurate preliminary assessment of case merit than the defendant or the court, many veteran appellate lawyers feel that they cannot fully assess the merit of a case until they have briefed it.

For these reasons, the attorney in an adversary system cannot make screening decisions about her own cases, even when her familiarity with the case puts in the best position to do so.[16] She has strong reason to believe that her involvement in the screening process will blunt her recognition of hidden error and complexity, and that her decision to fast-track an appeal will reduce its odds of success, by denying it adequate review and by conveying an adverse judgment on its merits.[17] If she is to participate in the screening process at all, it must be as an advocate of full review for every client's appeal.[18]

SCREENING BY THE COURT

Judicial screening procedures vary in the timing of the decision and the resulting disparity in treatment: at one extreme are "leave" systems, where the decision is made at the outset and an adverse decision means that the case is not heard at all; on the other extreme are internal screening mechanisms, which are generally made after the case has been briefed and sometimes after oral argument, and which have no affect on its presentation, only on the judicial procedure for deciding it. The earlier the screening decision, and the more extreme and irrevocable its consequences, the greater the risk that obscure or subtle errors will be overlooked. The later the decision, however, and the less the resulting disparity in treatment, the less the savings in time and attention.

In this section, we will focus on screening mechanisms that curtail or abridge the basic functions of appellate counsel in an adversary system: the opportunity to search the record for hidden errors and to present the fullest possible case for reversal or modification. We will concern ourselves with screening devices which affect the court's internal processing of the case only to the extent that they invite or discourage adversary input. We will also have little to say about measures to limit oral argument on fully briefed cases, which offer neither the economies nor the risks of more severe screening procedures.[19]

The strongest argument for formal screening procedures is that they rationalize a process which goes on informally in all overburdened courts. Lacking the resources to provide full review for all cases, the courts have already imposed drastic economies. As Harlon Dalton has observed, "the right to appeal has begun to shrink to a mere formality in many jurisdictions, as appellate judges severely restrict oral argument, deliberate alone, write skeletal opinions, write unpublished opinions, affirm without opinion, and in some cases rule from the bench."[20] A formal screening mechanism might allow the court to conserve its resources for more significant cases without further detracting from the cursory review it now gives to weak and routine ones.

There is considerable doubt, however, that case-screening procedures can be both accurate and efficient: accurate in identifying the cases that warrant close attention, efficient in making that determination without requiring too much additional effort from the attorneys and the courts. I will argue that screening decisions made without counsel's participation will be unreliable, while screening procedures which invite counsel's participation will add another round of adversary litigation to almost all cases. Because counsel will have to participate to protect his clients' interests, the screening procedure may well consume more attorney and judicial resources than it conserves.

SPECIFIC PROCEDURES AND A GENERAL DILEMMA

We will begin by examining the most extreme screening option, a leave system, and then consider less drastic curtailments of full dress appellate review. The British system of criminal appeal "by leave" illustrates the risk in making a preliminary assessment of merit with a very limited opportunity for an adversarial presentation. Next, we will consider a more moderate option, the Rhode Island system of expedited review, which involves less risk, but also provides less obvious economies. The difficulties encountered in Rhode Island illustrate the dilemma facing any judicial screening mechanism in an adversary system.

First-Level Criminal Appeal by Leave

A leave system grants appeals at the discretion of a judge or judges, with counsel initially limited to arguing the "leave-worthiness" of the case. Proponents of such a system claim that it affords considerable economy at relatively small cost, since the difference between the quality of review provided by an overloaded system of appeals-of-right and a flexible leave system is not as great as might appear. Daniel Meador has observed that:

> Functionally, there is little difference between the kind of review a defendant may get in the U.S. Fifth Circuit, where every appeal is in theory a matter of right, and in the Virginia Supreme Court, where in theory all appeals are discretionary. Indeed, it could be argued that greater review is afforded in the "discretionary" Virginia system than in the "obligatory" Fifth Circuit system, because an appellant in Virginia can argue his position orally, if he so desires, in addition to filing a brief.[21]

One major objection to a leave system is that even if it permitted briefing and oral argument, it would not give counsel the opportunity to review the record for significant but obscure errors—one of the critical functions underlying *Douglas*' guarantee of appellate counsel.[22] A leave application process which gave new counsel an opportunity to review the record and consult with trial counsel would not be likely to conserve appellate resources; one which denied her that opportunity might undermine her value to her client and the court in finding issues worthy of appellate review. The danger of overlooking issues would be magnified by the reliance on a single judge to make the leave decision—a reliance that seems necessary if the leave system is to conserve judicial resources.

Some insight into these risks is provided by Meador's study of the British system of criminal appeals, in which leave applications are decided by a single judge but can be renewed at the defendant's option before a three-judge panel. While Meador found that less than 10 percent of appealed leave denials were reversed by the three-judge panel, he also discovered that the issues on which the first judge granted leave were not always the ones which the reviewing court found significant.[23]

Based on this limited information, it is hardly possible to judge the accuracy of the British system in picking the most "leave worthy" cases. It is clear, however, that much of its economy depends on the limited participation of assigned counsel. While counsel is in theory available to all convicted indigents applying for leave, Meador found that many indigent leave applications were completely *pro se* and that only a small minority were prepared by counsel. Moreover, only 20 percent of the rejected applications were renewed before the three-judge panel.

In a system where assigned counsel was constitutionally required to provide the same basic services as retained counsel, the initial leave applications would be more thorough, and many or most leave denials would be appealed. The impact of counsel's participation in the screening process is suggested by Rhode Island's experience with a system in which a single judge makes an early screening decision after a full adversary proceeding.

Fast-Tracking in Rhode Island

Rhode Island has adopted one of the earliest and most comprehensive screening mechanisms of any American jurisdiction. Within twenty days of receiving the record, appellate counsel must file a prebriefing statement. A prebriefing conference is then held before a single judge of the state Supreme Court (Rhode Island has no intermediate appellate court), after which the case is either placed on the full-briefing calendar or "fast-tracked" for summary disposition, with the defendant/state required to "show cause" why the conviction should not be affirmed/reversed. The full court hears oral arguments on the show cause orders, permits additional briefing, and may either decide the case or reassign it for full briefing.

The Rhode Island system differs from the British not only in the less drastic consequences of its screening decisions, but in making that determination after a full adversary hearing. It also allows counsel to renew the argument for full briefing after the initial fast-tracking decision has been made. While judges, prosecutors, and public defenders alike seem happy with its results, there are several indications that it might be less accurate and efficient than hoped.

The accuracy of the process is called into question by the fact, reported by Olson and Chapper, that 25 percent of the cases selected for summary reversal in the first year of the program were restored to the regular calendar by the full court.[24] The prevailing belief was that this percentage would drop as judges became more proficient at making screening decisions. The problem, however, may lie not only in the inexperience of the judges but in the limited opportunity afforded counsel to research the case before the prebriefing conference. Olson and Chapper note that "many of the defense attorneys are concerned that significant issues may be overlooked when the appellate process is accelerated and shortened."[25]

The efficiency of the process is undermined by the duplication of effort involved in having to brief the same case twice, in the "prebriefing statement," and then in a full brief or supplemental papers for the show-cause determination. The same case may have to be briefed a third time if it is initially fast-tracked, and then restored to the full argument calendar. Olson and Chapper report that the attorney reactions to the program's economy were decidedly mixed.

Repetition will be a particularly severe problem because the attorney's obligation to her client requires her to contest all fast-tracking decisions for nonfrivolous appeals: in addition to arguing the merits in the prebriefing and supplementary papers, she will have to argue at both stages for full briefing, to avoid the adverse consequences of expedited disposition.[26] If such challenges to fast-tracking became routine, the obligation to make them would become stronger, since the court would be more likely to draw an adverse inference from the attorney's failure to do so. While some Rhode Island defense attorneys value the screening process because it eliminates the need to file *Anders* briefs in frivolous cases, that gain may be offset by the repetitive effort it requires in weak-but-nonfrivolous cases.[27]

The Dilemma of Judicial Screening

The Rhode Island experience suggests a general dilemma for judicial screening procedures: The less attorney input it permits, the less reliable the screening decision is likely to be. The more attorney input it permits, the more protracted the process will become, since the zealous attorney must take every opportunity the court provides to argue for full briefing. Proponents of judicial screening obscure this dilemma in two ways: by failing to recognize the scope of counsel's obligation to challenge adverse screening decisions and by underestimating the attorney and judicial resources required to adjudicate the screening decision.

Thus, consider a relatively modest proposal for issue screening made by Carrington, Meador, and Rosenberg, who recognize that "defense lawyers themselves cannot realistically be expected" to avoid briefing marginal issues and "over briefing" routine ones and urge the courts to "exercise control of the extensiveness of the argumentation."[28] They propose that counsel submit a statement of points shortly after the notice of appeal is filed; the court's staff attorneys would then decide which points require full briefing and which were "so lacking in merit that no further briefing is justified for a fair and just decision"—so lacking in merit, that is, that they should be summarily rejected.[29]

If counsel is not allowed to challenge this staff recommendation, reliability will suffer, since the threshold decision on merit will have to be made before counsel has had the opportunity to fully review the record or research the issues. But if counsel can contest the recommendation, any economy will be lost in the resulting litigation. Carrington et al. attempt to blunt the second horn of this dilemma by arguing that "most defense counsel would not object" to an adverse recommendation, since they often recognize meritless issues and would "welcome a court directive relieving them of the briefing burden."[30] But in almost all cases, counsel *should* object, since the summary rejection of one or more of the nonfrivolous issues she planned to raise might weaken the brief, particularly if she sought to claim cumulative error or prejudice.[31]

Because the conscientious attorney would be obliged to protest many or most recommendations for summary dismissal, the proposed scheme would be unlikely to conserve attorney or judicial resources. A system where issues were routinely "over briefed" would be replaced by a three-stage procedure, in which counsel proposed issues, then fought for permission to brief them fully, and finally briefed those issues on which permission had been granted. The economies of this alternative are, to say the least, not obvious.[32]

Similarly, in urging that counsel be given the opportunity to respond to staff memoranda recommending fast-tracking, Oakley and Thompson note that "the judges need spend very little time reviewing the memorandum when there is no response."[33] For precisely this reason, counsel must respond vigorously to every adverse memorandum. The authors claim that "where response is forthcoming, the judicial inquiry should be less time-consuming because of its narrower focus."[34] But this will not be the case if the judges make an independent search of the record, as they are required to do in New York. Even if the judges confine themselves to the issues raised by counsel, it is certainly a debatable proposition that their deliberation time will be reduced by vigorous adversary argument.

Even a critic of internal screening as perceptive as Thomas Davies fails to appreciate the danger of involving counsel in the screening process. Davies notes "the difficulty of assessing the legal merit of an appeal on a superficial basis," and warns that this difficulty may diminish the quality of review for internally screened cases.[35] He suggests that appellate counsel be permitted to receive information about internal screening decisions in criminal appeals "and perhaps *with discretion* to request traditional judicial processing if such lawyers believe that a particular case is inappropriate for staff processing."[36]

In these circumstances, zealous counsel would have to request full judicial processing for every case she found meritorious enough to brief in the first place. If she exercised the discretion that Davies desires, she would violate her obligation to the clients for whom she failed to make the request, since even weaker and more routine cases would benefit from full judicial processing—as Davies himself points out, the perceived merit of a case "can be a function of the amount of time and thought" the judges devote to it.[37] Moroever, the failure to flag a case for full judicial processing would convey the attorney's own judgment that it was not worthy of close attention, reinforcing the already strong presumption against its favorable treatment.

CONCLUSION

The moral of this chapter is that most judicial screening mechanisms offer an exaggerated, if not a false, economy. If the screening procedure excludes counsel, it is likely to overlook cases whose merits are at all obscure, at least if the screening decision occurs early in the appellate process.[38] If it permits counsel's participation, however, it will either compromise her adversary role, by requiring discrimination inconsistent with zealous advocacy for every nonfrivolous case, or add another round of adversary argument to the proceedings, nullifying any savings in judicial or attorney resources.[39]

The same dilemma confronts screening mechanisms for civil appeals, but the justification for screening is considerably stronger. Although the rate of appeal may be much higher in criminal cases and the frequency of close or novel issues much lower, the greater interests at stake make screening less appropriate. The law-making and institutional control functions of civil appeals may be best served by limiting the access of disappointed litigants. The overriding function of criminal appeals is the correction of error against the defendant: like proof beyond a reasonable doubt, searching appellate review is part of the heavy burden the state should have to bear to deprive a person of his liberty.[40]

One of the primary responsibilities of a first-level appellate court must be to review the fairness of *every* disputed criminal conviction, however weak, repetitive, and uninteresting the issues it presents. The appellate court serves a vital function by performing this review patiently and conscientiously, even if it ends up affirming most convictions and rarely finds serious error. If the need to provide full review for so many routine cases creates "a judicial *Weltschmerz*" as Robert Hermann laments, it may be a critical part of the judicial function to bear the pain.[41]

NOTES

1. Oakley and Thompson, "Screening, Delegation and the Values of Appeal: An Appraisal of the Ninth Circuit's Screening Docket During the Browning Years," in Hellman, ed., *Justice Restructured: The Innovations of the Ninth Circuit and the Future of the Federal Courts* (Ithaca, N.Y.: Cornell University Press, [forthcoming 1990]): 156.

2. Carrington, Meador, and Rosenberg, *Justice on Appeal* (St. Paul, Minn.: West, 1976): 93–95.

3. While he could always solicit the opinion of his trial attorney, trial attorneys, even very good ones, are often poor judges of appellate merit.

4. The alternative of paying defendants not to take the consultation would further equalize the positions of indigent and nonindigent defendants, but would add to the administrative complexity of the scheme and work against the goal of encouraging more informed decisions.

5. A scheme that offered payoffs inversely proportional to assess merit, somewhat like plea bargaining, would be a constitutional, administrative, and moral brier patch.

6. This a fortiori argument is raised in its strongest form when the payoff for not appealing *is* a plea discount—in other words, when the prosecution insists on waiver of the right to appeal as a condition of the defendant's guilty plea.

Two 1988 Appellate Division cases about the validity of such waivers revealed considerable judicial ambivalence. In *People v. Seaberg*, 139 AD 2d 53, the Second Department upheld a negotiated waiver on the ground that the defendant enjoyed the same freedom to waive his right to appeal as his right to trial. At the same time, the court insisted that waiver was fully consistent with public policy, since it "permits the conservation of judicial and prosecutorial resources for those cases where more substantial issues are raised."

In *People v. Ventura*, 139 AD 2d 196, decided only three days later, the First Department confronted a case in which the defendant had waived just such a substantial issue, involving a questionable stop and frisk. Faced with a situation in which the defendant's waiver conflicted with public policy, the court invalidated the agreement, denouncing "autocratic attempts by the prosecutorial branch to insulate convictions from appellate review when no legitimate State purpose is being served."

Admittedly, there are significant differences between the two cases that may justify a finding of waiver in one but not the other: In *Ventura*, the plea agreement which contained the waiver may have struck the court as unconscionable: the prosecutor had already made good on his threat to double the three-year minimum term offered the defendant if he insisted on a suppression hearing, and then demanded the waiver as a condition of a six-year minimum term. In pleading guilty, the defendant made it clear that he was accepting the waiver under protest. In *Seaberg*, defense counsel had aggressively negotiated an extremely favorable nonincarcerative sentence, for which an appellate waiver seemed a modest price. The defendant sought to appeal only after violating the terms of his probation and receiving a jail sentence. Nevertheless, both opinions evade the tension between defendant waiver and public policy.

7. 461 U.S. 1.

8. 463 U.S. 745. If any form of explicit merit screening by the defendant's attorney were viewed as a conflict of interest, as I argued in Chapter 8 that it should be, it might be held to violate the defendant's right to "conflict-free representation" under the Sixth Amendment. The Rehnquist Court, however, is not likely to take this view.

9. This alone might be reason enough to prohibit attorney screening. Jerry Goldman observes that "if litigants expect the traditional model of adversary adjudication, that includes oral argument, the denial of oral argument... will remove the sense of participation that appears vital to the long-term legitimacy of powerful institutions." Goldman, "Appellate Justice Economized: Screening and Its Effect on Outcomes and Legitimacy," (paper prepared for Law and Society Assn. 1989 Annual Meeting, Madison, Wisc.): ch. 5, 42. The litigant's estrangement will be all the greater if he sees his own attorney as denying him the opportunity to participate.

10. 372 U.S. 353.

11. Thomas Davies suggests that the effects of fast-tracking may be seen in a decline in the overall reversal rate. Such a decline might indicate that the affirmance rate for fast-tracked cases increased faster than the reversal rate for fully briefed cases. As Davies cautions, however, an overall decline could also be due to unrelated historical trends. Further, an absence of change in the overall rate would not rule out an adverse effect on the disposition of fast-tracked cases—it might indicate only that the losses to fast-tracked cases were offset by the gains to fully briefed cases. See Davies, "Gresham's Law Revisited: Expedited Processing Techniques and the Allocation of Appellate Resources," *Justice Systems Journal* 6 (1981): 372.

12. These studies are described in Goldman, "Appellate Justice Economized."

13. More striking effects might have been obtained by dividing up cases that had already been selected for regular tracking. Fast tracking may be more likely to

obscure the merits of strong cases than regular tracking is to exaggerate the merits of weak cases.

14. In a system where there was no presumption of correctness, in which the courts expected a large share of its cases to contain reversible error, it would frequently be in the interest of the appellant to request a summary appellate procedure. His case might be a sure winner, so that extended briefing would only give his adversary the chance to obscure its compelling merits, or his case might be only superficially strong and vulnerable to close inspection. This will often be the case in a leave-granting system, where the prior selection of the case as one warranting the court's attention creates a very different presumption. Defense attorneys who have obtained leave to appeal before the New York Court of Appeals will frequently not oppose summary disposition and will sometimes request it.

15. Simon, "The Ideology of Advocacy: Procedural Justice and Professional Ethics," *Wisconsin Law Review* (1978): 29.

16. Even if she knows the most about the case, however, the attorney may not be in the best position to determine the appropriate level of review. While she may know far more about the specific strengths, weaknesses, and ambiguities of the case than the court does, she may know far less than the court about its *comparative* complexity or ambiguity. The attorney also may not be well-positioned to judge the value of the case for law articulation or institutional control. Nevertheless, her opinion would often be valuable even in these areas.

17. This does not mean that an attorney would have to do everything for one client that she did for another. In a jurisdiction where the court did not fast-track submitted appeals or draw an adverse inference from the failure to request oral argument, the attorney could certainly forego argument in a simple case, in which her brief required no elaboration.

18. While the CPR prohibits counsel from presenting "truly frivolous" arguments and thus requires counsel to make a judgment of absolute merit, *Anders* weakened that requirement by making withdrawal sufficiently painful to encourage assigned counsel to resolve any doubts in favor of continued representation.

19. In the past decade, a number of American commentators have proposed schemes for consolidated review incorporating two features of the British system of criminal appeals—(1) an emphasis on discussion rather than briefing, which permits the attorneys to narrow the issues in response to the court's expressed concerns and (2) broad, flexible review powers, which permit the court to consider unpreserved errors and to enlarge the record with stipulations, affidavits, or testimony.

These schemes differ from the British system in requiring active attorney participation throughout the appellate process, avoiding the dangers of judgment made without counsel's examination of the record. They differ from the screening mechanisms discussed in the text because they do not involve a single tracking decision but a flexible determination about the level of review appropriate for each issue.

These proposals also challenge the assumption that the primary communication between the attorney and the court should be the brief, with oral argument merely serving as a supplement in complex, novel, or particularly close cases. This assumption has been reinforced by the observed quality or oral argument in the intermediate appellate courts, especially in criminal cases: most arguments seem to be hurried paraphrases of the briefs, interrupted by a few impatient questions. Oral argument may have this character, however, just because it has been relegated to a secondary role. Particularly in weak and routine cases, the briefs have already exhausted the issue, and the courts tend to regard argument as annoying surplusage. Several recent judicial experiments with strict briefing restrictions and expanded oral arguments have found that the shift in emphasis makes the arguments livelier, more focused, and more incisive, and the briefs sharper as well as leaner, an adequate substitute for full briefing in all but the most complex and novel cases.

Several judicial experiments have utilized screening procedures to select cases for expedited briefing and extended oral argument. In California's Third Judicial District, for example, a program was adopted in 1981 for civil appeals that placed simpler cases on an expedited disposition calendar, with strict briefing restrictions and filing deadlines but unlimited oral argument. Placement on the calendar was voluntary, and because of the speed with which decisions were rendered, actively sought by many civil litigants. Because expedited disposition was voluntary and was not seen as having adverse consequences, it did not generate the resistance that criminal fast-tracking will frequently provoke. More than half the unsettled appeals were placed on the calendar, and most lawyers and judges found the procedure appropriate for all but the most complex cases. Chapper and Olson, "Expedited Procedures for Appellate Courts: Evidence from California's Third District Court of Appeals," *Maryland Law Review*, 42 (1983): 696.

20. Dalton, "Taking the Right to Appeal (More or Less) Seriously," *Yale Law Journal* 95 (1985): 62, 63.

21. Meador, *Criminal Appeals: English Practice and American Reforms* (Charlottesville: University Press of Virginia, 1974): 57. Meador cautions against confusing the discretionary character of the appeal with the criteria for granting leave—the primary criterion in a first-level system would be the possibility of significant error, not the significance of the case for law articulation or institutional control. Nevertheless, Meador recognizes that a leave-judge may emphasize important doctrinal or institutional issues at the expense of case-specific errors, however prejudicial (58–59).

This emphasis may be inevitable when a judge is required to screen but not decide cases, since it may be considerably easier to appreciate the significance of a doctrinal issue without deciding it than to make a preliminary assessment of the merits of a case-specific error—in the latter case, it is not clear whether the leave judge is supposed to be assessing the plausibility of the allegation, the probability of reversal, or the gravity of the alleged error.

22. While trial counsel would be familiar with the record, he would often lack the perspective and expertise to represent the defendant in his leave application. New counsel, on the other hand, would need to review the record and would have to acquaint herself with the case merely to know what parts of the record to order. The problem would be particularly acute in jurisdictions where the appellate court had the power to review unpreserved and off-the-record issues.

23. Meador, *Criminal Appeals*, 45–46. Using the success rate of leave renewals as a measure of the reliability of the initial judgment, we get a fairly comforting picture: of the 7,013 leave applications made in 1970, 6,275 were denied by the single judge; of these, 1,100 were renewed before a three-judge panel, which granted leave in only 104. The fact that the panel took less than 10 percent of the renewals might suggest that there is little divergence between the single judge and the panel, particularly since the renewals constituted only 20 percent of all rejected applications

and may have been made by those defendants most confident about the leave-worthiness of their cases. On the other hand, the small divergence may merely reflect the reluctance of appellate judges to overrule each other. Moreover, the renewals may have come not from the most legitimately aggrieved, but the most litigious defendants.

The vagaries of single-judge leave decisions are more strongly suggested by Meador's detailed examination of a single appeal (136–61). In *Regina v. Chilcott*, the single judge granted leave on two of the four issues raised in the leave application; the case was heard by a three-judge panel and reviewed by three American appellate judges: though six judges disagreed on the merits, they gave at least as much attention to one of the issues that the screening judge passed over as either of the two on which he based his leave grant. Had it not been for their fortuitous conjunction, this issue would never have received the full review which most of the judges clearly felt they warranted. This divergence is not surprising, considering the sharp disagreement I found among New York judges concerning the merit of fully briefed issues.

24. Olson and Chapper, "Screening and Tracking Criminal Appeals: The Rhode Island Experience," *Justice System Journal* 8 (1983): 25, 28–29.

25. Ibid. 32.

26. While Olson and Chapper state that "the show-cause procedure does not appear to be affecting the outcome," they base this conclusion on the fact that the proportion of reversals and affirmances is "within the prior experience" of the court. Not only do the authors lack a statistical baseline for comparison, but they apparently neglect the fact that one-third of the show-cause orders were against the prosecution. A higher reversal rate for these cases may well have offset a higher affirmance rate for the show-cause orders issues against defendants.

27. Ibid.

28. Carrington et al., *Justice on Appeal*, 88.

29. Ibid. 89.

30. Ibid.

31. Of course, the recommendation might cause counsel to reappraise the merits of the issue, convincing her that it was not worth raising. In that case, she would clearly have no obligation to contest the recommendation.

32. Carrington et al., also propose a scheme in which cases with simple or frequently recurring issues would be slated for immediate oral argument rather than extended briefing. If the oral argument provided a full adversarial hearing—if it gave counsel adequate time for preparation and adequate opportunity to present his case and respond to his adversary's contentions—the screening decision could safely be made by the court without input from counsel. But if the conditions for a full adversary hearing were satisfied, it is not clear how much judicial or even attorney time would be saved by the elimination of written briefs.

33. Oakley and Thompson, "Screening, Delegation and the Values of Appeal," 193.

34. Ibid.

35. Davies, "Gresham's Law Revisited," 372, 398.

36. Ibid. 402.

37. Ibid. 398.

38. Where cases are screened after full briefing, counsel's input into a screening

decision on oral argument or mode of judicial disposition may be less critical, both because less is at stake once the case is fully briefed and because the brief itself can always argue explicitly or implicitly for oral argument or regular tracking. I am not convinced that oral argument has a significant effect on the outcome or review of fully briefed cases decided by traditional judicial conferencing, although close students of the appellate process have concluded otherwise. (See notes to Chapter 4.) While Goldman's First District study, discussed in the text, showed a higher affirmance rate for cases randomly assigned to the no-argument track, the judicial decision procedures on that track appeared to differ substantially as well.

Thus, I find little to object to in the California Third District screening procedure described by Hanson and Chapper, in *Judge's Journal* 27 (1988): 6, in which the central staff seeks waiver of oral argument in a large percentage of fully briefed cases. In these circumstances, counsel's agreement to waive oral argument may not have the adverse effects that it does in other jurisdictions. First, since the court is requesting waiver, counsel is less likely to be seen as "writing off" the case by acceding. Second, submitted as well as argued cases are decided by regular judicial conferencing and receive written opinions. Finally, counsel can move for reargument after the decision if she thinks that the court ignored or misconstrued a point in her brief; such motions are frequently granted.

39. Perhaps the strongest argument against judicial screening, though somewhat outside our purview, is that it does not save judicial resources at all. In a comprehensive study of appellate court productivity in 44 states, Thomas Marvell found that summary judgment procedures "have little or no impact on output." Marvell, "A Time Series, Cross Section Study of Methods to Increase Appellate Court Output," talk given at *Law & Society Association*, Annual Meeting, June 10, 1987.

40. See Dalton, "Taking the Right to Appeal," 101–2. The point might be made in another way, by noting, with David Neubauer, that

> definitions of "important" versus "routine" cases are open to conflicting interpretations. To a defendant facing up to ninety-nine years . . . for a conviction of armed robbery, the case is clearly more important than one where a defendant received probation following a conviction for a "minor" offense. But the legal issues in the robbery case may be straightforward, while the issues in the "minor" offense may be new or novel. Neubauer, "Published Opinions versus Summary Affirmances," *Justice Systems Journal* 10 (1985): 173, 188–89.

41. Hermann, "Frivolous Criminal Appeals," *New York University Law Review* 47 (1972): 701, 703.

11

Increasing the Impact of Indigent Appellate Representation

This concluding chapter considers three strategies for increasing the impact of appellate courts and lawyers on the quality of justice received by indigent defendants at the trial level: enlarging the powers of the appellate courts to engage in factfinding and hear new evidence, increasing the involvement of appellate counsel in trial-level adjudication, and exploiting the position and the resources of the appellate defender to monitor trial counsel, to control wayward police, prosecutors, and judges, and to reduce unwarranted variation in sentencing.

LOOKING INTO THE GATEHOUSE AND BEHIND THE TRIAL RECORD

The need for extending the reach of appellate review has been suggested several times in the course of this book. In Chapter 7, for example, we saw that only 17 percent of all favorable action concerned pretrial issues—the issues which will affect the vast majority of cases settled by plea as well as the small share going to trial. While this small percentage may reflect the relatively settled state of the law on confessions, searches, and line-ups, it may also result from the poverty of the record in many cases, where significant issues of police and prosecutorial misconduct go undetected or inadequately documented. We also noted, in Chapters 1 and 7, the growing insulation of guilty pleas from appellate scrutiny and the continuing barriers to the appellate review of counsel's effectiveness, particularly in plea cases. Again, these barriers are partly doctrinal, but they are reinforced by the reluctance or inability of the courts to consider, or counsel to obtain, constitutionally relevant off-the-record information.

This section considers two convergent means of strengthening the appellate review of "gatehouse" issues—first, by broadening the scope of appellate review to permit the court to receive new evidence, and second, by increasing the role of appellate counsel in enlarging and supplementing the record available for appellate review. Expanded factfinding by the appellate courts and increased activism by appellate counsel are expensive and uncertain undertakings; their cost and their limited prospects for success force us to consider alternatives to the direct appeal as avenues of redress and reform for indigent defendants.

EXPANDING THE SCOPE OF APPELLATE REVIEW

New factfinding by the appellate court is not as radical a proposition as it might sound to appellate lawyers and judges accustomed to thinking of "matters *dehors* the record" as taboo. It is routinely practiced by the British courts and it has been frequently proposed by American court reformers.[1] The restriction on the appellate review of factual matters arose in part from practical considerations that became frozen into a rule of law. While appellate courts might reasonably limit their factfinding to cases where it is not feasible to delegate that task to a tribunal set up for the purpose, there is no reason why they must regard the trial court record as sacrosanct—an attitude Roscoe Pound derided as "record worship."[2]

Perhaps the strongest argument against a blanket restriction on new factfinding by the appellate court is that it routinely occurs in some areas, from findings of mootness to detailed factual updates in desegregation cases. The British experience shows that appellate courts can exercise unrestricted factfinding powers very selectively. If appellate judges find it awkward, cumbersome, or inefficient to take testimony themselves, they can always delegate the task to magistrates or referees.

The two principal advantages of new appellate factfinding are that it would remove the decision to reopen the record from a trial court committed to the status quo, and that it would free the appellate court from its reliance on a trial record often tailored to suppress the errors and misconduct of those who create it. It is easy, however, to exaggerate these advantages: appellate courts may develop, if they do not already have, even stronger presumptions against belated complaints than the trial courts, and the desire and capacity of the appellate court to get behind the record created in the lower court may be quite limited.

A strong case can be made for removing the decision to reopen the record from the trial judge. However impartial the judge may have been up to the verdict or sentence, he is likely to have acquired a strong personal stake in finality that will bias him against a motion to enlarge the record. After a protracted trial or plea negotiations, he may recoil at the invitation to order another round of hearings. Although some states, including New York, allow the defendant to seek leave to appeal the trial court's refusal, he must then overcome the appellate court's presumption in favor of the court below as well as its own reluctance to reopen the record.[3]

Trial court bias may be particularly strong in the two areas where off-the-record information may be critical to a just resolution of the case: the effectiveness of trial counsel and the knowing and voluntary character of a guilty plea. In the former area, the trial judge may be reluctant to acknowledge the possibility that significant misrepresentation has occurred in proceedings under his control; although he has no direct responsibility for counsel's performance, he may take a claim of ineffectiveness, even one based on off-the-record omissions, as an implicit reproach to his trial management.

The trial judge is even more directly involved in the defendant's plea of guilty. He may have directly or indirectly pressured the defendant into taking the plea, and he will have elicited the defendant's own assurance that the plea was knowing and voluntary. Conscientious judges will often seek to fortify pleas against postconviction challenges with airtight allocutions, and they can hardly welcome claims that their efforts were in vain.

While appellate courts value finality as well, their detachment from the case may make them more dispassionate judges of requests to enlarge the record. At the same time, a sustained exposure to so many repetitive, suspect, and unprovable complaints of false promises, improper threats, and neglected defenses might well make them unduly skeptical. If appellate fact-finding became routine, appellate courts could develop an even stronger bias against such claims than the trial courts.

The second virtue of appellate evidence-taking is that it would reduce a debilitating reliance on the lower-court record, a record often tailored to conceal the very errors that the reviewing court is supposed to detect. Martin Shapiro suggests that a primary function of appeals is to bypass the usual flow of information from the bottom up, a "process of successive summarization [which] gives lower levels ample opportunity to suppress and distort information, particularly that bearing on their own insubordination and poor performance." The appeal serves to give the reviewing court a "slice of life" whose presentation generally cannot be controlled by the "family circles" directing the flow of summarized information to the top.[4]

Obviously, an appellate court cannot serve that function if its review is limited to the record created by those "family circles." The standard plea allocution is a perfect example of such a record: the judge, prosecutor, defense attorney, and the defendant himself all conspire to "suppress and distort information"—about unresolved factual and legal issues in the case, and often about "the insubordination and poor performance" of the defense attorney, prosecutor, and judge in protecting the defendant's constitutional rights. But the example of the standard plea allocution also reveals the limited potential for appellate factfinding to cut through a distorted record to the "facts."

First, the belief that the appellate judges can discover the facts behind the bargain by summoning the parties before them is somewhat naive. If the judge, prosecutor, and trial counsel can conceal a multitude of sins behind a paper record, they can keep them hidden in live testimony; anyone who has read police testimony at a suppression hearing knows that far less articulate and resourceful witnesses can usually stick to a practiced script in the face of relentless cross-examination. The defection of the defendant from the "family circle" will not open a serious breach; if the defendant can rarely prevail in a "swearing contest" with police witnesses, he stands almost no chance against lawyers and judges.

Second, the record in which the trial-level participants conceal their "insubordination and poor performance" has been written for them by the very appellate judges who are now supposed to look behind it. In the 15 years since *Boykin*, appellate courts have been giving trial courts precise and increasingly permissive instructions on what they must do to make their guilty pleas facially valid. It is certainly optimistic to expect that the appellate courts would now, given the power, strip away the facades they have worked so hard to erect.

Even if we assume that appellate courts have the capacity and motivation to look behind the lower-court record, the critical question remains of when they should do so. On the one hand, the court could conduct a hearing whenever the defendant made allegations which, if correct, would present a meritorious issue. The obvious danger in such a liberal approach is that defendants would quickly learn to tailor their applications accordingly. The availability of a de novo hearing for any defendant with a facially appropriate application might provoke a flood of baseless complaints from previously quiescent defendants. On the other hand, the court might make a preliminary assessment of the defendant's allegations to decide whether to hold a hearing, relying on its common sense and collective experience. The danger in such a restrictive approach is that the court's threshold judgments of plausibility would inevitably be subject to unacknowledged biases and unwarranted preconceptions.

To make these competing concerns less abstract, it is worth considering how the proposed system of consolidated review would handle the most challenging defendant allegations: those that are commonly made, often made-up, but too serious to ignore. Consider the following variations in a case involving a 19-year-old defendant with no prior record charged with first-degree robbery after one of the two gunmen in a bodega hold-up names him as the driver:

(1) The defendant takes a plea to second-degree robbery, receiving the

minimum 1–3 year sentence. In the allocution, he admits his guilt but says he had no part in planning the hold-up. In moving to enlarge the record, he claims that he had told his trial attorney that he had no idea his friends were going to rob the store, that they insisted they were stopping off to buy a six-pack of malt liquor. He claims that his attorney told him that if he went to trial, the prosecution would not have to prove that he knew anything about the robbery, and that he could get a life maximum if convicted.

(2) The situation is the same as in (1), except that the defendant asserts in his motion to enlarge the record that he told his lawyer he was at a friend's house at the time of the incident, and that the friend and his mother would testify to his presence. He claims that his lawyer never even spoke to these witnesses.

(3) The situation is the same as in (2), except that the defendant went to trial, with his lawyer arguing his unwitting participation but presenting no evidence.

In all three cases, the court would face a tradeoff between economy and reliability. In (1), it would be in a far better position to resolve the likely swearing match between the lawyer and client by having them testify; in (2) and (3), it would be better able to assess the credibility of the alibi witnesses by hearing them subjected to cross-examination. A court which felt obliged to hold a full-blown hearing in these circumstances, however, might reasonably fear that it would be overwhelmed by largely spurious claims, not only from defendants who would have appealed under a more restrictive system of review, but from others who could not resist the opportunity to make their trial attorneys account for perceived deficiencies.[5]

A court which declined to order full hearings to resolve such allegations, however, would have to decide them on the strength of clashing affidavits. It is hard to see how it could always do so, particularly in those cases where the trial attorney contradicted his former client or where the alibi witnesses told internally consistent stories untested by cross-examination.[6] A blanket presumption for the trial attorney over the defendant, or against prior acquaintances as alibi witnesses, would be indefensible.

The "compromise" solution of relying on appellate counsel's discretion to call witnesses only when appropriate would also be unacceptable. If counsel requested testimony, he would implicitly vouch for the truth of his client's allegations; if he failed to do so, he would implicitly denigrate them. The temptation to draw a favorable or adverse inference from counsel's actions would be particularly strong in this setting, in which she might be thought to have access to other, undisclosed information. The fairest standard would probably be the most liberal, since it would protect both the objectivity of the court and the zeal of appellate counsel. Clearly, however, the need to obtain further evidence in many cases, particularly testimonial evidence, would greatly increase the time and expense of the average appeal.

ENLARGING AND IMPROVING THE RECORD ON APPEAL

These difficulties with appellate factfinding suggest that the movement toward broader, more meaningful review must come from another direction: from the efforts of appellate counsel to create a more complete record for review than the plea and trial process presently generate. There are two different, and somewhat conflicting, approaches that appellate counsel could take: closer collaboration with trial counsel in creating a stronger record, and closer consultation with the defendant in reviewing the performance of trial counsel and discovering off-the-record improprieties. While both approaches might improve the performance of trial counsel, the first would be facilitated by institutional affiliation between trial and appellate counsel, the second by an arm's length relationship.

Increased Collaboration between Appellate and Trial Counsel

The mere presence of appellate lawyers in the trial courtrooms may improve the performance of trial counsel. Their curiosity and critical interest may make trial counsel more self-conscious, and more serious, about the routine tasks of criminal representation. On the other hand, the presence of appellate lawyers may be more of a nuisance than a tonic. It may be naive to expect trial attorneys to act their best for guests from the appeals bureau when they resist the monitoring and criticism of their own supervisors.

Whatever their general effect on trial counsel, appellate consultants can enhance the trial record in a number of specific ways: by expanding the inquiry into possible pretrial misconduct through motions and hearings, by preserving objections to judicial and prosecutorial errors, and by framing new or unresolved issues for appellate review. The first function is often critical, since some issues will only be apparent from the appellate record if they are recognized at the trial level. For example, the trial attorney must know the right questions to ask the defendant about his treatment by the police to even suggest a basis for raising certain search and confession issues. Timely and specific objections are obviously important as well, since they compel the Appellate Division to consider claimed errors as a matter of law and permit their review by the Court of Appeals. Even though it has the power to consider unpreserved errors in the interest of justice, the Appellate Division is far more likely to give serious consideration to an issue if it was already litigated at the trial level.

The most active and focused form of record creation by the defense is the "test case," which raises a novel or unresolved issue through a pretrial hearing or extensive trial testimony. Typically, the defense will bring a test case to challenge a recurring practice of the police, prosecutors, or judicial administrators through a pretrial hearing or extensive trial testimony. A case may be appropriate for such a test because the prejudice to the defendant is particularly clear, the dangers of the practice are especially visible, or simply because the trial judge is willing to permit a full factual inquiry into an issue which other judges have dismissed or summarily resolved. A good example of the last is the extensive pretrial hearing held on the exclusion of minorities by the grand jury selection process in Kings County, whose minutes filled thirteen volumes and were incorporated in the record of several major appeals, including the Court of Appeals case which finally decided the issue.[7] Such test cases permit the appellate courts to examine parts of the "gatehouse" normally closed to their scrutiny.

While the involvement of appellate lawyers in trial litigation would obviously facilitate record-making, preservation, and the development of test cases, it has several drawbacks. The greater the participation of the appellate attorney, the harder it may be for her to assume the detached perspective necessary for effective briefing. The appellate attorney may also find herself in an awkward position to invoke the court's interest of justice review if she or an appellate colleague missed an issue at the trial level. The court may be especially concerned about "sandbagging" in this setting, suspecting that an objection was deliberately withheld in the belief that it would do more good on appeal than at trial.[8] This suspicion may force the appellate attorney to become, in effect, a witness for her own innocent intentions. This situation should not arise very frequently, however, since appellate counsel should miss very few objections and should be able to make a trial court record of any error that she failed to object to at the appropriate moment.

The greatest problem with close collaboration between appellate and trial defenders is one of resources. An appellate attorney who is drafting a trial court motion, second-seating a trial, or collaborating on a test case is not engaged in her usual business of writing briefs. Although her familiarity with the trials she works on may facilitate her briefing of the case when *and if* they come up for appeal, her participation may also disqualify her from handling the appeal. Even if it does not, she will hardly be able to make up for the time she has invested in the trial proceedings. The routine involvement of appellate lawyers in trial litigation would require a larger appellate staff to produce the same number of briefs, significantly increasing the cost of appellate defense.

Both the potential and the limitations of increased collaboration are illustrated by the experience of CAB in the mid–1980s. Until 1985, CAB took little advantage of its affiliation with CDD to lay the groundwork for its appeals. The sheer size of LAS, and the physical isolation of CAB from any of the trial bureaus, precluded the kind of informal exchange and consultation between trial and appellate attorneys that is commonplace in smaller indigent defense organizations. The only cases on which CAB attorneys would routinely collaborate with CDD attorneys were those remanded to CDD after a CDD-procured reversal.[9] As we know from Chapter 5, however, such reversals are relatively uncommon events.

Starting in 1985, CAB began experimenting with a number of programs to increase its collaboration with CDD. It introduced a Coordinated Issue-Litigation Project, flagging new or neglected issues for CDD attorneys in the hopes of developing test cases. It offered lecture series for new CDD attorneys and CDD supervisors on preservation, record-making, and new developments in criminal law. The CAB staff attorneys set up a "hot line" for trial attorneys needing research assistance and updating on novel or complex issues. Finally, CAB began a "second-seating" program, assigning volunteers to work with CDD attorneys, to receive a basic exposure to trial work, and to take part in significant trials and hearings.

While some of these programs sparked considerable interest, they did not produce a major legal case or a significant change in the working relations between CAB and CDD. The Coordinated Issue-Litigation Project succumbed to poor publicity and a lukewarm response, generating few inquiries from CDD and no coordinated litigation. Part of the problem was apparently that the upper level CDD supervisors whose cooperation was essential had little interest in promoting a project they could not control. The lecture series were reportedly well-attended and well-received, but no attempt was made to gauge their effect on motion practice and trial performance. The "hot line" was used only infrequently, and mostly, CAB staffers suspected, by CDD attorneys too lazy to do their own research on routine issues. While trial and appellant participants found the second-seating program very rewarding, only a small number of attorneys took part and it is not clear if the program provided anything more than an exciting "field trip."

The mixed success and token character of these programs suggest some of the difficulties in achieving close and systematic collaboration. First, many trial attorneys may have little or no interest in providing laboratories for appellate research, either because they are preoccupied with doing as much as they can for their clients in the trial court or simply because, like the judges and prosecutors, they are mainly concerned with "moving" as many cases as quickly as possible.

Second, more concerted collaboration would be a very expensive proposition. Not only would it slow the disposition of cases at the trial level, requiring prosecutors and judges to devote more time to the resolution of more and better researched defense motions, but it would divert resources from appellate briefing. The trade-off is explicit in the second-seating program, which offers CAB attorneys the same credit for taking part in a trial as they receive for writing a brief.

Involving the Client in the Review Process

One effect of restricting the appellate court to the trial record has been to make the defendant himself largely irrelevant to the appellate process.

While he must initiate the appeal by hiring a lawyer or filing a poor person application and must be consulted if there is a risk in appealing or a possible conflict of interest, he does not need to be heard from again. When his attorney contacts him, it is mainly as a courtesy—to introduce herself, to send him a copy of the brief, to let him know when the appeal is calendared, and to tell him how the case came out.

The neglect of appellate clients by assigned counsel is not universal: the appellate defenders in some states visit all of their clients before the appeal is filed. CAB, however, has a policy authorizing client visits only when necessary to ensure the client's understanding of a risk involved in his appeal. While CAB attorneys are encouraged to pursue plausible client allegations of off-the-record improprieties or newly discovered evidence, they do not actively probe for this information. Given the limited education and legal understanding of most convicted indigents, CAB reliance on the client's initiative virtually guarantees that a significant number of serious improprieties will be overlooked.

A policy of personally interviewing every client for possible ineffectiveness and off-the-record improprieties would undoubtedly yield more dross than gold. Nevertheless, in a small number of cases, it would reveal critical facts concerning the advice given the defendant by counsel or the evidence available to the defense. While the courts might be reluctant to consider this information, particularly in plea cases, their refusal to do so would permit the defendant to raise the same claim in a federal habeas action. In a setting where the odds of reversal are extremely low to begin with, this seems a more than adequate justification for the expense and aggravation.

THE APPELLATE DEFENDER AS MONITOR AND GADFLY

Thus far, we have considered measures to improve the quality of appellate review on a case-by-case basis. Unfortunately, the success of these measures appears to depend on an improbable level of interest and cooperation from the appellate courts and the trial defender. In this section, we examine the possibilities for unilateral action by the appellate defender. I believe that there is a great deal an appellate defender organization (which I will refer to as an "appellate defender" in the rest of this chapter) could do on its own initiative to encourage and sometimes embarrass the official participants in the criminal justice system, including its affiliated trial attorneys, into treating indigent defendants with greater fairness and respect.

Specifically, I will consider three measures which would extend the role of the appellate defender beyond its prescribed task of representing individual defendants in their direct appeals and other postconviction challenges: (1) monitoring the performance of trial counsel in plea cases and other nontrial dispositions; (2) analyzing plea bargains to establish presumptive dispositions; and (3) seeking sanctions against officials who repeatedly violate defendants' rights. These measures have both a retrospective and a prospective aspect: they increase the information about trial-level practices that can be used in the direct appeal, and they improve those practices through the heightened scrutiny they offer.

While these measures are tailored for an institutional appellate defender with the resources to collect and analyze information from a large number of cases, they can be adapted by individual appellate attorneys working cooperatively with that defender. Although they would increase the workload of appellate attorneys, they would not require them to compromise their zealous representation of individual clients. In some cases, they would benefit clients in their direct appeals; in others, they would benefit indigent defendants generally, through better trial representation, more restrained prosecution, or fairer sentencing.

Monitoring the Performance of Trial Counsel

Rather than limiting itself to largely futile claims of ineffectiveness, an appellate defender can attempt to impose minimum standards of representation on the trial attorneys whose cases it inherits. Although such a monitoring function might be performed more effectively by an independent appellate defender, it is instructive to consider how an affiliated defender like CAB could assume a supervisory role within its own organization and then extend its supervision to unaffiliated trial attorneys.[10]

The simplest and most effective way of making trial attorneys accountable may be to demand an accounting from them in every case. An institutional appellate defender could reasonably insist that its affiliated trial attorneys keep a written summary of what was said by, said to, and done for each client. The format of these summaries could be standardized or left up to the individual trial attorney; their level of detail would evolve as a compromise between the trial attorneys' time constraints and the appellate attorneys' desire to know as much as possible about the course of trial-level representation.

Log-keeping would certainly add to the burdens on overworked trial attorneys. It would place greater demands on more zealous attorneys, who talk more to, and do more for, their clients. But most conscientious attorneys already keep some record of their conversations with clients, prosecutors, and judges, and checklists of motions and deadlines. A log would merely require a more complete and more formal record.

While some trial attorneys would be impervious to appellate oversight, and others resentful of it, the prospect of in-house review would be a stronger motivating factor than the remote possibility of an ineffectiveness claim by substitute counsel or the even remoter possibility of an ineffectiveness finding by the appellate court.[11] The motivating effect of internal review would be greatest in cases where the trial attorney was relieved at an early stage and the ultimate responsibility for the disposition devolved on substitute counsel:

the appellate attorney could ascertain whether the trial attorney had falsified or exaggerated a claim of conflict as a means of disposing of an unwanted case—a practice which McConville and Mirsky found to be distressingly common.[12]

Once log-keeping became an accepted practice within an institutional defense organization, it could be imposed on the assigned counsel panel, with trial panel attorneys required to keep case logs as a condition of compensation. If the panel administrators were reluctant to impose this requirement, the institutional defender could bring pressure to bear by refusing to take all cases in which the trial attorney had not kept an adequate record of his representation, severely burdening an appellate panel too small to handle its normal caseload. As a less drastic measure, the institutional defender could argue presumptive ineffectiveness in all such cases.

A record-keeping requirement, enforced by vigilant appellate defenders, would make wholesale neglect less profitable for the courthouse regulars who, in New York City, continue to take a disproportionate share of panel cases. It might encourage even hardened regulars to go through the motions, literally and figuratively, of adversary representation. Admittedly, such logs could hide more than they revealed, recording the formally correct advice given by the attorney to his client, while revealing nothing of the conflict and misunderstanding just below the surface. Still, even perfunctory consultation, investigation, and motion practice would be a vast improvement over the outright neglect found by McConville and Mirsky.[13]

If log-keeping became a standard part of assigned representation, case logs would inevitably be sought in making or rebutting ineffectiveness claims. While the threat to attorney-client confidentiality might prevent their widespread use, their mere existence might encourage the courts to demand greater accountability from trial counsel. Eventually, the acceptance of case logs as a device for internal monitoring and their occasional use in appellate litigation might encourage the courts to adopt the minimum standards or "checklist" approach to ineffectiveness urged by defendants' rights advocates.[14]

Reviewing the Outcomes of Plea Negotiation

Given the poor quality of indigent representation at the trial level, it is certainly important for the appellate defender to subject the plea-bargaining process to close scrutiny. The more a negotiated sentence exceeds the "going rate" for similar offenses by similar offenders, the closer appellate counsel should look for duress, misrepresentation, or incompetence that would invalidate the plea. Such procedural scrutiny, however, is of limited value in a system that depends on quickly transacted pleas for the bulk of its criminal dispositions.

The problem is not only that the courts tolerate a high level of coercion, deception, and bad representation in the bargaining process, but that the defendant can end up with a bad deal without suffering any procedural impropriety.[15] He may have the misfortune to be assigned a naive or risk-averse defender, a prosecutor out to make a reputation as tough and uncompromising, or a judge whose own standards for acceptable plea discounts are much stricter than the usual practice. He himself may cling to the belief that he can win further concessions by holding out, paying the price for his recalcitrance or naivete with a final offer two or three times higher than the first.

Although the New York Appellate Division has the power to reduce any sentence above the legal minimum, even a negotiated one, the defendant who has given his formal assent to a bad deal can presently expect no relief on appeal. The court is likely to be far more tolerant of disparities in negotiated sentences than in sentences imposed after trial—and it is extremely tolerant of the latter. Moreover, a negotiated sentence, usually for a lesser offense than the one charged, will look very lenient in absolute terms, however harsh it may be comparatively.

The appellate defender can play an important role in reducing and occasionally redressing these disparities. It can ensure that even the greenest trial attorney knows the going rates; it can present statistical evidence of disproportionality to the court. But, to achieve either of these objectives, an appellate defense organization must collect and analyze data on the actual patterns of plea bargaining in the jurisdiction, to establish what the defendant's "presumptive" sentence or disposition would have been, given the offenses he was charged with and his prior record.

This sort of information has been collected for the past fifteen years by sentencing commissions preparing judicial or legislative guidelines. New York's short-lived sentencing guidelines commission, for example, compiled and analyzed a great deal of relevant data in 1983–1984. If a state sentencing commission has collected this information, the appellate defender should use and update it; if not, the appellate defender should insist that the information be collected, or undertake the collection itself. To proceed on its own, the appellate defender would have to collect plea and sentencing information on all defendants convicted by plea, whether they were represented by assigned or retained counsel and whether or not they appealed.[16]

While the prosecution would obviously not be bound to accept a presumptive disposition in any particular case, such research would clarify the norms around which negotiation should take place. The effect of more explicit and documented norms would be to give defendants more consistent and predictable deals, not necessarily more favorable ones. The increased reliance on these norms should also serve to individualize plea negotiations, focusing the negotiations on special factors which warrant a departure.

Presumptive plea dispositions could also play a significant role on appeal. While the court would be very unlikely to reduce a defendant's sentence merely because it exceeded the going rate, a statistical disparity would give additional force to a strong excessiveness claim. In introducing a standard of outcome fairness, the appellate defender might also reduce the court's reliance on spurious procedural justifications for harshly negotiated sentences. At the same time, the court would be likely to adopt a very strong presumption in favor of any sentence within the presumptive range, making it even harder to make a successful excessiveness claim based on unusual circumstances. Nevertheless, the recognition of presumptive plea dispositions would almost certainly help more defendants than it hurt, at least in a jurisdiction which did not allow sentence appeals by the prosecution.

Discovering Patterns of Misconduct and Tracking Repeat Offenders

The volume of cases reviewed by an institutional appellate defender may enable it to discover and document patterns of police, prosecutorial, or judicial misconduct that would otherwise elude detection. Some misconduct will only be apparent in its repetition, like superficially credible police testimony about the suspect's movements that is repeated verbatim by different officers in different proceedings; other misconduct will merely be exacerbated by repetition, like inflammatory remarks by a judge or prosecutor.

At the present time, the research necessary to discover such patterns is conducted only informally and haphazardly—an individual appellate attorney will circulate a memo to his colleagues, asking if any of them has encountered a biased charge from judge X, an inflammatory summation from judge Y, or incredible testimony from officer Z. Far more evidence of this sort would be discovered if it was compiled centrally; an appellate attorney could simply punch up the "yellow sheet" on a particular judge, prosecutor, or police officer, or the file on a particular type of erroneous charge, inflammatory summation, or suspicious testimony.

The discovery of patterns of official misconduct will sometimes benefit the individual defendant in his direct appeal, for example, in rebutting a claim that the intemperate remarks of a judge or prosecutor were merely a response to defense provocation, or in convincing the appellate court to "make an example" of a recalcitrant prosecutor who has repeatedly flouted its rulings. More often, however, the information will be of little use in the defendant's direct appeal: police testimony, for example, cannot be "impeached" on appeal by information that was not available to the judge or jury, since the appellate court is not deciding the truth of the officer's testimony, but the validity of the ruling or verdict in light of the evidence presented.

Even if the discovery of such misconduct does not avail the injured defendant, however, it can be of prospective benefit to other defendants. Critics of the exclusionary rule have long insisted that official misconduct is more effectively deterred by sanctioning the official than by suppressing the evidence or reversing the defendant's conviction. Even if professional disciplinary proceedings are not an adequate substitute for reversal, they are certainly an under-utilized supplement.

Thus, appellate attorneys should bring their clients' well-founded complaints of official misconduct before the appropriate disciplinary bodies: in New York, the police civilian review board and internal affair divisions, the Appellate Division's Character and Fitness Committee, and the state's Judicial Conduct Committee.[17] The effectiveness of these complaints will not depend on harsh sanctions from the disciplinary bodies. As criminal defendants know all too well, the process can be the punishment. While even the most egregious and well-documented misconduct against indigent defendants is unlikely to receive more than a slap on the wrist, the aggravation and expense of a disciplinary hearing may be a far more effective deterrent than the remote threat of reversal.[18]

An institutional defender would obviously be much better equipped to collect such information than individual appellate attorneys, and the defender could be required to share its information with those attorneys. In return, assigned counsel would be expected to submit any offending or suspicious conduct they discovered to the "data bank." It would also be appropriate for the state to defray the cost of collecting this information, perhaps in the form of a contribution from the administrator of the assigned counsel panel to the institutional defender.

Why the Appellate Defender?

It might be argued that the proposed monitoring and data collection functions could be performed more effectively by an independent agency, unencumbered by the appellate defender's responsibilities to individual clients. Unfortunately, there is no agency in most jurisdictions with the inclination or capacity to act as a watchdog for indigent defendants.[19] Moreover, the appellate defender in New York already has a strong commitment to protecting the rights of indigent defendants and a history of skilled advocacy on their behalf. In a criminal justice system dominated by a corner-cutting, time-serving bureaucratic mentality, zeal is a precious commodity.

Several commentators have proposed the trial judge as a monitor of trial counsel, emphasizing the obvious advantages of contemporaneous monitoring.[20] While they acknowledge the threat to litigant autonomy and judicial neutrality, they ignore the more realistic danger that judicial oversight would be utterly pro forma in a system where judges are just as impatient as assigned counsel to "move" cases.[21] In contrast to trial judges, appellate counsel can monitor assigned counsel without fear for neutrality or case flow, and with full access to confidential information.

The critical question is whether the appellate defender can be enlisted in the cause of systematic reform without imposing too great a financial burden on its operation, jeopardizing the institutional support and good will it needs to maintain its effectiveness, or compromising its duties to individual clients. I will briefly consider the budgetary, political and ethical difficulties that will confront an appellate defender like CAB in its efforts to expand its role.

Workload. If the attorneys for the appellate defender monitor trial attorneys, meet with their clients, and bring disciplinary proceedings against police, prosecutors, and judges, they will obviously have less time to write briefs. The marginal effort needed for these other activities may not be very great, however, since most of the research they require will be carried out by the Managing Attorney's office or conducted in the course of preparing individual appeals.[22] The individual attorney will need only a few extra minutes to read over case logs and presumptive disposition tables, which will provide useful background information regardless of how she decides to proceed. While the grievances brought to a disciplinary board may have a different format and a wider scope than the issues raised on appeal, the essence of the complaint will usually be the same. The economy in having the appellate defender serve as monitor and watchdog arises from the fact that it already reviews the conduct of a wide range of trial-level participants in the course of its normal representation.

Institutional Position. The appellate defender must work with the trial attorneys whose performance it is scrutinizing, demand increased funding from the city or state to broaden its attacks on the conduct of public officials, and seek the often discretionary intervention of an appellate court whose supervision of the criminal justice system it subjects to continual reproach. Each of these constraints, however, may have an accompanying advantage. The appellate defender may have greater influence with its affiliated trial defender than an outside auditor; the city and state may recognize that policing by the appellate defender is a relatively cheap means of upgrading criminal defense and fear adverse publicity from a budgetary showdown; appellate judges may welcome the diversion of criminal justice housekeeping to other reviewing bodies.

Professional Obligations. In establishing presumptive plea dispositions and bringing disciplinary proceedings against public officials, the appellate defender may benefit some clients at the expense of others. If presumptive dispositions are utilized by the defense to claim disproportionality in some cases, they will inevitably be used by the prosecution to rebut that claim in others. If the courts are angered or threatened by the defender's recourse to disciplinary proceedings, clients with close and discretionary cases may suffer.

As I argued in Chapter 8, however, this kind of adverseness is inherent in representing a large proportion of the defendants appealing their convictions in a given jurisdiction.[23] This can be seen most clearly in the review of sentences: by definition, only a small fraction of all sentences can be found disproportionate, and a finding for one client marginally disadvantages the others. While the introduction of presumptive dispositions may shift the balance of advantages among the defender's clients, it will not make their interests any more adverse.[24] Thus, I see no barrier under existing conflicts rules to adopting measures that maximize the protection of indigent defendants as a class.

Although the practical and ethical barriers to the proposed measures appear to be surmountable, I recommend them only as an experimental supplement to the zealous representation of individual defendants. My hope is that the adoption of unorthodox tactics by appellate defenders will dramatize recurring injustices to indigent defendants and lead to the creation of permanent watchdog agencies to protect their interests. Even if these measures do not have a dramatic institutional impact, however, they will enhance appellate defense in routine cases, enlarging the record and allowing the defender to raise more frequent and more credible claims of ineffectiveness, excessive punishment, and official misconduct.

CONCLUSION: THE IMPORTANCE OF INDIGENT APPELLATE REPRESENTATION

The research presented in this book has provided a weak vindication of an expensive system of indigent appellate representation. It found that New York City's institutional appellate defender, CAB, was doing a good job of representing its clients, though a somewhat less satisfactory job of taking its intended share of the appellate caseload. It showed the system to be "working" in rectifying serious errors in a small proportion of cases, though often in an oblique and incomplete manner. The findings of Part II suggested that adversarial zeal played an important role in the present system of appellate review, increasing the probability of favorable action and perhaps also of significant error detection.

At the same time, this research has sharpened some of the concerns raised at the outset about the comparative importance of appellate representation in an under-funded system of indigent defense. The modest successes it revealed hardly explains why New York City should have increased the CAB staff by almost 50 percent at a time when there was an acute shortage of trial attorneys and investigators, criminal parts, and trial judges. The suspicion remains that the system provides its most zealous representation precisely where it can do the least damage—after the defendant has pleaded guilty or been convicted at trial on seemingly overwhelming evidence. The system may simply not be willing to pay the cost of providing every indigent defendant with zealous representation and individualized justice at earlier, more critical stages of criminal adjudication.

If this is true, however, it does not mean that the appellate function is merely cosmetic. The Appellate Division Justices certainly do not see their role this way, even if they affirm the overwhelming majority of the convictions brought before them. While they want to believe that the trial system is basically sound and may willfully blind themselves to some of its deficiencies, they are anxiously aware of the possibility of police misconduct, prosecutorial overreaching, and mistaken convictions. When they are forced to confront such errors and assured that they can correct them without threatening the basic operation of the trial system, they will seize the opportunity. The less frequently they reverse, the more important reversals may become as a vindication of their role. Because appellate judges believe at least some of what they say about their review function, they are susceptible to the influence of skilled counsel.

Throughout this book, we have observed the double-edged character of appellate review, in exposing error but refining its concealment. The due process revolution provides a number of striking illustrations: it has led to more professional and restrained police conduct but also encouraged police perjury, as in the notorious "dropsy" cases; it has reduced the frequency of prosecutorial misconduct, but it also increased its subtlety. These examples suggest the dialectic of appellate review: trial-level actors are subjected to stricter or more searching review; they learn, sometimes with appellate coaching, how to insulate their conduct from this heightened scrutiny; finally, new standards of review are adopted in response to the circumvention of old ones.

The process must repeat itself, because in instructing the trial participants how to act, the court also reveals how they can insulate their actions from further scrutiny. Sometimes the court will strive heroically to prevent the subversion of its directives; at other times it will invite it. In either case, that subversion will inevitably take place, and zealous appellate advocacy is necessary to begin another cycle of rectification.

Whatever impact they have on police, prosecutors, and trial judges, zealous appellate attorneys certainly play a role in keeping the appellate courts honest. They remind appellate judges that the rules they impose on lower-level functionaries are not self-enforcing; that the more demanding they are, the more likely they are to be circumvented. Perhaps most important, they help to individuate cases and issues that overburdened courts would be inclined to stereotype and summarily dismiss. The value of appellate counsel for indigent defendants cannot be measured in reversals or legal precedents, but in the frequency with which they get reluctant courts to render individualized justice.

NOTES

1. See Chapper and Hanson, "Expedited Procedures for Appellate Courts: Evidence from California's Third District Court of Appeals," *Maryland Law Review*

42 (1983): 696; Carrington, Meador, and Rosenberg, *Justice on Appeal* (St. Paul, Minn.: West Publishing Co., 1976).

2. Pound, "Appeal and Error—New Evidence in the Appellate Courts," *Harvard Law Review* 56 (1943): 1313.

3. Thus, the handicap to the defendant in bringing his motion to enlarge the record before the trial court would not be offset by granting him an appeal-of-right from the trial court's refusal, a feature of Paul Robinson's "Proposal and Analysis of a Unitary System for Review of Criminal Judgments," *Boston University Law Review* 54 (1974): 485.

4. Shapiro, "Appeal," *Law & Society Review* 14 (1980): 629, 641–42.

5. Many courts would simply dismiss the failure to investigate the alibi as a "tactical decision" by trial counsel, but this would almost certainly be mistaken in the trial case and very probably in the plea case. There is no apparent tactical reason for failing to interview the alibi witnesses for trial, to make an informed decision about which defense strategy to adopt. The only possible reason for not interviewing the witnesses in the plea setting is that an attractive offer might have been withdrawn in the time it took to do so, but that would be the exceptional case. The whole point of a record-enlarging hearing would be to determine if there actually was a tactical reason for costly actions or omissions by counsel, rather than to assume, as too many courts now do, that there was one.

6. Additionally, the specter of postconviction litigation might induce trial attorneys to practice a kind of "defensive lawyering" that would be beneficial to their clients as well as to the review process, for example, keeping a log of all offers conveyed to the defendant, of all legal information and advice given him, and of all the defendant's responses to these communications.

7. *People v. John Best and Marvin Winston* (Kings Co. Ind.# 811/78). See *People v. Guzman*, 89 AD2d 14 (2d Dept. 1983).

8. Of course, the court will have this concern whenever the same attorney handles the trial and appeal, which is common practice with retained counsel.

9. In such cases, the CAB attorney could bargain for any degree of participation, from an extended conference with the trial attorney to complete control of the trial proceedings.

10. On the one hand, it might seem that an appellate defender without institutional ties to the appellate defender would be in a better position to monitor its trial attorneys: it could judge their performance more objectively, and it would not have to be relieved when it was dissatisfied. On the other hand, trial attorneys might be more willing to accept an in-house review than an outside audit.

11. It might be useful to require appellate "monitors" to have some trial experience, the better to appreciate the pressures exerted by judges, the games played by defendants, and other factors hampering effective representation. Trial attorneys would be more likely to accept monitoring if they saw it as peer review rather than Monday-morning quarterbacking.

12. McConville and Mirsky, "Criminal Defense of the Poor in New York City," *New York University Review of Law and Social Change* 15 (1987): 581, 837–54.

13. Their use would raise a number of difficult evidentiary issues: Could the defendant subpoena the log in raising a civil or a collateral ineffectiveness claim? Could the trial attorney introduce the log in defending himself in a civil suit? Could the prosecution subpoena the log whenever the defendant claimed ineffectiveness in

a direct or collateral appeal? Would the log be accorded a presumption of accuracy or completeness? Would a "parole evidence" rule or estoppel preclude the trial attorney from arguing its incompleteness?

14. See Levine, "Preventing Defense Counsel Error—An Analysis of Some Ineffectiveness Claims and Their Implications for Professional Regulation," *Toledo Law Review* 15 (1984); Genego, "The Future of Effective Assistance of Counsel: Performance Standards and Competent Representation," *American Criminal Law Review* 24 (1987).

15. See *Bordenkircher v. Hayes* 434 U.S. 357 (1978).

16. Statistics based on the whole population of plea defendants would not only be more accurate, but more helpful to the appellate defender, since privately represented and nonappealing defendants may, on average, get better deals.

17. While it is not necessary that the attorney believe her client, she should have a substantial good faith basis for any charges she brings.

18. Such proceeding may also help to convince cynical defendants that their assigned attorney is really on their side, and that the appeals process is not merely part of a game in which they are the only losers.

19. In New York City, the Character and Fitness Committees of the Appellate Division respond to complaints of specific improprieties but lack the resources or the mandate to initiate investigations, let alone to engage in the routine monitoring of attorneys. The New York State Office of Court Administration is charged with collecting and analyzing data about the disposition of criminal cases, but its data is limited, unreliable, and poorly analyzed, and it has shown little inclination to provide information for defenders or independent researchers.

20. Meltzer, "State Court Forfeitures of Federal Rights," *Harvard Law Review* 99 (1986): 1235; Resnick, "Tiers," *Southern California Law Journal* 837 (1984): 1019; Schwartzer, "Dealing With Incompetent Counsel—The Judge's Role," *Harvard Law Review* 93 (1980).

21. Schwartzer and Meltzer suggest pretrial conferences as a vehicle for judicial oversight, neglecting the fact that such conferences are a luxury rarely afforded indigent criminal defendants in state court. Resnick offers the plea colloquy as a model for judicial inquiry into effectiveness, hardly an encouraging precedent.

22. The Managing Attorney's Office will certainly require a larger technical staff to carry out the necessary data collection and analysis, including several full-time programmers and a house statistician.

23. It might be argued that these tradeoffs do not involve a conflict of interest: a conflict only arises when the judgment or performance of the attorney is impaired, and there is no impairment in these settings, merely damage to one client's interests by actions taken on behalf of another. Under this standard, however, an attorney would never face a conflict in the representation of clients with sharply adverse interests as long as his actions and judgment on behalf of each was unimpaired. This is certainly not the prevailing view. It could also be argued that no conflict arises from displaced judicial hostility, since it is the court, not the attorney, who makes one client pay for actions taken on behalf of another. But this is merely to insist that the clients' interests should not be adverse, not to deny that they are.

24. Moreover, in adopting these measures, the appellate defender will not for the most part be making trade-offs between specific, identified clients, nor between groups of clients with distinct identities. All its clients, or at least those with close

or discretionary cases, may suffer from the court's hostility, and it is not disloyal to any of them to take appropriate and effective measures that run some risk of incurring judicial hostility. Similarly, the defender should not be thought of as owing a duty to the clients with above-average bargains as a class, a duty that would bar it from collecting statistics that would highlight their advantage.

Appendix: Suggestions for Further Research

In pursuing a narrowly focused research agenda, this book has made only a first pass at, or passing reference to, a number of important empirical issues that deserve extended investigation: the impact of appellate reversals on individual cases and the operation of the criminal justice system, the backgrounds and practices of institutional and assigned appellate defenders, the performance of assigned appellate counsel on discretionary appeals, and the craft of advocacy and persuasion in indigent criminal appeals. I will begin with the most conspicuous omission in a study of indigent appellate defense: the defendant himself.

THE DEFENDANT'S PERSPECTIVE ON CRIMINAL APPEALS

We know a great deal about the way that judges and lawyers view criminal appeals, but almost nothing about how the defendant understands them.[1] Studies of defendant attitudes usually stop at sentencing, while studies of appellate review generally focus on judges, clerks, and lawyers.[2] The defendant's perspective is easy to overlook because the defendant himself is almost invisible in the appellate process. Once he had filed the appeal and consented to any risks in pursuing it, he does not need to be heard from again.

When the incarcerated defendant does communicate with his attorney or the court, it is often through a jailhouse lawyer, who may function as scribe, in-house counsel, or consumer advocate. Sometimes, the presence of a third party is obvious; more often, it is merely suggested by the recurrence of certain issues and phrases in inmate letters. Jailhouse intermediaries not only shape the defendant's attitudes and expectations, but mute the expression of his personal beliefs, feelings, and values in his communications with the outside world.

Although the defendant is barely visible on appeal, he plays a critical role in the appellate process. He makes the threshold decision whether to appeal, and his decision has important consequences for the system of appellate review and for the criminal justice system as a whole. Large numbers of indigent defendants have taken advantage of the guarantee of free appellate counsel, contributing to an upsurge in criminal appeals over the past 25 years.[3] Equally important but less noticed, an even larger number of criminal defendants have *not* exercised their right to appeal; if they did, the volume of criminal appeals would be several times greater than it is now.[4] My own comparison of felony convictions with appellate dispositions indicates that the number of criminal appeals in New York City would quintuple if every convicted defendant appealed; if every defendant convicted at trial appealed, the number of criminal appeals would increase about 50 percent.[5]

The choices made by individual defendants are important not only for the administration of the appellate courts but for the development of the law. Constitutional rights are enforced and clarified through the complaints of convicted defendants, yet we have no idea how defendants perceive the uneasy alliance we have created between their self-interest and our public policy.

The dearth of information about the motives and expectations of criminal appellants became apparent when the Supreme Court was asked to decide, in *Jones v. Barnes* (1983), whether the constitutional guarantee of effective assistance required assigned counsel to brief every nonfrivolous issue pressed by the defendant.[6] The question was important because indigent defendants frequently insisted on raising issues that their attorneys felt would detract from the overall strength of their appeals; their attorneys frequently ignored these demands on the convenient assumption that they arose from misconceptions rather than deeply felt grievances. Lacking reliable information on the reasons why defendants pressed specific issues, the majority wrote as if appellants took a strictly instrumental view, concerned with nothing but the odds of a reversal or reduced sentence; the dissent treated convicted indigents as if they were more committed to their grievances than their freedom.

The debate over the psychological impact of criminal appeals on convicted defendants also rests on untested assumptions. Advocates of finality in criminal adjudication fear that prolonged appeals have a subversive effect on the defendant's adjustment, engendering false hopes and deferring rehabilitation.[7] Prison researchers are more inclined to see appeals and "writ-writing" as harmless and sometimes therapeutic distractions. Some academic critics suggest that appeals serve to "legitimate" assembly line justice to convicted defendants, placing a "fig leaf" of searching review over the vagaries of trial-level adjudication.[8] None of these positions has been buttressed by empirical research; the impact of the appeals process on defendants remains as uncertain as their motives for appealing.

To develop a comprehensive policy toward criminal appeals, we need to know a great deal more than we do about the prospective appellant. There are several critical areas in which we have only fragmentary or inconsistent information:

> *What percentage of convicted defendants actually appeal, by jurisdiction, mode of conviction, grade and type of offense, and sentence length? What discourages indigent defendants, particularly incarcerated ones, from taking a "free ride"?*

The data needed to answer these threshold questions typically fall between the cracks of two independent record-keeping systems: the trial courts rarely track defendants beyond sentencing, while the appellate courts usually keep records only for the unknown percentage of convicted defendants who retain or request counsel. While data from the two record-keeping systems could be compared, it might be difficult to match the two populations chronologically, particularly since there is no time limit in many jurisdictions for requesting assigned counsel. A more effective strategy would be to track a sample of convicted trial defendants, comparing the characteristics of those who completed and those who dropped out at each stage of the appellate process.

The information obtained from such a survey would obviously be valuable for criminal justice planning, since it would enable administrators to estimate the rate of appeal more accurately, not only from the sheer number of defendants convicted, but from various features of their convictions. The data would be valuable for explanatory purposes as well: the circumstances in which defendants appeal would suggest a variety of conflicting hypotheses about their motivation, which further research could help resolve. Thus, if most appeals came from incarcerated defendants, it might indicate that defendants usually appealed to escape prison sentences, that a defendant's sense of injustice was heavily influenced by the severity of his sentence, or that appeals generally reflected the norms of a prison culture more than the grievances of the defendant. A much higher rate of appeal among trial than among plea defendants might suggest that plea defendants were more satisfied with the procedure and outcome, that they were deterred by lower odds and greater risks, or that defendants who went to trial were simply more litigious.

The data would also be useful in approaching the question of defendant motivation from the opposite perspective, to discover why so many defendants did *not* appeal when it cost them nothing to do so. In some jurisdictions, like New York, the most significant attrition seems to occur between the filing of a notice of appeal with the trial court, which most defendants do through the agency of trial counsel, and the filing of a poor person application, which the indigent defendant must do at his own initiative after commencing his sentence.

During this period, the defendant may be deterred from pursuing his appeal by factors ranging from the paperwork to the risk of a higher sentence. In a study of California criminal appeals, Thomas Davies found that applications for counsel increased considerably after the state simplified its complicated application procedure.[9] Daniel Meador found that the rate of criminal leave applications in Britain dropped over 50 percent after a well-publicized announcement that defendants would lose "time served" if their applications were deemed frivolous.[10] In New York, however, an estimated 25 percent of convicted trial defendants failed to request counsel, even though the application procedure is very simple and there is virtually no risk of a higher sentence. There are clearly other disincentives that need to be understood.

What do defendants believe about appeals? What are their sources of information?

The defendant would be significantly misinformed about criminal appeals if he merely shared the misconceptions of the general public—that convictions were frequently reversed on the kind of technicalities that a smart appellate lawyer can find in almost any case; that when the conviction is reversed, the defendant usually "walks." But the defendant also has several other sources of information—his ex-convict friends, his cellmates, and his trial lawyer—who may correct or reinforce his preexisting misconceptions. Some appellate defenders send their clients pamphlets with basic facts on appeals, but these may be widely ignored or misunderstood.

A great deal could be learned about the sources of the defendants' expectations by interviewing the same defendants at different stages of the appellate process. It would be interesting to learn if defendants obtained more or less accurate information about appeals as they progressed through the correctional system, if there were shared misconceptions among defendants in the same custodial environments, and if there were systematic differences between defendants who pursued their appeals and those who did not.

Are defendants concerned about the kind of procedural issues that can be successfully raised on appeal?

It is doubtful that the issues of greatest concern to defendants are the ones most likely to succeed on appeal. For one thing, many defendants, particularly career criminals, apply a very different standard than their lawyers in assessing the conduct of police and prosecutors: not their official roles and duties, but the rules of a game in which both sides are expected to operate outside the written law. Thus, Jonathan Caspar has observed that a drug dealer may expect the police to plant narcotics on him when more orthodox methods of apprehension fail. Seeing this as part of the game, he lacks the "unequivocal indignation that the detached libertarian would be able to muster."[11] On the other hand, actions well within the law may outrage him: the same dealer might be furious at a politically motivated raid on a previously tolerated dope house, seeing it as vindictive or opportunistic.

There is some moral content to the defendant's responses: he is responding to the satisfaction or frustration of reasonable, if not "legitimate," expectations about how the game is to be played. At the same time, his grievances may provide little or no basis for an appeal: the politically motivated raid on the dope house will yield, at most, a very weak claim of desuetude. The counsel of fellow inmates and jailhouse lawyers may bring the defendant's expectations into line with the legal possibilities, or it may strengthen his preoccupation with unappealable grievances.

Because the beliefs and expectations of incarcerated defendants are continually shaped by their custodial environment, it may be impossible to tease out their spontaneous grievances from those cultivated by their fellow inmates. It seems more productive to compare the issues defendants raise themselves, in correspondence, motions, or *pro se* briefs, with those raised by their attorneys on their behalf. If the issues raised by the defendants differ little across cases, it may suggest that they reflect the idiosyncratic concerns of individual defendants less than the norms of jail and prison culture.

What motivates defendants to appeal?

Although the defendants who choose to appeal will have mixed and often complex motives for doing so, it may be helpful to consider four ideal types: the passive defendant, who takes the "free ride" offered by the system because everyone else does; the opportunistic defendant—Holmes's "bad appellant"—indifferent to substantive and procedural justice and only concerned with his chances for a more favorable disposition;[12] the substantively aggrieved defendant, who seeks full or partial exoneration for a crime of which he does not, or cannot, believe himself guilty; the procedurally aggrieved defendant, who is less disturbed by his conviction than by the manner in which it was procured.

The defendant's motivation will have an important, if not always an obvious, influence on the issues he wants to raise on appeal. The opportunistic defendant wants winning issues; he is indifferent to their content as long as they maximize his chances of favorable action. The substantively aggrieved defendant wants to protest his innocence, regardless of its merit as an appellate issue. Like the opportunistic defendant, he will judge the appeal largely by its outcome. Unlike him, however, he may prefer to win for the "right" reason and feel cheated by a victory that fails to exonerate him or acknowledge doubts about his guilt.

The procedurally aggrieved defendant will use the appeal as a forum for airing specific complaints about his treatment, which he will insist on raising regardless of their relative merit. His satisfaction with the appeal may not depend on the bottom line: he may feel vindicated by an admonition to a biased judge or overreaching prosecutor that does not result in reversal. Conversely, he may take little pleasure in a decision which gives him the right result for the wrong reason, since he is less concerned with the result than the means by which it is obtained. He may pose a significant challenge to appellate counsel, because his grievances often concern affronts to personal dignity and respect that the appellate process was not designed to redress.[13] Obviously, careful research is needed to assess the distribution of pure types and hybrids in the population of criminal appellants.

What are the psychological effects of the appellate process on convicted defendants?

The actual effects of the appellate process on the defendant may have little relation to the motives he had in appealing. An opportunistic defendant may get caught up in the process, ending up with an unexpected sense of indignation or satisfaction. A substantively or procedurally aggrieved defendant may find the appeal a rewarding experience, not because it eliminates his grievances but because it provides an outlet for his pent-up energy. His carefully nurtured grievances may disappear in the face of an appellate victory on completely unrelated grounds. The appeal may function as a form of denial, a harmless distraction or a cathartic release for defendants with very different conscious objectives.

From a procedural justice perspective, the appeal might be expected to have either of two opposing effects on defendant satisfaction. On the one hand, the procedural virtues of the appellate process may help to reconcile the defendant to adverse outcomes at the trial and the appellate level. The appeal may give the defendant a sense of participation which he previously lacked or provide him with the zealous adversary representation he had hitherto been denied.[14] On the other hand, the light cast by the appeal on the procedural vices of the trial proceedings may heighten the defendant's sense of injustice. A vigorous appellate challenge, particularly an unsuccessful one, may deepen his dissatisfaction, reinforcing his sense of unfair treatment at the trial level or making him aware for the first time of significant procedural violations.

The way the appeal is handled by the attorney and decided by the court may determine which effect predominates. The defendant is more likely to reconcile himself to adverse trial and appellate outcomes if his attorney has patiently explained the issues and the court has carefully addressed them than if his attorney has ignored him and the court has silently affirmed his conviction.

Who are jailhouse lawyers and how do they operate?

The appellate attorney is often involved in a ménage à trois. She writes to a 19-year-old Spanish-speaking client with a second-grade education and gets back a letter in Old Gothic typeface with florid expressions of gratitude and a long list of technical legal issues: several months later she gets a letter in barely legible scrawl, informing her in broken English that the client has been transferred to another prison. A client who from all previous correspondence seemed docile and acquiescent suddenly insists on filing a *pro se* supplemental brief that raises almost the same issues, in the same stilted language, as the brief filed by another client convicted of a different offense, incarcerated at the other end of the state. Three clients in different institutions write back after receiving a copy of their briefs, each declaring that "I couldn't have done better myself (smile)."

Eventually, the attorney gets used to the idea that she must communicate with a larger number of her clients through a jailhouse intermediary, who functions as scribe, counselor, and ombudsman. Sometimes, the presence of an intermediary will be obvious; more often, it will merely be suggested by the frequency with which far-flung defendants raise the same issues or use the same idioms. Jailhouse lawyers obviously play a critical role in shaping defendants' attitudes and expectations; to find out what defendants think and feel, it is not only necessary to get around these intermediaries, but to understand their influence.

Although jailhouse lawyers have frequently been disparaged, they have rarely been studied. A few anecdotal studies followed the Supreme Court's recognition of a qualified constitutional right to jailhouse lawyering in *Johnson v. Avery* (1969), but I have been unable to find any published research in the past 15 years. There is obviously a lot to be learned about the networks that provide inhouse legal assistance—their structure, self-regulation, and place in the larger prison community.[15]

It would be interesting to learn if the role of jailhouse lawyers has shifted to accommodate the guarantee of free counsel and the establishment of prisoner legal service groups—do they continue to function primarily as "writ-writers," or do they now serve mainly as liaisons with outside counsel and sources of second opinions? Do they continue to play a more active role in the collateral challenges that outside counsel rarely pursue?

WHAT DO REVERSALS ACCOMPLISH AND HOW DO THEY COME ABOUT?

Our analysis of favorable action in Chapter 7 provided some insight into the grounds for criminal appellate reversals but little information on their repercussions or on the role of appellate counsel in procuring them. We could learn a great deal about the impact and origins of appellate reversals through several simple inquiries. We could begin by tracking a sample of reversed cases like those examined in Chapter 7, noting the proportion subject to reprosecution, and, of those, the proportion resulting in dismissals, pleas, trial convictions, and acquittals. A study of federal reversals found the breakdown for cases subject to reprosecution to be 43.7 percent, 30 percent, 18.8 percent and 6.9 percent, respectively.[16] While the study noted that 85 percent of the dismissals resulted from prosecutor's motions, it did not examine whether those motions were prompted by infirmities in the original case or by new difficulties arising from the lapse of time since conviction.

A more comprehensive survey would also analyze the ultimate disposition of the case by a number of characteristics, including the specific grounds for reversal. Such an analysis that would require a larger sample of reversals than the 200 cases examined in Chapter 7.[17] It would be interesting to compare the plea bargains made on remand with a matched sample of initial pleas, to explore the extent to which reversals served to increase the defendant's bargaining power. Another follow-up study would look at the precedential impact of sampled reversals, to see if they had any wider effect. This could be accomplished simply by "shepardizing" the case and examining how it was invoked in subsequent decisions.

We could throw additional light on the impact of criminal appellate representation by starting in the other direction, by examining "leading cases" and seeing how they came about: who represented the defendant, how novel or close the winning issue appeared to be from the opposing briefs and the cases cited as precedent, how fully the court adopted the language or logic of the defendant's brief in its own opinion. The cases selected could be those most frequently cited from, or during, a specific time period, those featured in year end surveys on developments in the law, or those listed by judges, clerks, or law professors as the most significant. This survey might also yield some insight into the "attorney effect" on appellate dispositions, suggesting whether the momentum for resolving a given issue was imparted by the legal history of the issue or the initiative of the defense attorney. It would provide suggestive evidence on the extent to which appellate lawyers made important new law by their own initiative or simply managed to be in the right place at the right time.

DISCRETIONARY REVIEW AND ASSIGNED APPELLATE COUNSEL

The research reported in this book has focused on first-level appeals-of-right and referred only in passing to discretionary appeals to the state's highest court. Indigent appellate representation before the New York Court of Appeals would provide an interesting contrast to the Appellate Division practice we have studied. In some respects, it presents a setting similar to first-level indigent appeals before *Douglas*: the attorney is assigned to argue one of the small shares of cases that the Court has found to present a significant issue of law. We would expect the treatment of assigned counsel to be more gracious, the provisions for briefing and argument more generous, and the rate of favorable action much higher than in the Appellate Division.

According to CAB yearly reports on the Court of Appeals, the defense wins almost as often as the prosecution.[18] Prosecution appeals constitute a quarter to a third of the Court's criminal docket, however, and CAB statistics do not indicate what percentage of defendant appeals receive favorable action. While the high success rate for the defense might commend the Court of Appeals as a site to study attorney effects on appellate dispositions, its criminal docket is very small and the range of attorney skill may be fairly narrow. Leave is granted only in an estimated 5 percent of criminal applications, and the defense attorneys appearing before the court will already have demonstrated their proficiency in what *Ross v. Moffitt* (1974) described as the "somewhat arcane art of preparing petitions for discretionary review."[19]

THE BACKGROUNDS AND PRACTICES OF APPELLATE DEFENDERS

Much of this book has been devoted to examining the challenges and pressures facing appellate defenders, but very little has been said about the individuals who face them; about the lawyers who practice criminal appellate representation. The literature on indigent defense has given us contrasting and somewhat exaggerated profiles of public defenders and private assigned counsel: the former, young and idealistic but prone to demoralization and burnout; the latter, courthouse regulars with shoestring practices, subsisting on high-volume representation.

The McConville and Mirsky study of trial representation put some empirical flesh on both stereotypes. It found that, far from being sustained by the participation of the established bar, the private assignment system "relied on solo practitioners who organized themselves to obtain court assignments and depended on them for their livelihood." The study isolated a "core group of career defenders [who] took large numbers of assignments and received compensation greater than or equal to that received by full-time Society staff attorneys."[20] The study found LAS attorneys to be younger, better educated in criminal law, and less committed to remaining in the same line of work.

The contrast between the two types of defenders may be less stark on appeal. Because appellate work has lower entry barriers in training and overhead, it may attract a wider range of private practitioners. My own informal survey of the 18b appellate panel in AD1 found the caseload divided somewhat more evenly than at the trial level, with a smaller "core group" handling a more modest share of cases. Still, some disproportion is almost inevitable, since, with limited fact patterns and legal issues, appellate work has obvious economies of scale. It would be interesting to profile the two defenders in greater detail, particularly to see if the 1985 and 1987 rate increases had any effect on 18b demographics.

The research in this book has offered only fleeting glimpses of the retained appellate bar. A closer look would be useful both for an integrated view of criminal appellate practice and a fuller examination of attorney influence on appellate dispositions. We noted that retained appeals enjoyed a much higher rate of favorable action than CAB appeals in several areas. The high success rate for retained *plea* appeals suggested that the selectivity of paying clients contributed to their success. We were, however, not able to compare the quality of retained and assigned briefs, to test the other obvious explanation for the success of retained counsel—that they were superior appellate advocates.

It would be useful to have a panel of retired judges rate the quality of typical retained briefs, although it would be difficult to arrange the specific form of comparison we chose for assigned briefs, given the very small number of jointly tried pairs of paying/indigent defendants we would be likely to find. It would also be useful to compare the offense types in retained and assigned appeals, to see if retained counsel appealed a higher proportion of nonviolent, property, or "white-collar" crimes. Finally, it would be interesting to find out who retained appellate attorneys were: private trial attorneys handling the appeals of their convicted clients, appellate specialists in private defense firms, independent appellate specialists, or 18b attorneys supplementing their panel earnings with an occasional retainer?

HOW TO SUCCEED ON CRIMINAL APPEAL

Some of the country's leading appellate judges, including Justice Rehnquist in *Jones v. Barnes*, have volunteered advice to criminal attorneys about how to win on appeal. This advice needs to be taken skeptically, because judges may not be in the best position to know. Over the past two decades, social and cognitive psychologists have shown convincingly that lay and expert decision makers often have little idea of the factors that really influence their judgment processes; they tend to overestimate the influence of factors they think should matter and underestimate the influence of less recognized or acceptable factors.[21] Although we all prefer clever, understated commercials, for example, our buying behavior may be more affected by witless, hyperbolic, and repetitive ones. Similarly, appellate judges often complain about overwriting and hyperbole, but it is entirely possible that, at least up to a point, appellate counsel can be more effective by being less subtle.

Since appellate attorneys are, or should be, more interested in persuading judges than in pleasing them, this is an important area for empirical research. The ideal setting for pursuing it would be judicial seminars and conferences, at which appellate judges could be randomly assigned to different persuasive techniques in deciding hypothetical cases. There would be obvious problems in obtaining cooperation from a sufficient number of judges, in operationalizing argument styles, in generalizing from the specific arguments chosen, and in moving from hypothetical to actual decision-making. Nevertheless, the results of such simulations could prove quite valuable if they converged with more general findings emerging from the reviving field of opinion and persuasion research.[22]

A final area for research is the judicial perception of merit and frivolity. Appellate judges insist that, while they cannot define frivolity, they know it when they see it; some critics counter that the term is inherently ambiguous, a smokescreen for judicial impatience with criminal appeals. Our test brief results raised doubts about a judicial consensus on merit: one judge faulted an attorney for failing to raise an issue which two other judges deemed frivolous. This disagreement invites systematic research. Sitting or retired judges could be presented with a number of "borderline" issues, asked to rate their merit, and to give the reasons for their ratings.[23] It would be interesting to measure the extent to which judges diverged, and to attempt to discern patterns in their divergence—do their disagreements reflect different ideologies or judicial philosophies, divergent views on the legal merits of specific issues, or varying thresholds for briefing weak issues?

There is a need to test the widely held assumption that judges of sharply divergent ideologies will "recognize a frivolous appeal when they see one." This assumption has already been challenged by studies revealing the wide disagreement among federal judges over which claims warrant Rule 11 sanctions for frivolity.[24] It would be instructive to do the same kind of comparison for state appellate judges.

NOTES

1. See Carrington, Meador, and Rosenberg, *Justice on Appeal* (St. Paul, Minn.: West, 1976); Davies, "Affirmed: A Study of Criminal Appeals and Decision-making Norms in a California Court of Appeal," *American Bar Foundation Research Journal* (1983): 543; Davies, "Gresham's Law Revisited: Expedited Processing Techniques and the Allocation of Appellate Resources," *Justice Systems Journal* 6 (1981): 372; Marvell, *Appellate Courts and Lawyers: Information Gathering in the Adversary System* (Westport, Conn.: Greenwood Press, 1978).

2. See Caspar, "Having Their Day in Court: Defendant Evaluations of the Fairness of Their Treatment," *Law & Society Review* 12 (1978): 237; Caspar, *Criminal Courts: The Defendant's Perspective* (Washington D.C.: Government Printing Office, 1978); Caspar, *American Criminal Justice: The Defendant's Perspective* (Englewood Cliffs, N.J.: Prentice Hall, 1972).

3. See Carrington, "Crowded Dockets and the Courts of Appeal: The Threat to the Function of Review and the National Law," *Harvard Law Review* 82 (1969): 542; Bureau of Justice Statistics Bulletin, *The Growth of Appeals: 1973–1983 Trends* (February 1985).

4. The 1,670 criminal appeals decided by the Second Department in 1984 and the 1,876 decided in 1985 represented less than 20 percent of the roughly 10,000 felony convictions imposed yearly in Kings, Queens, and Richmond counties alone in 1982 and 1983. Thus, roughly 80 percent of all convicted defendants fail to file a notice of appeal, never complete a poor person application or hire counsel, or withdraw their appeal after counsel has been assigned or retained.

5. As noted in Chapter 2, court clerks estimate that 25 percent of eligible trial defendants never apply for counsel. If we assume that 50 percent of the decided appeals arise from trials—an estimate based on the disposition sample reported in Chapter 4—and that trials account for 15 percent of New York City felony convictions—then there are about 800 trial appeals for 1,500 trial convictions, an attrition rate of almost 50 percent. This rate of appeal is somewhat lower than in the federal courts between 1971 and 1976, where roughly 70 percent of those convicted in "contested cases" filed appeals. On the other hand, it is much higher than in Minnesota, which in 1976 reported only 200 requests for appellate counsel and 53 appeals filed for the *900* defendants committed to prison that year. American Bar Association, *Standards on Criminal Appeal* (1970): 1.1, 7 n.5.

6. 463 U.S. 745.

7. See Bator, "Finality in Criminal Law and Federal Habeas Corpus for State Prisoners," *Harvard Law Review* 76 (1963): 44.

8. Dalton, "Taking the Right to Appeal (More or Less) Seriously," *Yale Law Journal* 95 (1985): 62.

9. Davies, "Gresham's Law Revisited: Expedited Processing Techniques and the Allocation of Appellate Resources," *Justice Systems Journal* 6 (1981): 372, 390–91.

10. Meador, *Criminal Appeals: English Practice and American Reforms*, (Charlottesville: University Press of Virginia, 1974).

11. Caspar, *American Criminal Justice.*

12. Some instrumental defendants will seek to gain advantage from the mere act

of appealing as well as from its outcome: by appealing, a defendant may avoid the social stigma he would suffer in conceding his guilt of an unsavory offense, like child molesting, or delay the legal disabilities, such as deportation, he will suffer when his conviction becomes final.

13. Admittedly, these stereotypes are not only artificial but somewhat ambiguous—for the thoroughgoing proceduralist, the defendant protesting his innocence would merely be complaining about the violation of an imagined right to be acquitted if innocent, with no more of a legitimate complaint than the defendant indignant at being convicted on purely circumstantial evidence. At the same time, the proceduralist might find some moral content in the instrumental defendant's complaint about being punished in a system where enforcement is highly erratic.

14. As Dalton notes in "Taking the Right to Appeal," 100, the appeal "increases the level of participation by assuring every litigant a second day in court;" while for litigants who never went to trial, "the appeal may constitute, or at least feel like, her only day in court." Jerry Goldman has obtained some empirical support for this claim. In an informal survey of civil appellants in federal court, he found considerable sensitivity to the details of appellate procedure and the opportunities afforded for participation by the defendant or his attorney. "Appellate Justice Economized: Screening and Its Effects on Outcome and Legitimacy" (paper prepared for 1989 Annual Meeting, *Law and Society Assn.*, Madison, Wisc.).

15. The one field study of jailhouse lawyering I have been able to find described a professional structure in one medium size state prison remarkably similar to the private criminal bar. Wexler, "The Jailhouse Lawyer as a Paraprofessional: Problems and Prospects," *Criminal Law Bulletin* 7 (1971): 139.

The lower echelon "writ-writers" demanded payment in cigarettes—prison cash—and prepared boilerplate pleadings. The higher echelon consisted of eight to ten well-educated inmates who did high quality work for considerably higher fees. Like all smart criminal attorneys, they required the bulk of their payment up front. The preliminary interview was not even arranged until the "lawyer's" prison account had been credited with the agreed-upon sum, transferred by friends or relatives of the client to avoid the prison ban on fees for services.

This legal elite, which the author describes as the "Jailhouse Bar Association," even had its own code of ethics, prohibiting one member from stealing clients from another or criticizing his work, blackballing any inmate who would not pay his bills, and requiring concerted action against the prison authorities for sanctioning any member. Like private defense lawyers, these jailhouse practitioners had varying scruples about taking cases with no merit, but were generally fairly selective.

16. Roper and Melone, "Does Procedural Due Process Make a Difference?" *Judicature* 63 (1981): 136.

17. Some important preliminary work has been done by Hanson and Chapper, whose survey of reversals in five state appellate courts, discussed in Part II, examined conviction, offense, and attorney type. They found the highest success rate for sentencing issues and technical issues concerning lesser included offenses and merger. They did not examine the transcripts of the cases, however, for equitable and evidentiary factors that might have prompted the court to intervene.

18. On file with Andrew Fine, Associate Attorney in Charge.

19. 417 U.S. 400.

20. McConville and Mirsky, "Criminal Defense of the Poor in New York City," *New York University Review of Law and Social Change* 15 (1987): 581, 744.

21. See Nisbett and Ross, *Human Inference: Strategies and Shortcomings of Social Judgment* (Englewood Cliffs, N.J.: Prentice Hall, 1980).

22. See the studies cited in Linz and Penrod, "Increasing Attorney Persuasiveness in the Courtroom," *Law and Psychology Review* 8 (1984): 1.

23. This could be a dichotomous or scale judgment.

24. Schwartzer, "Rule 11 Revisited," *Harvard Law Review* 101 (1988): 1013, 1016–18.

Select Bibliography

American Bar Association. *Standards on Criminal Appeals* (1970).

Association of the Bar, City of New York, Committee on Criminal Advocacy. *The Crisis in Indigent Appeals in the First and Second Departments* (1985).

Association of the Bar, City of New York, Committee on Criminal Advocacy. *A System in Crisis. The Assigned Counsel Plan in New York: An Evaluation and Recommendations for Change* (1986).

Botler, J., M.C. DeVita, S. Kallas, W. Ruane, and L. Weisbrot. "Project. The Appellate Division of the Supreme Court of New York: An Empirical Study of Its Powers and Functions as an Intermediate State Court." *Fordham Law Review* 47 (1978): 929–1024.

Bureau of Justice Statistics Bulletin. *The Growth of Appeals. 1973–1983 Trends.* Washington D.C.: Government Printing Office, 1985.

Carrington, P. "Crowded Dockets and the Courts of Appeals: The Threat to the Function of Review and the National Law." *Harvard Law Review* 82 (1969): 542–617.

Carrington, P., D. Meador, and M. Rosenberg. *Justice on Appeal.* St. Paul, Minn.: West, 1976.

Caspar, J. *American Criminal Justice: The Defendant's Perspective.* Englewood Cliffs, N.J.: Prentice Hall, 1972.

Caspar, J. "Having Their Day in Court: Defendant Evaluations of the Fairness of Their Treatment." *Law & Society Review* 12 (1978): 237–51.

Chapper, Jr. and R. Hanson. *Understanding Criminal Reversals.* Williamsburg, Va.: National Center for State Courts, 1989.

Colloquium. "Effective Assistance of Counsel for the Indigent Criminal Defendant: Has the Promise Been Fulfilled?" *New York University Review of Law and Social Change* 14 (1986).

Dalton, H. "Taking the Right to Appeal (More or Less) Seriously." *Yale Law Journal* 95 (1985): 62–107.

Davies, T. "Gresham's Law Revisited: Expedited Processing Techniques and the Allocation of Appellate Resources." *Justice Systems Journal* 6 (1981): 372–404.

Davies, T. "Affirmed: A Study of Criminal Appeals and Decision-Making Norms in a California Court of Appeal." *American Bar Foundation Research Journal* 82 (1982): 543–648.

Geer, J. "Representation of Multiple Defendants: Conflicts of Interest and the Professional Responsibilities of the Defense Attorney." *Minnesota Law Review* 62 (1978): 119–162.

Gellis, S. "Reasons for Case Reversal in Texas: An Analysis." *St. Mary's Law Journal* 16 (1985): 299–327.

Genego, W. "The Future of Effective Assistance of Counsel: Performance Standards and Competent Representation." *American Criminal Law Review* 24 (1987): 181–212.

Godbold, J. "Fact Finding by the Appellate Courts: An Available and Appropriate Power." *Cumberland Law Review* 12 (1982): 365–89.

Goldman, J. "Appellate Justice Economized: Screening and Its Effect on Outcomes and Legitimacy." Paper prepared for 1989 Annual Meeting, *Law and Society Association*, Madison, Wisconsin.

Gregory, R. "Whose Reasonable Doubt? Reconsidering the Role of the Reviewing Court in the Criminal Decision Making Process." *American Criminal Law Review* 24 (1987): 911–82.

Hellerstein, W. "Appellate Advocacy for the Defense—A Joyful Challenge." *The Defender* 39 (Spring 1987): 37.

Hellman, A., ed. *Justice Restructured: The Innovations of the Ninth Circuit and the Future of the Federal Courts*. Ithaca, N.Y.: Cornell University Press (forthcoming 1990).

Hermann, R. "Frivolous Criminal Appeals." *New York University Law Review* 47 (1972): 701–21.

Hopkins, J. "The Role of An Intermediate Appellate Court." *Brooklyn Law Review* 41 (1975): 459–78.

Levine, B. *Indigent Appellate Defense: A Review of State Systems*. Report to the Michigan Supreme Court, March 1987.

Levine, B. "Preventing Defense Counsel Error—An Analysis of Some Ineffectiveness Claims and Their Implications for Professional Regulation." *Toledo Law Review* 15 (1984): 1275–1466.

Marvell, T. *Appellate Courts and Lawyers: Information Gathering in the Adversary System*. Westport, Conn.: Greenwood Press, 1978.

Mather, L. *Plea Bargaining or Trial? The Process of Criminal Case Disposition*. Lexington, Mass.: Lexington Books, 1979.

McConville, M. and C. Mirsky. "Criminal Defense of the Poor in New York City." *New York University Review of Law and Social Change* 15 (1987): 581–664.

McCrate, R., J. Hopkins, and M. Rosenberg. *Appellate Justice in New York*. Chicago: American Judicature Society, 1982.

Meador, D. *Appellate Courts: Staff and Process in the Crisis of Volume*. St. Paul, Minn.: West, 1974.

Meador, D. *Criminal Appeals: English Practice and American Reforms*. Charlottesville: University Press of Virginia, 1974.
Neubauer, D. "Published Opinions versus Summary Affirmances." *Justice Systems Journal* 10 (1985): 173–89.
Note. "Courting Reversal: The Supervisory Role of the State Supreme Courts." *Yale Law Journal* 87 (1978): 1191–1218.
Olson, R. and J. Chapper. "Screening and Tracking Criminal Appeals: The Rhode Island Experience." *Justice System Journal* 8 (1983): 20–34.
Orfield, L. *Criminal Appeals in America*. Boston: Little, Brown, 1939.
Pengilly, C. "Never Cry *Anders*: the Ethical Dilemma of Counsel Appointed to Pursue a Frivolous Appeal." *Criminal Justice Journal* 9 (1986): 45–64.
Roper, R. and A. Melone. "Does Procedural Due Process Make a Difference?" *Judicature* 63 (1981): 136–41.
Seidman, L. "Factual Guilt and the Burger Court: An Examination of Continuity and Change in Criminal Procedure." *Columbia Law Review* 80 (1980): 437–503.
Shapiro, M. "Appeal." *Law & Society Review* 14 (1980): 629–61.
Steinberg, H. "The Criminal Appeal." In Carpentier, ed., *Counsel on Appeal*. New York: McGraw-Hill, 1968.
Symposium. "The Appellate Judiciary: Its Strengths, Its Woes and Some Suggestions for Reform." *Maryland Law Review* 42 (1983).
Traynor, R. *The Riddle of Harmless Error*. Columbus: Ohio State University Press, 1970.
Wexler, D. "The Jailhouse Lawyer as a Paraprofessional: Problems and Prospects." *Criminal Law Bulletin* 7 (1971): 139–56.
Wheeler, S., B. Cartwright, R. Kagan, and L. Friedman. "Do the Haves Come Out Ahead?: Winning and Losing in State Supreme Courts, 1870–1970." *Law & Society Review* 21 (1987): 403–45.

Index

About the Author

DAVID T. WASSERMAN is a Research Scholar with the Institute for Philosophy and Public Policy, located at the University of Maryland, and a former staff attorney with the criminal appeals bureau of the New York Legal Aid Society. His articles have appeared in a number of legal journals, including *Philosophy and Public Affairs*, *North Carolina Central Law Journal*, and *Maryland Law Review*.